T0155890

Design Science Methodology for Information Systems and Software Engineering

Roel J. Wieringa

Design
Science
Methodology

for Information Systems
and Software Engineering

Springer

Roel J. Wieringa
University of Twente
Enschede
The Netherlands

ISBN 978-3-662-52446-6   ISBN 978-3-662-43839-8 (eBook)
DOI 10.1007/978-3-662-43839-8
Springer Heidelberg New York Dordrecht London

Printed on acid-free paper

Springer is part of Springer Science+Business Media (www.springer.com)

Preface

This book provides guidelines for doing design science in information systems and software engineering research. In design science, we iterate over two activities: designing an artifact that improves something for stakeholders and empirically investigating the performance of an artifact in a context. A key feature of the approach of this book is that our object of study is *an artifact in a context*. The artifacts that we design and study are, for example, methods, techniques, notations, and algorithms used in software and information systems. The context for these artifacts is the design, development, maintenance, and use of software and information systems. Since our artifacts are designed for this context, we should investigate them in this context.

Five major themes run through the book. First, we treat design as well as empirical research as *problem-solving*. The different parts of the book are structured according to two major problem-solving cycles: the design cycle and the empirical cycle. In the first, we design artifacts intended to help stakeholders. In the second, we produce answers to knowledge questions about an artifact in context. This dual nature of design science is elaborated in Part I.

Second, the results of these problem-solving activities are *fallible*. Artifacts may not fully meet the goals of stakeholders, and answers to knowledge questions may have limited validity. To manage this inherent uncertainty of problem-solving by finite human beings, the artifact designs and answers produced by these problem-solving activities must be justified. This leads to great emphasis on the validation of artifact designs in terms of stakeholder goals, problem structures, and artifact requirements in Part II. It also leads to great attention to the validity of inferences in the empirical cycle, treated in Part IV.

Third, before we treat the empirical cycle, we elaborate in Part III on the *structure of design theories* and the role of conceptual frameworks in design and in empirical research. Science does not restrict itself to observing phenomena and reporting about it. That is journalism. In science, we derive knowledge claims about unobserved phenomena, and we justify these fallible claims as well as possible, confronting them with empirical reality and submitting them to the critique of peers.

In this process, we form scientific theories that go beyond what we have observed so far.

Fourth, we make a clear distinction between case-based research and sample-based research. In *case-based research*, we study single cases in sequence, drawing conclusions between case studies. This is a well-known approach in the social sciences. In the design sciences, we take the same approach when we test an artifact, draw conclusions, and apply a new test. The conclusions of case-based research typically are stated in terms of the architecture and components of the artifact and explain observed behavior in terms of mechanisms in the artifact and context. From this, we generalize by analogy to the population of similar artifacts. In *sample-based research,* by contrast, we study samples of population elements and make generalizations about the distribution of variables over the population by means of statistical inference from a sample. Both kinds of research are done in design science. In Part V, we discuss three examples of case-based research methods and one example of a sample-based research method.

Fifth and finally, the appendices of the book contain checklists for the design and empirical research cycles. The checklist for empirical research is generic because it applies to all different kinds of research methods discussed here. Some parts are not applicable to some methods. For example, the checklist for designing an experimental treatment is not applicable to observational case study research. But there is a remarkable uniformity across research methods that makes the checklist for empirical research relevant for all kinds of research discussed here. The method chapters in Part V are all structured according to the checklist.

Figure 1 gives a road map for the book, in which you can recognize elements of the approach sketched above. Part I gives a framework for design science and explains the distinction between design problems and knowledge questions. Design problems are treated by following the design cycle; knowledge questions are answered by following the empirical cycle. As pointed out above, these treatments and answers are fallible, and an important part of the design cycle and empirical cycle is the assessment of the strength of the arguments for the treatments that we have designed and for the answers that we have found.

The design cycle is treated in Part II. It consists of an iteration over problem investigation, treatment design, and treatment validation. Different design problems may require different levels of effort spent on these three activities.

The empirical cycle is treated in Part IV. It starts with a similar triple of tasks as the design cycle, in which the research problem is analyzed and the research setup and inferences are designed and validated. Validation of a research design is in fact checking whether the research setup that you designed will support the inferences that you are planning to make. The empirical cycle continues with research execution, using the research setup, and data analysis, using the inferences designed earlier.

Examples of the entire empirical cycle are given in Part V, where four different research methods are presented:

- In *observational case studies*, individual real-world cases are studied to analyze the mechanisms that produce phenomena in these cases. Cases may be social

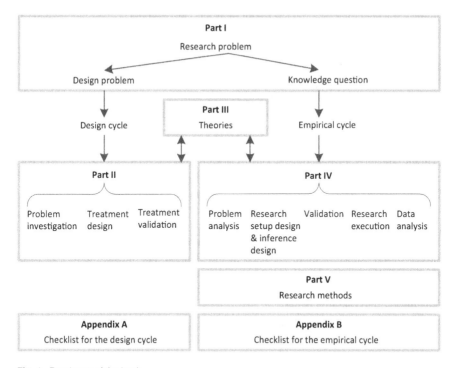

Fig. 1 Road map of the book

systems such as software projects, teams, or software organizations or they may be technical systems such as complex software systems or networks.
- In *single-case mechanism experiments*, individual cases are experimented with in order to learn which phenomena can be produced by which mechanisms. The cases may be social systems or technical systems, or models of these systems. They are experimented with, and this can be done in the laboratory or in the field. We often speak of *testing* a technical prototype or of *simulating* a sociotechnical system.
- In *technical action research*, a newly designed artifact is tested in the field by using it to help a client. Technical action research is like single-case mechanism experimentation but with the additional goal of helping a client in the field.
- In *statistical difference-making experiments*, an artifact is tested by using it to treat a sample of population elements. The outcome is compared with the outcome of treating another sample with another artifact. If there is a statistically discernable difference, the experimenter analyzes the conditions of the experiment to see if it is plausible that this difference is caused, completely or partially, by the difference in treatments.

In the opening chapter of Part V, we return to Fig. 1 and fill in the road map with checklist items. Each research method consists of a particular way of running through the empirical cycle. The same checklist is used for each of them, but not all items in the checklist are relevant for all methods, and particular items are answered differently for different methods.

The remaining chapters of Part V are about the four research methods and can be read in any order. They give examples of how to use the checklist for different research methods. They are intended to be read when you actually want to apply a research method.

Part III in the middle of the book is about scientific theories, which we will define as generalizations about phenomena that have survived critical assessment and empirical tests by competent peers. Theories enhance our capability to describe, explain, and predict phenomena and to design artifacts that can be used to treat problems. We need theories both during empirical research and during design. Conversely, empirical research as well as design may contribute to our theoretical knowledge.

References to relevant literature are given throughout the book, and most chapters end with endnotes that discuss important background to the chapter. All chapters have a bibliography of literature used in the chapter. The index doubles up as a glossary, as the pages where key terms are defined are printed in boldface.

The book uses numerous examples that have all been taken from master's theses, PhD theses, and research papers.

☐   Examples are set off from the rest of the text as a bulleted list with square bullets and in a small sans serif typeface.

The first 11 chapters of the book, which cover Parts I–III and the initial chapters of Part IV, are taught every year to master's students of computer science, software engineering, and information systems and an occasional student of management science. A selection of chapters from the entire book is taught every year to PhD students of software engineering, information systems, and artificial intelligence. Fragments have also been taught in various seminars and tutorials given at conferences and companies to academic and industrial researchers. Teaching this material has always been rewarding, and I am grateful for the patience my audiences have had in listening to my sometimes half-baked ideas.

Many of the ideas in the book have been developed in discussions with Hans Heerkens, who knows everything about airplanes as well as about research methods for management scientists. My ideas also developed in work done with Nelly Condori-Fernández, Maya Daneva, Sergio España, Silja Eckartz, Daniel Fernández Méndez, and Smita Ghaisas. The text benefited from comments by Sergio España, Daniel Fernández Méndez, Barbara Paech, Richard Starmans, and Antonio Vetrò.

Last but not least, my gratitude goes to my wife Mieke, who long ago planted the seed for this book by explaining the regulative cycle of the applied sciences to me and who provided a ground for this seed to grow by supporting me when I was endlessly revising this text in my study. My gratefulness cannot be quantified, and it is unqualified.

Enschede, The Netherlands   R.J. Wieringa
May 15, 2014

Contents

Part III   Theoretical Frameworks

Part IV   The Empirical Cycle

Part I
A Framework for Design Science

Chapter 1
What Is Design Science?

To do a design science project, you have to understand its major components, namely, its object of study and its two major activities. The object of study is an artifact in context (Sect. 1.1), and its two major activities are designing and investigating this artifact in context (Sect. 1.2). For the design activity, it is important to know the social context of stakeholders and goals of the project, as this is the source of the research budget as well as the destination of useful research results. For the investigative activity, it is important to be familiar with the knowledge context of the project, as you will use this knowledge and also contribute to it. Jointly, the two major activities and the two contexts form a framework for design science that I describe in Sect. 1.3. In Sect. 1.4, I show why in design science the knowledge that we use and produce is not universal but has middle-range scope.

1.1 The Object of Study of Design Science

Design science is the design and investigation of artifacts in context. The artifacts we study are designed to interact with a problem context in order to improve something in that context. Here are two examples, one technical and one organizational. We will use these examples many times later, and so I introduce acronyms for them:

☐ In the direction of arrival (DOA) project [10], algorithms for estimating the DOA of a satellite TV signal were tested. Each of the tested algorithms is an artifact, and the context for each of them is an IT infrastructure for watching TV in the backseats of a car.

☐ In the data location compliance (DLC) project [8], a method was developed that allows cloud service providers to show compliance to the European data location regulations. The method is an artifact, and the context consists of cloud service providers who want to offer their services on the European market.

© Springer-Verlag Berlin Heidelberg 2014
R.J. Wieringa, *Design Science Methodology for Information Systems and Software Engineering*, DOI 10.1007/978-3-662-43839-8_1

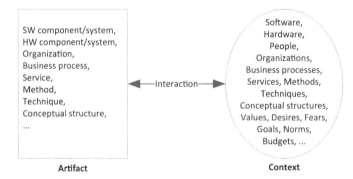

Fig. 1.1 The subject of design science: an artifact interacting with a context

The two examples illustrate that design science problems are *improvement problems*. Each of the problems has a context in which some improvement is aimed for, and to understand the design problem, this context has to be understood.

The examples also illustrate that the concept of an artifact is to be taken broadly, including algorithms and methods. We will even consider conceptual structures as artifacts, as tools for the mind, that may be usable and useful for particular purposes.

Figure 1.1 illustrates the wide variety of useful things that can be designed as an artifact. It shows by implication what can *not* be an artifact. People, values, desires, fears, goals, norms, and budgets appear in the context of an artifact but cannot be designed by a design researcher. They are given to the design researcher, as part of a problem context, and the researcher must investigate these elements of the context in order to understand them, but not to change them.

Finally, Fig. 1.1 shows that the artifact itself does not solve any problem. It is the *interaction* between the artifact and a problem context that contributes to solving a problem. An artifact may interact differently with different problem contexts and hence solve different problems in different contexts. It may even contribute to stakeholder goals in one context but create obstacles to goal achievement in another context. The design researcher should therefore study the interaction between artifacts and contexts rather than artifacts alone or contexts alone.

1.2   Research Problems in Design Science

The two parts of design science, design and investigation, correspond to two kinds of research problems in design science, namely, *design problems* and *knowledge questions* (Fig. 1.2). Table 1.1 lists a number of example design problems and knowledge questions.

Design problems call for a change in the real world and require an analysis of actual or hypothetical stakeholder goals. A solution is a design, and there are usually many different solutions. There may even be as many solutions as there are

Fig. 1.2 Design science research iterates over two problem-solving activities

Table 1.1 Some example design science research problems. In the top half of the table, the knowledge questions are motivated by the design problems. In the lower half, the design problems are motivated by the knowledge questions

Design problem	Knowledge question
Design a DOA estimation system for satellite TV reception in a car	Is the DOA estimation accurate enough?
Design an assurance method for DLC for cloud service providers	Is the method usable and useful for cloud service providers?
Design a DOA prototype Design a simulation of plane wave arrival at a moving antenna	Is the DOA estimation accurate enough?
Design a usability and usefulness test with consultants as subjects	Is the method usable and useful for cloud service providers?

designers. These are evaluated by their utility with respect to the stakeholder goals, and there is not one single best solution.

Knowledge questions, by contrast, do not call for a change in the world but ask for knowledge about the world as it is. The answer is a proposition, and when we try to answer a knowledge question, we assume that there is one answer only. We do not know the answer, and we may give the wrong answer; we may give a partial answer or an answer to a slightly different question than what was asked; we may have degrees of (un)certainty about the answer, and the answer may be true in most but not all cases. But answering a knowledge question would be meaningless if there would be as many answers as researchers. And answers to knowledge questions are evaluated by truth, which does not depend on stakeholder goals. Rational discourse implies the assumption of single truth but must be combined with the assumption of **fallibilism**: we can never be sure that we have actually found the answer to an empirical knowledge question.

The distinction between design problems and knowledge questions is often camouflaged in reports about design science research, because design problems are often formulated to look like a knowledge questions. We then read:

• " What is an accurate algorithm for recognizing DOA?"

instead of

• "Design an accurate algorithm for recognizing DOA."

Table 1.2 Heuristics to distinguish design problems from knowledge questions

Design problems	Knowledge questions
Call for a change of the world	Ask for knowledge about the world
Solution is a design	Answer is a proposition
Many solutions	One answer
Evaluated by utility	Evaluated by truth
Utility depends on stakeholder goals	Truth does not depend on stakeholder goals

This is confusing, because the way design problems must be treated differs from the way knowledge questions must be answered, and the results are evaluated differently. Design problems are treated by following the design cycle, which is the subject of Part II of this book. Knowledge questions may be analytical or empirical, and in this book we consider empirical knowledge questions. These can be answered by following the empirical cycle, which is the subject of Parts IV and V of this book. Table 1.2 summarizes the distinction in terms of heuristics that you can use to classify your problem.

Problems can create new problems, and a design science project is never restricted to one kind of problem only. This generates an iteration over design problems and knowledge questions in design science [2, 11]. One possible sequence is that starting from a *design problem,* we can ask *knowledge questions* about the artifact, about its problem context, and about the interaction between the two. For example, we can ask about the performance of the artifact and the effects it has on entities in the problem context. The knowledge-question-answering activity returns knowledge to the design problem-solving activity.

Conversely, the activity of answering a *knowledge question* can lead to new *design problems,* for example, to build a prototype of the artifact, to simulate its context, or to design a measurement instrument. The artifacts that result from these design activities are returned to the question-answering activity and can be used to answer knowledge questions.

1.3 A Framework for Design Science

The problem context of an artifact can be extended with the stakeholders of the artifact and with the knowledge used to design the artifact. This extended context is the context of the design science project as a whole. The resulting picture is a framework for design science, shown in Fig. 1.3. This is similar to the framework of Hevner et al. [3], but it contains some important differences, such as the separation of design and investigation [12].

The *social context* contains the stakeholders who may affect the project or may be affected by it. Stakeholders include possible users, operators, maintainers,

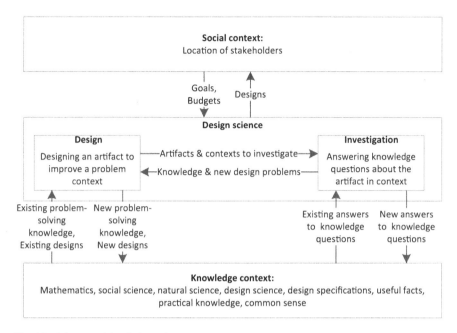

Fig. 1.3 A framework for design science

instructors, etc., of the artifact to be designed. They also include the sponsors of the design project. Sponsors provide the budget for the project and set goals to be achieved by the project. Sponsors may be government, in which case they will probably require the research project to have a goal that is relevant and useful for society, or they may be private enterprises, in which case they will probably require the project to deliver a design that is useful for the company.

The *knowledge context* consists of existing theories from science and engineering, specifications of currently known designs, useful facts about currently available products, lessons learned from the experience of researchers in earlier design science projects, and plain common sense [9, pp. 208–224]. The design science project uses this knowledge and may add to it by producing new designs or answering knowledge questions. Here is the context of our two examples:

☐   The stakeholders in the social context of the DOA project [10] are the chip manufacturer NXP (sponsor), car component suppliers, car manufacturers, garages, car drivers, and passengers.
The knowledge context is very diverse. The project uses a mathematical theory (matrix calculus) and a natural science theory (signal processing). Three existing algorithm designs are tested, and these are taken from the knowledge context too. The project also uses some basic theory of properties of algorithms. The knowledge context in addition contains useful facts, such as the maximum rotation speed of a car, and lessons learned from experience, such as how to use Matlab and how to program the experimental Montium processor used in this project.

☐ The stakeholders in the social context of the DLC project [8] are KPMG (sponsor), KPMG
  consultants (end users of the method), cloud service providers, and European companies who
  are or want to become clients of cloud service providers.
  In the knowledge context, we find theories about people and organizations: theories of auditing,
  cloud business models, knowledge about different designs of cloud computing architectures,
  and design theories about security properties of those architectures. Useful facts include facts
  about current cloud service providers in the market and their architectures and business models.
  Lessons learned from experience used in the project are how to do interviews, how to understand
  regulations, and consultancy.

Knowledge available prior to the project is called **prior knowledge**; knowledge
produced as a result of the project is called **posterior knowledge**. As shown in
Fig. 1.3, there are many sources for prior knowledge:

- Scientific literature: Scientific theories from the basic sciences and the engineering sciences, implementation evaluation studies, and problem investigations
- Technical literature: Specifications of artifacts used in a problem context, other
  than the artifact you are currently studying
- Professional literature: Experiences of others described in professional mag-
  azines, information about artifacts currently on the market, documentation
  provided by their vendors, etc.
- Oral communication: Lessons learned by others and heard in conferences, in the
  lab, or from their colleagues

If you need an answer supported by rigorous scientific evidence and current
scientific literature does not provide an answer, then you have to do your own
research. This usually scales up the budget of time and money needed to answer
your knowledge questions by an order of magnitude. Research is expensive. The
decision to do research to answer a knowledge is therefore in practice always made
together with the sponsor, who must provide the money and pay the time to do the
research.

1.4 Sciences of the Middle Range

We can further structure the knowledge context of design science research by
identifying different knowledge disciplines (Fig. 1.4). *Basic science* is the study of
the fundamental forces and mechanisms of nature and includes physics, chemistry,
and some parts of biology that can claim validity in the entire universe. Basic
sciences aim at universal generalizations, which are generalizations that start with
"for all x, ..." They achieve this goal at the cost of **idealizations,** which are
abstractions that are known to be false in the real world, such as point masses,
frictionless surfaces, etc. [1, 4, 5, 7]. Idealizations serve to make the research
problems conceptually manageable. One of the purposes of laboratory research is to
approximate these idealized conditions as much as possible.

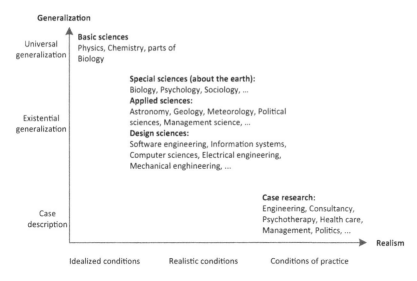

Fig. 1.4 The place of design sciences among other sciences

At the other extreme is *case research,* which is the knowledge acquisition about single cases that takes place in engineering, consultancy, psychotherapy, health care, and other professions. These professions must solve problems in the real world and cannot idealize away any of the factors or components that play a role in the problem they are trying to solve. Unmanageable conditions in the real world will not go away merely by the fact that a professional ignores them or builds an idealized model in the laboratory. We call these unignorable real-world factors and components **conditions of practice** [6, pp. 692–693].

The professions do not aim to generalize beyond the cases that they work with. Their primary aim is to help the cases they work with. But a side effect of solving particular cases is that the professional builds up generalizable knowledge. Even in the real world, there are plenty of justifiable generalizations to be made, but they do not have universal scope.

The production of these limited generalizations is the focus of the sciences of the middle range that sit between the extremes of basic sciences and case research. *Special sciences* such as parts of biology, psychology, and sociology are quite happy to generalize about interesting sets of objects of study but do not aim to generalize about the universe. They study phenomena under realistic conditions, and many of their generalizations are existential, which means that they start with "for some/many/most x, …."

In the middle range, we also find *applied sciences* such as astronomy, geology, and management science, which apply results from other sciences but also have developed considerable knowledge of their own. And we find the *design sciences* such as software engineering and information systems research. We call these sciences *middle range* because they do not aim at universal but at existential generalizations, and they do not make unrealistic idealizations in order to acquire knowledge, but aim to make only realistic assumptions about their object of study. We call these existential, realistic generalizations **middle-range generalizations**.

The lower-left part of the diagram is empty. It would contain sciences that aim to make idealized descriptions of individual cases. There are no such sciences, for they would produce no generalizable knowledge and, due to the high level of idealization, would not even produce knowledge of an individual case. However, in design science we may start with simple simulations of new technology under idealized conditions of the laboratory to see if something is possible at all. This is the start of a process called *scaling up* new technology.

The upper right of the diagram is empty too. It would contain sciences that produce universal generalizations about cases without making any idealizing abstractions. These sciences would say that despite the huge variety in conditions of practice in different problem contexts, some artifact will always produce the intended effect. Usually, this is an attempt to sell snake oil. The world is too complex, and our minds are too small, for us to produce such generalizations with certainty.

However, the design sciences do aim to push the limit of realism and generalizability. They are aiming to produce knowledge about the real world that does not make any unrealistic abstractions and that has a scope of validity that is as large as possible. We will never be able to reach the upper right corner, but when scaling up new technology from the idealized conditions of cases studied in the laboratory (lower left) to populations that live in the real world to conditions of practice (upper right), we aim to get as far as possible.

1.5 Summary

- Design science is the design and investigation of artifacts in context.
- Design science iterates over solving design problems and answering knowledge questions.
- The social context of a design science project consists of stakeholders who may affect or may be affected by the project.
- The knowledge context consists of knowledge from natural science, design science, design specifications, useful facts, practical knowledge, and common sense.
- Generalizations produced by design science research are middle range. They may abstract from some conditions of practice but do not make unrealizable idealizations. They generalize beyond the case level but are not universal.

References

1. N. Cartwright, *How the Laws of Physics Lie* (Oxford University Press, Oxford, 1983)
2. H. Heerkens, A. van Winden, *Geen Probleem: Een Aanpak voor Alle Bedrijfskundige Vragen en Mysteries* (Van Winden Communicatie, Utrecht, The Netherlands, 2012)
3. A.R. Hevner, S.T. March, J. Park, S. Ram, Design science in information system research. MIS Quart. **28**(1), 75–105 (2004)
4. R. Laymon, Applying idealized scientific theories to engineering. Synthese **81**, 353–371 (1989)
5. R. Laymon, Experimentation and the legitimacy of idealization. Philos. Stud. **77**, 353–375 (1995)
6. E.T. Layton, American ideologies of science and engineering. Technol. Cult. **17**, 688–701 (1976)
7. E. McMullin, Galilean idealization. Stud. Hist. Philos. Sci. **16**(3), 247–273 (1985)
8. J. Noltes, Data location compliance in cloud computing. Master's thesis, Faculty of Electrical Engineering, Mathematics and Computer Science, University of Twente, August 2011. http://essay.utwente.nl/61042/
9. W.G. Vincenti, *What Engineers Know and How They Know It. Analytical Studies from Aeronautical History* (Johns Hopkins, Baltimore, 1990)
10. J.D. Vrielink, Phased array processing: direction of arrival estimation on reconfigurable hardware. Master's thesis, Faculty of Electrical Engineering, Mathematics and Computer Science, University of Twente, January 2009. http://essay.utwente.nl/62065/
11. R.J. Wieringa, Design science as nested problem solving, in *Proceedings of the 4th International Conference on Design Science Research in Information Systems and Technology, Philadelphia* (ACM, New York, 2009), pp. 1–12
12. R.J. Wieringa, Relevance and problem choice in design science, in *Global Perspectives on Design Science Research (DESRIST)*. 5th International Conference, St. Gallen, Lecture Notes in Computer Science, vol. 6105 (Springer, Heidelberg, 2010), pp. 61–76

Chapter 2
Research Goals and Research Questions

To frame a research project, you have to specify its research goal (Sect. 2.1). Because a design science project iterates over designing and investigating, its research goal can be refined into design goals and knowledge goals. We give a template for design problems in Sect. 2.2 and a classification of different kinds of knowledge goals in Sect. 2.3.

2.1 Research Goals

To understand the goals of a design science research project, it is useful to distinguish the goals of the researcher from the goals of an external stakeholder. The researcher's goals invariably include curiosity and fun: curiosity what the answer to knowledge questions is and fun in the design and test of new or improved artifacts. In this sense, all design science research is *curiosity-driven* and *fun-driven research*.

The researcher may have additional goals, such as the desire to improve society or to promote the well-being of people. This kind of goal is similar to the goals that external stakeholders may have. One of the external stakeholders will be the *sponsor* of the project, which is the person or organization paying for the research. The sponsor allocates a budget to the research project in order to achieve some goals and expects to receive useful designs that serve these goals and useful knowledge about those designs. For most sponsors, design science research projects are *utility driven* and *budget constrained*. Some sponsors however may be willing to sponsor some researchers to do *exploratory research*. The sponsor may still hope that useful results will emerge, but whether this will happen is very uncertain.

Putting all of these motivations together gives us a wide variety of kinds of projects, ranging from market-oriented projects in which an enhancement to a particular product must be designed to exploratory projects where even the sponsor

© Springer-Verlag Berlin Heidelberg 2014
R.J. Wieringa, *Design Science Methodology for Information Systems and Software Engineering*, DOI 10.1007/978-3-662-43839-8_2

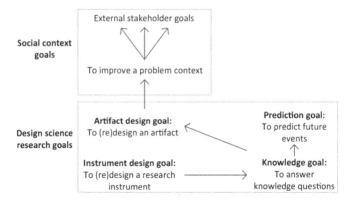

Fig. 2.1 Goal structure of a design science research project. The goals on the left concern improvement of the real world, and those on the right concern our beliefs about the world. In an exploratory project, there may be no higher-level improvement goals

has only a vague idea of the possible utility of the designs or knowledge that will come out of the project. These goals require different capabilities of the researcher and have a different risk profile for the sponsor.

In all these cases, design science research projects have a goal hierarchy with the characteristic contribution structure shown in Fig. 2.1. The goals on the right hand concern our beliefs about past, present, and future phenomena. The goals on the left are design goals or more generally improvement goals. We now discuss the goal structure in more detail, starting at the right-hand side.

Design science researchers often have a **prediction goal**. For example, we may want to predict how an artifact will interact with a problem context or how a problem would evolve if it were not treated. A prediction is a belief about what will happen in the future, which will turn out to be true or false. To make these predictions, we need knowledge.

Possible **knowledge goals** of a design science research project are to describe phenomena and to explain them. For example, a knowledge goal may be to describe what happens when an artifact interacts with a context and to explain this in terms of internal mechanisms of the artifact and context.

In order to answer the knowledge questions, some design science research projects may have to design instruments. For example, the researcher may have to build a simulation of an artifact in context or to construct a questionnaire to collect user opinions. These **instrument design goals** are the lowest-level design goals in Fig. 2.1.

Moving up in the diagram, design science research projects usually have a higher-level design goal such as to improve the performance of some artifact in a context. We call this an **artifact design goal** or, alternatively, a **technical research goal**.

The goal of artifact design is in turn to solve, mitigate, or otherwise improve some problem in the social context of the project, such as the goal to make viewing satellite TV in a car possible or to audit data location compliance in cloud computing.

No goal exists in a normative vacuum, and the problem improvement goal in turn often supports some higher-level stakeholder goals. There may be a range of different external stakeholder goals all served by the project improvement goal. For example, the parent's goal may be to keep children in the backseat of a car quiet, the children's goal is to watch TV in a car, and the car manufacturer's goal is to increase sales.

Market-driven projects have a very clear goal hierarchy. Exploratory projects may have a more fuzzy goal hierarchy where the higher-level goals are speculative or may even be absent:

☐ The DOA project is market driven. Starting from the bottom up in Fig. 2.1, the lowest level goal was to build simulations and prototypes of DOA algorithms and of an antenna array. This is an *instrument design goal*. These instruments were used to answer *knowledge questions* about the performance of different DOA algorithms—a knowledge goal. This knowledge was generalizable and could be used to *predict* the performance of all implementations of the algorithm—another knowledge goal. Answering these questions also contributed to the *artifact design goal* of designing a DOA estimation component. This in turn contributes the goal of *problem context improvement*. The DOA estimation component will be part of a directional antenna for satellite TV signal reception, which is to be used in a car to allow passengers on the backseat to watch TV. The *sponsor's goal* is to develop and sell components of the IT infrastructure needed for this.

☐ As an example of an exploratory project with only knowledge goals, a project that we will call ARE (for Agile Requirements Engineering) studied how requirements were prioritized in agile software engineering projects [1]. This is a knowledge goal that was achieved by answering *knowledge questions* about a sample of projects. Achieving this goal enabled another knowledge goal, namely, to *predict* how requirements were prioritized in similar projects. There was no artifact design goal, although the results would be potentially useful to improve requirements engineering in agile projects.

2.2 Design Problems

Goals define problems. How do we get from here to the goal? A **design problem** is a problem to (re)design an artifact so that it better contributes to the achievement of some goal. Fixing the goal for which we work puts us at some level in the goal hierarchy discussed in the previous section. An instrument design goal is the problem to design an instrument that will help us answer a knowledge question, and an artifact design goal is the problem to design an artifact that will improve a problem context.

Design problems assume a context and stakeholder goals and call for an artifact such that the interactions of (artifact × context) help stakeholders to achieve their goals. We specify requirements for the artifact that are motivated by the stakeholder goals. This gives us the schema for expressing design problems shown in Table 2.1.

Table 2.1 Template for design problems (aka technical research questions). Not all parts to be filled in may be clear at the start of the project

---

- Improve <a problem context>
- by <(re)designing an artifact>
- that satisfies <some requirements>
- in order to <help stakeholders achieve some goals>.

We discuss the role of stakeholder goals, requirements, and the problem context in more detail later on. Here, I give some illustrations only:

☐ The DOA design problem has this format:

- – Improve satellite TV reception in cars
- – by designing a DOA estimation algorithm
- – that satisfies accuracy and speed requirements
- – so that passengers can watch TV in the car.

At the start of the project, the requirements on the algorithms were not known yet.

☐ In a project that we will call MARP (multi-agent route planning), Ter Mors [2] designed and investigated multi-agent route planning algorithms for aircraft taxiing on airports. The design problem was to:

- – Improve taxi route planning of aircraft on airports
- – by designing multi-agent route planning algorithms
- – that reduces taxiing delays
- – in order to increase passenger comfort and further reduce airplane turnaround time.

This was an exploratory project where the interest of the researcher was to explore the possibility of multi-agent route planning. The aircraft taxiing was a hypothetical application scenario used to motivate the research and used as an example in simulations.

Not all elements of the design problem template may be known at the start of the project, and some may be invented as part of a hypothetical application scenario. Stating your design problem according to the template is useful because it helps you to identify missing pieces of information that are needed to bound your research problem. Table 2.2 lists some heuristics by which the elements of a design problem can be found.

We can now see what is the problem with masquerading a design problem as a knowledge question. Take the following knowledge question:

- "What is an accurate algorithm for recognizing direction of arrival?"

This is really a design problem. Using the template, we see what is missing:

- Improve <a problem context>
- by designing a DOA estimation algorithm
- that satisfies accuracy requirement
- so that <stakeholder goals>.

Table 2.2 Guidelines for filling in missing parts of the design problem statement template

• What must be designed by the researcher?	$\longrightarrow$ The artifact
• What is given to the researcher? • With what will the artifact interact?	$\longrightarrow$ The problem context
• What is the interaction? • What desired properties must it have?	$\longrightarrow$ The requirements
• To whom should this interaction be useful? • To achieve which of their goals?	$\longrightarrow$ The stakeholder goals

The problem context and stakeholder goals are missing, so that we have no clue about the required accuracy and miss one important requirement, namely, execution speed. We also miss the information needed to set up a test environment.

Many researchers do not want to be perceived as solving "mere" design problems and insist on stating their research problem as a question, with a question mark. The following template does that:

- How to <(re)design an artifact>
- that satisfies <requirements>
- so that <stakeholder goals can be achieved>
- in <problem context>?

It contains exactly the same information as our design problem template. Instead of calling it a design problem, we may now call it a "technical research question." However, I have reserved the word "question" for knowledge questions. If you want to give design problems a more dignified status, I propose to use the term **technical research problem**.

2.3 Knowledge Questions

The knowledge goals of a project should be refined into knowledge questions. A knowledge question asks for knowledge about the world, without calling for an improvement of the world. All knowledge questions in this book are **empirical knowledge questions**, which require data about the world to answer them. This stands in contrast to **analytical knowledge questions**, which can be answered by conceptual analysis, such as mathematics or logic, without collecting data about the world. Analytical knowledge questions are questions about the conceptual frameworks that we can use to structure our descriptions of the world. To answer an analytical knowledge question, we analyze concepts. But to answer an empirical knowledge question, we need to collect and analyze data. There are several ways to classify empirical knowledge questions, discussed next.

2.3.1 Descriptive and Explanatory Questions

One important classification of knowledge questions is by their knowledge goal: description or explanation. **Descriptive questions** ask for what happened without asking for explanations. They are journalistic questions, asking *what* events were observed, *when* and *where* they happened, *who* was involved, *which* devices were affected, etc. Imagine yourself a journalist at the scene of the happening. Your goal is not to judge nor to explain, but to just observe without prejudice.

Explanatory questions ask *why* something happened. We will distinguish three sorts of why questions:

- "What event *caused* this event?" Here we ask which earlier event made a difference to a current event:

    □ For example, if a program crashes, we may ask which input caused this crash. This means that we ask which input *made a difference* to the behavior of the program. It also means that we assume that with another input, the program might not have crashed.

- "What mechanism *produced* the event?" A mechanism is an interaction between system components, and here we ask what system components interacted to produce the event:

    □ For example, if we have identified the input that caused a program to crash, we can trace this input through the program to find the component (procedure, function, statement, etc.) that failed to respond properly to its input. We may be able to eliminate the failure mechanism by repairing the defective component or by replacing it with another one.

- "What are the *reasons* these people or organizations did that?" Biological and legal persons have goals and desires that motivate their actions, and we can explain their behavior by indicating these motivations.
    Reasons contain an element of choice, and we hold people and organizations responsible for actions that they performed for a reason. This is not the case for causes:

    □ For example, someone may push you in a swimming pool. That push is the cause of your being in the pool, but it is not your reason for being in the pool. You had no choice. You had no reason to jump in, and you are not responsible for being in the pool.
    □ If consultants refuse to use a method because it requires them to change their way of working, then we hold them responsible for this, because they could have chosen otherwise.
    □ A consultant may use a method incorrectly because he or she does not understand the method. Misunderstanding is the cause of incorrect use, not the reason. Given the misunderstanding, the consultant had no choice, desire, or goal to use the method incorrectly.

2.3.2 An Aside: Prediction Problems

Descriptive and explanatory questions ask what has happened and how this came to be. But what about the future? Can we have a knowledge question that asks what will happen in the future? We are asking questions like this all the time. For example,

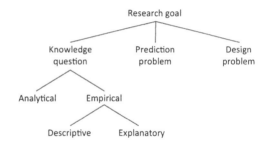

Fig. 2.2 A classification of research goals

what will be the average satisfaction of users of this system? How accurate will this algorithm be when used in a car?

However, these are not knowledge questions but **prediction problems**. A prediction is a belief about what will happen, and this belief does not constitute knowledge. We cannot *know* the future. There is no time travel: we cannot peek at a future event and then return to the present to answer our question. Instead, we must wait and see what happens.

But we can try to predict the future by using our knowledge of what has happened so far and generalizing from this:

☐   If system X is going to be implemented in organization A next month, we may ask what percentage of the users will be satisfied. This is a prediction problem. We have no knowledge about this percentage yet.

However, we can ask another question, namely, what percentage of users of X are satisfied with the system in organizations where X has been implemented. This is a descriptive knowledge question.

After empirical research, we find that in a sample of 30 organizations where implementation of X has been attempted, on the average, 80 % of the users are satisfied and give or take 5 %. This describes a fact.

Next, we can generalize: In organizations where implementation of X is attempted, on the average, 80 % of the users are satisfied and give or take 5 %. If sampling has been done in a statistically sound way, then this generalization has statistical support in the above fact. If we can explain it in terms of properties of X and of the users, then it has additional support. In the absence of these kinds of support, it is an informed guess based on the fact reported above.

Whatever the degree of support is, we can use the generalization to make a prediction: In the next organization where X will be implemented, on the average, 80 % of the users will be satisfied and give or take 5 %. The degree of support for this prediction depends on the degree of support for the generalization, and on the similarity of the next organization to the past organizations. In any case, we do not know whether the prediction is correct. In the future, we will know whether it is true.

Knowledge is created by answering knowledge questions, and scientific theories are created by generalizing from this. These generalizations can be used to solve prediction problems. We discuss ways to generalize from empirical research in Parts IV and V.

This gives us the classification of research goals shown in Fig. 2.2. Knowledge questions ask about the past and present, prediction problems ask about the future, and design problems ask for a change of the future. This book is about answering empirical knowledge questions and treating design problems. There are additional classifications of knowledge questions, treated next.

Table 2.3 Examples of empirical knowledge questions

	Descriptive questions	Explanatory questions
Open questions	• What is the execution time in this kind of context?	• What input causes the dip in the graph of recall against database size? • Is there a mechanism in the algorithm that is responsible for this?
	• What do the consultants think of the usability of this method for advising their clients?	• Why do these consultants have these opinions about usability? What reasons do they have? • How is this related to context of use? Can we find a social or psychological mechanism for this?
Closed questions	• Is the execution time of one iteration less than 7.7 ms?	• Why is the execution time of the method in these test data more than 7.7 ms? • Is this loop responsible for the high execution time?
	• Do the consultants think method A is more usable than method B in this context?	• Do consultants prefer method A over method B because method A resembles their current way of working more than method B does?

2.3.3   Open and Closed Questions

A second way to classify knowledge questions is by the range of possible answers that is prespecified. An **open question** contains no specification of its possible answers. It is exploratory. A **closed question** contains hypotheses about its possible answers.

This gives us in total four kinds of empirical knowledge questions. Table 2.3 lists some examples. Note that in research that uses statistical inference, closed descriptive questions are often stated as positive hypotheses, to be confirmed or falsified by empirical observations:

☐ Instead of the closed descriptive question "Do consultants prefer method A over method B?," we may state the following hypothesis about a population of consultants:

– Consultants prefer method A over method B.

This hypothesis is then tested on a sample of consultants. The data may provide support for or against this hypothesis.

Table 2.4 Four important kinds of knowledge questions about designs, with variations

Effect questions: (artifact × context) produce effects?

- What effects are produced by the interaction between the artifact and context?
- How does the artifact respond to stimuli?
- What performance does it have in this context? (Different variables)

Trade-off questions: (alternative artifact × context) produce effects?

- What effects do similar artifacts have in this context?
- How does the artifact perform in this context compared to similar artifacts?
- How do different versions of the same artifact perform in this context?

Sensitivity questions: (artifact × alternative context) produce effects?

- What effects are produced by the artifact in different contexts?
- What happens if the context becomes bigger/smaller?
- What assumptions does the design of the artifact make about its context?

Requirements satisfaction questions: Do effects satisfy requirements?

- Does the stimulus-response behavior satisfy functional requirements?
- Does the performance satisfy nonfunctional requirements?

2.3.4 Effect, Trade-Off, and Sensitivity Questions

The above two classifications of empirical knowledge questions are not restricted to design science research and are usable in any kind of empirical research. But the following classification is specific to design science research, because it classifies empirical knowledge questions according to subject matter. What is the question about?

The subject of design science is an artifact in context, and hence design science research questions can be about artifacts, their properties, their context, stakeholders and their goals, etc. Among all these possible questions, we single out four that are asked in virtually every design science research project. They are listed, with variations, in Table 2.4.

Effect questions ask what effect an artifact in a context has. The generic effect question is:

- What effects are produced by the interaction between artifact and context?

Trade-off questions ask what is the difference between effects of different artifacts in the same context, and **sensitivity questions** ask what is the difference between effects of the same artifact in different contexts. **Requirements satisfaction questions**, finally, ask whether the effects satisfy requirements. Requirements satisfaction is a matter of degree, and different requirements may be satisfied to a different degree or may even be violated to some degree where others are satisfied to some degree:

☐ The DOA project has the following knowledge questions:

    Q1   (Effect) What is the execution time of the DOA algorithm?

    Q2   (Requirements satisfaction) Is the accuracy better than $1°$?

    Q3   (Trade-off) How do the MUSIC and ESPRIT algorithms compare on the above two questions?

    Q4   (Sensitivity) How do the answers to the above questions vary with car speed? With noise level?

☐ Here are three knowledge questions from the DLC project:

    Q1   (Effect) What is the usability (effort to learn, effort to use) of the data compliance checking method? Why?

    Q2   (Trade-off) Which parts of the proposed method can be omitted with the remaining part still being useful?

    Q3   (Sensitivity) What assumptions does the method make about consultants, e.g., experience, required knowledge, and competence?

2.4 Summary

- Different stakeholders in a design science research project may have different kinds of goals. Researchers are usually at least driven by curiosity and fun and may be driven by utility too. Sponsors are usually driven by utility and constrained by budgets but may occasionally allow researchers to do exploratory research.
- Each design science research project has a goal tree containing design goals and knowledge goals. There is always a knowledge goal, and usually there are design goals too.
- A knowledge goal can be related to other research goals and questions in several ways:
  - A knowledge goal can be refined into knowledge questions. These express the same goal but in a more detailed way. Knowledge questions are descriptive or explanatory, they can be open or closed, and they may be effect, trade-off, sensitivity, and requirements satisfaction questions.
  - A knowledge goal may contribute to the ability to solve prediction problems.
  - A knowledge goal may be decomposed into lower-level instrument design goals. These are lower-level design goals that help you to achieve your knowledge goal.
  - A knowledge goal may contribute to an artifact design goals (aka technical research goals), which in turn may contribute to some improvement goal in the context, which in turn may contribute to some stakeholder goals. In exploratory research, some of these goals may be absent.
- A prediction problem is a problem to predict what phenomena will occur in the future. It is answered by applying a theoretical generalization. For example, we may use a design theory to predict what would happen if a treatment would

be implemented or to predict what would happen if a problem would remain untreated.

- A design problem is a problem to (re)design an artifact so that it better contributes to the achievement of some goal. The template for design problems relates the artifact and its requirements to the stakeholders and their goals. Some of this information may be missing at the start of a project or may be speculative.

References

1. Z. Racheva, M. Daneva, A. Herrmann, K. Sikkel, R.J. Wieringa, Do we know enough about requirements prioritization in agile projects: insights from a case study, in *18th International IEEE Requirements Engineering Conference, Sydney* (IEEE Computer Society, Los Alamitos, October 2010), pp. 147–156
2. A.W. ter Mors, The World according to MARP. Ph.D. thesis, Delft University of Technology, March 2010. http://www.st.ewi.tudelft.nl/~adriaan/pubs/terMorsPhDthesis.pdf

Part II
The Design Cycle

Chapter 3
The Design Cycle

A design science project iterates over the activities of designing and investigating. The design task itself is decomposed into three tasks, namely, problem investigation, treatment design, and treatment validation. We call this set of three tasks the design cycle, because researchers iterate over these tasks many times in a design science research project.

The design cycle is part of a larger cycle, in which the result of the design cycle—a validated treatment—is transferred to the real world, used, and evaluated. We call this larger cycle the engineering cycle. In Sect. 3.1, we start with the engineering cycle and present the design cycle as a subset of the engineering cycle. In Sect. 3.2, the design and engineering cycles are contrasted with the process of managing research and development.

3.1 The Design and Engineering Cycles

The **engineering cycle** is a rational problem-solving process with the structure shown in Fig. 3.1.[1] It consists of the following tasks:

- Problem investigation: What phenomena must be improved? Why?
- Treatment design: Design one or more artifacts that could treat the problem.
- Treatment validation: Would these designs treat the problem?
- Treatment implementation: Treat the problem with one of the designed artifacts.
- Implementation evaluation: How successful has the treatment been? This may be the start of a new iteration through the engineering cycle.

In implementation evaluation, we ask the same questions as in problem investigation but with a different goal. The goal of implementation evaluation is to evaluate a treatment after it has been applied in the original problem context. The goal of

© Springer-Verlag Berlin Heidelberg 2014
R.J. Wieringa, *Design Science Methodology for Information Systems and Software Engineering*, DOI 10.1007/978-3-662-43839-8_3

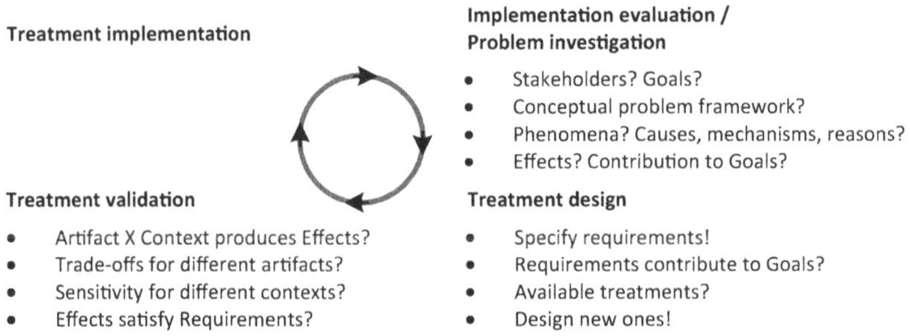

Treatment implementation

**Implementation evaluation /
Problem investigation**

- Stakeholders? Goals?
- Conceptual problem framework?
- Phenomena? Causes, mechanisms, reasons?
- Effects? Contribution to Goals?

Treatment validation

- Artifact X Context produces Effects?
- Trade-offs for different artifacts?
- Sensitivity for different contexts?
- Effects satisfy Requirements?

Treatment design

- Specify requirements!
- Requirements contribute to Goals?
- Available treatments?
- Design new ones!

Fig. 3.1 The engineering cycle. The question marks indicate knowledge questions, and the exclamation marks indicate design problems

problem investigation, by contrast, is to prepare for the design of a treatment by learning more about the problem to be treated.

Figure 3.1 shows the engineering cycle. The question marks indicate knowledge questions, and the exclamation marks indicate design problems. The terminology of the engineering cycle is overloaded, and I define the key terms below. First, I give two examples:

☐ The MARP project [11] was curiosity driven, and there was no *problem investigation*. *Treatment design* consisted of the design of several versions of a multi-agent route planning algorithm. The algorithms were *validated* analytically, by proving deadlock freedom under certain conditions and, empirically, by testing them on a simulation of an extremely busy day on Schiphol airport.

☐ The DLC project was utility driven. In the *problem investigation*, the researcher investigated the structure of the cloud provision market and current cloud provisioning technology used, European data location regulations, and the goals of auditors, European companies, and cloud service providers. As part of *treatment design*, the researcher made a survey of proposals for advanced methods to be used for auditing information technology. Based on this and on the results of the problem investigation, the student designed a new auditing method for data location compliance. The proposed method was *validated* by interviewing some IT consultants to ask their opinion about usability and utility of the method.

3.1.1 Treatment

It is customary for engineers to say that they are designing *solutions,* but we avoid this term because it may blind us for the possibility that an artifact may solve a problem only partially or maybe not at all. Artifacts may even introduce new problems. In the social sciences, the term *intervention* is used, in risk management the term *mitigation* is used, and in health-care *treatment* is used. The last term has the advantage that it naturally suggests an artifact (medicine) interacting with a problem context (the human body) to treat a real-world problem (contribute to healing), and so we will use the term "treatment." The treatment is the interaction between the artifact and the problem context, as indicated in Fig. 1.1 at the beginning of Chap. 1. The design science researcher designs not just an artifact, but designs a desired interaction between the artifact and the problem context, intended to treat the problem:

☐ For example, the DOA algorithm interacts with its context to provide an accurate and speedy estimation of direction of arrival. This treats, and actually solves, with the desired level of accuracy and speed, the problem of knowing what this direction is.

☐ The MARP algorithms interact with their context by updating route plans dynamically based on the current state of the context of each agent. This treats the problem of delays, by reducing these delays a bit.

☐ The compliance checking method is used by consultants in the context of cloud service provisioning. It treats the problem how to audit data location compliance.

3.1.2 Artifacts

An **artifact** is something created by people for some practical purpose. Examples of artifacts designed and studied in information systems and software engineering research are algorithms, methods, notations, techniques, and even conceptual frameworks. They are used when designing, developing, implementing, maintaining, and using information systems and software systems. When an artifact is used, it is used by people, which means that it interacts with a context that, along with other things, contains people.

3.1.3 Design and Specification

Treatments, and hence artifacts, are designed, and these designs are documented in a specification. There is considerable diversity in the use of these terms in software engineering and other branches of engineering. For example, in industrial product engineering, a product specification describes the *decomposition* of the product into its parts. In software engineering, a specification describes the *external behavior* of the software.

In this book, we stay close to the dictionary definition of these words. A **design** is a decision about what to do, and a **specification** is a documentation of that decision. For example, we can design the decomposition of a product into parts, but we can also design its external behavior. We will see later that we even design the requirements for a project. In all these cases, the designer makes decisions about what to do. And all these decisions can be documented in a specification.

3.1.4 Implementation

The word "implementation" can create confusion if researchers and practitioners from different fields talk to each other. For a software engineer, an implementation is a running software program. For an information systems engineer, implementations consist of databases and people collaborating to achieve an organizational goal. For a business manager, an implementation is an organizational change.

The confusion disappears if we define an **implementation** of a treatment as *the application of the treatment to the original problem context.* So instead of the word "implementation," we can always read "transfer to the problem context." What counts as an implementation depends on what problem context we have in mind.

With respect to real-world problems, design science projects are always restricted to the first three tasks of the engineering cycle: problem investigation, treatment design, and treatment validation. We call these three tasks the **design cycle**, because design science research projects usually perform several iterations through this cycle.

The confusion about what constitutes an implementation appears in design science projects as follows: From the point of view of an external stakeholder, the researcher performs a few iterations through the design cycle and never produces an implementation in the social problem context of the research project. But from the point of view of the researcher, he or she produces many implementations and tests them all. The confusion is resolved if we realize that the external stakeholder and the researcher are thinking of different problems and therefore mean something different when talking about an "implementation":

☐   In the DOA project, the researcher implemented several prototypes of DOA algorithms and of simulations of plane waves that arrive at an antenna array. The researcher's goal was to investigate properties of these algorithms. So he *investigated* the problem of estimating direction of arrival of a plane wave, *designed* a prototype and context simulation to do this estimation, *validated* the design, and *implemented* it. He then used it for his goal, which was to investigate the performance of the algorithms. During this use, he may have *evaluated* the quality of the prototypes and context simulations and may have improved them in light of this evaluation.

For the sponsor, a manufacturer of processors, the researcher never did more than validate possible treatments of the problem of DOA recognition in a TV reception system of a car. No implementation was produced, because none of the prototypes produced by the researcher was used in any of their products. From the sponsor's point of view, the researcher did not even have to do any *problem investigation* or *treatment design*. Rather, the researcher merely had to learn what is already known about the problem of TV signal reception in a moving car and about the available algorithms for DOA estimation. The original part of the research, from the point of view of the manufacturer, was to *validate* these algorithms for the goal of TV signal reception in a moving car.

In the rest of the book, I will assume that there is a problem context of external stakeholders, and unless otherwise stated, "implementation" is transfer to that problem context. So henceforth, unless otherwise stated, implementation is the same as technology transfer.

Design science research projects do not perform the entire engineering cycle but are restricted to the design cycle.[2] Transferring new technology to the market may be done after the research project is finished but is not part of the research project. Appendix A summarizes the design cycle in the form of a checklist.

3.1.5   Validation and Evaluation

To **validate** a treatment is to justify that it would contribute to stakeholder goals if implemented. In the engineering cycle, validation is done before implementation. It consists of investigating the effects of the interaction between a prototype of an artifact and a model of the problem context and of comparing these with requirements on the treatment. Based on this, we develop a *design theory*, which is a theory of the properties of the artifact and its interaction with the problem context. Using this theory, we then predict what would happen if the artifact were implemented, i.e., if it were transferred to the problem context.

Validation is contrasted with **evaluation**, which is the investigation of a treatment as applied by stakeholders in the field. In the engineering cycle, evaluation is done after implementation. In implementation evaluation, we have the benefit of hindsight and can use experience of external stakeholders with the implemented artifact to improve our design theory of it.

Validation and evaluation are different research goals that require different research approaches. The goal of validation is to predict how an artifact will interact with its context, without actually observing an implemented artifact in a real-world context. Validation research is experimental and is usually done in the laboratory. In validation research, we expose an artifact prototype to various scenarios presented by a model of the context, to see how it responds. Frequently used research methods are modeling, simulation, and testing, methods that are called "single-case mechanism experiments" in this book (Chap. 18).

The goal of evaluation research, by contrast, is to investigate how implemented artifacts interact with their real-world context. Evaluation research is field research of the properties of implemented artifacts. Frequently used research methods are statistical surveys and observational case studies (Chap. 17), but experimental research can be used too, as we will see later.

A special case is technical action research, which is a method to test a new artifact in the real world by using it to solve a real-world problem (Chap. 19). This is validation research, done in the field. The artifact is still under development and is not used by stakeholders independently from a research context. The artifact is used by researchers to test its properties under real-world conditions.[3]

3.2   Engineering Processes

The engineering and design cycles provide a logical structure of tasks but do not prescribe the process of engineering or of designing. They tell us that to design a treatment, we must understand the problem to be treated and that to justify the choice for a treatment, we must validate it before it is implemented. The engineering cycle also tells us that to learn from an implementation, we must evaluate it.

The engineering and design cycles do not tell us how to *manage* these processes. Management is achieving goals by the work of others, and managers must acquire resources, organize them, make plans, motivate people, and check results [1, 7]. None of these tasks are mentioned in the engineering cycle.

In particular, the engineering cycle does not prescribe a rigid sequence of activities. Possible execution sequences include, but are not limited to, the following sequences [13, pp. 348 ff]:

- In the linear *waterfall development process*, one sequential pass through the engineering cycle is made, without backtracking. This is possible if the problem is fully understood at the end of problem investigation, and treatment validation or treatment implementation do not give reason to redesign the treatment.
- In *agile development*, many sequential passes through the cycle are made. In each pass, a problem is treated of a size small enough to pass through the entire engineering cycle in about two calendar weeks.
- When *scaling up* new technology from the laboratory to real-world conditions, many passes through the engineering cycle are made. Initially, simplified problems are treated in idealized conditions. Later, simplifying assumptions are dropped until real-world conditions are approached. Each iteration through the engineering cycle aims at treating a problem at some level of realism or idealization, and the artifact designed and tested is a prototype geared to treating that problem.
- In *systems engineering*, first a number of iterations through the design cycle are performed, in which a problem and its possible treatments are described, specified, and validated conceptually, but no implementation is attempted. After each iteration, a decision is made to stop or to go ahead with the next iteration. Later, one or more passes through the entire engineering cycle are made, all of which are aimed at treating the same complex problem that is the goal of the entire systems engineering process. Each iteration through the engineering cycle uses knowledge about the problem and treatment generated by the previous ones. The next iteration may be started when the previous iteration is still running, leading to the concurrent but asynchronous execution of the engineering cycle for increasingly sophisticated versions of the artifact, all aimed at treating the same complex problem.

This does not exhaust the possible ways in which the engineering cycle can be executed in practice, but it suffices to remove the impression that the engineering cycle prescribes a single sequence of activities.

In design science, only the first three tasks of the engineering cycle are performed. This too must be managed. The research manager must manage the interface with the social context to acquire resources and align goals with stakeholders, as well as ensure that design problems and knowledge questions are formulated properly and answered in a methodologically sound way. The different activities in the design cycle are iterated over and may even be performed simultaneously for different aspects of the problem and for alternative treatments. Knowledge questions must be answered, which may require doing empirical research. All of this requires managing resources and time within the project budget. Managing this is very important, but it is not treated in this book.

3.3   Summary

- The design cycle consists of problem investigation, treatment design, and treatment validation.
- The design cycle is part of the engineering cycle, in which a designed and validated treatment is implemented in the problem context, and the implementation is evaluated.
- Implementation evaluation may be the problem investigation of a new engineering cycle.
- Managing the research and development process includes deciding what to do when, how to align with stakeholders, and how to use finite resources to achieve the research goal. This is out of scope of the engineering and design cycles.

Notes

[1]**Page 27, the engineering cycle.** The engineering cycle is well known in industrial product engineering as described, for example, by Cross [3], Jones [6], and Roozenburg and Eekels [10]. The engineering cycle is also present in Hall's [5] classical description of systems engineering, Archer's analysis of the architecture design process [2], and the logic of mechanical engineering described by Pahl and Beitz [8]. It sometimes goes by different names in different disciplines, but the structures recognized in different disciplines are virtually the same. Van Strien [12] calls it the *regulative cycle* and argues that it is the structure of action in practical disciplines such as consulting and psychotherapy.

[2]**Page 30, the design cycle.** Peffers et al. [9] define a design science research methodology (DSRM) that is a slightly elaborated design cycle.

Peffers et al. [9]	Design cycle
Problem identification and motivation	Problem investigation
Objectives of a solution	Treatment design: specify requirements
Design . . .	Treatment design: the rest
. . . and development	Validation: instrument development. Develop prototype and model of context
Demonstration	Validation: effects, trade-offs, sensitivity?
Evaluation	Validation: do effects satisfy requirements?
Communication	

Peffers et al. elaborate validation into some of its subtasks. To answer the validation questions, research instruments must be developed, namely, artifact prototypes and models of the context. They also include a communication task, which in this book is viewed as part of research management.

Gorschek et al. [4] discuss a technology transfer process that consists of the design cycle followed by a release of the technology for implementation. We discuss this process in Chap. 16.

[3]**Page 31, validation versus evaluation.** Another potentially confusing boundary case is that we may validate artifacts that are already implemented in the real world. For example, we may investigate a programming technique that is already in widespread use by software engineers. If we investigate properties of this technique in the laboratory, for example, by means of students who use the technique in the laboratory, then we are doing validation research. We are not investigating a real-world implementation of the technique but are investigating a model of the real world, namely, a student project in which the technique is used. Results from this study may provide additional insight in real-world properties of the technique.

The key point in distinguishing validation from evaluation is that in evaluation researchers study an artifact in the real world that is used by stakeholders independently from the researchers, whereas in validation, researchers experiment with a model of how stakeholders would use the artifact in the real world.

References

1. R.N. Anthony, *Planning and Control Systems: A Framework for Analysis* (Harvard University Graduate School of Business Administration, Boston, 1965)
2. B.L. Archer, The structure of the design process, in *Design Methods in Architecture*, ed. by G. Broadbent, A. Ward (Lund Humphries, London, 1969), pp. 76–102
3. N. Cross, *Engineering Design Methods: Strategies for Product Design*, 2nd edn. (Wiley, Hoboken, 1994)
4. T. Gorschek, C. Wohlin, P. Garre, S. Larsson, A model for technology transfer in practice. IEEE Softw. **23**(6), 88–95 (2006)
5. A.D. Hall, *A Methodology for Systems Engineering* (Van Nostrand, New York, 1962)
6. J.C. Jones, *Design Methods: Seeds of Human Futures* (Wiley, New York, 1970)
7. R.A. MacKenzie, The management process in 3–D, in *Software Engineering Project Management*, ed. by R.H. Thayer (IEEE Computer Science Press, Los Alamitos, 1988), pp. 11–14. First appeared in *Harvard Business Review*, November/December 1969
8. G. Pahl, W. Beitz, *Konstruktionslehre. Handbuch für Studium und Praxis* (Springer, Heidelberg, 1986)
9. K. Peffers, T. Tuunanen, M.A. Rothenberger, S. Chatterjee, A design science research methodology for information systems research. J. Manag. Inf. Syst. **24**(3), 45–77 (2007–2008)
10. N.F.M. Roozenburg, J. Eekels, *Product Design: Fundamentals and Methods* (Wiley, Hoboken, 1995)
11. A.W. ter Mors, The World According to MARP. Ph.D. thesis, Delft University of Technology, March 2010. http://www.st.ewi.tudelft.nl/~adriaan/pubs/terMorsPhDthesis.pdf
12. P.J. Van Strien, Towards a methodology of psychological practice: the regulative cycle. Theory Psychol. **7**(5), 683–700 (1997)
13. R.J. Wieringa, *Requirements Engineering: Frameworks for Understanding* (Wiley, Hoboken, 1996). Also available at http://www.ewi.utwente.nl/~roelw/REFU/all.pdf

Chapter 4
Stakeholder and Goal Analysis

Design science research projects take place in normative context of laws, regulations, constraints, ethics, human values, desires, and goals. In this chapter, we discuss goals. In utility-driven projects, there are stakeholders who have goals that the research project must contribute to. In exploratory projects, potential stakeholders may not know that they are potential stakeholders, and it may not be clear what their goals are. Nevertheless, or because of that, even in exploratory projects, it is useful to think about who might be interested in the project results and, importantly, who would sponsor the project. After all, design research should produce potentially useful knowledge. We therefore discuss possible stakeholders in Sect. 4.1 and discuss the structure of stakeholder desires and goals in Sect. 4.2. In Sect. 4.3, we classify possible conflicts among stakeholder desires that may need to be resolved by the project.

4.1 Stakeholders

A **stakeholder** of a problem is a person, group of persons, or institution affected by treating the problem. Stakeholders are the source of goals and constraints of the project, which are in turn the source for requirements in the treatment, and so it is important to identify relevant stakeholders (Fig. 4.1).

The goal of treatment design is that some stakeholders are better off when the problem is treated. However, for any treatment, some stakeholders may be better off in some respects and worse off in others. Even more troubling, for some treatments, some stakeholders may be worse off overall when the problem is treated that way.

© Springer-Verlag Berlin Heidelberg 2014
R.J. Wieringa, *Design Science Methodology for Information Systems and Software Engineering*, DOI 10.1007/978-3-662-43839-8_4

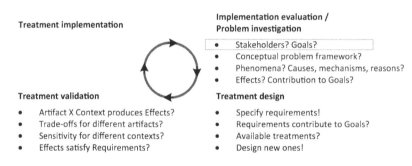

Fig. 4.1 The place of stakeholder and goal analysis in the engineering cycle

Table 4.1 gives a checklist of possible stakeholders in a design science research project, based on a checklist for engineering projects provided by Ian Alexander [1]. Another list is given by Clements and Bass [3], shown as a diagram in Fig. 4.2. Here are some examples:

☐ The DOA project to develop a satellite TV reception system for cars is an engineering project. Stakeholders in the project are the chip manufacturer NXP (sponsor), car component suppliers (responsible for interfacing systems), car manufacturers (functional beneficiary of the TV satellite reception system), garages (maintenance operators), car drivers (functional beneficiary), and passengers (normal operators).
  In the research project that investigated DOA algorithms, only the sponsor was important (the sponsor is always important), and the passenger goal to watch satellite TV in a car was important. The passenger goal motivates the requirement that accuracy of the DOA algorithm should be 1° and execution time of one iteration less than 7.7 ms.
☐ Stakeholders of the DLC project are KPMG (sponsor), KPMG consultants (end users, i.e., normal operators), and two classes of functional beneficiaries, namely, cloud service providers and European companies who are or want to become clients of cloud service providers (see also p. 8). Representatives of all of these stakeholders were interviewed for the project.

4.2 Desires and Goals

Stakeholders may have different levels of awareness of a problem and its possible treatments [2]. At the lowest awareness level, a stakeholder is *not aware* of the problem nor of the need of a treatment. For example, a car driver may feel fine with the audiovisual equipment in his or her car and not be aware of any problem with it.

At the second level of awareness, a stakeholder is aware of an improvement possibility but is *not interested* in actually carrying out the improvement. For example, a car driver may be aware that there is an improvement possibility in the audiovisual equipment in his car but not be interested in realizing this: He or she has no children who may want to watch TV in the backseat of his car. The stakeholder is indifferent, and there is still no problem.

Table 4.1 List of possible stakeholders of an artifact, based on the list given by Ian Alexander [1]

The system under development (SUD) consists of the artifact and these stakeholders interacting with the artifact

- **Normal operators** give routine commands to the artifact, sometimes called "end users"
- **Maintenance operators** interact with the system to keep it running
- **Operational support** staff support normal operators in their use of the system and help to keep the system operational

Stakeholders in the immediate environment of the SUD, interacting with the SUD

- **Functional beneficiaries** benefit from the output produced by the system, sometimes called "users" of the artifact
- Stakeholders responsible for **interfacing systems** have an interest in the requirements and scope of the artifact

Stakeholders in the wider environment of the SUD

- A **financial beneficiary** benefits from the system financially, such as a shareholder or director of the company that will manufacture the artifact
- A **political beneficiary** benefits from the system in terms of status, power, influence, etc.

- A **negative stakeholder** would be worse off when the artifact is introduced in the problem context
- A **threat agent** is a stakeholder who wants to hurt the system, e.g., by compromising its integrity or stealing confidential information from it

Stakeholders involved in the development of the SUD

- The **sponsor** initiates and provides a budget for developing the artifact. Important source of goals and requirements for the artifact
- The **purchaser** is, in this taxonomy, a stakeholder responsible for terminating development successfully. The purchaser could be a project manager or a product manager responsible for a wider range of projects all related to one product
- **Developers** such as requirements engineers, designers, programmers, and testers build the system. They are not normal operators of the system and do not benefit from its output during normal operation
- **Consultants** support development of the artifact
- **Suppliers** deliver components of the artifact

Fig. 4.2 List of possible stakeholders of an organization given by Clements and Bass [3]

Or the stakeholder may be aware of the improvement possibility and *desire* it. But still, he or she does not want, or is not able, to commit resources to realize this. The stakeholder may have no time or no money to realize this desire, or the desire is not strong enough to commit the time or money needed to achieve the desire. In this case, the stakeholder desires an improvement but has not set it as a goal to achieve. Most of us are in this state for most of our desires. We may like the option to have satellite TV in a car, but not desire it so much that we want to spend the money to actually acquire a car with satellite TV. It is too expensive, so we forget about it. There is a latent improvement possibility, and we do not spend attention to it.

We define a **stakeholder goal** as a desire for which the stakeholder has committed resources. The stakeholder is willing to achieve this goal and has committed money and/or time to achieve it. All stakeholders have finite resources, and only a few desires will be promoted to the status of goal. Here are two examples:

☐ In the DOA project, the manufacturer had committed a budget to achieve the goal of producing a directional antenna system for satellite TV. The other stakeholders were either not aware of the possibility to receive satellite TV or were aware but had not committed budget to achieve it.

☐ In the DLC project, the sponsor was an auditing company that had committed budget to develop and implement a method for auditing data location compliance. The other stakeholders had not yet committed budget to offer or to use data location compliant cloud services but were ready to do so if regulatory obstacles were out of the way.

4.3   Desires and Conflicts

Goals are desires for which resources are committed. Because stakeholders acquire artifacts to contribute to their goals, engineers and design science researchers will have to know about human desires. If there were no human desires, there would be no need for artifacts, and engineers and design science researchers would be out of a job.

The first thing to note is that *anything* can be the object of desire. Even desires can be the object of desire, such as when I wish I would desire to play a game with the pleasure that my grandson does. I can also desire to have a fear, as when I visit a scary movie, or desire to have a goal entertained by other stakeholders but to which I have not committed myself because I do not have enough budget. Figure 4.3 lists all elements of the context of an artifact as a possible objects of desire. Comparing this with Fig. 1.1 (p. 4) of the context of an artifact, we see that all possible context elements are possible objects of desire. By implication, any element of the context can be a stakeholder goal.

Second, desires can conflict with each other, and therefore goals can conflict with each other. A conflict among desires may be a reason to cancel a design project or to change its goals. Here are a few important kinds of conflicts between desires:

• Two desires are in *logical conflict* if it is logically impossible to realize them both. This means that there is no possible state of the world that could satisfy both desires and that this can already be shown by analyzing a description of

Fig. 4.3 Any element of the context of an artifact can be the object of stakeholder desire

both desires. For example, the desire to spend your money logically conflicts with the desire to keep it. The meaning of the words "spend" and "keep" are in logical conflict. It makes no sense to try to develop technology that harmonizes these desires.

- Two desires are in *physical conflict* if it would violate the laws of nature to satisfy them both. This means that there is no possible state of the world that could satisfy both desires, and this can be shown by empirically validated knowledge about the real world (the laws of nature). For example, the desire to eat more is in physical conflict with the desire to lose weight. The human body does not work that way. It is impossible to develop technology that would make these desires compatible.

- Two desires are in *technical conflict* if it would be physically possible to realize them both, but we currently have no technical means to achieve this. This points at an opportunity for new technical development. For example, it is at the time of writing not technically possible to receive satellite TV in cars, but new technical developments will probably make this possible in the near future. Until then, the desire to watch TV is in technical conflict with the desire to travel in a car at the same time.

- Two desires are in *economic conflict* if it is technically possible to realize them both, but this exceeds the available budget of the stakeholder. For example, a stakeholder may wish to have a 30 in. screen for his PC, but this exceeds his budget. He has to settle for a cheaper screen or a cheaper PC. This indicates a potential for further technical improvement that would make artifacts cheaper.

- Two desires are in *legal conflict* if it would be illegal to realize them both. For example, it is illegal for a European company to store privacy-sensitive data in the cloud outside Europe. The desire to store privacy-sensitive data legally conflicts with the desire to save cost by storing them noncompliantly in the cloud.

- Two desires are in *moral conflict* if satisfying them both would be morally wrong. For example, storing privacy-sensitive data and selling it to third parties may be legal, especially if this is announced in the conditions of use that the user subscribed to by clicking on a button. But many stakeholders would consider this morally wrong. For these stakeholders, the desire to store the data is in moral conflict with the desire to sell them.

For design researchers, the technical and economic conflicts are the interesting ones because design research may resolve these by making new things possible or by reducing the cost of artifacts.

4.4   Summary

- The actual and potential stakeholders of a design science project may motivate some project goals.
- A stakeholder of a problem is a person, group of persons, or institution who is affected by treating the problem.
- A stakeholder goal is a desire for the achievement of which the stakeholder has committed a budget of time, money, or other resources.
- Stakeholder desires and hence stakeholder goals may conflict. Some conflicts cannot be resolved; others may be resolvable by technical means or by increasing the budget. Resolution of some conflicts may be illegal or immoral.

References

1. I. Alexander, A taxonomy of stakeholders: Human roles in systems development. Int. J. Technol. Human Interact. **1**(1), 23–59 (2005)
2. M.I. Bossworth, *Solution Selling: Creating Buyers in Difficult Markets* (Irwin, Burr Ridge, 1995)
3. P. Clements, F. Bachmann, L. Bass, D. Garlan, J. Ivers, R. Little, P. Merson, R. Nord, J. Stafford, *Documenting Software Architectures: Views and Beyond*, 2nd edn. (Prentice-Hall, Upper Saddle River, 2010)

Chapter 5
Implementation Evaluation and Problem Investigation

Treatments are designed to be used in the real world, in the original problem context. Once they are implemented in the original problem context, this is an important source of information about the properties of the artifact and about the treatment that it provides. This may or may not trigger a new iteration through the engineering cycle.

In the social sciences, the study of real-world implementations of social programs is called an evaluation study. We follow this practice but attach a broader meaning to this term so that it includes the study of real-world implementations of artifacts. In Sect. 5.1, I distinguish and illustrate the two research goals of implementation evaluation and problem investigation, and in Sect. 5.2 we look at some examples of design theories that can be used and produced by this research. In Sect. 5.3, a few research methods that can be used for this kind of research are listed.

5.1 Research Goals

In *implementation evaluation*, the research goal is to evaluate an implementation of a treatment *after* it has been applied in the original problem context. The research goal is not necessarily to prepare for further improvement but to describe, explain, and evaluate the effects of a past improvement.

In *problem investigation*, the research goal is to investigate an improvement problem *before* an artifact is designed and when no requirements for an artifact have been identified yet. The research goal is to improve a problematic situation, and the first task is to identify, describe, explain and evaluate the problem to be treated.

Implementation evaluation and problem investigation are both real-world research. To study implementations and problems, you have to visit the real world. Implementation evaluation and problem investigation both contain the identification

© Springer-Verlag Berlin Heidelberg 2014
R.J. Wieringa, *Design Science Methodology for Information Systems and Software Engineering*, DOI 10.1007/978-3-662-43839-8_5

Table 5.1 Example knowledge questions in implementation evaluation and problem investigation

Implementation evaluation	Problem investigation
• Descriptive: What effects does the implemented artifact have?	• Descriptive: What are the phenomena?
• Explanatory: How does the artifact cause these effects? By what mechanisms?	• Explanatory: How are they caused? By which mechanisms are they produced? For what reasons are effects created?
• Evaluative: Do the effects contribute to and/or detract from stakeholder goals?	• Evaluative: Do the phenomena contribute to and/or detract from stakeholder goals?
• Explanatory: Why do they contribute and/or detract this way?	• Explanatory: Why do they contribute and/or detract this way?

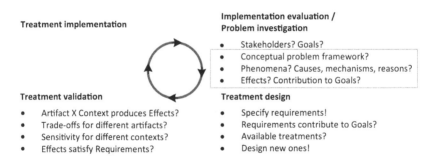

Fig. 5.1 The place of problem investigation and implementation evaluation in the engineering cycle

of stakeholders and goals, as discussed in the previous chapter. This is different from the investigation and evaluation of phenomena, which is the focus of this chapter.

Table 5.1 lists some typical research questions of both kinds of studies. Note the presence of evaluation questions, which are important in design science. An evaluation question is a special kind of descriptive question, in which we compare observed phenomena with a norm. As indicated by the questions in Fig. 5.1, in implementation evaluation and problem investigation, we are interested in the contribution, positive or negative, of phenomena and of their effects to stakeholder goals.

The research questions and methods used for both kinds of research goals are the same, but as we saw, the top-level goals are different: evaluation in one case and improvement in the other. Also, their object of study may be different. Implementation evaluations by definition study an artifact in context, whereas a problem investigation does not necessarily have to do so. These distinctions are gradual, and there are many intermediate cases, as the following examples illustrate:

☐ In the DLC project, the following problem research questions can be asked [7, p. 14]:

– What technical solutions do cloud service providers currently use to satisfy these goals?
– What obstacles do cloud service providers experience that prevent them to show data location compliance? How do these obstacles come about?

These questions evaluate the state of the practice of cloud service provision (an artifact) with respect to the goal of data location compliance (a context), and so this is an implementation evaluation.

☐ In the ARE problem, we can ask the following questions about implementations of agile practices [8]:

– Who are the decision-makers in the prioritization process?

  ∗ What roles do they play in the organization?
  ∗ What are their responsibilities in the decision-making process? Why these?

– Which value-based criteria do companies use to perform value-driven decisions during agile prioritization? Why?
– What characteristics of the project settings influence the way a requirements prioritization process is carried out in a project? How do they influence this?

These questions investigate the state of the practice of the implementation of agile requirements engineering but do not ask for an evaluation, so we can view this as an implementation *investigation* but not necessarily as an implementation *evaluation*.

☐ Our third example is from a project that we will call SPI, for software process improvement [10]. The goal of this research project was to evaluate the effect of SPI programs based on empirical evidence from one company. The core research questions of the project are [10, p. 11]:

– What are the quantitative effects of software process improvement on software development productivity?
– How are these effects produced?

The goal was to use the understanding gained by these empirical evaluations to improve the effectiveness of SPI programs and gain continuing support from management for SPI programs. So this was an implementation evaluation as well as a problem investigation project.

5.2 Theories

The goal of implementation evaluation and problem investigation is to build a scientific theory of real-world implementations and real-world problems, respectively. We discuss the structure and function of scientific theories in Part III and here only give examples. But to understand the examples, I give a crash course on the nature, structure, and function of scientific theories:

A scientific theory is a belief about a pattern in phenomena that has survived testing against empirical facts and critical reviews by peers. It consists of a *conceptual framework* plus *generalizations* about patterns in phenomena. The conceptual framework can be used to *frame* a research problem, *describe* phenomena, and *analyze* their structure. The generalizations may be useful to *explain* the causes, mechanisms or reasons for phenomena. This in turn may be useful to *predict* phenomena, or to justify artifact *designs*. Not each generalization may be useful for each of these purposes.

This finishes the crash course. It mentions the major elements of implementation evaluation and problem investigation such as a conceptual framework and explanations of phenomena (Fig. 5.1). Examples are given below, and a more detailed treatment, with literature references, is given in Part III of the book.

The crash course talks about scientific theories in general. This includes design science. Is there anything specific we can say about design science? Two things. First, design science studies the interactions between an artifact and its context. We call theories about (artifact × context) **design theories**.

Second, the phenomena studied in implementation evaluation and problem investigation are real-world phenomena. Theories developed in this kind of research can make less *idealizations* and must make more realistic assumptions about conditions of practice than theories developed in basic science. We discussed the need to balance idealizations against conditions of practice in design science research earlier, in Chap. 1. See also Fig. 1.4 (p. 9).

With this background, let us now look at a number of examples, in which we emphasize the words italicized above:

☐ In the DLC project, literature was studied, and experts were interviewed to develop a *conceptual framework* that defined key concepts such as that of cloud computing, private cloud, public cloud, infrastructure as a service, etc. This framework could be used to *frame* the research problem, i.e., to state the knowledge goal and formulate knowledge questions. It could also be used to *analyze* the structure of the cloud service provision market and to *describe* goals and problems of stakeholders in this market. The theory contained some simple descriptive *generalizations*, namely, that these phenomena usually occur in cloud service provision markets.

☐ In the ARE project, the researcher did a literature study and performed observational case studies to develop a *conceptual framework* of requirements engineering in agile projects done for small- and medium-sized enterprises (SMEs). The framework defines key concepts such as business value, business requirement, risk, and priority [8]. These concepts can be used to *analyze* and *describe* phenomena in agile requirements engineering.

One *generalization* found was that SMEs have a limited budget for software development, and their business priorities are not in favor of putting a customer on-site, even though putting a customer on-site is required by all agile development methods. This is a *design theory*: it says something about the interaction between an artifact (agile development) and a context (SMEs). The generalization contains an *explanation*: limited budgets and different business priorities are causes and reasons, respectively, for not putting as customer on-site of the project. The generalization can be used to *predict* that this will happen in other SMEs too. This is useful if we want to *redesign* an agile method to cater for this circumstance.

☐ The SPI project used a *conceptual framework* for software productivity measurement and measurement of requirements engineering activities. Statistical research produced some *generalizations*, such as that for larger projects in the case organization, facilitated workshops increase project productivity, whereas for smaller projects one-on-one requirements interviews appeared to be more productive [10, p. 62]. This is a *design theory*, as it is about artifacts (requirements engineering techniques) in a problem context (in-house software development). No *explanation* was given of this relationship. Nevertheless, the statistical generalizations can be used to *predict* the effect of introducing requirements engineering in some projects.

☐ The DOA project used a well-established signal theory found in textbooks. The *conceptual framework* contains concepts such as wave, wave front, plane wave, frequency, wave length, bandwidth, noise, etc. A *generalization* of the theory is that $\phi = 2\pi \, (d/\lambda) \sin \theta$, where θ is the direction of arrival of a plane wave with wavelength λ, d is the distance between antennas in an antenna array, and ϕ the phase difference between the waves arriving at two adjacent antennas in the array. It is a *design theory* how an artifact (antenna array) interacts with a context (plane waves). It can be used to *explain* why, for example, ϕ changes when θ changes and to *predict* that it will change when θ changes. This is used in the *design* of antenna arrays.

The theory makes some *idealizations* that may be violated in practice: waves are perfectly plane, bandwidth is narrow, etc. [13, pp. 6–7]. However, these idealizations are still realistic enough for the theory to be used to design antenna arrays.

5.3   Research Methods

There are many ways to investigate implementations and problems: you can read the scientific, professional, and technical literature, and you can interview experts. If none of this provides sufficient knowledge and you want to add to the published body of scientific knowledge, then you can decide to do scientific research yourself. Below is a brief description of some of the frequently used research methods for implementation evaluation and problem investigation. Most of these are described in detail in Part V of the book, and here I give only a few examples.

5.3.1   Surveys

Instances of an implementation or of a problem can be surveyed statistically, to find real-world performance data and identify statistical regularities. Anything about which data can be obtained in large numbers can be surveyed. Surveys can be taken by paper questionnaires, web forms, oral interviews, or other data collection means.

We can survey bug reports, change requests, problem reports, company memos, meeting notes, twitter messages, chat messages, emails, Internet traffic, intrusion attempts, log-in attempts, etc. We can also survey people's memory of past events, expectations of the future, opinions about company strategies, subjective theories about causes and effects of problems, etc.

Surveys are useful for implementation evaluation and problem investigation because they can provide information about real-world phenomena. Their disadvantage is that they may disturb the phenomena investigated (answering a question is disturbing and takes time) and can investigate only a few aspects of the phenomena.

Survey methods are not discussed in this book. Useful references to find out more are Babbie [3, Chap. 12], Robson [9, Part III], and Denscombe [4]. Here is an example:

☐ Agner et al. [1] surveyed the use of UML in embedded software development in Brazil using a web questionnaire. The research goal was to learn about the use of UML and model-driven development, the practice of embedded software development, and so this was an implementation evaluation.

Completed questionnaires were received from 209 respondents out of a total of 1,740 software developers and researchers contacted. Findings included the observation that among the respondents, UML is used mostly by experienced software developers (more than 5 years experience) and that among the factors that prevent the use of UML for embedded software development are short lead time for software development and lack of knowledge about UML among developers.

5.3.2   Observational Case Studies

In an observational case study, we observe a single case without intervening. We try to minimize any influence we may have on the case. Case study research can extend over several cases that are each studied in detail. The difference with statistical surveys is that in case study research, the sampled cases are studied one by one, whereas in statistical research, samples are selected and studied as a whole.

Observational case studies are useful for implementation evaluation and problem investigation because they give potential access to the underlying mechanisms that produce real-world phenomena. Their advantage is that they may give access to *all* aspects of the studied phenomena. Their disadvantages are that they may disturb the phenomena (being observed is disturbing), that they give information about only a few cases, and that about each case an unanalyzable mountain of data may be collected. Chapter 17 gives more information on how to do observational case studies. Here are two examples:

☐ Aranda et al. [2] interviewed managers of seven small companies to find out how they managed their software projects and elicited customer requirements. The companies were selected in a so-called snowball sampling procedure, which means that each company suggested other companies to visit as well. The focus of the study was on requirements engineering and not on any particular artifact used in this context, so this is a problem investigation.
   One of the findings was that it was often the entrepreneur, i.e., the one who started the company, who did the requirements engineering. One explanation for this is that a characteristic competence of an entrepreneur is the ability to translate customer needs in technical solutions, which is the goal of requirements engineering too.
☐ Myers [6] describes a study of an information systems implementation project performed for the New Zealand government. His study is a detailed implementation evaluation, where the focus is on social mechanisms that were responsible for the failure. Data was collected through primary documents and interviews, and the findings were that this project was highly politicized, where some stakeholders found it in their own interest to make this project fail and to publicized this failure in the media.

5.3.3   Single-Case Mechanism Experiments

A single-case mechanism experiment is a test of a single case in which the researcher applies stimuli to the case and explains the responses in terms of mechanisms internal to the case. This is what you do when you test a program: You feed it some input, observe the output, and explain how the output could have been produced by mechanisms internal to the program. It is also what a physician does when investigating a patient: The patient is exposed to some stimuli, responses are observed, and these are explained by mechanisms internal to the patient. And it is what we do to test artifacts in the real world. For example, to understand the IT network of a company, we can expose it to an input scenario, measure its performance, and then explain this in terms of the mechanisms internal to the architecture of the network.

The difference between single-case mechanism experiments and observational case studies is that in a single-case mechanism experiment, the researcher intervenes in the case, i.e., performs an experiment, whereas in an observational case study, the researcher does not intervene. In an observational case study, the research tries to influence the case as little as possible. In the literature, both kinds of studies are often referred to as "case studies," but in this book we will distinguish them clearly. Single-case mechanism experiments require the specification of an experimental treatment; observational case studies require a specification of ways in which the researcher reduces his or her influence on the case.

Single-case mechanism experiments are useful for implementation evaluation and problem investigation because they can provide insight into the behavior of artifacts and problematic phenomena in the real world. The researcher can create a scenario of stimuli that helps her to understand the mechanisms that produce phenomena. The researcher needs to have permission to apply these artificial stimuli.

Single-case mechanism experiments can be done in the lab or in the field. The advantage of lab research is that you can control the stimuli that the case is exposed to. The disadvantage is that the responses in the lab may not be similar to the responses in the field. If done in the field, the situation is reversed. Responses may now be similar to those of other real-world cases, but in the field there may be many other uncontrolled events happening at the same time that can make it difficult to interpret what is going on. Chapter 18 discusses single-case mechanism experiments in detail:

☐ Terwellen [12] extended a software system called SIL that is used by Océ, a manufacturer of printers and copiers, to simulate parts of a printer. This is used during new printer development. As a preparation for the extension of SIL, the researcher wanted to understand the mechanisms and performance properties of SIL and so he tested it. This part of the project is an implementation evaluation, and the test is a single-case mechanism experiment done in the real world. It is single case, because only one system, SIL, is tested. It is an experiment, because the researcher exposed SIL to a series of stimuli in order to learn something from its behavior. And it is a mechanism experiment, because outputs were explained in terms of mechanisms internal to the architecture of SIL.

5.3.4 Statistical Difference-Making Experiments

In a statistical difference-making experiment, we apply a treatment to a sample of cases selected from a population and compare the average outcome with the average outcome of another treatment on another sample drawn from the same population. If there is a difference, the researcher analyzes the experiment to see if this is caused by the difference in treatments or by another cause. This is the logic of controlled trials of medicines, where a new medicine is compared to an existing medicine or a placebo. It is also used in empirical software engineering to compare the effects of two software engineering techniques.

There are many variations of this design, of which the following must be mentioned here. In this variant, samples are drawn from *different* populations and receive the *same* treatment. Any observed difference between average outcomes is analyzed to see if it is produced by a difference in the populations. For example, we can give the same medicine to different groups to see if the medicine has different effects on different kinds of people. The logic and statistics of difference-making by treatments or by groups are the same.

Statistical difference-making experiments can be used in implementation evaluation and problem investigation by doing field experiments in the population of interest. The advantage is that this allows us to show a causal effect without relying on knowledge of internal mechanisms that produce this effect. The disadvantage of real-world research is that field experiments in software engineering and information systems are extremely expensive [11], because many resources are needed to build samples of sufficient size. Also, uncontrolled field conditions may make it hard to interpret the outcome. Statistical difference-making experiments are described in detail in Chap. 20:

☐ Hannay et al. [5] investigated the effects of personality, expertise, task complexity, and country of employment on pair programming performance, by creating pairs of professional software engineers exhibiting different combinations of these variables. The researchers studied the difference in performance of these pairs in terms of the quality of the program and the effort it took to produce it.

 This is an implementation evaluation because it was a field study of an artifact (pair programming) evaluated on some performance parameters. It was extremely expensive, because participants were paid professional software engineering wages. The situation was still somewhat artificial because some real-world aspects were missing, such as group dynamics and long-duration cooperation.

 The findings were that personality traits have modest predictive value for pair programming performance compared to expertise, task complexity, and country.

5.4 Summary

- Implementation evaluation is the investigation of artifacts that have been transferred to their intended real-world problem context. The research goal is to evaluate them with respect to actual stakeholder goals.
- Problem investigation is the investigation of real-world problems as a preparation for the design of a treatment for the problem. The research goal is to learn about stakeholder goals and to understand the problem to be treated.

- Both kinds of empirical study ask the same research questions that are about phenomena, causes and effects, and the contribution of phenomena to stakeholder goals. Questions can be open or closed and descriptive or explanatory.
- Implementation evaluation and problem investigation aim to develop theories of phenomena. A theory consists of a conceptual framework and generalizations. If the theory is about the interaction of an artifact with its context, we call it a design theory.
- Implementation evaluation and problem investigation are real-world research. Different research methods can be used, including surveys, observational case studies, single-case mechanism experiments, and statistical difference-making experiments.

References

1. L.T.W. Agner, I.W. Soares, P.C. Stadzisz, and J.M. Simão, A Brazilian survey on UML and model-driven practices for embedded software development. J. Syst. Softw. **86**(4), 997–1005 (2013)
2. J. Aranda, S.M. Easterbrook, G. Wilson, Requirements in the wild: how small companies do it, in *Proceedings of the 15th IEEE International Requirements Engineering Conference (RE 2007)*. (Computer Science Press, New York, 2007), pp. 39–48
3. E. Babbie, *The Practice of Social Research*, 11th edn. (Thomson Wadsworth, Belmont, 2007)
4. M. Denscombe, *The Good Research Guide For Small-Scale Social Research Projects*, 4th edn. (Open University Press, Maidenhead, 2010)
5. J.E. Hannay, A. Arisholm, H. Engvik, D.I.K. Sjøberg, Effects of personality on pair programming. IEEE Trans. Softw. Eng. **36**(1), 61–80 (2010)
6. M.D. Myers, A disaster for everyone to see: An interpretative analysis of a failed IS project. Accounting Manag. Inf. Technol. **4**(4), 185–201 (1994)
7. J. Noltes, Data location compliance in cloud computing. Master's thesis, Faculty of Electrical Engineering, Mathematics and Computer Science, University of Twente, August 2011. http://essay.utwente.nl/61042/
8. Z. Racheva, M. Daneva, A. Herrmann, K. Sikkel, R.J. Wieringa, Do we know enough about requirements prioritization in agile projects: insights from a case study, in *18th International IEEE Requirements Engineering Conference, Sydney*, October 2010 (IEEE Computer Society, Los Alamitos, 2010), pages 147–156
9. C. Robson, *Real World Research*, 2nd edn. (Blackwell, Oxford, 2002)
10. J. Schalken, Empirical investigations of software process improvement. Ph.D. thesis, Vrije Universiteit, Amsterdam, 2007. http://www.cs.vu.nl/en/research/Dissertations-1995-now/index.asp
11. D.I.K. Sjøberg, B. Anda1, E. Arisholm1, T. Dybå, M. Jørgensen1, A. Karahasanovicacutel, M. Vokáccaron, Challenges and recommendations when increasing the realism of controlled software engineering experiments, in *Empirical Methods and Studies in Software Engineering*, ed. by R. Conradi, A.I. Wang, LNCS, vol. 2765 (Springer, New York, 2003), pp. 24–38
12. C. Terwellen, Evaluating the behavior of embedded control software – using a modular software-in-the-loop simulation environment and a domain specific modeling language for plant modeling. Master's thesis, Faculty of Electrical Engineering, Mathematics and Computer Science, University of Twente, November 2012. http://essay.utwente.nl/62824/
13. J.D. Vrielink, Phased array processing: Direction of arrival estimation on reconfigurable hardware. Master's thesis, Faculty of Electrical Engineering, Mathematics and Computer Science, University of Twente, January 2009. http://essay.utwente.nl/62065/

Chapter 6
Requirements Specification

In design science projects, there may be uncertainty about stakeholders and their goals, and so treatment requirements may be very uncertain. It nevertheless pays off to spend some time on thinking about the desired properties of a treatment before designing one (Fig. 6.1). The requirements that we specify provide useful guidelines for searching possible treatments.

In Sect. 6.1, requirements are defined as desired treatment properties. The desirability of a requirement must be motivated in terms of stakeholder goals by a so-called contribution argument, which is explained in Sect. 6.2. In Sect. 6.3, several ways to classify requirements are discussed. One important class is the class of nonfunctional requirements, which are usually not directly measurable. Nonfunctional requirements must be operationalized if we want to measure them. This is discussed in Sect. 6.4. This section is also important for the design of measurement procedures in empirical research, treated later.

6.1 Requirements

A **requirement** is a property of the treatment desired by some stakeholder, who has committed resources (time and/or money) to realize the property. In other words, it is a goal for the to-be-designed treatment. As we will see, treatment requirements are always decomposed into artifact requirements and context assumptions:

☐ In the DLC problem, the following requirements for the data location compliance checking method were specified:

   R0   The method must allow auditors to audit data location.
   R1   The method must be usable for KPMG consultants, i.e., the effort to learn and effort to use are acceptable. KPMG is the company that sponsored the project.
   R2   The method must be useful for KPMG consultants, i.e., by using the method, consultants help CSPs and their clients.

© Springer-Verlag Berlin Heidelberg 2014
R.J. Wieringa, *Design Science Methodology for Information Systems and Software Engineering*, DOI 10.1007/978-3-662-43839-8_6

Design implementation

Implementation evaluation /
Problem investigation

- Stakeholders? Goals?
- Conceptual problem framework?
- Phenomena? Causes, mechanisms, reasons?
- Effects? Contribution to Goals?

Design validation

- Artifact X Context produces Effects?
- Effects satisfy Requirements?
- Trade-offs for different artifacts?
- Sensitivity for different contexts?

Treatment design

- Specify requirements!
- Requirements contribute to Goals?
- Available treatments?
- Design new ones!

Fig. 6.1 The place of requirements specification in the engineering cycle. The exclamation mark indicates that requirements are produced by design actions, not found as answers to knowledge questions

RO is a functional correctness requirement, and the other two are performance requirements. These requirements are motivated by stakeholder goals, and the stakeholder has committed a budget to realize the requirements. They are meaningful under some assumptions about the context, such as that the method is going to be used by KPMG auditors and that they will be applied in the European union where data location regulations are in force. The requirements motivate research questions that we have encountered earlier, in Chap. 5 (p. 43).

☐   Three requirements for the DOA algorithm are:

RO   The component must recognize DOA of a plane wave.
R1   The resolution of the algorithm need not be smaller than $1°$.
R2   One iteration of the estimation algorithm must not take more 7.7 ms.

RO is a functional correctness requirement; the other two are performance requirements. The requirements are motivated by a stakeholder goal, receiving satellite TV in a moving car, and the manufacturer has committed a budget to realize the requirements. They are meaningful under certain context assumptions, such as that all waves are plane and that the algorithm will be used in a car that drives. The requirements motivate the research questions about DOA algorithms that we have encountered earlier, in Chap. 2 (p. 21).

6.2   Contribution Arguments

Stakeholders rarely if ever are able to specify requirements. Instead, specifying requirements is an important design activity of the design researcher. The requirements are not answers to questions that we ask the stakeholders. Instead, they are the result of design choices that we make jointly with, or on behalf of, the stakeholders.

To justify your choice for some requirement, you have to give a **contribution argument**, which is an argument that an artifact that satisfies the requirements would contribute to a stakeholder goal in the problem context.[4] A contribution argument has the form

(Artifact Requirements) × (Context Assumptions) contribute to (Stakeholder Goal).

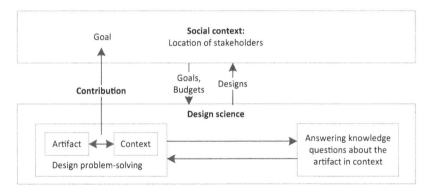

Fig. 6.2 The interaction of an artifact with its context should contribute to a stakeholder goal. Questions about goal contribution are prediction problems

Figure 6.2 shows where the contribution takes place in our design science framework. Note that in a design science project, there may be several contribution arguments for a requirement. A treatment that satisfies some requirement may, because of that, contribute to several different goals of different stakeholders.

A contribution argument is a prediction, because it argues that when the artifact would be inserted in its problem context, it would interact with it in a way that contributes to stakeholder goals. The contribution argument is fallible, because it does not provide deductively certain support to its conclusion. Here are some examples:

☐   In the DLC problem, the following contribution argument is given:

  – If the compliance checking method allows auditors to audit location of data stored in the cloud and is usable and useful for KPMG auditors in their auditing practice,
  – and assuming that the cloud provision market and infrastructure has the architecture as modeled in our project,
  – then the method contributes to KPMG's goal of acquiring more customers in the cloud provisioning market.

  This argument is fallible, as the cloud provisioning market may have been modeled incorrectly by the researcher, and the method may turn out not to be as usable and useful to consultants as initial research suggested that it is.

☐   The contribution argument for the DOA algorithm is as follows:

  – If the DOA algorithm satisfies the requirements that it can recognize DOA of a plane wave, with a resolution not worse than 1°, and an iteration time of at most 7.7 ms,
  – and assuming that the DOA algorithm is part of a beamforming system, which is used to receive satellite TV in a car,
  – then the DOA estimation component of such a beamforming system contributes to the goal of car passengers to watch satellite TV in a moving car.

This argument appears to be quite certain, but it is not. Cars drive very fast in some countries, and display screens may get a very high resolution, making the numbers used in the argument obsolete. And some of the unstated assumptions about the distance of sources and the nature of noise may be false in some contexts.

6.3 Kinds of Requirements

Requirements can be classified in many ways. For example, we may classify them according to the stakeholder goals that they contribute to, according to the importance of the goal (priority), or according to the deadline (urgency) by which they should be realized [1, 7].

Sometimes, *constraints* on the internal composition of the artifact are distinguished from requirements on the externally observable properties of an artifact. Both are desired properties of the artifact, and what is a constraint for one stakeholder can be a negotiable requirement for another:

☐ For example, an enterprise architect may view a global architecture of the IT infrastructure of a company as hard constraint on any system development project. A project manager may view this as a negotiable requirement that might be dropped from the project.

Another classical distinction is that between the so-called functional and nonfunctional requirements. An artifact **function** is a terminating part of the interaction between an artifact and its context that contributes to a service to a stakeholder [8]:

☐ For example, estimating direction of arrival is a function of the DOA estimation component of a satellite TV reception system, because it contributes to the service of the system.
☐ Methods are artifacts too and have functions too. For example, it is the function of a compliance checking method to support its user in assessing compliance.

A **functional requirement** is a requirement for desired functions of an artifact.

A **nonfunctional property**, sometimes called a *quality property*, is any property that is not a function. Nonfunctional properties are usually global properties of the interaction between an artifact and its context. The term "nonfunctional property" is awkward, but it is here to stay and I will use it too:

☐ Examples of nonfunctional properties are utility for a stakeholder, accuracy of output, efficiency in time or space, security, reliability, usability by a stakeholder, interoperability with other systems, maintainability for a maintainer, and portability across platforms. See Table 6.1.

A **nonfunctional requirement** is the requirement that an artifact has a specified nonfunctional property. We have seen a number of examples of nonfunctional requirements:

☐ The estimation algorithm should have a spatial resolution of $1°$ (accuracy).
☐ The estimation algorithm should recognize direction of arrival within 7.7 ms (time efficiency).
☐ The method must be usable by consultants in their daily practice (usability).
☐ The method must be useful for consultants who want to check data location compliance (utility).

Table 6.1 Some examples of properties and indicators, based on ISO standard 9126 [4]

Property	Some possible indicators
Utility	Stakeholder opinion about utility
Accuracy of output	Domain-dependent indicators, such as spatial resolution
Efficiency in time or space	Execution time, Memory usage
Security	Availability, Compliance to standards
Reliability	Mean time between failures, Time to recovery
Usability by a stakeholder	Effort to learn, Effort to use
Interoperability with other systems	Effort to realize interface with other systems
Maintainability for a maintainer	Effort to find bugs, Effort to repair, Effort to test
Portability across platforms	Effort to adapt to new environment, Effort to install, Conformance to standards

6.4 Indicators and Norms

An **operationalization** of a property is a measurement procedure by which evidence for the presence of the property can be established. Functional properties are operationalized by specifying tests for them. Nonfunctional properties are usually operationalized by defining one or more **indicators** for them, variables that can be measured and that indicate the presence of the property. In software engineering research, indicators are usually called *metrics*. Table 6.1 gives some examples of nonfunctional properties and some of their possible indicators.

Note that none of the indicators completely establishes all of the aspects of the property that they operationalize. If a property must be operationalized by indicators, then we may always question the validity of the operationalization. This kind of validity is called *construct validity*, and it is part of the validity of conceptual frameworks. We discuss it in Chap. 8.

A **norm** for an indicator is a set of required values of the indicator. Indicators operationalize properties, and norms operationalize requirements. In software engineering research, norms may be called *acceptance criteria*. Here are a few examples:

☐ "The algorithm should recognize the direction of arrival of a plane wave." This defines an indicator, namely, *ability to recognize DOA*. It has two possible values, *present* and *absent*, and the norm is that it should be *present*. This norm operationalizes a functional requirement.
☐ "The estimation algorithm should have a spatial resolution of 1° or less (accuracy)." The property *accuracy* is operationalized by the indicator *spatial resolution*. The norm *not worse than one degree* operationalizes a requirement.
☐ "The interviewed consultants must not find any elements of the method that make it unusable." This is an indicator for usability by consultants. The indicator is *opinion about usability*, and the norm that operationalizes the requirement is *opinion is favorable*.

In many research projects, nonfunctional requirements are not operationalized. The research goal may be to make something possible (such as data location compliance checking) or to see if something can be improved (such as delay reduction for aircraft taxiing) without being very clear about the performance norm to be achieved. In other cases, requirements may be operationalized into a testable norm (such as having an execution time of less than 7.7 ms).

6.5   Summary

- Requirements are treatment goals. They are desired by some stakeholder who has committed a budget to realize them.
- Requirements are specified by the design researcher. To justify requirements, there should be a contribution argument of the form

    (Artifact Requirements) × (Context Assumptions) contributes to (Stakeholder Goal).

- Requirements can be classified in many ways. One classification is the distinction between functional and nonfunctional requirements:

    - To make a nonfunctional property measurable, it must be operationalized by indicators.
    - To make a nonfunctional requirement measurable, it must be operationalized by indicators and norms.
    - Sometimes a norm is crisp, but often it just indicates the direction of improvement.

Notes

[4] **Page 52, the contribution argument.** The concept of a contribution argument corresponds closely to the concept of a satisfaction argument introduced by Jackson [5]. Satisfaction arguments are part of Jackson's problem-solving approach to software engineering using problem frames [6]. A brief explanation with formalization is given by Gunter et al. [2], and a philosophical argument that this is one of the core achievements of software engineering is given by Hall and Rapanotti [3].

References

1. D.C. Gause, G.M. Weinberg, *Exploring Requirements: Quality Before Design* (Dorset House, New York, 1989)
2. C.A. Gunter, E.L. Gunter, M.A. Jackson, P. Zave, A reference model for requirements and specifications. IEEE Softw. **17**(3), 37–43 (2000)
3. J. Hall, L. Rapanotti, Beauty in software engineering. Computer **46**(2), 85–87 (2013)
4. ISO/IEC JTC1/SC7/WG6, *ISO/IEC 9126-1 Information technology – Software Quality Characteristics and Metrics – Quality Characteristics and subcharacteristics*. International Organization for Standardization, June 9, 1995
5. M.A. Jackson, *Software Requirements and Specifications: A Lexicon of Practice, Principles and Prejudices* (Addison-Wesley, Boston, 1995)
6. M.A. Jackson, *Problem Frames: Analysing and Structuring Software Development Problems* (Addison-Wesley, Boston, 2000)
7. S. Lauesen, *Software Requirements: Styles and Techniques* (Addison-Wesley, Boston, 2002)
8. R.J. Wieringa, *Design Methods for Reactive Systems: Yourdon, Statemate and the UML* (Morgan Kaufmann, Burlington, 2003)

Chapter 7
Treatment Validation

To validate a treatment is to justify that it would contribute to stakeholder goals when implemented in the problem context. If the requirements for the treatment are specified and justified, then we can we validate a treatment by showing that it satisfies its requirements. The central problem of treatment validation is that no real-world implementation is available to investigate whether the treatment contributes to stakeholder goals. Still, we want to predict what will happen if the treatment is implemented. This problem is explained in Sect. 7.1. To solve it, design researchers build validation models of the artifact in context, and investigate these models (Sect. 7.2). Based on these modeling studies, researchers develop a design theory of the artifact in context, and use this theory to predict the effects of an implemented artifact in the real world (Sect. 7.3). We review some of the research methods to develop and test design theories in Sect. 7.4. These methods play a role in the process of scaling up an artifact from the idealized conditions of the laboratory to the real-world conditions of practice. This is explained in Sect. 7.5.

7.1 The Validation Research Goal

The goal of validation research is to develop a design theory of an artifact in context that allows us to predict what would happen if the artifact were transferred to its intended problem context (Fig. 7.1). For this, it is essential that the design theory can be used for prediction. Explanation is desirable too, but not essential.

The core validation research questions have been treated in Chap. 2 and are repeated in Table 7.1.

The central problem of validation research is that it is done *before* implementation. The artifact is not interacting with any problem context yet and perhaps never will. A realistic implementation does not even exist. So what is there to investigate? In design science research, we use validation models to simulate implementations.

© Springer-Verlag Berlin Heidelberg 2014

R.J. Wieringa, *Design Science Methodology for Information Systems and Software Engineering*, DOI 10.1007/978-3-662-43839-8_7

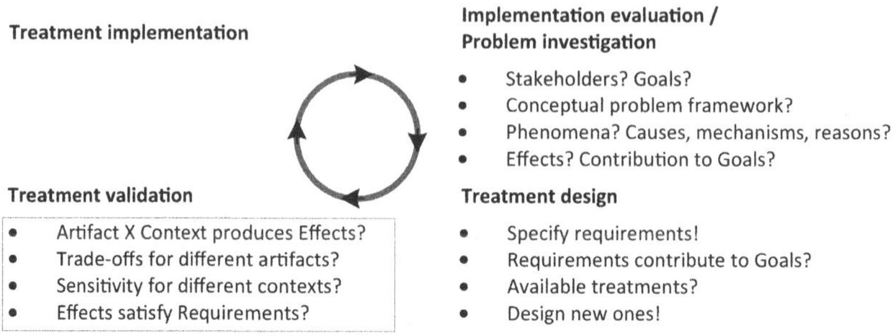

Treatment implementation

**Implementation evaluation /
Problem investigation**

- Stakeholders? Goals?
- Conceptual problem framework?
- Phenomena? Causes, mechanisms, reasons?
- Effects? Contribution to Goals?

Treatment validation

- Artifact X Context produces Effects?
- Trade-offs for different artifacts?
- Sensitivity for different contexts?
- Effects satisfy Requirements?

Treatment design

- Specify requirements!
- Requirements contribute to Goals?
- Available treatments?
- Design new ones!

Fig. 7.1   The place of treatment validation in the engineering cycle

Table 7.1   Four important kinds of knowledge questions in validation research. Repeated from Table 2.4

Effect questions: (artifact × context) produce Effects?

- What effects are produced by the interaction between the artifact and context?
- How does the artifact respond to stimuli?
- What performance does it have in this context? (Different variables)

Trade-off questions: (alternative artifact × context) produce effects?

- What effects do similar artifacts have in this context?
- How does the artifact perform in this context compared to similar artifacts?
- How do different versions of the same artifact perform in this context?

Sensitivity questions: (artifact × alternative context) produce Effects?

- What effects are produced by the artifact in different contexts?
- What happens if the context becomes bigger/smaller?
- What assumptions does the design of the artifact make about its context?

Requirements satisfaction questions: do effects satisfy requirements?

- Does the stimulus-response behavior satisfy functional requirements?
- Does the performance satisfy nonfunctional requirements?

For example, we study a prototype of an artifact, interacting with a model of the intended problem context, to develop a design theory about the interaction between the artifact and a context.

We can do this even if implementations already exist. For example, after an effort estimation technique is implemented and is used in real-world projects, we may continue to validate it by testing its accuracy in student projects in the laboratory. It is therefore not entirely accurate to say that validation research is done before implementation. We can even study existing implementations by studying validation models that represent existing real-world implementations. The central problem of validation research exists by definition: In validation research, we want to study the interaction between an artifact and its context by studying a model of it.

7.2   Validation Models

The word "model" is overloaded, and in this book we use it in one of its many meanings, namely, that of an analogic model. An **analogic model** is an entity that represents entities of interest, called its **targets,** in such a way that questions about the target can be answered by studying the model. Henceforth, unless otherwise stated, the term "model" always refers to analogic models.[5]

Examples of models in science are the use of an electrical network as a model of a network of water pipes, the use of water waves as a model of light waves, and the double-helix model of DNA, among others. Models are used in science to make complex phenomena understandable and to reduce the cost of investigating the phenomena. In engineering, scale models are routinely used to simulate the behavior of artifacts under controlled circumstances. And in drug research, animals are used as natural models of human beings to test the effect of drugs [16].

A **validation model** consists of model of the artifact interacting with a model of the problem context (Fig. 7.2). The targets of a validation model are all possible artifact implementations interacting with real-world problem contexts.

There is a wide variety of models that are used for validation purposes in software engineering and information systems research. To simulate aspects of software systems, we can use executable specifications, Matlab simulations, software prototypes, or user interface mock-ups, and we can even do a role-play in which people act as software components. To simulate the interaction between an IT artifact and its context, we can use students or real-world stakeholders, who we ask to perform tasks in a simulated environment in the laboratory. In technical action research, as we will see later, we investigate the effect of a new technique by applying it to a real-world case that is used as model for other real-world cases.

All of these uses of models are based on a relevant similarity between the model and its target, which is used to generalize by analogy from observations of the model to properties of its target. Reasoning by analogy is discussed further in Chap. 15:

☐   In a project to design a new goal-oriented enterprise architecture (EA) design method that we
     will call EA, the researcher performed two validations, using two validation models [3]. In the first
     validation, he used the method himself to design a new EA for a client. In this study, the model

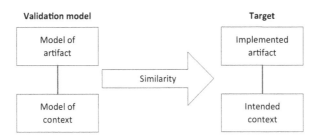

Fig. 7.2 A validation model represents its targets by similarity. It is used to answer questions about its targets

of the artifact was the then current description of the method. The model of the intended problem context was the client and the small EA project performed by the researcher for the client.

In the second validation, the researcher taught the method to architects in another client company, after which they used it to redesign the EA of their organization. In this study, the model of the artifact was the description of the method used by the architects. The model of the context was the client organization who performed the EA project.

☐ In the DLC project, the researcher presented a prototype of the newly designed data location compliance auditing method, in the form of a number of slides and a text on paper, to a panel of consultants, who gave their opinion about the usability and utility of the method. Each consultant constructed a validation model in their head, consisting of an imagined problem context in which they applied the prototype of the method. The targets of these partly imagined validation models are all real-world uses of the method for data location compliance assessment, independently from the designer of the method.

☐ In the DOA project, two kinds of validation studies were done. In the first validation, the validation models were Matlab simulations of algorithms to estimate direction of arrival and Matlab simulations of the context. In the second validation, the artifact was prototyped in a particular version of C, and the various contexts were simulated in the same programming language.

7.3 Design Theories

The goal of validation is to build a theory of the implemented artifact in a real-world context, based on study of validation models. Once we have a theory that has successfully survived tests and criticism, we use it to make predictions. We will discuss the structure and function of scientific theories in more detail later and here repeat the crash course given earlier, in slightly different words:

- A scientific theory is a belief about a pattern in phenomena that has survived testing against empirical facts and critical reviews by peers. This survival does not imply that the theory is final or even that it is completely true. Any scientific theory is fallible and may be improved in the future.
- A scientific theory contains a *conceptual framework* that can be used to *frame* a research problem, *describe* and *analyze* phenomena, and generalize about them.
- A scientific theory also contains *generalizations* about patterns in phenomena that may be usable to *explain* the causes, mechanisms, or reasons of phenomena. This in turn may be useful to *predict* phenomena or to justify artifact *designs*. Not each generalization may be usable for each of these purposes.

In validation research, we develop *design theories*, which are theories of the interaction between an artifact and its intended problem context:

☐ The *conceptual framework* of the design theory in the EA project is the conceptual framework of the artifact, the ARMOR method. This framework defines concepts such as goal, stakeholder, requirement, etc. The *generalization* of the design theory is that the steps of the ARMOR method are sufficient to create an enterprise architecture that links architecture components to the relevant business goals. This is a kind of functional correctness. The generalization *predicts* what will happen if the ARMOR method is used and *explains* the expected result in terms of the steps of the method.

The greatest threat to this design theory is that it may be true of simple EA projects performed under controlled conditions but may be false of complex projects performed under conditions of practice. In other words, the major goal of validation research is to check whether the theory holds under conditions of practice.

☐ In the DOA project, the artifacts being investigated are algorithms to estimate direction of arrival. The *conceptual framework* of the design theory of these artifacts contains concepts from matrix calculus, linear algebra, and signaling theory. The conceptual framework of the DOA design theory is used to specify the design of estimation algorithms and to *analyze* their properties. The conceptual framework is also used to *describe* measurements of the performance of the algorithms.

The major *generalization* is about functional correctness: When used in the proper context (plane waves, narrow bandwidth, etc.), the algorithms produce an accurate estimate of the direction of arrival of plane waves.

For one particular algorithm, called MUSIC, more research was done. A generalization about MUSIC is that DOA is recognized up to an accuracy of 1 degree and within 7.7 ms execution time. Additional generalizations were found too, such as that increasing the number of antennas in an array produces a higher spatial resolution [14, page 24] and that a particular set of nested loops caused performance degradation under certain conditions [14, page 59]. Some of these generalizations can be used to *predict* performance of the algorithm in the real world. Some can be used to *explain* the behavior of the algorithm or to improve the *design* of the systems in which the DOA algorithm was used.

7.4 Research Methods

There are many methods to study validation models, and some lists of methods have been published, for example, by Zelkowitz and Wallace [17] and by Glass et al. [4]. Closer inspection reveals that these lists can be reduced to the list of methods below and the measurement techniques and data analysis techniques discussed later [15].[6]

Most of the methods discussed below are explained in more detail later, in Part V.

7.4.1 Expert Opinion

The simplest way to validate an artifact is by expert opinion. The design of an artifact is submitted to a panel of experts, who imagine how such an artifact will interact with problem contexts imagined by them and then predict what effects they think this would have. If the predicted effects do not satisfy requirements, this is a reason to redesign the artifact. This approach to validation is very similar to code inspections, where a number of software engineers read code produced by someone else in order to find any bugs. An example is the DLC project, in which experts were asked to give their opinion about a data location compliance auditing method.

Note that the goal of expert opinion is *not* to give a survey of all opinions of all experts. Rather, the experts are used as instruments to "observe," by imagining, a validation model of the artifact. The model exists in the imagination of the experts.

Validation by expert opinion only works if the experts understand the artifact, imagine realistic problem contexts, and make reliable predictions about the effects of the artifact in context. Positive opinions may indicate socially desirable remarks, or they may indicate that the experts cannot imagine why this artifact would not work in practice. To rule this out, you have to ask the experts to explain their predictions in terms of the mechanisms that they think will produce the effects.

Negative opinions are more useful than positive opinions, because they give early indications of improvement opportunities for the artifact. Negative opinions can indicate conditions of practice not thought of by the researcher. Expert opinion is useful to weed out bad design ideas early.

We will not further discuss the use of expert opinion in this book. It is similar to the use of focus groups in requirements engineering, explained by, for example, Alexander [1] and Lauesen [10].

7.4.2 Single-Case Mechanism Experiments

A single-case mechanism experiment in validation research is a test in which the researcher applies stimuli to a validation model and explains the response in terms of mechanisms internal to the model. For example, you build a prototype of a program, build a model of its intended context, and feed its test scenarios to observe its responses. The responses, good or bad, are explained in terms of the mechanisms internal to the program or to the environment.

Single-case mechanism experiments are useful for validation research, because they allow us to expose the model to controlled stimuli and analyze in detail which mechanisms are responsible for the responses. Depending on the realism of the model, we may study the effects of mechanisms in the artifact as well as mechanism in the context and their interaction. Single-case mechanism experiments are discussed in Chap. 18. They are not restricted to testing software, as illustrated by the second example below:

☐ In the MARP project, the planning algorithms were tested in a simulation of an extremely busy day on Schiphol airport. The validation model consisted of a set of agents using MARP in a simulation of Schiphol airport. The model showed a reduction of delays with respect to the fixed planning algorithms used currently at the airport. By contrast, simulations on arbitrary road networks with random arrival and destination points showed very large delays. These phenomena were explained in terms of the behavior of the agents that were using MARP, as well as of the architecture of Schiphol airport compared to that of random route networks.

☐ Land et al. [9] proposed and validated a mechanism for code inspections, called procedural roles. In code inspection, inspectors first search for defects in code individually and then meet to discuss findings. Defects found individually may be lost in the group meeting. Land et al. explained this phenomenon using theories from social dynamics and then proposed a meeting format in which inspectors play procedural roles. This format was tested in two mechanism experiments with students. The validation model consisted of an artifact model (a preliminary description of the inspection process using procedural roles) and a model of the context (the students and the code to be inspected). As predicted, less defects were lost in the group meeting when procedural roles were used. Note that in this example, one of the relevant mechanisms is the method being tested.

7.4.3 Technical Action Research

Technical action research (TAR) is the use of an artifact prototype in a real-world problem to help a client and to learn from this. Usually this is one of the last stages in scaling up a technology from the laboratory to the real world. For example, a cruise control algorithm can first be tested in a simulated car, next in a real car on a test drive, and finally in a real car used by a volunteer in his daily commuting to work. This last test would be technical action research.

Technical action research is really a special case of a single-case mechanism experiment, because single validation models are tested and the results are explained in terms of mechanisms. The validation model in TAR consists of a realistic version of the artifact interacting with a real-world context. The difference with other single-case mechanism experiments is that in addition to investigating the responses of the validation model to stimuli, the researcher also uses the artifact to help a client. This gives TAR a special structure, different from all other single-case mechanism experiments. It is discussed in Chap. 19:

☐ The conceptual framework developed in the ARE project was taught to a project manager of a small software engineering project, managed in an agile way. The manager used it to structure project tasks, specify requirements, manage their alignment with business goals, and decide on priorities for each next agile iteration. This process was observed by the researcher and used to validate the usability of the conceptual framework in practice.

7.4.4 Statistical Difference-Making Experiments

Statistical difference-making experiments compare the average outcome of treatments applied to samples. They can be used in validation research by selecting samples of validation models and comparing the average outcome of treatments in different samples.

The advantage of statistical difference-making experiments for validation research is that they do not require full understanding of the mechanisms that produce responses. The disadvantage is that conditions are very hard to control completely, even in validation models, and that it may be difficult to attribute an observed difference to a difference in treatments or to a difference in groups or to some other difference. Statistical difference-making experiments are discussed in Chap. 20:

☐ Prechelt et al. [13] investigated the use of the so-called pattern comment lines (PCLs) to enhance the understanding of the use of patterns by programmers. PCLs describe pattern usage in a few comment lines, where applicable. A treatment group consisting of students performed some maintenance on programs containing PCLs in the classroom, and the control group performed the same maintenance tasks on the same programs minus the PLCs.

The artifact studied was the PCL, and the context with which it interacted was a student maintaining a program in the classroom. The maintenance assignments performed by the students were the treatments. All groups received the same treatments, and the goal was to find out if there is a difference between the groups using PCLs and the groups not using PCLs.

A statistically discernable difference was found: Programs containing PCLs took less effort to maintain. This difference was explained by a theory of program comprehension that postulates some cognitive mechanisms used by programmers to understand programs. The explanation of the difference in effort is that PCLs trigger these mechanisms so that it is easier to understand a program.

7.5   Scaling Up to Stable Regularities and Robust Mechanisms

New technology is always developed by designing and testing it under idealized laboratory conditions first, incrementally scaling this up to conditions of practice later. In this **scaling up** approach, we follow two lines of reasoning, illustrated in Fig. 7.3.

Along the horizontal dimension, our research goal is to test an increasingly realistic model of the artifact under increasingly realistic conditions of practice. We reason by analogy from the investigated model to real-world cases. This is **case-based inference.**

We will see that case-based inference gains plausibility if it is based on similarity of architecture. The reasoning is then that if a stimulus of a validation model triggers an interaction among architectural components of the model, which has an effect, then this mechanism will also occur in real-world implementations with a similar architecture, with a similar effect.

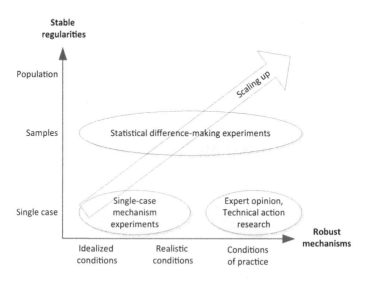

Fig. 7.3 Scaling up to stable mechanisms under conditions of practice, by investigating validation models using different research methods

Along the vertical dimension, our research goal is to show that an effect exists on the average in a population. If all artifact implementations would be identical and if they would operate in identical contexts, then this research goal would be superfluous. In the real world, though, artifact implementations and contexts differ, and there is nondeterminism. We use statistical research to average out this nondeterminism by observing average outcomes in samples and to make plausible that this average effect also exists in the population. This is **sample-based inference.** In it, we reason from samples to a population.

Sample-based inference is statistical inference and is based on random sampling and allocation of treatments. We do not have to rely on knowledge of the mechanisms that produce different responses. Even if we have this knowledge, we cannot use it in statistical inference.

How can these strategies be combined? By designing different experiments with different validation models. We can start by filtering out bad designs by submitting our design to expert opinion. We can perform single-case mechanism experiments on single validation models under idealized laboratory conditions to increase our understanding of the mechanisms that produce responses. We can scale up to conditions of practice to test whether the mechanisms are robust. We can study the response of samples of validation models to average out nondeterministic behavior and identify stable effects on the average. Finally, we can test our artifact under conditions of practice by doing technical action research. Gorschek et al. [6] describe such a process of scaling up. We will look closer at this process in Chap. 16.

7.6 Summary

- In treatment validation, we develop a design theory of the interactions between the artifact and its context.
- Important validation research questions are what the effects of the interaction are and whether these satisfy requirements. Trade-off questions test the generalizability over different versions of the artifact; sensitivity questions test the generalizability over differences in context.
- Since we cannot, by definition, validate real-world implementations, we investigate validation models. A validation model consists of a model of the artifact interacting with a model of the context.
- Research methods to investigate validation models include expert opinion, single-case mechanism experiments, technical action research, and statistical difference-making experiments:

  - Expert opinion can be used to weed out bad designs early.
  - Statistical difference-making experiments can be used to provide empirical support for the existence of stable population-level average effects.
  - Single-case mechanism experiments and technical action research can be used to investigate the mechanisms that produce these effects.

Table 7.2 Validation methods identified by Zelkowitz and Wallace [17] and by Glass et al. [5]

This book	Zelkowitz and Wallace [17]	Glass et al. [5]
Validation research methods		
• Expert opinion		
• Single-case mechanism experiment	• Simulation • Dynamic analysis	• Field experiment • Laboratory experiment—Software • Simulation
• Technical action research	• Case study	• Action research
• Statistical difference-making experiment	• Replicated experiment • Synthetic environment experiment	• Field experiment • Laboratory experiment—human subjects
Other research methods		
• Observational case study	• Case study • Field study	• Case study • Field study
• Meta-research method	• Literature search	• Literature review/analysis
Measurement methods		
• Methods to collect data	• Project monitoring • Legacy data	• Ethnography
Inference techniques		
• Techniques to infer information from data	• Static analysis • Lessons learned	• Data analysis • Grounded theory • Hermeneutics • Protocol analysis

Notes

[5]**Page 61, analogic models.** This is based on a definition by Apostel [2] and one by Kaplan [8, p. 263]. It is very similar to the concept of a model in software engineering used by Jackson [7]. Müller [12] recounts an insightful history of the concept of a model, in which he identifies many different relevant meanings of the term. Morrison and Morgan [11] review the many different functions models can have. The function of validation models is to simulate and represent implementations.

[6]**Page 63, validation research methods.** Table 7.2 compares the different classifications. The table shows that Zelkowitc and Wallace and Glass et al. also list other research methods that are useful for implementation evaluation and problem investigation but cannot be used for investigating

validation models. They additionally include measurement methods and inference techniques that can be combined with various research methods, as will be shown later in this book. I discuss this comparison in more detail elsewhere [15].

References

1. I. Alexander, L. Beus-Dukic, *Discovering Requirements: How to Specify Products and Services* (Wiley, Hoboken, 2009)
2. L. Apostel, Towards a formal study of models in the non-formal sciences, in *The Concept and Role of the Model in the Mathematical and the Natural and Social Sciences*, ed. by H. Freudenthal (Reidel, Dordrecht, 1961), pp. 1–37
3. W. Engelsman, R.J. Wieringa, Goal-oriented requirements engineering and enterprise architecture: Two case studies and some lessons learned, in *Requirements Engineering: Foundation for Software Quality (REFSQ 2012), Essen, Germany*. Lecture Notes in Computer Science, vol. 7195 (Springer, Heidelberg, 2012), pp. 306–320
4. R.L. Glass, V. Ramesh, I. Vessey, An analysis of research in the computing disciplines. Commun. ACM **47**(6), 89–94 (2004)
5. R.L. Glass, I. Vessey, V. Ramesh, Research in software engineering: an empirical study. Technical Report TR105-1, Information Systems Department, Indiana University, September 2001
6. T. Gorschek, C. Wohlin, P. Garre, S. Larsson, A model for technology transfer in practice. IEEE Softw. **23**(6), 88–95 (2006)
7. M.A. Jackson, *Problem Frames: Analysing and Structuring Software Development Problems* (Addison-Wesley, Boston, 2000)
8. A. Kaplan, *The Conduct of Inquiry. Methodology for Behavioral Science* (Transaction Publishers, Piscataway, 1998); First edition 1964 by Chandler Publishers
9. L.P.W. Land, C. Sauer, R. Jeffrey, The use of procedural roles in code inspections: An experimental study. Empir. Softw. Eng. **5**(1), 11–34 (2000)
10. S. Lauesen, *Software Requirements: Styles and Techniques* (Addison-Wesley, Reading, 2002)
11. M.S. Morgan, M. Morrison, Models as mediating instruments, in *Models as Mediators. Perspectives on Natural and Social Science*, ed. by M.S. Morgan, M. Morrison (Cambridge university Press, Cambridge, 1999)
12. R. Müller, The notion of a model: A historical overview, in *Philosophy of Technology and Engineering Sciences*, ed. by A. Meijers (Elsevier, Amsterdam, 2009), pp. 637–664
13. L. Prechelt, B. Unger-Lamprecht, M. Philippsen, W.F. Tichy, Two controlled experiments assessing the usefulness of design pattern documentation in program maintenance. IEEE Trans. Softw. Eng. **28**(6), 595–606 (2002)
14. J.D. Vrielink, Phased array processing: Direction of arrival estimation on reconfigurable hardware. Master's thesis, Faculty of Electrical Engineering, Mathematics and Computer Science, University of Twente, January 2009. http://essay.utwente.nl/62065/
15. R. Wieringa, Empirical research methods for technology validation: Scaling up to practice. J. Syst. Softw. (2013). http://dx.doi.org/10.1016/j.jss.2013.11.1097
16. P. Willner, Methods for assessing the validity of animal models of human psychopathology, in *Animal Models in Psychiatry I*, ed. by A. Boultin, G. Baker, M. Martin-Iverson. Neuromethods, vol.18 (The Humana Press, New York, 1991), pp. 1–23
17. M.V. Zelkowitz, D. Wallace, Experimental models for validating technology. Computer **31**(5), 23–31 (1998)

Part III
Theoretical Frameworks

Chapter 8
Conceptual Frameworks

When we design and investigate an artifact in context, we need a conceptual framework to define structures in the artifact and its context. In Sect. 8.1, we look at two different kinds of conceptual structures, namely, architectural and statistical structures. In information systems and software engineering research, the context of the artifact often contains people, and researchers usually share concepts with them. This creates a reflective conceptual structure that is typical of social research, discussed in Sect. 8.2. Conceptual frameworks are tools for the mind, and the functions of conceptual frameworks are discussed in Sect. 8.3. In order to measure constructs, we have to operationalize them. This is subject to the requirements of construct validity, discussed in Sect. 8.4.

8.1 Conceptual Structures

A **conceptual framework** is a set of definitions of concepts, often called **constructs.** The constructs are used to define the structure of an artifact and its context, to describe phenomena in the artifact and context, to formulate questions about these phenomena, to state generalizations, etc. The structure of a conceptual framework can be analyzed in itself, without doing empirical observations, by mathematical or conceptual analysis. Conceptual frameworks are an important part of scientific theories.

Table 8.1 lists and illustrates a number of conceptual structures frequently encountered in design science. These structures are familiar from conceptual modeling and ontologies, and I will not give precise definitions of them here. More about them can be found in the relevant literature [3, 13, 19, 20, 30, 31].

The table shows two overlapping but different kinds of conceptual structures:

- In **architectural structures,** the world is a hierarchy of interacting systems. Each system is an entity that can be decomposed into components that interact to

© Springer-Verlag Berlin Heidelberg 2014
R.J. Wieringa, *Design Science Methodology for Information Systems and Software Engineering*, DOI 10.1007/978-3-662-43839-8_8

Table 8.1 Examples of conceptual structures found in conceptual frameworks. The list is not exhaustive

---

- Entities

    - Wave, wave source, antenna, beam-forming system
    - Cloud service provider, client, auditor

- Events

    - Arrival of an aircraft, incident, departure
    - Sprint deadline

- Composition relations

    - Decomposition of beamforming system
    - Enterprise architecture decomposition

- Processes

    - Trip from arrival to departure point
    - Sprint in a development process

- Procedure specifications

    - Audit method specification
    - ARMOR method specification

- Constraints

    - EU privacy regulation
    - Constraints on a route plan

- Taxonomic relations

    - Taxonomy of antennas
    - Taxonomy of different kinds of project risks

- Cardinality relations

    - Each location in a road network is connected to at least one road
    - Cloud service provider uses more than one cloud server

- Variables

    - Frequency, distance, angle of arrival
    - Compliance
    - Usability, effort, goal

- Probability distributions

    - The failure probability of a project
    - Correlation between failure and size of a project

- Populations

    - The population of ERP systems
    - The population of software engineering projects.

---

produce overall system behavior. Components too may be systems of lower-level components. Conversely, components can be composed into composite systems. One possible research goal is to predict or explain overall system behavior from knowledge of its architecture. Another possible research goal is to discover a system's architecture from observations of its behavior.

- In **statistical structures,** the world is a collection of phenomena that can be described by variables. The values of a variable have a probability distribution over the set of all possible phenomena. One possible research goal is to predict or explain phenomena from knowledge of the probability distribution of variables. Another possible research goal is to estimate properties of the probability distribution of variables from observations of samples of phenomena.

The common element in both kinds of structures is the concept of a variable. In an architectural structure, variables are properties of systems or of their interactions.

In a statistical structure, they are aspects of phenomena with a probability distribution. One conceptual framework can define both kinds of structures.

The distinction between these two kinds of structures is a core element in the rest of the book. Architectural structures support **case-based research,** in which we investigate individual cases, study their architecture, identify mechanisms by which overall system-level phenomena are produced, and generalize case by case. Statistical structures support **sample-based research,** in which we infer properties of the distribution of a variable over a population of phenomena, by observing the variable in a sample of the population. Case-based and sample-based research should deliver mutually consistent results, because they are about the same real world. But research design and inference differ for the two kinds of research:

☐ For example, we can define the variable *data location compliance* for the cloud service offered by a provider. This is a property of the interaction between one system (a cloud service provider) and another system (a client). We can investigate how the cloud service provider organized this service. Which organizational components play a role, by which processes? What software components play a role, and how is this coordinated? This is an *architectural* analysis because we study components and their interactions.

From a sample of observations of the variable across a population of services delivered by one provider, we can try to derive information about the distribution of the variable over this population. What percentage of services in this population is judged compliant? This is a *statistical* analysis because we are trying to discover a property of the distribution of a variable.

Both analyses, if done properly, should deliver mutually consistent information. For example, the statistical analysis can provide information about the effectiveness of the mechanisms by which compliance is realized.

8.1.1 Architectural Structures

A **system** is a collection of elements that interact and form a whole. The systems concept is very general and applies to software systems, physical systems, social systems, and even symbolic systems such as the law, a development method, or a notation. What makes all these entities systems is that the *organization of their components* produces overall properties of the system. A collection of elements forms a system by virtue of their organization.

Almost all of the conceptual structures of Table 8.1 are actually systemic structures: Systems are *entities* that can be decomposed into *components* that perform *processes* to respond to *events*. Systems and components can be classified in *taxonomies* and have *cardinality relations* with each other [31]. Systems can behave nondeterministically according to a probability distribution. We next discuss the concepts of an architecture, component, and mechanism.

Architecture

A system **architecture** is the organization of the system's components that produces overall system behavior.[1] The central idea is that an architecture is *responsible* for some system-level phenomena. If we throw all components of a car on a heap, the heap will not behave as a car. If we put them together according to the architecture specified by its designers, we get a system that behaves as a car. The difference is made by the architecture.

Components

An architecture consists of **components** that interact to produce system behavior. The components of an architecture are defined by their capabilities and limitations.

A **capability** is an ability to respond to stimuli, to changes in conditions, or to temporal events such as deadlines or periodic events [31]. If we designed and built a component in order to realize some capability, then usually this component has additional capabilities, not known to us:

☐ For example, a software component that is constructed to realize some stimulus-response behavior may respond in unexpected ways to stimuli for which no response was specified. It may crash, or it may show interesting behavior.

☐ And an employee, which is a human component of an organization, may perform some job role, which is a specified capability. But people have more competencies than those specified in a job role, and the employee may respond intelligently to many situations not specified in the job role.

At the same time, components have **limitations.** They may fail, respond incorrectly, or reach the boundary of their performance capabilities. To say that a component has capabilities is equivalent to saying that it has limitations. We will sometimes talk about capabilities and limitations, capabilities/limitations, plain limitations, or simply capabilities. All of these phrases mean the same thing in this book.

Mechanisms

When a system receives a stimulus, a pattern of interaction among system components is produced that leads to system responses. This is called a **mechanism.** There are software mechanisms and hardware mechanisms but also cognitive mechanisms that produce understanding in human beings and social mechanisms that produce phenomena in social systems. Mechanisms in hardware and software may be deterministic, but social and psychological mechanisms are always nondeterministic. Nondeterministic mechanisms produce different responses with different probabilities.

By what mechanisms a system produces responses depends on the system architecture and the capabilities and limitations of its components. If we change a system's architecture, this may change the mechanisms by which responses are produced, and hence it may change the capabilities of the system as whole. If

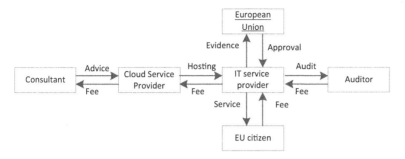

Fig. 8.1 Architecture of the compliant cloud service provision market. The European Union is an individual component; the other boxes represent types of components

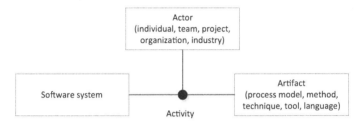

Fig. 8.2 Generic architecture of software projects [27]

we preserve a system's architecture but replace some components by others with different capabilities, then this too may change the mechanisms by which responses are produced and hence the capabilities of the system as a whole. Here are some examples:

☐ In the DLC problem, the cloud service provision market is a system, containing providers, clients, auditors, and governments as components. Each of these has characteristic capabilities, such as the ability to offer cloud storage services, the ability to pay for these services, the ability to audit them, etc. The number of components is dynamic, because actors can enter and exit the market. The properties of this market change if some components change their capabilities or if the architecture of the market is changed.

Figure 8.1 represents the architecture of the cloud service provision market and some interactions. The European Union is an individual component of the system, and the other rectangles represent types of components.

Some mechanisms in the system are the processes by which clients and providers find each other and do business, the mechanism by which governments issue regulations, and the processes by which auditors check compliance. All of these mechanisms are nondeterministic. This produces system-level phenomena such as the total flow of goods and services through a market, the formation of networks of suppliers and clients, and the compliance-producing and compliance-checking behavior.

☐ Any development project is a system containing actors, a software system, and software engineering artifacts as components (Fig. 8.2) [27]. Social mechanisms among actors produce project-level behavior. The interaction between the software engineering artifacts and software engineers may trigger cognitive mechanisms in the actors and may create social mechanisms by

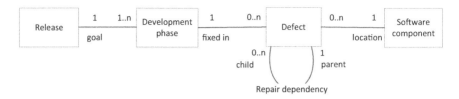

Fig. 8.3 Conceptual model used to define multicomponent defects by Li et al. [14]. To fix a parent defect, children defects need to be fixed too. Defects have a location, and they are fixed in a development phase for a particular release

which the actors interact. All of these mechanisms, and more, are nondeterministic and can be the object of empirical study.

☐ Li et al. [14] studied multicomponent defects and architectural hotspots in a large software system. This topic had not been studied before, and in order to describe important phenomena, the authors defined the concepts of *multicomponent defect* and of *architectural hotspot*.

The case being studied is a long-running development project of a large software system. This case is itself a (sociotechnical) system. Some components of the case are shown in the entity-relationship diagram of Fig. 8.3. The components have capabilities. For example, a defect can break the behavior of a software component. Stimuli may trigger mechanisms. For example, the repair of one defect may trigger the repair of another defect. Thus, the conceptual model of Fig. 8.3 allows us to describe important phenomena in the project.

Architectures are useful structuring mechanisms for design researchers both when designing artifacts and when doing empirical research. First, architecture is used in *design* to decompose a complex design problem in simpler subproblems, solve these subproblems, and compose the entire system from components that solve subproblems. Second, if a system architecture is known, designers can use it to trace undesirable behavior of a system to that of one or more components and try to repair the system by replacing some components with others that have capabilities more suitable for the production of desirable system behavior. Third, designers can explore design options for a system by experimenting with alternative components, with different capabilities, and with different ways of organizing them in order to produce desirable overall system behavior.

Architectures are used in *empirical research* too. First, a major aim of empirical science is to discover the architecture of the system of nature [1, 5, 15, 29]. Second, in order to reduce complexity, a researcher can study one component of an artifact or its context at a time in order to understand its capabilities in detail and ignore the rest. Third, just as an engineer, a researcher can abstract from the internal structure of system components and try to explain system phenomena in terms of component capabilities and the architecture of the system.

The investigation of architectures is always case-based research. We observe, analyze, and experiment with the architecture of single cases and then generalize by analogy to cases with a similar architecture. More on this in Chap. 15. The examples given above illustrate that this may be combined with statistical research, discussed next.

8.1.2 Statistical Structures

In statistical structures, we omit all structures listed in Table 8.1 except variables, probability distributions, and populations. A statistical structure is a population of elements and one or more variables with a probability distribution over the population. We first discuss populations and then variables and distributions.

Populations

A **population** is a set of all objects that satisfy some predicate and that are possible objects of study for a researcher. The researcher usually does not study a population as a whole, but a subset called a **sample,** and uses sample observations to statistically infer properties of the population:

☐ A researcher may be interested in the population of all ERP (enterprise resource planning) systems, all software engineers, all software development projects, etc. Any of these population is too large to study as a whole, and the researcher studies instead a sample of ERP systems used in a few companies, a sample of software development projects, etc. From the sample data, the researcher will infer population properties.

Looking at a sample only, we cannot know from which population it was drawn. In order to draw an inference from the sample to the population, we need to know from which population the sample has been selected and how it was selected. Without such a specification, we cannot do statistical inference from the sample to the population:

☐ Given a set of distributed software projects in the insurance business, we could guess that it was drawn from the population of all software projects, of all distributed software projects, of all software projects done in the insurance business, etc. In order to use the sample to statistically infer properties of a population, we must know from which population it was selected and how it was selected, for example, by simple random sampling.

All population elements are similar in some respects, and this similarity is expressed in a **population predicate.** The population predicate should make clear what *counts as* a population element, in more than one sense of this phrase [31, p. 98]:

* How do we recognize a population element when we see one?
* How do we count population elements?

There is a deep connection between counting and classification [32]: If we change a population definition, we may change the way we recognize and count population elements.

A population predicate can be surprisingly hard to define, even for concepts that we think we know well:

☐ For example, how do we recognize an agile project? When do they follow a method generally accepted as agile? Many projects follow a method only partially. And when is a method "generally accepted" as agile? What about unknown agile methods?

☐ How do we count agile projects? Is a global project that is agile at two of its three locations one or two projects? What if a project at one location delivers two systems? What if it is terminated and taken over by another company? What if the project follows one agile method first and another one later?

In sample-based research, we need a clear definition of the population to sample from. If this is not possible to give, we simply define a list of population elements called a *sampling frame*. Sampling then consists of selecting elements from this list, and statistical inference allows us to draw conclusions about the population described by the sampling frame.

In case-based research, we have populations too, but they need not be defined as crisply as populations in sample-based research. We will see that in case-based research, we select cases by (dis)similarity and that we study them one by one. Part of the research goal may be to discover more about the relevant similarity relation among population elements, which allows us to improve our definition of the population predicate.

Random Variables

Any construct that can be measured is a variable. Examples are wave frequency, data location compliance, and project effort. Mathematically, we speak of a **random variable,** defined as a mapping from observations to a set of numbers. In information systems and software engineering research, random variables are usually defined in terms of a population:

☐ We can define the variable *project effort* for a population of software projects as the time, in person-hours, that has been spent on a project so far. Whenever we measure the effort of a project, we get a value of this variable for this project.

The definition of a random variable over a population is called a **chance model** of the variable. We can visualize a chance model of a random variable X as a box filled with tickets, where each ticket has a number written on it, which is a measurement of X in a population element [7]. Different tickets may have the same number written on them. The numbers on the tickets have a probability distribution. Measurement is drawing a sample of tickets from the box.

A **probability distribution** of a random variable is a mathematical function that summarizes the probability of selecting a sample of values in a random draw from the X-box. To make this precise, mathematics is needed [28]. Here, it suffices to say that if X is discrete, the probability distribution gives for each

Table 8.2 Elements of a chance model for a random variable

1. What is the meaning of the numbers on the tickets? You define this as part of the *conceptual framework* of your research
2. What is assumed about the probability distribution of the numbers over the tickets in the box? For example, how many tickets (population elements) are there? What do we assume about the functional form of the distribution of numbers on the tickets? These assumptions are specified as part of the *population definition*
3. How are the numbers measured? This is part of *measurement design*
4. When sampling, how many tickets are drawn from the box? Are they drawn randomly? With or without replacement? This is part of *sampling design*

value of X the probability of selecting that value in a random draw from the X-box. If X is continuous, the probability of drawing any particular value is 0. The probability distribution of a continuous variable summarizes something else, namely, the probability of selecting a range of values in a random draw from the X-box. Mathematicians speak of selecting a sample *from a distribution*. Empirical researchers usually speak of selecting a sample *from a population*. In both cases, we can visualize this as a selection of a sample from a box of tickets.

A chance model for X is defined by answering the questions listed in Table 8.2. Here are two examples of chance models. Because we want to define chance models over a population, we include the definition of the population as the zeroth part of the definition of the chance model:

☐ Huynh and Miller [11] investigated implementation vulnerabilities of open-source web applications.

0. The population is the set of all open-source web applications.

One random variable defined over this population is *ImpV*, which stands for implementation vulnerabilities. The chance model of *ImpV* is this:

1. The numbers on the tickets are proportions of implementation vulnerabilities among total number of vulnerabilities in a web application.
2. The numbers have the probability distribution *binomial*(n, p) where n is the number of vulnerabilities in a web application and p the probability that a vulnerability is an implementation vulnerability. *Binomial*(n, p) is the distribution of the number of successes in a series of n independent Bernoulli experiments with fixed probability p of success. A Bernoulli experiment is an experiment with two possible outcomes, arbitrarily called "success" and "failure." The assumptions made here are that the proportions of implementation vulnerabilities in different web applications are independent and that the probability that a vulnerability is an implementation vulnerability is constant across all web applications.
3. *ImpV* is measured by counting and classifying the vulnerabilities in a web application. The paper does not reveal who did the counting and classifying.
4. Huynh and Miller selected a sample of twenty applications to do their measurements. The paper explicitly lists all twenty applications but does not reveal how they were selected.

☐ Hildebrand et al. [9] investigated the effect of feedback from a social network on the creativity by which a consumer customized a mass-customizable product and on the satisfaction of the consumer with the final product:

0. The population is the set of all consumers who design a product by selecting options in a web interface.

One random variable defined over this population is $\mathrm{Pref}\Delta_{ij}$, the difference between the preference of a consumer i and the preference of the social network member j who commented on the consumer preference. Each consumer i received feedback from exactly one peer j. $\mathrm{Pref}\Delta_{ij}$ is defined by a chance model as follows:

1. The numbers on the tickets are Euclidean distances between the initial choice of consumer i and the feedback about the choice received from member j of a social network. Slightly simplified, the numbers are computed by the distance measure $\sum_c \sqrt{(\tau_{i,c} - \tau_{j,c})^2} \times \omega_{i,c}$, where $\tau_{i,c}$ is the preference of consumer i on attribute c, $\tau_{j,c}$ is the preference of social network member j about attribute c, and $\omega_{i,c}$ is the importance of c to i, based on the proportion of the total price of the product allocated to c.
2. Initially, nothing is assumed about the distribution of the numbers, except that they have a finite population mean and standard deviation. Some of the statistical inferences used in the paper assume that $\mathrm{Pref}\Delta_{ij}$ is distributed normally over the population.
3. The numbers are computed from measurements of selections by consumers on the web page where they can customize the product.
4. Hildebrand et al. selected a sample of 149 consumers who customized a vehicle using a car manufacturer's web-based mass customization interface and received feedback on this from another consumer.

Chance models contain simplifying assumptions, which are unavoidable in any study. Is the proportion of implementation vulnerabilities independent from the type of application and from the year the application was first developed? Is the response to feedback from one person the same as the response to possibly contradictory feedback from many people? If we would study the real world in its unconstrained complexity, every phenomenon would be unique. To generalize is to simplify.

We can define chance models for more than one random variable. For two random variables X and Y, we can define their X-box and Y-box, as well as their (X, Y)-box. If there are dependencies between X and Y, then the (X, Y)-box contains more information than just the Cartesian product between the X-box and the Y-box:

☐ Hildebrand et al. [9] define a number of random variables of consumers, such as *own expertise* and *self-expression*. There may be dependencies between these variables, so their measurements across all consumers in the population would be collected in an *(own expertise, self-expression)* box.

Statistical structures are used in *sample-based research* to investigate properties of the distribution of variables over a population. Statistical concepts such as mean and variance are properties of samples and populations, but not of individual elements of the population.

The results of sample-based research are useful for *decision-makers* who must decide about large numbers of objects. For example, managers must decide whether and, if so, how to invest in social network support for mass customization. Politicians must decide on the allocation of public money to public infrastructures. Project managers can use knowledge of the distribution of vulnerabilities to decide which designs must be improved next.

With repeated sampling from the same population, sample statistics may vary around a mean with a small variance, even if the variance of individuals in a sample is much larger. This can make phenomena visible at the sample level that were invisible at the individual level. For *empirical researchers,* statistical structures reveal a new layer of reality, not visible at the individual level. Even where the behavior of an individual element may be nondeterministic, samples of elements can show stable behavior in the long run.

8.1.3 Mixed Structures

Architectural and statistical frameworks can be mixed. For example, you follow up a sample-based, statistical study with a few case studies. Here is an example:

☐ You can do a statistical survey of the use of role-based access control in organizations and follow this up with an in-depth study of a few organizations from the survey. The survey would be statistical and, if the sample would be random, would support statistical inference to the population. This would be a sample-based generalization. The follow-up study would be case based and support analogic inference to other cases. This would be a case-based generalization. If done properly, the results of the studies should be mutually consistent and should enrich each other's conclusions.

Importantly, the population in both studies is the same, but the target of generalization is different. The target of sample-based inference is a statistical model of the *population,* such as the mean and variance of a random variable over the population. The target of a case-based inference is an architectural model of *elements* of the population.

The next example is about statistical research *inside* a case study. Here, the population of interest for the case-based generalization is different from the population of interest for each statistical study inside a case:

☐ Bettenburg and Hassan [2] present two case studies of social interactions preceding and following a software release. The case studies are about the development of the Eclipse system and of the Mozilla Firefox system. The population of interest is the population of software development projects, from which these two cases have been selected.
In each of the two case studies, data sources were the issue tracking and version control repositories of the studied project. In each case study, the researchers analyzed discussions stored in these repositories to find information about code churn, source code regions talked about, patches, etc. They also analyzed issue reports in the 6 months following a release. Altogether, they measured 23 random variables.
The samples selected in each case were the set of issues in the 6 months preceding and following a release. The sample size for the Mozilla case was 300,000, and the sample size for the Eclipse system was 977,716.
The information in each sample was used to estimate a linear equation that expressed post-release defect probability in terms of a linear combination of the prerelease variables. Thus, in each case study, the authors inferred a statistical model of the population of all issues in the issue tracking and version control system of this case. As there are two case studies, there are two populations, and there are two statistical models. The two populations are of course different from the population of software projects.

8.2 Sharing and Interpreting a Conceptual Framework

The conceptual framework of a scientific theory is used for communication between researchers themselves. If the framework is standardized and available in textbooks, a research report does not have to explain the constructs. If it is shared by only a few researchers or if readers of a report may misinterpret constructs in the framework, then a research report must contain definitions of the constructs.

But a conceptual framework may also be shared with people in the studied domain. For example, the researcher may adopt and formalize concepts used by people in the investigated domain, or conversely, people in the investigated domain may adopt new constructs first defined by the researcher. This happens quite a lot in information systems and software engineering research:

☐ In the DLC project, concepts of cloud computing and of the EU privacy regulation, used in the domain, were adopted by the researcher. The researcher designed a method that uses some of these concepts without modifications, so that people in the domain using the method could understand them.

☐ In the ARE project, the researcher reviewed the literature on agile requirements engineering and constructed a conceptual framework from domain concepts using a grounded theory approach [21]. The resulting framework contains concepts such as *business value, negative value, requirements value, risk,* and *priority.* The researcher then taught these concepts and the associated way of working to a project manager, who used them in his project.

☐ Goal-oriented requirements engineering (GORE) methods used everyday concepts such as *goal, conflict, concern,* and *assessment* and redefined them somewhat (Fig. 8.4). In the EA project, they were then further redefined a bit and included in the ARMOR method [6]. When the architects in a case study used ARMOR, these concepts were adopted by these architects. However, some of the concepts in ARMOR had received a very specific meaning that does not agree with the way these concepts are normally used in the domain, and these concepts were misunderstood, and misused, by the architects.

☐ Most variables defined by Bettenburg and Hassan [2] were concepts used by the participants in the discussions stored in the issue tracking system. Other concepts were not used in the domain but were borrowed from social network theory, such as *closeness* and *centrality,* that were not used by the discussion participants. And some concepts had to be operationalized in a way that may have departed from the intended meaning in the domain. For example, *interestingness* was measured by the length of the notification list of an issue. This is a very rough measure of the level of interest that each of the members of the list may have had in the issue.

These examples illustrate a phenomenon that must be carefully managed by researchers who study social phenomena: Researchers may study the conceptual frameworks of subjects [23]. Doing this, they have to *interpret* concepts used by subjects, and they may even adopt them. This produces an additional layer of understanding that is not expressed in terms of causes or mechanisms but in terms of first-person meaning for people in the domain [16].

Some methodologists treat this in an exclusionary way, for example, the influential nineteenth-century philosopher Dilthey:

mechanistic explanation[s] of nature explain only part of the contents of external reality. This intelligible world of atoms, ether, vibrations, is only a calculated and highly artificial abstraction from what is given in experience and lived experience (quoted by Makkreel [16]).

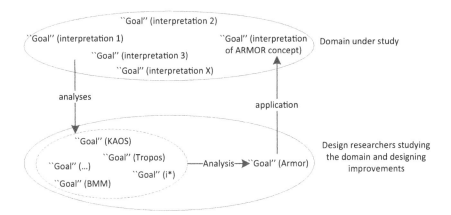

Fig. 8.4 The history of a concept. A concept can have many interpretations in the domain. It may be reconstructed in various ways by researchers, to be used in different methods such as KAOS, BMM, Tropos, and i*. A further reconstruction of the concept may be introduced in the domain, where it may or may not be understood in its reconstructed way

My view is that each kind of understanding adds to other kinds of understanding. The real world is complex and it does not help the progress of knowledge if we disregard insights provided by causal, architectural, or rational explanations or insights provided by first-person experience.

Concepts can be shared by people in the domain and may be shared between researchers and subjects. But even though concepts are shared, we cannot assume that they are shared by all people in the domain or that they are interpreted in the same way. Different people may interpret the same concept differently, and some concepts may be so ambiguous that one person interprets it in different ways at the same time. In addition, the meaning of concepts may change over time. This has three consequences for design researchers, corresponding to the three arrows in Fig. 8.4:

- If your research goal is to learn which concepts are used by people in the domain and how they interpret these concepts, you need methods for collecting and analyzing data that help you to put aside for the moment your own interpretation of these concepts, so that they do not influence your interpretation of the domain concepts. We discuss some of these methods in Chap. 12.
- Regardless of your research goal, if a construct is not standardized and available to your readers, you must define it in your research report and motivate the definition. The motivation may include a review of the alternative definitions of a construct currently used by researchers.
- If your research goal is to introduce an artifact in the domain, then you must ensure that the conceptual framework required to use the artifact is understood by the users. This is not only true for methods, which consists primarily of a structured set of concepts, but also of hardware and software, which may require that the user be aware of some special concepts.

8.3   The Functions of Conceptual Frameworks

Conceptual frameworks are tools for the mind. What can they be used for? They can be used to ask questions, describe observations, do measurements, interpret past events, issue instructions, express opinions, give permissions, make plans, specify artifacts, define methods, interpret specifications, etc. We here focus on the use of concepts in designing treatments and investigating phenomena.

First of all, they can be used to **frame** design problems and knowledge problems. In design problems, a conceptual framework can define the concepts needed to identify stakeholders, state their goals, and specify requirements on a treatment. A conceptual framework can also provide the concepts by which to specify a treatment and talk about the architecture, components, capabilities, and mechanisms of an artifact and of its context. In software engineering, this has been called a problem framing [12].

In addition to framing a design problem, conceptual frameworks can be used to frame a research problem. A conceptual framework can provide the language in which to define a population, define variables, state knowledge questions, and specify hypotheses. Defining a conceptual framework for the research problem is part of the research problem investigation task in the research methods described later in the book.

Once a problem is framed, we can use the concepts of a framework in design to **specify** a treatment and in empirical research to **describe** phenomena and **generalize** about them. Descriptions and generalizations can be case based or sample based, as illustrated in Table 8.3.

Finally, a conceptual framework itself can be the subject of mathematical or conceptual **analysis.** This is not strictly spoken a function of conceptual frameworks but can provide greater computational and reasoning capability during empirical research and hence enhances the functions of conceptual frameworks.

We now look at an extended example of the different uses of a conceptual framework:

Table 8.3 Examples of case-based and sample-based descriptions and generalizations. It is not our concern here whether these descriptions are true or false

Case description	In this agile project performed for a small company, there is no customer on-site
Case-oriented generalization	In all agile projects performed for small companies, there is no customer on-site
Sample description	In our sample of agile companies performed for small companies, 86% of the projects have no customer on-site
Statistical generalization	In the population of agile companies performed for small companies, 86% ± 5% of the projects have no customer on-site (95% confidence interval)

☐ In the MARP problem [18], multi-agent planning algorithms were developed for planning aircraft taxi routes on airports. Concepts from the fields of robot motion planning and multi-agent route planning and algorithmics were used to *specify* and *analyze* MARP algorithms.

Examples of constructs introduced in the report are *infrastructure* (a set of intersection and locations, connected by lanes) and *resource graph* (showing the connectivity between edges and nodes in an infrastructure) [18, p. 32]. A *plan* is a consecutive sequence of plan steps through adjacent resources, where each *plan step* is the occupation of a resource for a time interval by the agent [18, p. 34]. The *cost* of a plan is the difference between planned start and planned finish time [18, p. 35]. These concepts are defined formally.

Slightly less formal is the concept of *robustness*, which is the property of a plan to remain efficient even after "moderate" revisions [18, p. 3]. The concept of a moderate revision is left undefined. An *incident* is a period that an agent must stand still, i.e., acquires a delay with respect to its plan [18, p. 99]. The *delay* actually acquired during the execution of a plan is defined as *(finish time) minus (planned finish time)*. So an agent with a negative delay is ahead of schedule.

These concepts were used to frame the research problem:

– The population of interest is the set of all multi-agent planning systems, but the research is focused on one such kind of system, namely, aircraft taxiing on airports.
– The researcher used the constructs to state research questions that ask how the robustness of agent plans is influenced by changes in the topology of the infrastructure and by the frequency and severity of incidents [18, p. 98].

The constructs defined so far were used to describe delays for different sets of agents [18, p. 105]. More interesting structure could be described by distinguishing *mechanism delay* from *incident delay*. To avoid deadlock, priorities among agents must not be changed during replanning, and this makes it unavoidable that an agent acquires some delay while waiting to enter a resource because a higher-priority agent must enter first [18, p. 101]. This may cause other agents to wait behind the waiting agent as well. This is *mechanism delay*. *Incident delay* occurs when an agent has a temporary breakdown or is waiting behind an agent with incident delay.

With these additional constructs, it became possible to show that mechanism delay and incident delay respond differently to different parameter settings of the simulation model. For example, it could be shown that on airports, the MARP algorithms produce fewer mechanism delays than other planning tools. We return to these explanations in Chap. 14, when we discuss architectural explanations.

8.4 Construct Validity

If constructs are to be measured, they must be operationalized. This is subject to the requirements of construct validity. Construct validity is defined by Shadish et al. [24, p. 506] as the degree to which inferences from phenomena to constructs are warranted. However, phenomena are not given independently from the constructs by which we observe them. We observe execution times, project effort, the percentage of implementation vulnerabilities, etc. We cannot observe phenomena without already structuring them in terms of constructs. There is no way we can talk about phenomena independently from our constructs, and hence there is no inference from phenomena to constructs.

We here define **construct validity** instead as the degree to which the *application* of constructs to phenomena is warranted with respect to the research goals and questions. Before explaining this and giving examples, please note that construct

Table 8.4 Construct validity requirements and threats

Requirements	Threats
Are the constructs defined explicitly so that researchers can classify and count all and only the instances of the concept?	**Inadequate definition:** there is no definition that allows researchers to clearly classify and count all and only the instances of the concept
Can instances be classified unambiguously?	**Construct confounding:** an instance that satisfies the concept and satisfies other concepts too
Do indicators of constructs capture the intended meaning of the constructs?	**Mono-operation bias:** the indicators defined for a concept do not fully capture the concept
Does the method of measurement of an indicator avoid bias?	**Mono-method bias:** the indicators defined for a concept are all measured or applied in the same way

validity is a matter of degree. This is also true for the validity concepts that we will encounter later, namely, conclusion validity and internal and external validity. Constructs can be valid to some extent but are never valid totally. Science is fallible. The memorable remark of Gordon [8, p. 667] about total objectivity and total certainty deserves to be quoted and framed here:

> "That these ideals cannot be attained is not a reason for disregarding them. Perfect cleanliness is also impossible, but it does not serve as a warrant for not washing, much less for rolling in a manure pile."

It is customary to discuss construct validity by means of its threats. Shadish et al. [24, p. 73] list 14 threats to construct validity, of which we discuss four (Table 8.4). We also give the positive requirements that justify why some construct definitions, applications, or measurements threaten construct validity.

The first requirement is that the definition of a construct should allow a researcher to classify and count instances of the constructs. An **inadequate definition** is a threat to the satisfaction of this requirement. Many constructs start their life inadequately defined:

☐   We have seen earlier that the concept of an agile project is not defined explicitly to the extent that it provides clear criteria of classification and counting. There are many clear cases of agile projects, but there are also borderline cases where it is not clear whether or how the concept should be applied. The problem can be mitigated by providing a definition that allows researchers to at least classify and count clear cases of agile projects, even though for borderline cases the definition may not be of much help.

Not only a construct may be ambiguous; a case can be ambiguous too. This is called **construct confounding**:

☐ A clearly agile project, in addition to clearly being an agile project, may also clearly be an instance a project that is over time and budget and clearly be a global software engineering project. To which population can we generalize our observations? In other words, what is the relevant similarity relation over which we can generalize?

One way to mitigate this problem is to analyze on which architectural properties your results depend and check whether all and only the elements of the population that is the target of your generalization have this architecture.

Some constructs are not directly measurable, such as usability or maintainability. For these concepts, we need to define measurable indicators. If we define only one indicator for a construct, then we may not have operationalized the construct sufficiently, which would introduce bias. This risk is called **mono-operation bias**:

☐ Operationalizing *maintainability* only as *time to correct a fault* does not fully characterize maintainability. To better characterize maintainability, we should define more indicators, including the *effort to find a fault* and the *effort to test a resolution*.

Each indicator must be measurable. If we measure an indicator in only one way, we may introduce a systematic bias. This risk is called **mono-method bias**:

☐ Measuring *time to correct find a fault* by analyzing the log of the programming environment used by maintainers would be fine if the time stamps in the log are correct. But if maintainers are regularly interrupted for other tasks, then this method systematically overstates the time to correct a fault, and it is better to supplement it with other measurement methods.
But other methods may create their own bias. For example, monitoring a maintainer by camera so that interrupts are registered probably influences the speed by which a maintainer discovers a fault. Combining measurements obtained with multiple methods with different biases may give better results.

8.5 Summary

- A conceptual framework defines concepts, called constructs, that define structures for phenomena. Two important kinds of structures are architectural structures and statistical structures:

  - An architectural structure consists of components with capabilities and limitations. They are organized in such a way that they exhibit patterns of interaction among components, called mechanisms, by which system-level phenomena are produced.
  - A statistical structure consists of a population and one or more random variables defined over those populations. Each random variable has a probability distribution over the population. The distribution is usually unknown, but we can make assumptions about it.

- Architectural structures are good for describing individual cases. Statistical structures are good for describing populations. Both kinds of structures can be present in one conceptual framework.
- Conceptual frameworks are shared among people. If a researcher wants to understand the conceptual framework used by people, he or she has to bracket his or her own framework (temporarily set it aside).
- Conceptual frameworks are tools for the researcher. They can be used to frame design problems and knowledge problems, specify and describe phenomena, and generalize about them. Mathematical or conceptual analysis of a framework enhances these functions.
- Construct validity is the extent to which an application of a construct to phenomena is warranted. Construct validity is a matter of degree.

Notes

[1] **Page 76, system architecture.** The concept of system architecture is widely applicable, from industrial product design [22, p. 39] to organizational design [17,26]. The concept also aligns with the concept of a software architecture as a high-level structure of a software system [25].

Software architecture researchers emphasize that there is not a single, privileged architecture of a software system [4,10]. This corresponds to the idea that different system-level phenomena may require different conceptual frameworks to understand them. I consider this to be a *reframing of the artifact,* redescribing it in a different conceptual framework. The ability to reframe an object by changing the conceptual framework to describe it is important both in design and in empirical study.

References

1. W. Bechtel, A. Abrahamsen, Explanation: a mechanistic alternative. Stud. Hist. Philos. Biol. Biomed. Sci. **36**, 421–441 (2005)
2. N. Bettenburg, A.E. Hassan, Studying the impact of social interactions on software quality. Empir. Softw. Eng. **18**(2), 375–431 (2013)
3. A. Borgida, V. Chaudhri, P. Giorgini, E. Yu, *Conceptual Modelling: Foundations and Applications* (Springer, Heidelberg, 2009)
4. P. Clements, F. Bachmann, L. Bass, D. Garlan, J. Ivers, R. Little, P. Merson, R. Nord, J. Stafford, *Documenting Software Architectures: Views and Beyond*, 2nd edn. (Addison-Wesley, Boston, 2010)
5. E.J. Dijksterhuis, *The Mechanization of the World Picture* (Oxford University Press, Oxford, 1961). Transl. C. Dikshoorn
6. W. Engelsman, R.J. Wieringa, Goal-oriented requirements engineering and enterprise architecture: Two case studies and some lessons learned, in *Requirements Engineering: Foundation for Software Quality (REFSQ 2012), Essen, Germany.* Lecture Notes in Computer Science, vol. 7195 (Springer, Heidelberg, 2012), pp. 306–320
7. D. Freedman, R. Pisani, R. Purves, *Statistics*, 4th edn. (Norton & Company, New York, 2007)
8. S. Gordon, *History and Philosophy of Social Science* (Routledge, London, 1992)

9. C. Hildebrand, G. Häubl, A. Herrmann, J.R. Landwher, When social media can be bad for you: Community feedback stifles consumer creativity and reduces satisfaction with self-designed products. Inf. Syst. Res. **24**(1), 14–29 (2013)
10. C. Hofmeister, R. Nord, D. Soni, *Applied Software Architecture* (Addison-Wesley, Boston, 2000)
11. T. Huynh, J. Miller, An empirical investigation into open source web applications' implementation vulnerabilities. Empir. Softw. Eng. **15**(5), 556–576 (2010)
12. M.A. Jackson, *Problem Frames: Analysing and Structuring Software Development Problems* (Addison-Wesley, Boston, 2000)
13. R. Kaschek, L. Delcambre (eds.), *The Evolution of Conceptual Modeling*. Lecture Notes in Computer Science, vol. 6520 (Springer, Heidelberg, 2011)
14. Z. Li, N.H. Madhavji, S.S. Murtaza, M. Gittens, A.V. Miranskyy, D. Godwin, E. Cialini, Characteristics of multiple-component defects and architectural hotspots: A large system case study. Empir. Softw. Eng. **16**, 667–702 (2011)
15. P. Machamer, L. Darden, C.F. Craver, Thinking about mechanisms. Philos. Sci. **67**, 1–25 (2000)
16. R. Makkreel, Wilhem Dilthey, in *The Stanford Encyclopedia of Philosophy*, ed. by E.N. Zalta. Summer 2012 Edition (2012)
17. G. Morgan, *Images of Organization* (Sage Publications, Thousand Oaks, 1986)
18. A.W. ter Mors, *The World According to MARP*. PhD thesis, Delft University of Technology, 2010. http://www.st.ewi.tudelft.nl/$\sim$adriaan/pubs/terMorsPhDthesis.pdf
19. A. Olivé. *Conceptual Modeling of Information Systems* (Springer, Heidelberg, 2007)
20. R. Poli, J. Seibt, M. Healy, A. Kameas (eds.), *Theory and Applications of Ontology. Computer Applications*, vol. 2 (Springer, Heidelberg, 2011)
21. Z. Racheva, M. Daneva, A. Herrmann, K. Sikkel, R.J. Wieringa, Do we know enough about requirements prioritization in agile projects: Insights from a case study, in *18th International IEEE Requirements Engineering Conference, Sydney* (IEEE Computer Society, Los Alamitos, 2010), pp. 147–156
22. N.F.M. Roozenburg, J. Eekels, *Product Design: Fundamentals and Methods* (Wiley, Boston, 1995)
23. A. Sayer, *Method in Social Science: A Realist Approach*, 2nd edn. (Routledge, London, 1992)
24. W.R. Shadish, T.D. Cook, D.T. Campbell, *Experimental and Quasi-Experimental Designs for Generalized Causal Inference* (Houghton Mifflin Company, Boston, 2002)
25. M. Shaw, D. Garlan, *Software Architecture: Perspective on an Emerging Discipline* (Prentice Hall, Upper Saddle River, 1996)
26. H.A. Simon, *The Sciences of the Artificial* (MIT Press, Cambridge, 1969)
27. D.I.K. Sjøberg, T. Dybå, M. Jörgensen, The future of empirical methods in software engineering research, in *Future of Software Engineering* (IEEE Computer Society, Los Alamitos, 2007), pp. 358–378
28. L. Wasserman, *All of Statistics. A Concise Course in Statistical Inference* (Springer, Heidelberg, 2004)
29. R.S. Westfall, *The Construction of Modern Science: Mechanisms and Mechanics* (Cambridge University Press, Cambridge, 2005); First printing Wiley, 1971
30. R. Wieringa, Real-world semantics of conceptual models, in *The Evolution of Conceptual Modeling*, ed. by R. Kaschek, L. Delcambre. Lecture Notes in Computer Science, vol. 6520 (Springer, Heidelberg, 2011), pp. 1–20
31. R.J. Wieringa, *Design Methods for Reactive Systems: Yourdon, Statemate and the UML* (Morgan Kaufmann, Burlington, 2003)
32. R.J. Wieringa, W. de Jonge, Object identifiers, keys, and surrogates—object identifiers revisited. Theory Pract. Object Syst. **1**(2), 101–114 (1995)

Chapter 9
Scientific Theories

Like all scientific research, design science aims to develop scientific theories. As explained earlier in Fig. 1.3, a design science project starts from a knowledge context consisting of scientific theories, design specifications, useful facts, practical knowledge and common sense. This is called **prior knowledge.** The set of scientific theories used as prior knowledge in a design research project is loosely called its **theoretical framework.** When it is finished, a design science project should have produced additional knowledge, called **posterior knowledge.** Our primary aim in design science is to produce posterior knowledge in the form of a contribution to a scientific theory. In this chapter, we discuss the nature, structure and function of scientific theories in respectively Sects. 9.1, 9.2, and 9.3.

9.1 Scientific Theories

A **theory** is a belief that there is a pattern in phenomena.[1] This includes all kinds of theories, including my theory why the Dutch lost the most recent European Championship, conspiracy theories about the causes of the credit crisis, economic theories about the causes of the same crisis, the theory of classical mechanics, the theory of thermodynamics, and string theory. We will here define a theory to be **scientific** if it has been submitted to, and survived, two kinds of tests [7, 36]:

- **Justification to a critical peer group** The theory has been submitted to, and survived, criticism by critical peers. This is organized in a peer review system, in which the author of a theory submits it to a peer-reviewed publication process and the quality of the justification of the theory is critically assessed by peers before publication. Critical peers have the competence to criticize a paper and will try to find flaws in the justification of the theory, much as a lawyer would try to find flaws in the argument of his or her opponent.

© Springer-Verlag Berlin Heidelberg 2014
R.J. Wieringa, *Design Science Methodology for Information Systems and Software Engineering*, DOI 10.1007/978-3-662-43839-8_9

• **Empirical testing** The theory has been submitted to, and survived, tests against experience. This can be done in observational research or in experimental research. Part of the justification to critical peers is that these tests do not depend on the person of the researcher and hence are repeatable: Critical peers must be able to repeat the empirical tests. They will try to do so.

Surviving criticism and empirical testing is never final. Even for a theory that survived criticism and testing for a long time, it is always possible that someone will find a flaw or that a test will falsify part of the theory. Scientific theories are fallible.[2]

9.2   The Structure of Scientific Theories

The belief that there is a pattern in a class of phenomena is a **generalization.** Scientific generalizations are stated in terms of an explicitly specified conceptual framework and have a scope. Therefore, theories have the structure shown in Table 9.1.[3]

The conceptual framework of a theory, as we have seen in the previous chapter, serves to frame research problems, to describe phenomena, to analyze the structure of phenomena, and to state generalizations. Scientific generalizations, in turn, can be used to explain or predict phenomena or to justify design decisions, although not each generalization can be used for each of these purposes. More on this below. First, consider the scope of a scientific theory.

9.2.1   The Scope of Scientific Theories

The **scope** of a scientific theory is the set of all cases about which it generalizes. It is the set of possible targets of generalization. The scope of a theory may be fuzzy, even if we think it is not. Scientific research can produce surprises about what exactly is inside and what is outside the scope of a theory.

For example, the classical theory of mechanics was thought to have universal scope until Einstein showed that bodies close to the speed of light are outside its scope. And what is "close to the speed of light"? There is some fuzziness here. Closer to home, theories about effort estimation, coordination in global software

Table 9.1 Structure of scientific theories

• Conceptual framework
• Generalization(s)
• Scope

engineering, and organizational change all have a fuzzy scope. Research may produce incrementally better insights in what the scope of these theories is.

In sample-based research, the *population* is the set of all possible objects of study, from which we select a sample. This is the scope of our statistical generalizations. But even here there is fuzziness:

☐ For example, Huynh and Miller [24] concluded from their data that about 73 % of the vulnerabilities in web applications are implementation vulnerabilities. The population here is the set of all web applications, and this is also the scope of the generalization. Population and scope are identical. But what is the set of all web applications? The applications that existed at the time of research? Or of today? Or all possible web applications, past, present, and future? How can we draw a random sample from this set?

The solution to this puzzle is to define a *sampling frame,* which is a list of objects of study from which we will select a sample. This is a crisp set, exhaustively listed by the sampling frame. It is called the *study population.* If we select a random sample from the study population, we can generalize from the sample to the study population using statistical inference.

The study population is a subset of a larger population, called the *theoretical population,* that may be fuzzily defined and that is nevertheless the intended scope of the generalizations of our theory. To generalize from sample observations to a theoretical population, we first generalize to the study population using statistical inference and then from the study population to the theoretical population by analogy. This is explained at length in Part IV, and it is illustrated in Chap. 13 when we discuss statistical difference-making experiments.

In case-based research, we do not use the concept of a study population, but sample our cases one by one, based on similarity, from a theoretical population that may be fuzzily and incompletely defined. We generalize by analogy from the sampled cases to all "similar" cases, which is the imperfectly understood theoretical population. This process is called *analytical induction,* and it is discussed in Chap. 14:

☐ The ARE project investigated agile software development projects done for small- and medium-sized enterprises (SMEs). This population predicate defines a fuzzy theoretical population, because the concepts of agile and SME are fuzzy. Nevertheless, the developed theory is applicable to the many clear cases of agile projects done for SMEs. The theory was developed incrementally by doing a series of case studies.

9.2.2 The Structure of Design Theories

A design theory is a scientific theory about the interactions between an artifact and its context [48]. We may have a design theory about a composite system in its context or about a component of a system and *its* context. As indicated in Table 9.2, a design theory contains generalizations about the effects of the interactions between an artifact and its context and, possibly, about the satisfaction of requirements.[4]

Table 9.2 Structure of design theories

- Conceptual framework
- Generalization(s)

    - **Effect generalization:** (An artifact designed like this) interacting with (a context satisfying these assumptions) produces (effects like these).
    - **Requirements satisfaction generalization:** (Effects like these) satisfy (these requirements) to some extent.

- Scope

An **effect generalization** says what the effects of the interactions between an artifact and its context are. It is developed by answering effect questions, trade-off questions, and sensitivity questions. The result is a generalization over a class of similar artifacts and a class of similar contexts:

- (specification of artifact) $\times$ (assumptions about context) $\rightsquigarrow$ effects,

abbreviated $S \times A \rightsquigarrow E$. Informally, we can read this as (an artifact designed like this) interacting with (a context satisfying these assumptions) produces (effects like these). The specification S of the artifact design is incomplete, as it includes some implementation freedom as well as the design freedom explored by answering trade-off questions. The assumptions A about the context likewise leave freedom to choose different contexts, as explored by answering sensitivity questions.

A **requirements satisfaction generalization** says to what extent effects satisfy a requirement:

- The effects satisfy these requirements to some extent.

Satisfaction is a matter of degree, and it may be negative, i.e., an effect may violate a requirement. A design theory may not contain any requirements satisfaction generalization. What the requirements are depends on the context of stakeholder goals, and this is independent from what effects are produced by the interactions between artifacts and context. Generalizations may be descriptive or explanatory. Here are some examples:

☐   The theory about the DOA estimation algorithm describes, explains, and predicts what the output of the algorithm in the intended problem context is: an estimate of direction of arrival of plane waves. The explanation of this effect specifies the essential structure of the estimation algorithm but does not specify it down to the last design choice. There are many different implementations of the algorithm, and these are all in the scope of the generalization. The assumptions about the context are that waves are plane, distances among antenna's are equal and constant, bandwidth is narrow, etc. There are a lot of contexts that satisfy these assumptions, and they are all in scope of the generalization.

The generalization is descriptive, as it describes the responses to stimuli. But it also explains this in terms of the structure of the algorithm, and so this is also an explanatory effect generalization.

In another generalization, the theory describes that the accuracy of the estimation is best when the signal-to-noise ratio is 60 Db. It does not give an explanation of this, so this is a descriptive effect generalization.

In yet another generalization, the theory says that the MUSIC algorithm executes faster than 7.7 ms and has an accuracy of one degree. So it satisfies the requirement on execution speed. There is no explanation of this, so this is a descriptive requirements satisfaction generalization.

☐ Prechelt et al. [31] compared the maintenance effort of programs commented by a technique called pattern comment lines (PCLs) with the maintenance effort of programs not commented this way. The research supported the effect generalization that on the average, programs with PCLs are easier to maintain than programs without PCLs that are otherwise similar. The design specification of PCLs leaves a lot of freedom. The specification is that PCLs describe pattern usage where applicable. All comments that describe pattern usage could be in the scope of this generalization. There are no assumptions about the program other than that they are object-oriented programs written in Java or C++, so at least these programs are in scope. Identifying more assumptions about the programs in which PCLs are used is one topic of further research, intended to get more clarity about the scope of the generalization.

The effect generalization is descriptive. An additional generalization about cognitive mechanisms of program comprehension is offered as explanation of the descriptive generalization. Note that this is a mechanism in the context (the programmer) of the artifact (the PCLs).

There is no requirements satisfaction generalization. However, it is understood that in any stakeholder context, lower maintenance effort is better.

9.3 The Functions of Scientific Theories

Scientific theories can be used to explore, frame, describe, explain, predict, specify, design, control, and organize phenomena [8]. In this book, we discuss only a few of these functions, and we divide these into two groups, the functions of conceptual frameworks and the functions of generalizations. In the previous chapter, we looked at the use of conceptual frameworks to frame, specify, and describe phenomena and to generalize about them. Here we look at three core functions of generalizations: explanation, prediction, and design.

9.3.1 Explanation

An **explanation** is a hypothesis about the way that a phenomenon came about. Explanations take us beyond hard observable facts. Explanations, like all scientific theories, are always fallible, but we try to raise the quality of the support of explanations by submitting them to the test of practice and to the critique of competent peers.

We distinguish three kinds of explanations that ask for causes, mechanisms, and reasons, respectively. This classification corresponds to the three kinds of explanatory questions listed in Chap. 2 (p. 18). We give the definitions first and then give some extensive examples:

- Suppose you want to explain why a variable Y changed. A **causal explanation** would say that Y *changed because, earlier, a variable X changed in a particular way.* This is a **difference-making** view of causality, because it says that a difference in X makes a difference for Y. We leave open whether the change is deterministic or not. If it is nondeterministic, Y changes with some probability, and possibly even the probability distribution of Y as a whole may change.[5]

    In the difference-making view of causation, it is meaningless to ask why Y has some value. The only meaningful causal explanatory question to ask is why it has *changed* its value or more generally why it has a *different* value than elsewhere:

    ☐ For example, it is meaningless to ask why maintenance effort is low. We can ask why it has become low or why it is lower than in other cases that seem to be similar. We may then offer as causal explanation that, for example, a particular software engineering technique A is used, and introduction of A usually reduces maintenance effort. Our explanation is that A makes the difference.

- An **architectural explanation** says that phenomenon E *happened in the object of study because components $C_1, \ldots, C_n$ of the object of study interacted to produce E.* The interactions that produced E are collectively called the **mechanism** that produced E. Mechanisms may be deterministic or nondeterministic.[6]

    Architectural explanations can explain a hypothesized causal relationship. For example, if we have support for the causal generalization that a change in property X of an object of study causes a change in property Y, we may investigate the components and organization of the object of study to see by which mechanism X influences Y:

    ☐ Suppose after some experimentation with light bulbs and switches in the rooms of a building we have come to the following causal generalization: Flipping a light switch causes a light to switch on. We can use this generalization to give a causal explanation of an observation that a light is on: The switch was flipped. This made the difference between the light being on rather than off.
    Next, we ask a new kind of why question: Why does flipping a switch make a difference to the light? By which mechanism does this happen? After some more research, we propose an explanation in terms of a mechanism involving the switch, the light, the wiring that connects the two, and the electricity supply. This is an architectural explanation.

- A **rational explanation** explains phenomena in terms of the goals of the actor. It says that *a phenomenon occurred because an actor wanted to achieve a goal:*

    ☐ A rational explanation why the light could be this: It is on because someone wanted to read a book.

The actor can be a legal or biological person and is assumed to have goals and be rational about them. A rational explanation gives *reasons* for action, not *causes* of action. In Dutch winters, I have no reason to jump into a swimming pool, but your pushing me may cause me to jump into the pool.

Note that reasons are unobservable. Information about reasons for action can be gotten by interviewing the actor that performed the action or by observing an actor's behavior and interpreting it in terms of the conceptual framework of the actor. Rational explanations are important in design science because we need to discover how an artifact in a context contributes to stakeholder goals.

We will be strict in our terminology. Causes **cause** effects; mechanisms **produce** system-level phenomena; goals **provide** reasons. Here are some examples:

☐ In the example of Prechelt et al. [31] given above, it was found that on the average, programs with PCIs are easier to maintain than programs without PCIs that are otherwise similar. The causal explanation of this was that PCLs cause maintenance effort to reduce.
 The architectural explanation of this causal influence was that PCLs focus the attention of the maintainer to patterns, which are beacons that are familiar and allow the maintainer to switch from a labor-intensive bottom-up understanding of the program to a faster top-down approach to understanding the program. This reduces the psychological effort of the maintainer.

☐ In the EA project, the design theory said that using the ARMOR method will result in an enterprise architecture that is well aligned with business goals [12]. This is a causal generalization. If a company uses ARMOR to define their enterprise architecture and ends up with a well-aligned enterprise architecture, then the causal explanation of this is that they used the ARMOR method (and not some other method).
 This causal influence is in turn explained architecturally by referring to the steps and supporting tools and techniques of the ARMOR method. The architectural explanation says that **the method is the mechanism** by which the effects are produced.

• In the ARE project, it was observed in six case studies that if the client of an agile project is a small, or medium-sized enterprise (SME), they will not put a customer on-site of the project. Earlier, we have given an *architectural explanation* of this, namely, that the capabilities of SMEs are limited. Because the company is small, it will have a limited budget for the project, and its business priorities will not be in favor of putting a customer on-site.
 We now extend and support this by a *rational explanation,* namely, that one of the goals of an SME is to use their resources as effectively and efficiently as possible. In the perception of the entrepreneur who leads the SME, developing a software or information system is the business of the developer, not of SME's employees.

9.3.2 Prediction

Like explanations, predictions take us beyond the facts that have been observed. But where explanations look at the past and hypothesize a possible cause, mechanism, or reason that has brought about the observed facts, predictions look at the future and claim that something will happen in the future. Often we can use a generalization to explain as well as to predict, but this is not always the case. Some explanations may be too incomplete to allow us to base predictions on them [26, p. 349]. Here are a few examples:

☐ The generalizations in the examples above, namely, in the study by Prechelt [31], in the EA project, and in the ARE project, can all be used as explanations and as predictions. This is good because they are design theories, and the primary function of design theories is to predict what will happen if an artifact is implemented.

☐ As an example of a generalization that explains but does not predict, consider a project failure. After it occurred, we investigate it, and we develop a theory about what caused it and by which social mechanisms the failure was produced. Then we have explained the failure.

But this does not mean we are now able to predict that these social mechanisms will lead to project failure in the future. There are too many factors that influence project success, and the social mechanisms that were responsible for the failure in the project that we investigated may not be responsible for failure in the next project. They may be counterbalanced by other mechanisms, and we do not know how all these social mechanisms interfere with each other. Many of our explanations of social phenomena are incomplete.

☐ There are also generalizations that can be used for prediction that are purely descriptive and give no explanation. Statistical generalizations are like that. The average percentage of implementation vulnerabilities found in web applications by Huynh and Miller [24] is about 73 % with a small standard deviation of less than 4 %. This may be used to predict that other web applications have a similar percentage of implementation vulnerabilities, without understanding why.

☐ Performance measurements too may give us descriptive generalizations that may be used to predict but not to explain. For example, in the DOA project, performance measurements showed that on a range of test problems, execution time was below 7.7 ms. There is no explanation for this. Why not 7.5 or 7.8?

Since this performance was repeatable, it was stated as a descriptive generalization and used to predict that in other implementations of the same algorithm, in contexts satisfying the same assumptions, the same performance will be achieved.

9.3.3 Design

Design theories are tools to be used in design practice, and as all tools, they must be usable and useful. Suppose the design theory says that $S \times A \rightsquigarrow E$ where S is an artifact specification, A are context assumptions, and E describes effects. *Usability* of this theory in design depends on the capabilities of the practitioner. The practitioner must have the competence, time, money, and other resources to use a design theory for his or her purposes. The practitioner must at least have the following two capabilities:

1. The practitioner has the capability to acquire or build an artifact that satisfies specification S of the theory.
2. The practitioner has the capability to ascertain that the context satisfies the assumptions A of the theory.

Utility depends on whether the effects will actually occur in the practitioner's context and whether they will serve the goals of stakeholders:

3. The predicted effects E will occur.
4. E will satisfy requirements or at least will contribute to the goals of stakeholders in the practitioner's context.

Why would predicted effects not occur? Because the theory may be false of the practitioner's context. The theory is middle range and may abstract from components and mechanisms in a concrete situation that interfere with the predicted effect.

To assess whether a theory is usable and useful, a practitioner must assess the following risks:

1. The risk to acquire or build an incorrect artifact, i.e., one that does not satisfy specification S
2. The risk that a given context does not satisfy the assumptions A
3. The risk that mechanisms in the actual context of the artifact, not accounted for by the theory, will prevent the predicted effects to occur
4. The risk that the predicted effects E will not satisfy the requirements or not contribute to stakeholder goals

To make this concrete, here are two examples:

☐ In the EA project, the enterprise architecture design method ARMOR was developed to help enterprise architects design architectures that are well aligned with, and traceable to, business goals. The theory says that using ARMOR improves alignment between business goals and enterprise architecture. Is this theory usable?

First, is it in the capability of the architects to use ARMOR? First, experience suggests a qualified yes [13]. The architects in one case were able to use ARMOR but also misused considerable parts of it, because those parts of the conceptual model of ARMOR were misunderstood by them. So in fact this implementation of ARMOR was not correct. This posed little risk because ARMOR was an addition to their existing design practice and the only effect of misusing an ARMOR construct is that a diagram does not mean what it is supposed to mean according to the language definition. However, among themselves, they knew what was meant by the diagram.

Second, can the architects recognize whether their context satisfies the assumptions of ARMOR? The only assumption made by ARMOR is that the organization has a mature architecture department, and this could be ascertained by the architects themselves.

Third, could the architects trust the prediction of the theory in their case? They were aware of the many interfering conditions of practice of real-world enterprise architecture contexts, such as incomplete documentation, political pressure, and limited time. They accepted these risks, because they trusted their own experience and competence in dealing with unexpected conditions. They believed that despite this interference, the predicted effects would occur.

Finally, did the predicted effects contribute to stakeholder goals? At the time of writing, it is too early to say, but it was rational for the architects to expect this. The business goals were to reduce the cost of enterprise architecture and increase flexibility, and linking an enterprise architecture to business goals by means of ARMOR would contribute to these goals.

☐ In the MARP problem, the design theory for the dynamic route planning algorithms predicts reduction of delays in taxi routing on airports.

Who would be the user of this theory? To produce the predicted effect on an airport, all airplanes taxiing on the airport should use these algorithms. It is not within the capability of an airport to realize this, nor is it in the capability of any individual airline company. It is in the capability of an aircraft manufacturer to implement these algorithms, but no single aircraft manufacturer could force other manufacturers to use the same algorithms. An international standardization body could enforce this. So possibly, the design theory could be usable by an international standardization body. It is not usable by the other stakeholders by themselves.

Would the predicted effects occur on any airport under all circumstances? More validation would have to be done to provide support for this.

Would it be useful for a standardization body to use the design theory? That depends on their goals. If reducing delays caused by taxiing on airports is an important goal, they may consider committing their resource to realizing MARP and its design theory in all airplanes.

9.4   Summary

- A theory is a belief that there is a pattern in phenomena. Scientific theories are theories that survived the test of peer criticism and the test of practice.
- A scientific theory consists of a conceptual framework and generalizations with a scope:
    - In design theories, there are two kinds of generalizations, namely, effect generalizations and requirements satisfaction generalizations.
    - The scope of a theory is a population of objects of study of which it is true. The population may be fuzzily and incompletely defined.
- Theories are used to explain or predict phenomena. There are three kinds of explanations:
    - A causal explanation says that a variable Y changed because a variable X changed in a particular way earlier.
    - An architectural explanation says that a phenomenon was produced by the interactions among a number of architectural components. These interactions are the mechanism that produced the phenomenon.
    - A rational explanation says that an actor performed an action in order to achieve some goal.
- Theories can be used for design:
    - A design theory is usable by practitioners if it is in their capability to acquire or construct the artifact and to recognize whether their context satisfies the assumptions of the theory.
    - A design theory is useful for a practitioner if the predicted effects will occur and will contribute to stakeholder goals.

Notes

[1]**Page 93, definition of theories.** Taken from Craver [8, p. 55]. After adoption of a theory, what appeared to be a chaotic bundle of phenomena turns out to exhibit a pattern. Kaplan [26, p. 295] contrasts theory with unreflective habit. Habit exploits regularities in phenomena but never pauses to reflect and identify the underlying pattern.

Very usefully, Craver [8] reviews three philosophical perspectives on theories:

- The "once received view" (ORV), according to which a theory is an axiomatic system in a formal language. The laws of nature are nonlogical axioms, correspondence rules relate non-observable constructs to phenomena, and predictions are deductions of observation statements from the theory plus initial conditions. This view has been shown to be false (no scientific theory is like this) and incoherent (e.g., it is logically impossible to define a theory-free observation language). Craver reviews some well-known arguments against the ORV.
- According to the model-based view, a theory is a semantic rather than a linguistic structure. Scientists build semantic models of phenomena.
- The third view is a specialization of the second view and says that theories are models of mechanisms found in phenomena.

Machamer [32] reviews how these views came to succeed each other. Godfrey-Smith [16] gives a readable book-length introduction, running through the whole story from logical positivism to the views of Popper, Kuhn, Lakatos, Laudan, and Feyerabend and treating some special topics such as scientific realism and Bayesian theories of evidence.

[2]**Page 94, fallibility of theories.** Fallibilism should not be confused with falsificationism. Fallibilism is the belief that theories are fallible and that every theory is a potential subject of improvement. Falsificationism is a guideline for dealing with falsification. The guideline says that if a theory is falsified, i.e., if it fails a test, it should be rejected. This guideline is the centerpiece of Popper's philosophy of science [41].

Kuhn [28] showed that in practice, scientists try to replicate falsifications before they believe it is a stable falsification. If they believe it is a stable falsification, they may shelve the falsification as a puzzling result to be studied in more detail later, or they may reframe their conceptual framework to see if the falsification can be defined away. Historical examples of reframing after falsification are given by Kuhn [28] and also by Lakatos [29, 30] and Bechtel and Richardson [2]. Reframing the problem and revising theoretical generalizations are core strategies in analytical induction [42].

[3] **Page 94, structure of theories.** Gregor [18] presents a very similar structure of theories in information systems. The elements above the line in the following table are obligatory in Gregor's framework; the ones below the line are optional in her framework.

Gregor [18]	This book
Means of representation	Not part of a theory in this book. One and the same theory can be represented in many different ways without changing the theory
Constructs	Conceptual framework
Statements of relationship	Generalizations
Scope	Scope
Causal explanation	This is one kind of explanation, next to architectural and rational explanations
Testable propositions (hypotheses)	Theories must be empirically testable, but testable propositions derived from the theory are not part of the theory
Prescriptive statements	Scientific theories do not prescribe anything

Sjoberg et al. [46] present a theory of UML-based development consisting of (1) a conceptual framework, (2) propositions, (3) explanations, and (4) an indication of scope. This parallels the structure of theories in this chapter. The similarity goes further, for their propositions and explanations seem to be causal and architectural explanations, respectively, introduced later in this chapter.

[4] **Page 95, structure of design theories.** Gregor and Jones [19] outline a structure for design theories in eight components that is more complex than the structure proposed here. All of the elements of their structure are covered by the approach in this book, but not all are part of design theories as defined here. The elements above the line in the following table are part of design theories in this book. The elements below the line are accounted for in other ways.

Gregor and Jones [19]	This book
Constructs	Conceptual framework
Testable propositions	Generalizations
Scope	Scope
Justificatory knowledge	Prior knowledge
Purpose	Artifact requirements, stakeholder goals
Principles of form and function	Design choices
Artifact mutability	Artifact variants (trade-offs)
Principles of implementation	Could be part of implementation theory
Expository instantiation	Validation model

The testable propositions of Gregor and Jones here seem to take the place of generalizations. Justificatory knowledge is part of the body of knowledge that a theory builds on. It is sometimes called a *reference theory,* which is a theory from another discipline to understand the interactions between an artifact and its context. The other elements in the list are products of a design process, such as artifact requirements, design choices, artifact variants, and a validation model. Principles of implementation could be a part of a theory of implementation but not of a design theory as defined in this book.

⁵ **Page 98, causal explanation.** The literature on causality is vast. It contains many fragments of insights but no unifying theory. Some sources that I have found very helpful, and that influenced the treatment of causality in this book, are the following. First, in order not to get lost in abstraction, it helps to see how the concept is used in various sciences. Parascandola and Weed give a very relevant overview of five different concepts of causation in epidemiology [38]. One is the concept of production, which corresponds to the architectural view in this book, and the other four are different concepts of deterministic and nondeterministic causation, which are variants of the difference-making view in this book. Another interesting source is Goldthorpe's [17] practical summary of the different views on causality for sociology researchers, where we see the same distinction between generative mechanisms on the one hand and causation as difference-making on the other hand. Russo and Williamson [44,45] give very readable introductions to causality and mechanisms in the health science, with practical examples.

The above papers give useful insights for the practicing researcher. A second group of sources is more philosophical. Cartwright [5,6] gives a deep philosophical analysis of the use of causality in physics and economics that is worth reading. The concept of capacity discussed by Cartwright [6] inspired the concept of capability used in this book.

Much of the philosophical literature, however, is domain independent. A useful starting point is Woodward's essay on the manipulability theory of causality [50], which is a version of the difference-making view that is well suited to the causal analysis of experiments. A much more elaborate treatment is given in his book [49]. Menzies [35] summarizes classical theories of counterfactual causation.

A third group of sources relates causality to probability and statistics. Hitchcock [22] gives a brief and readable introduction to probabilistic views of causality. A classic paper by Holland relates the difference-making view of causality presented here to randomized controlled trials [23]. Berk [3] gives a more methodological treatment, with examples from applied statistics in sociology, from the school of Freedman. The counterfactual theory of probabilistic causation described in these papers is based on work by Rubin [43], who himself traces it to original work by Neyman. Pearl [40] presents an integration of the counterfactual view of probabilistic causation with his own graphical approach. If you find the book overwhelming, you could start with his overview paper [39]. Morgan and Winship [37] give a clear introduction to Rubin's counterfactual approach to causal inference, integrating it with Pearl's [40] graphical approach.

⁶ **Page 98, architectural explanation.** Architectural explanations are called **mechanistic explanations** in the methodology of biology and of the health sciences [44, 45, 47], of psychiatry [27], of psychology [9], and of the social sciences [10, 11, 20, 21].

Glennan [14, 15] and Machamer et al. [33] give different definitions of the concept of mechanism. Illari and Williamson [34] survey these and other definitions and integrate them in a unifying definition. In this definition, a mechanism for a phenomenon consists of "entities and activities organized in such a way that they are responsible for the phenomenon." This is close to the software engineering concept of an architecture [25], with the special twist that Illari and Williamson treat entities and activities on the same footing. I view both as components, one more stable than then other.

Bechtel and Abrahamsen [1] and Bechtel and Richardson [2] give many historical examples of how biologists discovered the components of biological and biochemical processes, such as fermentation and biological inheritance. Bunge [4] and Elster [10, 11] give examples of social mechanisms, which are nondeterministic.

References

1. W. Bechtel, A. Abrahamsen, Explanation: a mechanistic alternative. Studies in the Hist. Philos. Biol. Biomed. Sci. **36**, 421–441 (2005)
2. W. Bechtel, R.C. Richardson, *Discovering Complexity: Decomposition and Localization as Strategies in Scientific Research* (MIT Press, Cambridge, 2010); Reissue of the 1993 edition with a new introduction
3. R.A. Berk, Causal inference for sociological data, in *Handbook of Sociology*, ed. by N.J. Smelser. (Sage, Thousand Oaks, 1988), pp. 155–172
4. M. Bunge, How does it work? The search for explanatory mechanisms. Philos. Soc. Sci. **34**(2), 182–210 (2004)
5. N. Cartwright, *How the Laws of Physics Lie* (Oxford University Press, Oxford, 1983)
6. N. Cartwright, *Nature's Capacities and Their Measurement* (Clarendon Press, Oxford 1989)
7. A. Cournand, M. Meyer. The scientist's code. Minerva **14**(1), 79–96 (1976)
8. C.F. Craver, Structure of scientific theories, in *The Blackwell Guide to the Philosophy of Science*, ed. by P. Machamer, M. Silberstein (Blackwell, Oxford, 2002), pp. 55–79
9. R. Cummins, 'How does it work?' versus 'What are the laws?': two conceptions of psychological explanation, in *Explanation and Cognition*, ed. by F.C. Keil, R.A. Wilson (MIT Press, Cambridge, 2000), pp. 117–144
10. J. Elster, *Nuts and Bolts for the Social Sciences* (Cambridge University Press, Cambridge, 1989)
11. J. Elster, A plea for mechanisms, in *Social Mechanisms. An Analytical Approach to Social Theory*, ed. by P. Hedström, R. Swedberg (Cambridge University Press, Cambridge, 1998), pp. 45–73
12. W. Engelsman, D.A.C. Quartel, H. Jonkers, M.J. van Sinderen, Extending enterprise architecture modelling with business goals and requirements. Enterp. Inf. Syst. **5**(1), 9–36 (2011)
13. W. Engelsman, R.J. Wieringa, Goal-oriented requirements engineering and enterprise architecture: Two case studies and some lessons learned, in *Requirements Engineering: Foundation for Software Quality (REFSQ 2012), Essen, Germany*. Lecture Notes in Computer Science, vol. 7195 (Springer, Heidelberg, 2012), pp. 306–320
14. S. Glennan, Rethinking mechanistic explanation. Philos. Sci. **69**, S342–S353 (2002)
15. S.S. Glennan, Mechanisms and the nature of causation. Erkenntnis **44**, 49–71 (1996)
16. P. Godfrey-Smith, *Theory and Reality. An Introduction to the Philosophy of Science* (The University of Chicago Press, Chicago, 2003)
17. J.H. Goldthorpe, Causation, statistics, and sociology. Eur. Sociol. Rev. **17**(1), 1–20 (2001)
18. S. Gregor, The nature of theory in information systems. MIS Q. **30**(3), 611–642 (2006)
19. S. Gregor, D. Jones, The anatomy of a design theory. J. AIS **8**(5), 312–335 (2007)
20. P. Hedström, R. Swedberg (eds.), *Social Mechanisms. An Analytical Approach to Social Theory* (Cambridge University Press, Cambridge, 1998)
21. P. Hedström, P. Ylikoski, Causal mechanisms in the social sciences. Ann. Rev. Sociol. **36**, 49–67 (2010)
22. C. Hitchcock, Probabilistic causation, in *The Stanford Encyclopedia of Philosophy*, ed. by E.N. Zalta. Spring 2010 edition (2010)
23. P.W. Holland, Statistics and causal inference. J. Am. Stat. Assoc. **81**(396), 945–960 (1986)
24. T. Huynh, J. Miller, An empirical investigation into open source web applications' implementation vulnerabilities. Empir. Softw. Eng. **15**(5), 556–576 (2010)
25. ISO, *Systems and Software Engineering — Architecture Description*. ISO/IEC/IEEE (2007)
26. A. Kaplan, *The Conduct of Inquiry. Methodology for Behavioral Science* (Transaction Publishers, Pscataway, 1998); First edition 1964 by Chandler Publishers
27. K.S. Kendler, Explanatory models for psychiatric illness. Am. J. Psychiatry **6**, 695–702 (2008)
28. T. Kuhn, *The Structure of Scientific Revolutions*, 2nd edn. (University of Chicago Press, Chicago, 1970)

29. I. Lakatos, Falsification and the methodology of scientific research programmes, in *Criticism and the Growth of Knowledge*, ed. by I. Lakatos, A. Musgrave (Cambridge University Press, Cambridge, 1970), pp. 91–196

30. I. Lakatos, *Proofs and Refutations* (Cambridge University Press, Cambridge, 1976); Edited by J. Worall and E. Zahar

31. L. Prechelt, B. Unger-Lamprecht, M. Philippsen, W.F. Tichy, Two controlled experiments assessing the usefulness of design pattern documentation in program maintenance. IEEE Trans. Softw. Eng. **28**(6), 595–606 (2002)

32. P. Machamer, A brief historical introduction to the philosophy of science, in *The Blackwell Guide to the Philosophy of Science*, ed. by P. Machamer, M. Silberstein (Blackwell, Oxford, 2002), pp. 1–17

33. P. Machamer, L. Darden, C.F. Craver, Thinking about mechanisms. Philos. Sci. **67**, 1–25 (2000)

34. P. McKay Illari, J. Williamson, What is a mechanism? Thinking about mechanisms *across* the sciences. Eur. J. Philos. Sci. **2**, 119–135 (2012)

35. P. Menzies, Counterfactual theories of causation, in *The Stanford Encyclopedia of Philosophy*, ed. by E.N. Zalta. Fall 2009 edition (2009)

36. R.K. Merton, The normative structure of science, in *Social Theory and Social Structure* (The Free Press, New York, 1968), pp. 267–278. Enlarged Edition

37. S. Morgan, X. Winship, *Counterfactuals and Causal Inference. Methods and Principles for Social Research* (Cambridge University Press, Cambridge, 2007)

38. M. Parascandola, D.L. Weed, Causation in epidemiology. J. Epidemiol. Commun. Health **55**, 905–912 (2001)

39. J. Pearl, Causal inference in statistics: an overview. Stat. Surv. **3**, 96–146 (2009)

40. J. Pearl, *Causality. Models, Reasoning and Inference*, 2nd edn. (Cambridge University Press, Cambridge, 2009)

41. K.R. Popper, *The Logic of Scientific Discovery* (Hutchinson, London, 1959)

42. W.S. Robinson, The logical structure of analytic induction. Am. Sociol. Rev. **16**(6), 812–818 (1951)

43. D.B. Rubin, Bayesian inference for causal effects: The role of randomization. Ann. Stat. **6**(1), 34–58 (1978)

44. F. Russo, J. Williamson, Interpreting causality in the health sciences. Int. Stud. Philos. Sci. **21**(2), 157–170 (2007)

45. F. Russo, J. Williamson, Generic versus single-case causality: The case of autopsy. Eur. J. Philos. Sci. **1**(1), 47–69 (2011)

46. D.I.K. Sjøberg, T. Dybå, B.C.D. Anda, J.E. Hannay, Building theories in software engineering, in *Guide to advanced empirical software engineering*, ed. by F. Shull, J. Singer, D.I.K. Sjøberg (Springer, Heidelberg, 2008), pp. 312–336

47. P. Thagard, Explaining disease: correlations, causes, and mechanisms, in *Explanation and Cognition*, ed. by F.C. Keil, R.A. Wilson (MIT Press, Cambridge, 2000), pp. 255–276

48. R.J. Wieringa, M. Daneva, N. Condori-Fernandez, The structure of design theories, and an analysis of their use in software engineering experiments, in *International Symposium on Empirical Software Engineering and Measurement (ESEM)* (IEEE Computer Society, Los Alamitos, 2011), pp. 295–304

49. J. Woodward, *Making Things Happen. A Theory of Causal Explanation* (Oxford University Press, Oxford, 2003)

50. J. Woodward, Causation and manipulability, in *The Stanford Encyclopedia of Philosophy*, ed. by E.N. Zalta. Summer 2013 edition. http://plato.stanford.edu/cgi-bin/encyclopedia/archinfo.cgi?entry=causation-mani

Part IV
The Empirical Cycle

Chapter 10
The Empirical Cycle

We now turn to the empirical cycle, which is a rational way to answer scientific knowledge questions. It is structured as a checklist of issues to decide when a researcher designs a research setup, and wants to reason about the data produced by this setup.[1]

Our checklist covers the context of empirical research as well as the cycle of empirical research itself. The first and last parts of the checklist consist of questions about the context. These parts are discussed in Sect. 10.1. The rest of the checklist is about the cycle of empirical research, and a bird's-eye view of this is presented in Sect. 10.2. The cycle starts with a list of questions about framing the research problem, and this is presented in Sect. 10.3. The rest of the checklist is about designing the research setup and the inferences from it, about research execution, and about data analysis. Sections 10.4–10.6 give a preview of this, and in the following chapters, these parts of the checklist are treated in detail. Appendix B summarizes the checklist.

Not all items of the checklist are relevant for each research method. In part V, we will explain and illustrate four different research methods using the relevant parts of the checklist. We have already encountered these methods when discussing research methods for implementation evaluation (Chap. 5) and treatment validation (Chap. 7).

The checklist of the empirical cycle is a logical grouping of questions that help you to find justifiable answers to scientific knowledge questions. It is not necessarily a sequence of tasks to be performed exactly in the order listed. This is similar to the design cycle. In Chap. 3, we saw that the design cycle is a rational way to solve design problems but that design managers may organize the design process in many different ways. In Sect. 10.7, we will see that research managers can organize the research process in different ways but that they should respect some basic rules of scientific knowledge acquisition that prohibit cheating and require full disclosure of the knowledge acquisition process.

© Springer-Verlag Berlin Heidelberg 2014
R.J. Wieringa, *Design Science Methodology for Information Systems and Software Engineering*, DOI 10.1007/978-3-662-43839-8_10

A final preliminary remark is that the empirical cycle is a heavyweight tool to answer knowledge questions. There are much easier and less resource-consuming ways to answer a knowledge question, for example, by reading the literature, asking experts, or testing a prototype without the elaborate conceptual framework and safeguards against wrong conclusions needed for scientific research. The choice to follow the empirical cycle depends on your knowledge goal and available budget. Henceforth, we assume that your goal is to advance scientific knowledge and to publish about it and that your budget provides the money to acquire the necessary resources and the time to do the required scientific research.

10.1   The Research Context

Table 10.1 shows the checklist questions for the research context. The first question asks what the (1) *knowledge goal* of this research is. The knowledge goal summarizes in one phrase all knowledge questions that you want to answer in the study. In curiosity-driven research, your knowledge goal may be to learn more about an artifact. If you are working in the context of a higher-level design or engineering

Table 10.1 Checklist for the research context

1. Knowledge goal(s)

    – What do you want to know? Is this part of an implementation evaluation, a problem investigation, a survey of existing treatments, or a new technology validation?

2. Improvement goal(s)?

    – If there is a higher-level engineering cycle, what is the goal of that cycle?
    – If this is a curiosity-driven project, are there credible application scenarios for the project results?

3. Current knowledge

    – State of the knowledge in published scientific, technical, and professional literature?
    – Available expert knowledge?
    – Why is your research needed? Do you want to add anything, e.g., confirm or falsify something?
    – Theoretical framework that you will use?

17. Contribution to knowledge goal(s)

    – Refer back to items 1 and 3

18. Contribution to improvement goal(s)?

    – Refer back to item 2
    – If there is no improvement goal, is there a potential contribution to practice?

cycle, your knowledge goal may be related to a task in the engineering cycle. Typical knowledge goals in the engineering cycle are:

- To investigate an improvement problem in the field
- To survey possible treatments
- To validate a design
- To evaluate an implementation in the field

The second question of the checklist asks whether you are working in the context of a higher-level design or engineering cycle with an (2) *improvement goal*. If you do, you are doing utility-driven research, and it is useful to state this design context in a research report. If you are not working in the context of a higher-level design cycle, you are doing curiosity-driven research.

To assess whether or not existing knowledge is sufficient to answer your questions, you must summarize (3) *current knowledge*. This is the summary of the review of scientific, technical, and professional literature relevant to your knowledge goal. In a research report, this may be called "related work" or "theoretical background."

The context checklist continues at the point where you have finished your research. At that point, you have to return to your knowledge goal. What is the (17) *contribution to the knowledge goal*? What do you give back to the knowledge context of your research? In a research report, this is often called "implications for research."

If there was an improvement goal that motivated your project, then you have to return to it now. What is your (18) *contribution to the improvement goal*? For curiosity-driven research too, the knowledge acquired by the study may have practical use. In a research report, the section describing these possible uses is often called "implications for practice."

10.2   The Empirical Cycle

After summarizing current knowledge, you may assess whether your knowledge goal has already been achieved sufficiently. If your research goal is to advance scientific knowledge beyond current knowledge and to publish about it and if your budget allows it, then you can use the checklist questions of the empirical cycle to structure your research (Fig. 10.1). You may also use the empirical cycle to decide what to put in a research report and to analyze the contents of a research report.

The empirical cycle has the structure of a rational decision cycle, just like the engineering cycle:

- **Research problem analysis**. What is the research problem to be solved? Here you frame the research problem. We treat this part of the checklist in the next section.

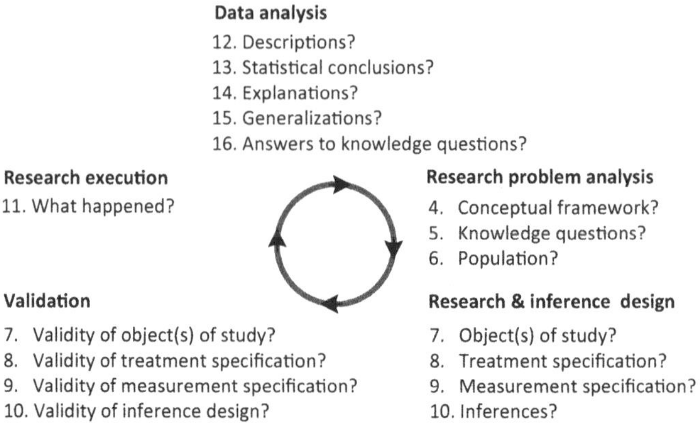

Data analysis
12. Descriptions?
13. Statistical conclusions?
14. Explanations?
15. Generalizations?
16. Answers to knowledge questions?

Research execution   **Research problem analysis**
11. What happened?   4. Conceptual framework?
                                                            5. Knowledge questions?
                                                            6. Population?

Validation   **Research & inference design**
7. Validity of object(s) of study?   7. Object(s) of study?
8. Validity of treatment specification?   8. Treatment specification?
9. Validity of measurement specification?   9. Measurement specification?
10. Validity of inference design?   10. Inferences?

Fig. 10.1 The empirical cycle

- **Research design and inference design**. What are you going to do to solve the knowledge problem? This is the research setup, and its design is treated in the next chapter. And how you are going to draw conclusions from the data generated by the research setup? This is inference design, and it is treated in Chaps. 12–15.
- **Validation of research and inference design**. The research setup and inferences must match each other, and they must be sufficient to answer the knowledge questions.
- **Research execution**. Research is executed according to the research design, but unexpected events may happen. Events relevant for the interpretation of the results must be reported.
- **Data analysis**. The data generated by the research is analyzed according to the inference design. Examples of execution and data analysis for different research methods are given in part V.

Validation in the empirical cycle is about the match between the research setup and inferences from the data. The major question is to what extent the research setup can support the inferences that we plan to do from the data. We extend this with two other fundamental questions that ask about repeatability and ethics. Repeatability is a condition of scientific knowledge acquisition (Sect. 9.1), and ethical norms are applicable whenever people are involved. This gives us three kinds of validity questions about a research design:

- *Inference support.* To what extent does the research setup support the planned inferences?
- *Repeatability.* Is the design specified in such a way that competent peers could repeat the research?
- *Ethics.* Does the treatment of people respect ethical norms?

Discussion of inference support belongs both to research design and inference design, because it is about the match between the two. When the design of the research setup is discussed in the next chapter, inference support cannot be discussed in detail because this would require familiarity with inference design. So validity is touched upon very lightly. Then, when we look at inference design in Chaps. 12–15, support given to inferences by different research setups is discussed in detail. Finally, in the explanation of the research methods in part V, validity of each research setup is treated when we look at research designs.

There is a potential ambiguity in the word "validation." In the design cycle, validation is the justification that a designed treatment contributes to stakeholder goals. In the empirical cycle, validation is the justification that a designed research setup would provide answers to the knowledge questions. Both kinds of meanings are used when we discuss the validity (empirical cycle) of the design of validation research (design cycle). Context will make clear in which sense we use the word.

10.3 The Research Problem

Table 10.2 gives the checklist for framing an empirical research problem. To state the research problem: you need a (4) *conceptual framework* that defines the relevant constructs. The framework can define architectural and statistical structures, and it is subject to the requirements of construct validity.

Using a conceptual framework, you can state (5) *knowledge questions* and define a (6) *population*. The checklist distinguishes different kinds of knowledge questions as we have done in Chap. 2. We have also seen that there are three kinds of explanatory questions that can ask for causes, mechanisms, or reasons, respectively.

Your knowledge questions are about the *population*, not only about the object that you are studying. If phenomena in the object of study would have no implication

Table 10.2 Checklist for the research problem statement

4. Conceptual framework

    - Conceptual structures? Architectural structures, statistical structures?
    - Chance models of random variables: semantics of variables?
    - Validity of the conceptual framework? Clarity of definitions, unambiguous application, avoidance of mono-operation and mono-method bias?

5. Knowledge questions

    - Open (exploratory) or closed (hypothesis-testing) questions?
    - Effect, satisfaction, trade-off, or sensitivity questions?
    - Descriptive or explanatory questions?

6. Population

    - Population predicate? What is the architecture of the elements of the population? In which ways are all population elements similar to each other and dissimilar to other elements?
    - Chance models of random variables: assumptions about distributions of variables?

for phenomena in any other object, then they would be random. Why should we want to publish a random fact, or why would anyone want to read about it? The aim of research is to find systematic relations among phenomena that can be generalized beyond the particular cases in which these phenomena were observed. These generalizations are fallible, and if our goal is total certainty, we should not make them. But if we accept fallible generalizations, then we should generalize, and we should support our generalizations with the best arguments that we can produce to survive the test of practice and the criticism of competent peers. This point is important, so I illustrate with an example:

☐   It is good to know that in one organization, global software engineering projects use a gatekeeper to maintain a consistent information state across different project locations, but if this would have no implication whatsoever for similar projects in similar companies, then this would be a random fact. Why should we publish about a random fact? But if it is not a random fact, then it is a fact about a population larger than just the single project that was studied. For example, it could be a fact about coordination mechanisms in global software engineering projects. The population would then be the population of global software engineering projects. Support for this generalization can be sought by repeating the research on different global software engineering projects.

10.4   The Research Setup

To answer a knowledge question about a population, the researcher needs one or more objects of study (OoSs). As indicated in Fig. 10.2, these have some relationship with the population, so that knowledge questions about the population can be answered by studying OoSs. In **case-based research**, the researcher studies OoS separately. Each studied object is called a case. To generalize from a case to a population, the similarity between the studied cases and other cases from the population must be assessed. In **sample-based research**, the researcher studies a

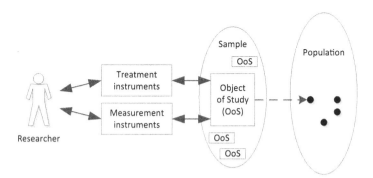

Fig. 10.2 Empirical research setup. In observational research, there is no treatment. Case-based research studies individual objects of study; sample-based research studies samples of objects of study

sample of cases. To generalize statistically from a sample to a population, the sample selection procedure must be understood.

The difference between case-based and sample-based research is that in case-based research we study individual objects and aim to generalize, by analogy, to similar objects. In sample-based research, we do not study individuals but samples and aim to generalize to the population from which the sample was drawn. Case-based research studies architectural structures; sample-based research studies statistical structures (Chap. 8).

Sampling plays a role in both kinds of research, but differently. Case-based research studies cases separately, and often in series, in a process of *analytical induction*. After studying one case, the conceptual framework and generalization based on the case population may be revised before a next case is studied. This revision may even include a redefinition of the population. Sample-based research, by contrast, studies samples as a whole, in other words studies all objects in the sample at the same time. Sampling must be finished before the sample as a whole can be studied. After studying a sample, *statistical inference* is used to draw conclusions about the population.

A second classification of research setups is into observational and experimental research. In **experimental research**, the researcher applies an experimental treatment to the OoS and measures what happens. In **observational research**, the researcher refrains from intervening and just measures phenomena in the OoS:

☐   If you study a software engineering project to see how requirements are managed, then you do an observational case study. If you take a web-based survey of projects to collect statistics about how requirements are managed, you are doing a sample-based observational study. You measure phenomena, but you do not intervene.
   If on the other hand you test a new requirements management technique in a pilot project, you are doing an experiment, because you intervene in the project. In the terminology of this book, it is a single-case mechanism experiment. If you compare two requirements management techniques by asking one group of student projects to use one technique and the other group of projects to use the other, then you are doing a sample-based experiment. In the terminology of this book, you are doing a statistical difference-making experiment.

Treatment and measurement are both interactions between the researcher and the OoS. When applying an experimental treatment, the researcher applies a specific intervention and tries to minimize any other influence. When doing a measurement, the researcher observes OoS while attempting to minimize any influence. Instruments are needed for both. In the next chapter, we discuss the checklist for designing a research setup.

Combining the two distinctions that we made, we get the classification of research designs shown in Table 10.3. As shown by the chapter numbers, all research designs except surveys are treated in this book.

Table 10.3 Some different research designs. Between brackets are the numbers of the chapters where these designs are explained

	Observational study **(no treatment)**	**Experimental study** **(treatment)**
Case-based research	• Observational case study (17)	• Single-case experiment (18) • Comparative-cases experiment (14) • Technical action research (19)
Sample-based research	• Survey • Quasi-experiment (20)	• Randomized controlled trial (20) • Quasi-experiment (20)

10.5   Inferences from Data

Measurements generate data. The process of drawing conclusions from these data is called inference. All of the inferences that we discuss are **ampliative**, which means that their conclusions may be false while their premises are true. This is the opposite of a **deductive inference**, of which the conclusions are guaranteed to be true when its premises are true. To manage the fallibility of ampliative inferences, they must be accompanied by a discussion of their degree of support, which is usually called a discussion of their *validity*.[2] In the following chapters, we discuss the following kinds of inferences, each with their own set of validity constraints:

- **Descriptive inference** summarizes the data into descriptions. It is subject to the constraints of **descriptive validity**.
- **Statistical inference** is the inference of population characteristics from sample statistics. It is subject to the constraints of **conclusion validity**.
- **Abductive inference** postulates the most plausible explanations for your observations. It is subject to the constraints of **internal validity**.
- **Analogic inference** is the generalization of your explanations to similar OoS. It is subject to the constraints of **external validity**.

Here is an example that contains all these sorts of inferences:

☐   Suppose you do a case study on requirements management in global software engineering. You study one global software engineering project by collecting data from email logs, version management systems, chat logs, interviews with engineers and other stakeholders, project meetings, etc.

Descriptive inference is the extraction of informative descriptions from this mountain of data. For example, you collect statistics about subjects of emails, draw a social network diagram of software engineers, transcribe and code interviews into concept maps, etc.

If you infer, from the subjects of a random sample of email messages, what the distribution of subjects in the entire population of email messages is, then you are doing *statistical inference*.

If you explain why some topics were discussed more frequently than others by means of social mechanisms of the project, then you do *abductive inference*.

If you then generalize that similar projects will exchange emails about the same topics by similar mechanisms, then you are doing *analogic inference*.

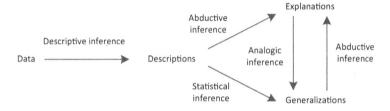

Fig. 10.3 Road map of inferences

Table 10.4 Case-based and sample-based inference strategies

Case-based inference	Sample-based inference
1. Descriptive inference: Describe the case observations.	1. Descriptive inference: Describe sample statistics.
	2. Statistical inference: Estimate or test a statistical model of the population.
2. Abductive inference: Explain the observations architecturally and/or rationally.	3. Abductive inference: Explain the model causally, architecturally and/or rationally.
3. Analogic inference: Assess whether the explanations would be true of architecturally similar cases too.	4. Analogic inference: Assess whether the statistical model and its explanation would be true of populations of architecturally similar cases too.

Figure 10.3 gives a road map of inferences, and Table 10.4 shows how we walk the map in case-based and in sample-based research. Each of the steps in the inferences is discussed in a separate chapter.

10.6 Execution and Data Analysis

Research execution is the execution of your research design. Usually the design cannot be executed exactly as designed, and unplanned events may happen. OoS may interact even if you planned for them not do so, treatments may be delivered imperfectly, measurements may fail or may disturb the OoS, subjects may drop out, etc. You must keep a diary of all events that may be relevant for data analysis.

In data analysis, you perform the inferences that were planned during your design. The validity of these inference designs is affected by unplanned events during research execution, and this means that the validity discussion must be revisited during data analysis, with all of the information you now have about research execution. It is usually this revised validity discussion that is included in a research report.

Data analysis results in descriptions, statistical generalizations, explanations, and analogic generalizations of the results, with varying degrees of support in the data. Jointly, this should provide enough information to answer the knowledge questions that were to be answered by the research. Examples of execution and analysis of research are given for different research methods in part V.

10.7   The Empirical Cycle Is Not a Research Process

The checklist is a logical grouping of questions, not a temporal sequence of tasks that you must perform. Some questions may not be relevant for the research you are planning, and questions may be answered in an order different from that in which they are asked.

Even at the top level of the cycle, you may interleave tasks. For example, during research execution, you may find that the conceptual framework needs to be elaborated further or that you may have to redesign a measurement instrument. The rule here is that almost anything goes.

Almost anything goes. Two things are prohibited, because they defeat the purpose of knowledge acquisition:

> **Rule of posterior knowledge**: Knowledge created by the research is present *after* execution of the research, and it is absent before executing the research.

For example, you cannot test a hypothesis that has been formulated *after* you have done the research. If your question was "What is the execution time?" and your data tells you that execution time is less than 7.7 ms, then you cannot act as if you have actually been testing the hypothesis "The execution time is less than 7.7 ms." You had no such hypothesis. If your goal is to acquire knowledge, then you must not claim to have had that knowledge at a point in time when you hadn't. This has to do with causality: If the research outcome caused us to have some knowledge, we must not act as if "really" that knowledge caused us to set up the research in the way we did.

There is a dual to this rule:

> **Rule of prior ignorance**: Any knowledge present *before* doing the research may influence the outcome of the research.

The only knowledge that cannot influence the outcome of research is knowledge that did not exist before doing the research. This is the reason why in double-blind experiments, the researcher observing the outcome of a treatment should not know which particular treatment has been allocated to which object of study. If the researcher would know, we would have to assume that this will influence the measurements and the measured phenomena.

What about knowledge questions? We might find interesting data that answer questions that we had not asked. Can we still state these knowledge questions? Yes you can, but you have to say that you formulated these questions after you did the research. Knowledge that these questions are relevant was created by the research and was absent before doing the research. The rule is this:

> **Rule of full disclosure**: All events that could have influenced research conclusions must be reported.

A special case of this rule is that all data that you collected for your research should be disclosed. If some data is confidential, then this should be anonymized first, of course. The information that was removed from the data can then not be used to draw inferences.

10.8 Summary

- In design research, we try to answer knowledge questions about implementations, problems, or treatments. The research context may be utility driven or curiosity driven.
- Empirical research is expensive, and before you attempt it, you should check other ways of answering knowledge questions, including literature study and asking experts.
- The research problem to be solved consists of a list of knowledge questions that presuppose a conceptual framework and assume a population of interest. The goal of research is to find support for a generalization to that population.
- The empirical cycle is a logical grouping of questions to ask about your research. You may also use it to decide what to put in a report and to analyze a report.
- The empirical cycle is not a list of tasks to be performed in a certain order. Almost anything goes, but two things are forbidden:
  - Rule of posterior knowledge: Knowledge created by the research is present *after* execution of the research, and it is absent before executing the research.
  - Rule of prior ignorance: Any knowledge present *before* doing the research may influence the outcome of the research.

  To ensure this, publication is required:

  > Rule of full disclosure: All events that could have influenced research conclusions must be reported.

- Research setup and inference are closely coupled, because the setup must support the inferences to be done later. Both must be designed before you start the research.

Notes

[1]**Page 109, checklists for empirical research.** Several checklists have been published in software engineering, notably by Kitchenham et al. [3] and Wohlin et al. [10] for experimental research and Juristo and Moreno for statistical research and inference design. Jedlitschka and Pfahl [2] integrated the then extant checklists for controlled experiments. Runeson et al. [4, 5] present a checklist for case study research.

For the checklist in this book, I have compared and integrated these checklists [7, 8]. We have performed an empirical validation of usability by students [1, 9], which led to a considerable simplification of the integrated checklist. Further simplifications have been found in the preparation of this book when I applied the checklist to a growing number of research reports that used different research methods.

[2]**Page 116, validity as degree of support.** Validity is defined by Shadish et al. [6, p. 513] as "the truth of, correctness of, or degree of support for an inference." I interpret this as *three* different definitions, not one. My definition follows the third of these three, degree of support.

References

1. N. Condori-Fernandez, R. Wieringa, M. Daneva, B. Mutschler, O. Pastor, Experimental evaluation of a unified checklist for designing and reporting empirical research in software engineering. Technical Report TR-CTIT-12-12, Centre for Telematics and Information Technology University of Twente, 2012
2. A. Jedlitschka, D. Pfahl, Reporting guidelines for controlled experiments in software engineering, in *Proceedings of the 4th International Symposium on Empirical Software Engineering (ISESE 2005)* (IEEE Computer Society, Los Alamitos, 2005), pp. 94–104
3. B.A. Kitchenham, S.L. Pfleeger, D.C. Hoaglin, K.E. Emam, J. Rosenberg, Preliminary guidelines for empirical research in software engineering. IEEE Trans. Softw. Eng. **28**(8), 721–733 (2002)
4. P. Runeson, M. Höst, Guidelines for conducting and reporting case study research in software engineering. Empir. Softw. Eng. **14**, 131–164 (2009)
5. P. Runeson, M. Höst, A. Rainer, B. Regnell, *Case Study Research in Software Engineering: Guidelines and Examples* (Wiley, Hoboken, 2012)
6. W.R. Shadish, T.D. Cook, D.T. Campbell, *Experimental and Quasi-Experimental Designs for Generalized Causal Inference* (Houghton Mifflin Company, Boston, 2002)
7. R.J. Wieringa, Towards a unified checklist for empirical research in software engineering: first proposal, in *16th International Conference on Evaluation and Assessment in Software Engineering (EASE 2012)*, ed. by T. Baldaresse, M. Genero, E. Mendes, M. Piattini (IET, 2012), pp. 161–165
8. R.J. Wieringa, A unified checklist for observational and experimental research in software engineering (version 1). Technical Report TR-CTIT-12-07, Centre for Telematics and Information Technology University of Twente, 2012
9. R. Wieringa, N. Condori-Fernandez, M. Daneva, B. Mutschler, O. Pastor, Lessons learned from evaluating a checklist for reporting experimental and observational research, in *International Symposium on Empirical Software Engineering and Measurement (ESEM)*. IEEE Computer Society, Los Alamitos, September 2012), pp. 157–160
10. C. Wohlin, P. Runeson, M. Höst, M. C. Ohlsson, B. Regnell, A. Weslén, *Experimentation in Software Engineering*, 2nd edn. (Springer, Heidelberg, 2012)

Chapter 11
Research Design

Figure 11.1 shows again the architecture of the empirical research setup. In this chapter, we discuss the design of each of the components of the research setup, namely, of the object of study (Sect. 11.1), sample (Sect. 11.2), treatment (Sect. 11.3), and measurement (Sect. 11.4).

11.1 Object of Study

11.1.1 Acquisition of Objects of Study

An **object of study** (OoS) is the part of the world that the researcher interacts with in order to learn something about population elements. It is the entity where the phenomena occur from which measurements are taken. An OoS can be a population element or a *model* of population elements. Remember that a model was defined in Chap. 7 (p. 61) as an entity whose behavior can be measured and that represents entities of interest, called its *targets*:

☐ In the DOA problem, the OoS is a *validation model* of real-world implementations of an algorithm to estimate direction of arrival. It consists of a model of the artifact and a model of the context. The model of the artifact is a prototype implementation of the DOA algorithm, and the model of the context consists of a prototype beamforming system, a simulated antenna system, and simulated signals from plane waves. The validation model represents real TV reception systems in a cars driving on a road.

☐ In the ARE problem, eight software development companies were investigated. There were eight OoSs, and each OoS is a case. These cases are population elements, and they are used to represent other population elements. The population is the set of all agile software projects done for small- and medium-sized companies.

☐ Prechelt et al. [9] used two samples of students to compare different ways of commenting programs. The objects of study consisted of students who performed maintenance tasks on programs. The students were elements of the population of students, and the programs were

© Springer-Verlag Berlin Heidelberg 2014
R.J. Wieringa, *Design Science Methodology for Information Systems and Software Engineering*, DOI 10.1007/978-3-662-43839-8_11

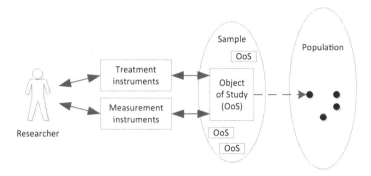

Fig. 11.1 Empirical research setup, repeated from Fig. 10.2. In observational research, there is no treatment

Table 11.1 Checklist for the Object of Study.

7.1   Acquisition of Objects of Study

– If OoS's are selected: How do you know that a selected entity is a population element?
– If OoS's are constructed: How do you construct a population element?
– Validity of OoS

- *Inference support.* Which inferences would be valid with respect to this design? See checklists for validity of descriptive statistics, abductive and analogic inferences.
- *Repeatability.* Could other researchers use your report to construct or select a similar OoS?
- *Ethics.* Are people informed that they will be studied, and do they consent to this? Are they free to stop at any time without giving reasons, and do they know this?

constructed models of the set of all programs. So each OoS consisted of a natural part (a student) and an artificial part (a program) constructed by the researchers.

Table 11.1 gives the checklist for selecting or constructing an OoS. An OoS can be constructed by the researcher, as in the DOA example, or selected from a population, as in the ARE example, or it can contain a natural and a constructed part, as in the study by Prechelt et al.

11.1.2   Validity of Objects of Study

In order for the OoS to support an inference, it must support the validity requirements of the inference. We look at these requirements in detail in the chapters to come and here only give a brief preview.

For *descriptive* and *statistical inference*, a chance model must be defined for the variables. This implies that the variables must be observable properties of the objects of study and that the objects of study must satisfy the population predicate.

For *causal inference* in experiments, the OoS should not be influenced by anything else than the experimental treatment. For *architectural inference* as well as *analogic inference*, the OoS should match the architecture as specified in the population predicate. For *rational inference*, goals and motivations of actors should be observable. Of course, real objects of study will satisfy these requirements to some extent, but not completely.

Acquisition of an OoS should be *repeatable* in the sense that other researchers could acquire similar objects. And it should respect the norms of *ethics* for the people involved. For example, people should only participate after informed consent and should be free to stop any time without giving reasons [1, 8, 10, 11].

11.2 Sampling

In the following, we discuss sampling for case-based studies, sampling for sample-based studies, and the validity of the sampling procedures. Table 11.2 gives the checklist for sampling.

11.2.1 Sampling in Case-Based Research

In case-based research, sampling is done sequentially in a process of analytical induction. The population in case-based research is usually not crisply defined, and we sample cases by similarity, where the similarity concept may be revised between case studies. After defining a theoretical framework and formulating knowledge

Table 11.2 Checklist for the sampling procedure.

7.2 Construction of a sample

- Case-based research: What is the analytical induction strategy? Confirming cases, disconfirming cases, extreme cases?
- Sample-based research: What is the sampling frame and probability sampling strategy? Random with or without replacement, stratified, cluster? What should the size of the sample be?
- Validity of sampling procedure

  - *Inference support.* Which inferences would be valid with respect to this design? See the applicable parts of the checklists for validity of statistical, abductive and analogic inferences.
  - *Repeatability.* Can the sampling procedure be replicated by other researchers?
  - *Ethics.* No new issues.

questions, a case is selected from the intended population and studied. This may lead to an update of the theoretical framework and even a redefinition of the population predicate. With this new theoretical framework and population predicate, a new case is selected and studied.

Assuming sufficient research resources, this process continues, until the theoretical framework can deal with all cases studied so far that are element of the final population, and the definitions did not have to be changed after the most recently studied case. Generalization in analytical induction is by analogy. Examples of analytical induction are given in Chap. 15 on analogic inference.

11.2.2 Sampling in Sample-Based Research

In sample-based research, a sample as a whole is studied. For statistical inference from a sample, you need a **random sample**, which is a sample selected randomly with replacement from the population. Each time a sample element is selected, each population element has the same probability of being selected. This means that the sample is a multiset, as one population element may be selected more than once.

In practice, we work with **simple random samples**, which are selected without replacement. After each selection, the probability of the remaining population elements of being selected increases slightly, because the set to be selected from has become smaller. If the population is large compared to the sample, then the difference with random sampling is negligible, but if it is small compared to the sample, statistical inferences must include a correction factor to compensate for the fact that sampling was done without replacement. We give the correction factor in Chap. 13 on statistical inference.

More complicated sampling schemes are stratified sampling and cluster sampling, which are used in observational research. We will not use these here. More information about them can be found in the literature [4, 7].

How do we actually select elements of a population? For this, we need a list of population elements from which you can select elements, called a **sampling frame**. This list often does not describe the entire population. The entire population is now called the **theoretical population**, and the subset described by the sampling frame is called the **study population** (see Fig. 11.2). The theoretical population may be just as fuzzily defined as in case-based sampling.

To select a simple random sample from a sampling frame, you could enter the sampling frame in a column of a spreadsheet, generate random numbers from the interval [0, 1] in the column next to it, and then sort on the random column. The first n rows then give you a simple random sample of size n.

Generalization in sample-based research now is a two-step process: Statistical inference takes you from a random sample to the study population, and analogic inference takes you from the study population to the theoretical population. Chapter 20, on statistical difference-making experiments, gives an example.

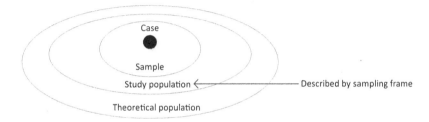

Fig. 11.2 Cases, samples, populations, and sampling frames

11.2.3 Validity of Sampling Procedure

Statistical inference from a sample to the study population requires random sampling, with or without replacement. Random sampling is very difficult to achieve, and there will often be a nonrandom, and therefore systematic, influence on the sample too. This creates a systematic error.

To spell this out, suppose some variable X is defined over a population and we repeatedly select a random sample from this population. Each time, we compute the sample average of X. All of these sample averages are probably different, a fluctuation that is the consequence of the fact that we are computing the average of finite samples of randomly drawn population elements. But because we are sampling randomly, the central-limit theorem says that these differences are random fluctuations around the real population mean and not the effect of some systematic mechanism in the sampling procedure. We discuss the central-limit theorem in Chap. 13 on statistical inference. The theorem says that if we repeatedly select random samples from the population, then in the long run, the sample means will cluster randomly around the population mean:

Sample mean = population mean + random fluctuation.

If sampling is not fully random, then it contains some systematic mechanisms, and the sample mean is [4]:

Sample mean = population mean + systematic displacement + random fluctuation.

An example is a statistical difference-making experiment (Chap. 20), where all sample elements receive the same treatment, and the goal is to estimate the systematic displacement caused by this treatment, which is called the **treatment effect**. The major methodological problem here is to ensure that the treatment is the *only* systematic influence on the outcome. Any mechanism other than random selection should be accounted for in the analysis of the data, because otherwise it will be mistakenly held to be part of the treatment effect. Examples of such additional treatment effects are given in Chap. 14 on abductive inference, when we discuss threats to the validity of causal inference.

Statistical inference only deals with random part of the measurements, not with any systematic part. The systematic displacement in the above equation is usually called **bias**, and the fluctuation is usually called **sampling error** [4]. Both terms are unfortunate, since they suggest prejudice and mistakes, but actually refer to systematic displacements and random fluctuations. But they are here to stay. Whenever I use them, I will give a warning not to misinterpret them.

If sampling is not random and not all mechanisms by which a sample is selected are known, then it is not possible to know which systematic displacement is part of the results. It is then not possible for other researchers to repeat the research. So if other researchers repeat the known steps of the research, then it is not possible to draw conclusions from a comparison of the outcomes. The replication has a systematic displacement that is unknown and must be assumed different from the systematic displacement in the original experiment that is also unknown:

☐ *An example is self-selection into a sample. If students volunteer to participate as subject in a study because of a small monetary reward, then this reward is part of the selection mechanism and may influence the outcome systematically. A replication with different students may show a different effect.*

11.3 Treatment

11.3.1 Treatment Design

An **experimental treatment** is a treatment of an OoS by a researcher, performed with the goal of finding out what the effects of the treatment are:

☐ Exposing a DOA algorithm to a simulated context in order to learn about its performance is an experimental treatment of the algorithm.

☐ Exposing students to programs with particular kinds of program comments in order to learn about the effects of the commenting techniques on maintainability is an experimental treatment of the students.

Compare this with the concept of a problem treatment in the engineering cycle. A problem treatment in the engineering cycle is the insertion of an artifact in a problem context in order to improve something for some stakeholders. An experimental treatment in the empirical cycle, by contrast, is the exposure of an OoS to a treatment in order to answer a knowledge question of the researcher. The stakeholder is here the researcher, who wants to answer a knowledge question. Both kinds of treatment are special cases of the more general concept of an intervention.

Conceptual frameworks in statistical research often distinguish among independent, dependent, extraneous, and confounding variables. The **independent variable** then represents the different possible treatments that can be applied to an OoS. Each possible treatment is then one level of this variable:

☐ For example, in the PCL experiment, we may define the independent variable C with two possible values *PCL* and *no-PCL* that represent the two treatments.

This is misleading. Treatments are interventions, not levels. We may view a treatment as the *action* of setting the level of an independent variable, but not as merely the resulting level. The difference can be illustrated as follows:

☐ Suppose in a random sample we observe different values of Y for every different value of X. So there is some correlation between X and Y in the sample. If we were to view the different values of X as "treatments" of Y, then we might conclude that the differences in Y are effects of differences in X. But the correlated differences in X and Y might be the effect of differences in an underlying, unobserved variable U. So this causal inference is not warranted by these observations.
The situation would be different if we could manipulate the values of X. Suppose we would set X to a different value and would observe no difference in Y. Then it would have become clear that differences in Y are not caused by differences in X. Manipulation is essential for the demonstration of causality.

A **dependent variable** is a variable believed to be influenced by differences in the independent variable. Jointly with the term "independent variable," this suggests that the researcher knows that changes in the independent variable cause changes in the dependent variable. However, often, we do not know this. In their standard work on mutltivariate statistics, Tabachnick and Fidell admit from the start that the terminology of dependent and independent variables is used for convenience and has no causal implication [13, p. 2]. However, this is a very misleading convenience. It is the same as describing two people as married just because it is convenient for you to describe them this way but without wanting to imply that they are really married. We will use a more neutral terminology and talk of **experimental treatments** and **measured variables**.

In the same terminology of dependent and independent variables, an **extraneous variable** is any other variable than the treatment, which may or may not influence the "dependent" variable. In a randomized controlled experiment, extraneous factors will cancel out in the long run when we average the results of many replications of the experiment. **Confounding variables** are extraneous variables believed to influence the dependent variable. Just as all other extraneous variables, in truly randomized experiments, these will cancel out in the long run. But often it is not possible to randomize over all confounding variables. Then these factors will have to be kept constant, to block their effects on the dependent variable, or else they have to be blocked out in the computations of the statistical inference. More information can be found in the methodological literature on statistical inference, especially on the inference technique called ANCOVA (analysis of covariance) [3, 5].

Table 11.3 shows the checklist for treatment design. The first part of the list shows that treatments must be specified, instrumented, allocated to sample elements, and scheduled for delivery. There are many allocation schemes in experimental research

Table 11.3 Checklist for treatment design.

8. Treatment design

- Which treatment(s) will be applied?
- Which treatment instruments will be used? Instruction sheets, videos, lessons, software, computers, actuators, rooms, etc.
- How are treatments allocated to OoS's?

    - In sample-based research: blocking, factorial designs, cross-over designs? Between-subjects or within-subject designs?
    - In case-based research: Are treatments scaled up in successive cases?

- What is the treatment schedule?
- Validity of treatment design:

    - *Inference support.* Which inferences would be valid with respect to this design? See the applicable parts of the checklists for validity of statistical, abductive and analogic inferences.
    - *Repeatability.* Is the specification of the treatment and the allocation to OoS's clear enough so that others could repeat it?
    - *Ethics.* Is no harm done, and is everyone treated fairly? Will they be informed about the treatment before or after the study?

that have a major influence on causal inference. The major choice is whether or not to randomize allocation. In a **randomized controlled trial** (RCT), allocation is random, and in a **quasi-experiment**, it is not. Within these two options, there are still many possibilities, leading to many different possible allocation schemes. Some of these are discussed in Chap. 14 on abductive inference, and pointers to the literature are given there too. Here it suffices to give an example:

☐ Suppose two software engineering techniques are to be compared. In an RCT, we would draw a random sample of students and allocate the two treatments randomly to the sample elements.
If on the other hand we would allocate the techniques based on student competence measured in a pretest, we would be doing a quasi-experiment in which the experimenter selected the subjects into a treatment group systematically rather than randomly.

11.3.2 Treatment Validity

Treatment allocation is relevant for statistical, causal, and analogic inference. For *statistical inference*, treatment allocation must be random. For *causal inference*, the ideal research setup is to apply exactly the treatment and only the treatment. This is rarely possible, and causal inference must account for all confounding influences in addition to the treatment. For *analogic inference*, the applied treatment must be similar to the treatments of the target of generalization. More on this is discussed in the chapters on statistical, abductive, and analogic inference.

11.4   Measurement

Measurement of a variable is the assignment, according to a rule, of a value to the phenomenon denoted by the variable [6]:

☐   For example, when we measure the duration of a project, we assign a value to the phenomenon denoted by the variable *project duration*. We do this according to a fixed rule. The rule could be that we count the number of days from the kickoff meeting to the day when the final deliverable is produced. Or it could be that we count the number of days from the day that an account number for the project was created to the day that the account was closed. It is important to fix the rule, stick to it, and describe it in the project report.

11.4.1   Scales

Definition of a measurement rule involves defining a **measuring scale**. Like a data type, a scale is a set of values with manipulation rules. But unlike a data type, the values and manipulation rules must have real-world meaning, and this meaning is considered to be part of the scale:

☐   For example, we may decide to estimate the likelihood of an accident on a scale of 1–5 and to estimate the impact caused by the accident on a scale from 1 to 5 too. Suppose we estimate a particular accident to have likelihood 3 and impact 4. Using operations available in the data type of natural numbers, we now compute the product of likelihood and impact 12. However, this product has no real-world meaning. The real-world meaning of the two scales is that they provide an ordering of likelihood and impact, respectively, but do not provide estimates of size. Multiplication in these scales is meaningless.
☐   We may measure a software execution time in terms of seconds or in terms of milliseconds. These are two different scales with a meaning-preserving transformation between them. For example, an execution time of 3.000 s is an execution time of 3,000 ms. Treated as elements of the data type of natural numbers, $3.000 \neq 3,000$, but as measurements in a scale, they are equal.

The real-world meaning of a scale is captured by the set of meaning-preserving transformations of scale. Once we have indicated what the meaning-preserving operations of a scale are, we know which operations can be applied in a scale, namely, those preserved by a meaning-preserving operation [12, 14]. Table 11.4 lists a number of frequently used types of scales and gives examples:

• In a **nominal scale**, different phenomena are given different labels, and we can test whether two phenomena have received the same or a different label. This test will receive the same answer under any one-one mapping of the scale to another scale. This shows that the names themselves are not meaningful but their identity and difference are.
• In an **ordinal scale**, phenomena are given ordered labels, and in addition to equality, we can test which order two labels have. (All examples of ordinal scales that we will encounter are totally ordered, but other orderings are possible.) Ordinal scales represent phenomena that have a natural ranking. Examples are levels of (dis)agreement, order of arrival of jobs, etc.

Table 11.4 Some well-known scales of measurement.

Scale	Meaning-preserving transformations	Permissible operations	Examples
Nominal	$S' = f(S)$ where f is any bijection	$=$	*Classifications, such as type of software, role of stakeholder*
Ordinal	$S' = f(S)$ where f is any monotonically increasing function	$=, <$	*Severity of impact, Opinion (agreement), Order of arrival*
Interval	$S' = aS + b$ for $a > 0$	$=, <, +, -$	*Fahrenheit temperature scale, Celcius temperature scale, calendar system for measuring date*
Ratio	$S' = aS$ with $a > 0$	$=, <, +, -, *, \div$	*Execution time in seconds, Memory usage in bits, Kelvin temperature scale*

- In an **interval scale**, distances between numbers are meaningful, but the position of the 0 is arbitrary. This means that the scale has a unit for addition, but not for multiplication. Interval scales are used for phenomena that have a natural degree of difference. Examples are Fahrenheit and Celcius temperature scales, calendar systems as a scale to measure dates, closeness of a system to satisfying a requirement, etc.
- A **ratio scale** is used for a measurement that measures how much of a unit scale goes into the measured phenomenon. There is a zero, and the unit of measurement is a unit of multiplication. Examples are execution time in seconds, Kelvin temperature scale, etc.

11.4.2 Measurement Design

Table 11.5 gives the checklist for measurements. You have to define and operationalize your constructs, find data sources, acquire instruments, plan your measurements, and decide how you are going to store the data once you have collected them. Construct definition includes the definition of chance models for variables. Measurement planning involves scheduling them as measurements of one state of the objects of study (cross-sectional study) or as a historical study of a sequence of states of the objects of study (longitudinal study). If there is a treatment, measurement planning involves decisions about what measurements to do before and after the treatment, called pretests and posttests. Data storage involves maintaining traceability between

Table 11.5 Checklist for the measurement procedure.

9. Measurement design

- Variables and constructs to be measured? Scales, chance models.
- Data sources? People (e.g. software engineers, maintainers, users, project managers, politically responsible persons, etc.), primary data (e.g. source code, log files, bug tracking data, version management data, email logs), primary documents (e.g. project reports, meeting minutes, organization charts, mission statements), etc.
- Measurement instruments? Interview protocols, questionnaires, video recorders, sound recorders, clocks, sensors, database queries, log analyzers, etc.
- What is the measurement schedule? Pretests, posttests? Cross-sectional or longitudinal?
- How will measured data be stored and managed? Provenance, availability to other researchers?
- Validity of measurement specification:

    - *Inference support.* Which inferences would be valid with respect to this design? See the applicable parts of the checklists for validity of abductive and analogic inferences.
    - *Repeatability.* Is the measurement specification clear enough so that others could repeat it?
    - *Ethics.* Which company data must be kept confidential? How is privacy of persons respected?

the data and the data source, called **provenance**, and deciding who else can use the data. There may be a conflict between the scientific requirement that peers must be able to check and reanalyze your data and the ethical requirements of confidentiality and privacy.

A popular measurement approach in software engineering is Goal Question Metric (GQM) [2]. In the framework of this book, GQM is an approach to defining indicators to use in implementation evaluation or problem investigation. This corresponds to a thread of three items in our checklist for the empirical cycle:

☐ Suppose the timeliness of change request processing must be improved [2]. The GQM approach now corresponds to asking questions 2, 4, and 9 of our empirical cycle checklist:

2. The first step is to specify the goal:

    • To improve the timeliness of change request processing from the project manager's viewpoint

    This is a top-level improvement goal that a stakeholder wants to achieve, which corresponds to item 2 in the checklist.

9. As a consequence of setting an improvement goal, some property of some object needs to improve, and knowledge questions are formulated about the property. The second step is then to ask a relevant question:

    • What is the current change request processing speed?

    This is a knowledge question in a problem investigation. It corresponds to item 4 of the empirical cycle checklist.

9. To answer the question, indicators must be defined that allow one to measure the current state and any improvement that might occur later on. This is done in step three of the GQM method. Remember that indicators are called "metrics" in software engineering research:

- By what metrics can processing speed be measured?

  This corresponds to item 9 of our checklist. Possible metrics are average cycle time, standard deviation of cycle time, and % of cases outside upper limit.

To summarize, the GQM approach is part of an implementation evaluation or problem investigation that is done as an observational study, following our checklist for empirical research. The problem investigation itself is the first task in an engineering cycle where the problem will be treated and the treatment implementation will be evaluated.

11.4.3 Measurement Validity

Measurements are used to support inferences. The major requirement for supporting a *causal inference* is that the act of measurement itself does not influence the OoS. If influence cannot be avoided, this must be included in the causal inference. To support *analogic inference*, measurements should provide information about the measured constructs, and the measured values should be representative of the range of values in the target of generalization. More on this in the Chaps. 14 and 15 on abductive and analogic inference.

11.5 Summary

- An OoS is an object that is measured. Objects of study can be population elements or models of the population elements. They must satisfy the population predicate.
- Case-based research samples OoSs in sequence in a process of analytical induction.
- Sample-based research studies objects in a sample all at once, where the sample is selected according to some sampling scheme. Sampling starts from a sampling frame that lists the study population.
- In experimental research, treatments must be specified, instrumented, allocated, and scheduled. Treatments can be allocated randomly in RCTs or systematically in quasi-experiments.
- Measurement requires the definition of a measurement rule and of scales. Data sources and instruments must be selected, storage of data must be decided on, and measurements must be scheduled.

References

1. M. Bailey, D. Dittrich, E. Kenneally, D. Maughan, The Menlo report. IEEE Secur. Privacy **10**(2), 71–75 (2012)
2. V.R. Basili, G. Caldiera, H.D. Rombach, Goal question metric paradigm, in *Encyclopedia of Software Engineering*, vol. 1, ed. by J.J. Marciniak (Wiley, Hoboken, 1994), pp. 528–532
3. A. Field, *Discovering Statistics Using SPSS*, 3rd edn. (Sage, Thousand Oaks, 2009)
4. D. Freedman, R. Pisani, R. Purves, *Statistics*, 4th edn. (Norton & Company, New York, 2007)
5. N. Juristo, A. Moreno, *Basics of Software Engineering Experimentation* (Kluwer, Dordrecht, 2001)
6. A. Kaplan, *The Conduct of Inquiry. Methodology for Behavioral Science* (Transaction Publishers, Piscataway, 1998). First edition 1964 by Chandler Publishers
7. L. Kish, *Statistical Design for Research* (Wiley, Hoboken, 2004)
8. D. Moher, S. Hopewell, K. Schulz, V. Montori, P.C. Gøtzsche, P.J. Devereaux, D. Elbourne, M. Egger, D.G. Altman, for the CONSORT Group, CONSORT 2010 Explanation and Elaboration: updated guidelines for reporting parallel group randomised trials. Br. Med. J. 340:c869 (2010)
9. L. Prechelt, B. Unger-Lamprecht, M. Philippsen, W.F. Tichy, Two controlled experiments assessing the usefulness of design pattern documentation in program maintenance. IEEE Trans. Softw. Eng. **28**(6), 595–606 (2002)
10. K.F. Schulz, D.G. Altman, D. Moher, CONSORT 2010 Statement: updated guidelines for reporting parallel group randomised trials. Ann. Intern. Med. **152**(11), 1–7 (2010)
11. J.A. Singer, N.G. Vinson, Ethical issues in empirical studies of software engineering. IEEE Trans. Softw. Eng. **28**(12), 1171–1180 (2002)
12. S.S. Stevens, On the theory of scales of measurement. Science **103**(2684), 677–680 (1946)
13. B.G. Tabachnick, L.S. Fidell, *Using Multivariate Statistics*, 5th edn. (Pearson, Upper Saddle River, 2007)
14. P.F. Velleman, L. Wilkinson, Nominal, ordinal, interval and ratio typologies are misleading. Am. Stat. **47**(1), 65–72 (1993)

Chapter 12
Descriptive Inference Design

Descriptive inference summarizes the data into descriptions of phenomena (Fig. 12.1). This requires data preparation (Sect. 12.1). Any symbolic data must be interpreted (Sect. 12.2), and quantitative data can be summarized in descriptive statistics (Sect. 12.3). The descriptions produced this way are to be treated as **facts**, and so ideally there should not be any amplification in descriptive inference. But in practice there may be, and descriptive validity requires that any addition of information to the data be defensible beyond reasonable doubt (Sect. 12.4).

12.1 Data Preparation

Data preparation is the transformation of the data into a form that makes it easier to process. It may involve transcription of interviews in written text, entering data into a database for qualitative or quantitative data analysis, transforming scales to facilitate quantitative analysis, removal of outliers, removal of records with missing data, and cleaning up primary data. Usually, it involves some amount of interpretation:

- For example, when transcribing an interview, you may interpret pauses, tone of voice, inaudible words, etc.
- When collecting returned questionnaires, you may judge some of them unusable and put them aside.
- When analyzing a database with software maintenance data, you may have to remove incorrect or incomplete records from the database. This involves some judgment.

In quantitative research, part of data preparation is the *removal of outliers*. The goal is to remove measurements that cannot possibly represent the measured phenomenon but must be the result of measurement mistakes. Any data point could be the result of a measurement mistake, including the data points that look normal. Outliers are conspicuous data points that deviate from the crowd of data

© Springer-Verlag Berlin Heidelberg 2014
R.J. Wieringa, *Design Science Methodology for Information Systems and Software Engineering*, DOI 10.1007/978-3-662-43839-8_12

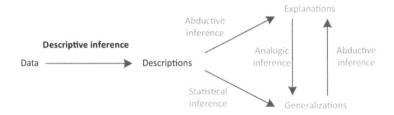

Fig. 12.1 Descriptive inference produces descriptions of phenomena from measurement data

Table 12.1 Validity of data preparation

- Will the prepared data represent the same phenomena as the unprepared data?
- If data may be removed, would this be defensible beyond reasonable doubt?
- Would your scientific opponents produce the same descriptions from the data?

points. They can be removed if there is no conceivable way in which the measured phenomenon could have produced such a measurement:

☐ In the MARP simulation, scenarios with a low rate of low-duration incidents show a delay close to zero. Suppose one agent had experienced a delay of 10 min in such a scenario, whereas all others had a delay close to zero. Then the researcher would have investigated this scenario to see what happened to this agent. He would have investigated simulation log files and possibly execution traces to see if this is an anomaly of the simulation or a true consequence of the route planning algorithm. If it would have been a simulation error, this data point would have been removed as an outlier. But if it would have been a true consequence of the route planning algorithm, it would have been an informative data point to be included in the observations.

☐ Suppose that in a software engineering experiment, the programming productivity of subjects is measured. Suppose all subjects produce between 10 and 30 lines of code per hour, except one, who produces 50 lines of code per hour. Just as for the route planning agents, the researcher would like to know whether this is a measurement error or some other artifact of the experiment that does not represent the phenomenon to be measured. Is there a mechanism in the object of study that could have produced this measurement? There are no brain dumps of the subject to analyze. Cognitive psychology or brain science does not provide any arguments to exclude the possibility of this measurement either. So the outlier cannot be removed.

Data preparation is valid if it does not change what phenomena are described by the data. A change of scale does not change what phenomena are represented; removal of an outlier changes what phenomena are represented, unless the outlier could not possibly represent a phenomenon. We return to the validity of outlier removal in Chap. 13 on statistical inference.

The validity questions listed in Table 12.1 ask about validity with respect to the phenomena and defensibility with respect to the peer group. This corresponds to the two criteria of scientific research mentioned in Chap. 9: empirical testing and justification to a peer group.

12.2 Data Interpretation

Symbolic data, such as interview transcripts, log files, databases, or video material, needs to be interpreted. This must be done by people according to an explicit interpretation method. Three popular interpretation methods are conceptual analysis, content analysis, and grounded theory. What follows is a very brief description of these methods. Denscombe [2] gives useful short summaries of many methods, including grounded theory and content analysis. Robson [8] describes less methods but gives more information about each. Other useful sources are Miles et al. [5] and Patton [6].

- In **conceptual analysis** of documents, you search for examples of entities, events, processes, procedures, constraints, taxonomic relations, composition relations, cardinality relations, etc., that are defined in the conceptual framework of your research. These examples are interpretations of the symbolic data in terms of your conceptual research framework. They look like stories about the OoS that illustrate your research concepts:

  ☐ Warne and Hart [10] report an observational case study of organizational politics in an information systems development project. Relevant concepts from their conceptual framework are *alignment with business needs*, *top management support*, and *user involvement*. They give illustrations of these concepts by summarizing some phenomena in the case, illustrated by some quotes from participants in the case. These and other concepts are used to interpret and analyze the otherwise unstructured mass of textual data about the case. They used their conceptual framework to analyze the case.

- In **content analysis**, you start from your conceptual research framework but add concepts found in the interpretative analysis. The interpreter breaks down a textual or multimedia document in smaller units, develops relevant categories for classifying the data, and codes the units in these categories. These categories are added to the conceptual research framework in terms of which the phenomena are interpreted and analyzed. The set of categories can be treated as a nominal scale, and the number of times a category appears in a unit of the document can be counted:

  ☐ Karlström and Runeson [3] report on an observational case study of extreme programming practices in a project, which was part of a larger project that was structured into a number of stages performed sequentially, with a decision point between stages. They interviewed project participants about their experience with using an extreme programming practices within a larger stage-gated project. Interviews with subjects were transcribed, coded, and analyzed by two researchers independently from each other, and any differences between the analyses were resolved to produce a set of concepts extracted from the interview transcripts. The concepts identified from the interviews were added to their research framework.

- In **grounded theory**, the interpreter tries to bracket his or her own conceptual framework, which means that he or she tries *not* to use it. The interpreter then explores the symbolic data by reading, listening to, or watching the text and multimedia documents several times. Any interpretation emerging from the text is written on a memo, one memo per interpretation decision. Next, codes for pieces of the document are developed, and these are classified into categories.

Table 12.2 Validity of interpretations

- Will the interpretations that you produce be facts in your conceptual research framework? Would your scientific peers produce the same interpretations?
- Will the interpretations that you produce be facts in the conceptual framework of the subjects? Would subjects accept them as facts?

These are organized in a network, and concepts and hypothesis are extracted. At every step, the interpretations of the interpreter must be checked against the recorded data. The result is a conceptual framework that the interpreter has found embedded in the documents. The researcher may also extract relationships between concepts from the documents, which constitute a theory about the world that was found embedded in the documents:

☐ Racheva et al. [7] analyzed interviews with developers about requirements prioritization in agile software projects. The interviews were analyzed using the grounded theory approach of Charmaz [1]. This resulted in a conceptual model of agile requirements prioritization, including a model of the stages of requirements engineering and of some of the factors that influence the decisions made in each stage. This conceptual framework and theory about agile requirements prioritization was extracted from the interviews, and it was not part of the research framework that the authors started with.

To improve consistency of the interpretation, the interpretation rules developed during the analysis should be written down and followed once written down. In some cases, the rules must be automated:

☐ For example, analyzing email logs or bug report databases must be automated due to the amount of data to be interpreted, and hence the interpretation rules are specified in an automatable form. In general, you may use database queries, log analyzers, and text processing software to analyze primary data and primary documents.

The bottom line of the validity question in data interpretation is whether you have identified facts or not. Table 12.2 lists the two criteria for this.

There are several ways to increase the support for, and hence the validity of, your interpretations:

- **Triangulation** is the use of multiple, independent ways of producing your interpretation. For example, you can use multiple independent data sources, multiple independent methods to collect the data, and multiple researchers to interpret the data independently from each other. Differences between the interpretations produced must be analyzed and resolved.
- In **member checking**, you check the interpretations with the subjects themselves.
- In **peer debriefing**, you submit the interpretation process to independent scientific peers for critical analysis. This is facilitated by keeping an audit trail of decisions that you made during the interpretation process.

12.3 Descriptive Statistics

Statistics are quantitative summaries of data. Examples of descriptive sample statistics are the mean and variance of a variable in a sample and the correlation between variables in a sample. Descriptive statistics usually includes data visualization using box plots, scatterplots, bar graphs, pie charts, graphs, etc. Using powerful graphics processors, data visualization has become a discipline on its own, which goes far beyond visualizing descriptive statistics. We will not discuss data visualization techniques in this book and define only two descriptive statistics that we will use in statistical inference later.

For descriptive and inferential statistics, I follow the notation of Wasserman [11]. We use upper case letters X, Y, ... to indicate random variables and lower case letters x, y, ... to denote arbitrary values of those variables. In Chap. 8, we saw that the chance model of a variable defines an X-box, which is a box with tickets that have measurements written on them. The value written on a particular ticket is denoted x. For a variable X, we define the *sample* $X_1, \ldots, X_n$ as a set of variables that have the same distribution as X. A draw from the X-box gives a set of tickets that contains values $x_1, \ldots, x_n$.

If X has an interval or ratio scale, the **sample mean** is itself a random variable, denoted $\overline{X}_n$, defined as the arithmetic mean:

$$\overline{X}_n = \frac{1}{n} \sum_{i=1}^{n} X_i.$$

The **sample variance** is another random variable, defined as

$$S_{X,n}^2 = \frac{1}{n-1} \sum_{i=1}^{n} (X_i - \overline{X}_n)^2.$$

$S_{X,n}$ is called the **sample standard deviation of** X. Sample mean and variance are the basic statistics used in statistical inference in the next chapter.

If you made no computation mistake, then the mean and variance of sample are valid: They are the mean and variance of a finite multiset of numbers. But to count as descriptive statistics of a measured sample of a population, a chance model must be defined (Table 12.3). This imposes two requirements on the sampled objects of study: They must satisfy the population predicate, and the variables must be observable properties of the objects of study.

Table 12.3 Validity of descriptive statistics

- Is the chance model of the variables of interest defined in terms of the population elements?

12.4 Descriptive Validity

Descriptive validity is the degree of support for a descriptive inference. Some methodologists call it *factual accuracy* [4, p. 285], and some call it *credibility* [9]. The checklists in Tables 12.1, 12.2, and 12.3 jointly form our checklist for descriptive validity. They are written in the future tense, which is the point of view that you have during research design. This is useful for planning your measurement procedures and for acquiring the resources to do descriptive inference.

After you completed the data collection, when you start data analysis, these questions have to be answered again, but now in view of the events that happened during the study.

12.5 Summary

- Data preparation is the transformation of data into a form that makes it easier to process. It may involve transcription and coding of symbolic data, changes of measurement scale, and removal of outliers. The result must still describe observed phenomena and no other phenomena.
- There are several methods for interpreting symbolic data, such as conceptual analysis, content analysis, and grounded theory. Interpretation must be done as intersubjectively as possible, so that different interpreters would assign the same interpretation to symbolic data and would treat the result as descriptions of facts.
- Description of sample statistics requires a chance model of the variables that are described.

References

1. K. Charmaz, *Constructing Grounded Theory: A Practical Guide Through Qualitative Research* (Sage, Thousand Oaks, 2007)
2. M. Denscombe, *The Good Research Guide For Small-Scale Social Research Projects*, 4th edn. (Open University Press, Maidenhead, 2010)
3. D. Karlström, P. Runeson, Integrating agile software development into stage-gated managed product development. Empir. Softw. Eng. **11**, 203–225 (2006)
4. J.A. Maxwell, Understanding and validity in qualitative research. Harv. Educ. Rev. **62**(3), 279–300 (1992)
5. M.B. Miles, A.M. Huberman, J. Saldaña, *Qualitative Data Analysis. A Methods Sourcebook*, 3rd edn. (Sage, Thousand Oaks, 2013)
6. M.Q. Patton, *Qualitative Research and Evaluation Methods*, 3rd edn. (Sage, Thousand Oaks, 2001)
7. Z. Racheva, M. Daneva, A. Herrmann, K. Sikkel, R.J. Wieringa, Do we know enough about requirements prioritization in agile projects: insights from a case study, in *18th International IEEE Requirements Engineering Conference, Sydney*. (IEEE Computer Society, Los Alamitos, October 2010), pp. 147–156

8. C. Robson, *Real World Research*, 2nd edn. (Blackwell, Oxford, 2002)
9. S.B. Thomson, Qualitative research: validity. J. Adm. Gov. **6**(1), 77–82 (2011)
10. L. Warne, D. Hart, The impact of organizational politics on information systems project failure-a case study, in *Proceedings of the Twenty-Ninth Hawaii International Conference on System Sciences*, vol. 4, pp. 191–201 (Jan 1996)
11. L. Wasserman, *All of Statistics. A Concise Course in Statistical Inference* (Springer, Heidelberg, 2004)

Chapter 13
Statistical Inference Design

Statistical inference is the inference of properties of the distribution of variables of a population, from a sample selected from the population (Fig. 13.1). To do statistical inference, your conceptual research framework should define the relevant statistical structures, namely, a population and one or more random variables (Chap. 8, Conceptual Frameworks). The probability distributions of the variables over the population are usually unknown. This chapter is required for Chap. 20 on statistical difference-making experiments, but not for the other chapters that follow.

There are many statistical inference techniques that all have at least these three shared elements: They start from sample measurements, they make an assumption about how the sample is related to the population, and they infer a property of the population distribution of one or more random variables. The property is called a statistical model (Sect. 13.1).

Statistical inference is based on the central-limit theorem (CLT), which says that the distribution of the means of samples selected randomly from a distribution varies normally around the distribution mean. We explain this informally in Sect. 13.2.

There are two classes of inference strategies: statistical hypothesis testing and statistical parameter estimation. In *statistical hypothesis testing,* you hypothesize one or more statistical models and, for each model, test the probability of the data given that model. Based on this, you make a decision about the models. We review three techniques for statistical hypothesis testing in Sect. 13.3. In *statistical parameter estimation,* you do not start with a hypothesis but directly estimate a property of the statistical models that best accounts for your data statistically. There are many estimation techniques, and in Sect. 13.4 we look at one, namely, estimation of a confidence interval for the population mean of a variable.[1]

Statistical hypothesis testing is used widely in the social sciences, but it is also much criticized because its use can be accompanied with reasoning mistakes and meaningless results. The conclusion of Sect. 13.3 is very critical about statistical hypothesis testing, and in Sect. 13.4 we will see that confidence interval estimation is a more informative and uncontroversial alternative. So why treat hypothesis

© Springer-Verlag Berlin Heidelberg 2014
R.J. Wieringa, *Design Science Methodology for Information Systems and Software Engineering*, DOI 10.1007/978-3-662-43839-8_13

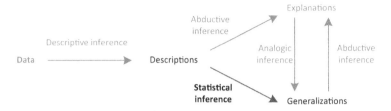

Fig. 13.1 Statistical inference is the inference of properties of the probability distribution of variables

testing at all? Because it is needed to read the many research papers that do use the statistical hypothesis testing techniques discussed here.

Statistical inference of whatever kind is fallible. In Sect. 13.5, we discuss the validity of inferences from samples to statistical models and give a checklist for assessing statistical conclusion validity of estimating confidence intervals.

13.1   Statistical Models

A **statistical model** of the distribution of one or more random variables is some characteristic of their (joint) distribution (Fig. 13.2). Examples of statistical models are the distribution mean and variance of a random variable and the correlation between two random variables.

A statistical model needs a chance model in order to give information about a population. The chance model defines the meaning of a random variable in a population, contains assumptions about the population distribution of X, and

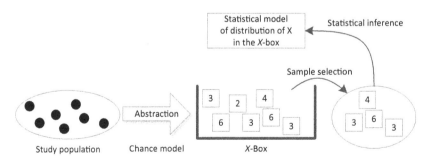

Fig. 13.2 A chance model for X abstracts away almost all properties of a population and leaves us with a box with tickets, on which values of X are written. The numbers on the tickets are values of X on population elements. The distribution of values in the box is usually unknown. In statistical inference, we use the values found in a sample that is drawn randomly from the box to draw conclusions about a statistical model of the distribution. The model may, for example, give us information about the mean of the distribution of X. Using the chance model, we can interpret this in the population. With a different chance model, the statistical model would have a different meaning in the population

contains information about measurement and sampling procedures. A chance model abstracts away all physical properties of a population and leaves us with a box with tickets, where each ticket stores the value of X in a population element. The numbers on the tickets in the box have a probability distribution. The starting point of statistical inference is a sample of tickets drawn randomly from this box.

In Chap. 8 (Conceptual Frameworks, p. 81), we have given two examples of chance models. We now extend these examples with statistical models:

☐   Huynh and Miller [32] studied implementation vulnerabilities in open-source web applications. They defined a random variable *ImpV* that stands for the proportion of implementation vulnerabilities among all vulnerabilities in a web application. The chance model of this variable defines the meaning of this variable, makes an assumption about its distribution, and describes how it is measured. The authors do not state how a sample is selected, and they proceed as if the sample were selected randomly. They measured *ImpV* in a sample of 20 web applications. From this, they used statistical inference to estimate the mean μ and standard deviation σ of the distribution of *ImpV*. These are statistical models of *ImpV*. Using the chance model, this provides information about the mean number of implementation vulnerabilities in open-source web applications and about the variance around this mean.

☐   Hildebrand et al. [30] studied the preferences of consumers who customized a mass-configurable product, both before and after they received feedback from a peer on a social network. They defined the random variable $\mathrm{Pref}\Delta_{i,j}$ as the difference between the initial preferences of consumer i and the feedback received from peer j and the aggregate deviation index ADI_i as the distance between the initial and final preferences of consumer i. Each consumer i received feedback from only one peer j, so the index j is superfluous. They defined chance models for these variables, in which they assumed that $\mathrm{Pref}\Delta_{i,j}$ is normally distributed. They measured these variables in a sample of 149 consumers and treated this sample as a random sample. They hypothesized a parameterized statistical model of the relationship between the two variables, namely, $\mathrm{ADI}_i = \alpha + \beta \times \mathrm{Pref}\Delta_{i,j}$, and estimated the coefficients α and β from their data. This is their statistical inference. The resulting equation, with estimated coefficients, is their statistical model of the relation between ADI_i and $\mathrm{Pref}\Delta_{i,j}$.

13.2   The CLT

We now forget about the population and only talk about the distribution of the values of a random variable in a box of tickets. Statistical inference derives information about the distribution of the variable from a finite sample of tickets selected randomly from the box. This is possible, thanks to two powerful results in mathematical statistics, the law of large numbers (LLN) and the CLT. The LLN says that the mean of a random sample of values of a variable X approximates the distribution mean of X when the sample gets larger. The approximation gets more accurate when the sample gets larger. The CLT says that the means of random samples of the same size are approximately normally distributed around the distribution mean and that the approximation gets better when the sample size gets larger. The following paragraphs introduce the core concepts and show how they can be used. A useful mathematical introduction is given by Wasserman [51].

13.2.1   Distribution Mean and Variance

We assume that X has at least an interval scale and define the mean and variance of the distribution of X intuitively as follows:

- The *distribution mean* μ_X is the mean of the numbers on the tickets in the X-box. (A number can be counted more than once, because it can be on more than one ticket.)
- The *distribution variance* σ_X^2 is the mean of the squared differences between the numbers on the tickets and μ_X. We call σ_X the *standard deviation* of X.

μ_X and σ_X are parameters of the distribution of X. If there is no danger of confusion, we drop the suffix X.

There are examples of distributions that do not have a mean [51, p. 48] and hence no defined variance, but the distributions that we work with can be assumed to have one.

13.2.2   Sampling Distribution, Mean, and Variance

A random sample selected from a X-box is denoted $X_1, \ldots, X_n$. The sample mean $\overline{X}_n$ is a random variable too, and it has its own box model that we call an $\overline{X}_n$-box. This box contains the means of all samples of size n selected randomly from the X-box. The distribution of numbers in the $\overline{X}_n$-box is called a **sampling distribution**, and it has a **sampling mean** and **sampling variance**.

It can be proven that the sampling distribution of $\overline{X}_n$ has the same mean as X and that its variance is $1/n$ times that of the parent distribution:

- $\mu_{\overline{X}_n} = \mu_X$
- $\sigma^2_{\overline{X}_n} = \sigma_X^2/n$

So the sample means vary around μ_X with a variance that gets smaller when the samples get larger. This is the basis of statistical inference, because it implies that we can estimate a population mean from a sample mean, with an accuracy that improves with sample size.

The above theorem assumes random sampling (with replacement). If we draw simple random samples from the same population, then we need to apply a correction factor if the population is finite. Simple random sampling does not replace the sampled elements, and if the population is small compared to the sample, this may produce a noticeable reduction of the variance of the sampling mean. Each removal of an element from the population removes some of the variance in the population. If $\mathbb{V}(\overline{X}_{n,\text{simple}})$ is the variance of the mean of a simple random sample and $\mathbb{V}(\overline{X}_{n,\text{random}})$ the variance of the mean of a random sample, then for a population of size N and a sample of size n, the correction is [20, p. 368]

$$\mathbb{V}(\overline{X}_{n,\text{simple}}) = \frac{N - n}{N - 1} \times \mathbb{V}(\overline{X}_{n,\text{random}}).$$

Here are a number of correction factors for a sample size of 30:

Sample size	Population size	Correction factor for variance	Correction factor for standard deviation
30	1,000	0.97	0.99
30	100	0.71	0.84
30	50	0.41	0.64

We will apply these correction factors for simple random samples from small populations.

13.2.3   Normal Distributions

A normally distributed variable with mean μ and standard deviation σ has a probability distribution with a shape as shown in Fig. 13.3. The curve shows a so-called probability density, which tells us something about the probability of the event that $X \geq x$. If we select a ticket from the X-box, then the event that the value on the ticket is $\geq x$ is denoted $X \geq x$. The probability that this happens is denoted $\mathbb{P}(X \geq x)$. In a probability density curve, $\mathbb{P}(X \geq x)$ is the area under the curve to the right of x. For example, if the values in the X-box are symmetrically distributed around μ_X, then $\mathbb{P}(X \geq \mu_X) = 0.5$.

As suggested by the figure, if X is normally distributed, then about two-thirds (68 %) of the tickets in the X-box have a value less than σ_X away from μ_X, and about 95 % of the tickets have values less than $2\sigma_X$ away from μ_X.

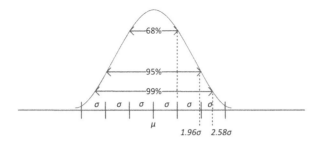

Fig. 13.3 The shape of normal distributions. The numbers are approximate. The figure does not show that any value more than 3σ away from μ is possible, although these values happen very rarely

13.2.4 The CLT

Consider an X-box with mean μ_X and variance σ_X^2. This defines the set of $\overline{X}_n$-boxes for all n. Each $\overline{X}_n$-box contains the sampling means of random samples of size n from the X-box. If we put the $\overline{X}_n$-boxes in sequence of increasing n, the central-limit theorem (CLT) says that

> the sampling distribution of $\overline{X}_n$ approaches a normal distribution with mean μ and variance σ^2/n when n gets larger.

In other words, the further we go down the sequence of $\overline{X}_n$-boxes, the closer the distribution of tickets in the box approximates a normal distribution. We already knew that $\mu_{\overline{X}_n} = \mu_X$ and $\sigma_{\overline{X}_n}^2 = \sigma_X^2/n$. The CLT adds a convergence result, namely, that the sampling distribution approaches a normal distribution as the sample size increases.

Figure 13.4 illustrates the CLT. If we sample repeatedly from an arbitrary distribution with mean μ and standard deviation σ, then after a finite number of repetitions the distribution of sample means will start resembling a normal distribution. For small sample sizes, the resemblance is very bad, but for larger samples, the resemblance gets better. At the same time, the variance of the sample means gets smaller when the samples get bigger. In general, if we double the sample size, the variance of the sample means is halved.

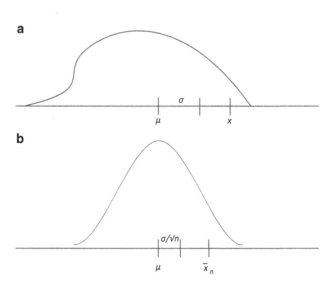

Fig. 13.4 An arbitrary distribution with mean μ_X and standard deviation σ_X. The CLT says that the means of samples of size n have approximately a normal distribution with mean μ_X and standard deviation $\sigma_X/\sqrt{n}$. The approximation gets better for larger n. (**a**) Arbitrary distribution with standard deviation σ. x is a measurement. (**b**) Normal distribution with mean μ and standard deviation $\sigma/\sqrt(n)$. The means $\overline{X}_n$ of random samples of size n from any distribution with a finite mean and standard deviation, approximate this normal distribution. $\overline{x}_n$ is the mean of one sample

The CLT is a remarkable theorem because no assumptions are made about the distribution of X other than that it has a mean and variance. The price to be paid is that we must select samples randomly (with replacement) and must be able to sample from the same distribution an indefinite number of times.

We can use the CLT to approximate the real distribution of $\overline{X}_n$ with a normal distribution. At what sample size can we do this? In other words, at what sample size does the distribution of X_n get close to a normal distribution? That depends on the distribution of X and on what can be considered "close."

The distribution of X is usually unknown. It has been shown that for some distributions of X and for some applications of the CLT, the distribution of $\overline{X}_n$ is close enough to a normal distribution already when $n = 30$. However, if the distribution of X is heavy at the tails or nonsymmetric or has several peaks, sample sizes must be much larger for $\overline{X}_n$ to be treated as close to normally distributed. The sample size may have to be several hundred before the distribution of $\overline{X}_n$ can be treated as close to normal. There are freely available simulations of the CLT on the web that show you what happens for different distributions of X and different sample sizes.[2]

13.2.5 Standardization

The CLT says that the sampling distribution of the mean converges on a normal distribution but does not say which normal distribution. Each different μ and σ define a different normal distribution. To make the use of the CLT easier, we standardize variables and work with a standardized normal distribution, of which there is only one. It has mean 0 and standard deviation 1. A variable that has the standard normal distribution is usually denoted Z.

By convention, $z_{0.025}$ is the value of Z which cuts off 2.5 % of the area under the standard normal curve at the right tail of the curve. So $\mathbb{P}(Z \geq z_{0.25}) = 0.25$. Looking at Fig. 13.3, we see that $z_{0.025} \approx 1.96$. The area cut out by the interval $(-z_{0.025}, z_{0.025})$ is 0.95, which is another way of saying that 95 % of the tickets in the Z-box have a number in this range.

For every random variable X with mean μ_X and standard deviation σ_X, we can define a **standardized** counterpart Z_X by the linear transformation:

$$Z_X = \frac{X - \mu_X}{\sigma_X}.$$

Z_X does not necessarily have a normal distribution. If the distribution of X is unknown, then so is the distribution of Z_X. But we know that Z_X has a similar distribution to X, scaled so that it has mean 0 and standard deviation 1. Importantly, Z_X is a dimensionless number that expresses the size of X using σ_X as unit.

The sampling distribution of $\overline{X}_n$ can be standardized too and is

$$Z_{\overline{X}_n} = \frac{\overline{X}_n - \mu_X}{\sigma_X / \sqrt{n}}.$$

This is called the z-**statistic** of the sample. The CLT says that

the distribution of $Z_{\overline{X}_n}$ approaches the standard normal distribution as n gets larger.

13.2.6   The t-Statistic

We would like to get rid of the σ, which is usually unknown. We can do this by estimating σ by sample standard deviation S_n. This gives us the t-**statistic** of a sample, defined by

$$T_{\overline{X}_n} = \frac{\overline{X}_n - \mu}{S_n / \sqrt{n}}.$$

Happily, the CLT still holds for the t-statistic:

The distribution of $T_{\overline{X}_n}$ approaches the standard normal as n gets larger.

But the approach is slower because it uses sample-based estimations of σ.

The CLT tells us what happens when sample sizes get arbitrarily large, but in practice we can only draw small samples. For statistical inference, the following theorem is important, because it gives us the exact distribution of the mean of small samples of normally distributed variables:

If X is normally distributed, then $T_{\overline{X}_n}$ has a so-called t_{n-1} distribution, which is a t-distribution with $n - 1$ degrees of freedom.

t_{n-1} distributions resemble a standard normal distribution but are fatter at the tails (Fig. 13.5). The probability that $T_{\overline{X}_n}$ is far away from the mean is larger than it is for the standard normal distribution, and this difference is noticeable for small n.

The above theorem says that for normally distributed X, the distribution of $\overline{X}_n$ is a t-distribution with the appropriate number of degrees of freedom. Starting from about $n = 100$, probabilities estimated with the t_{n-1} distribution closely approximate those estimated with the standard normal distribution. If $n > 100$, the probabilities estimated with t and with z are equal in the first two decimals.

Note that we have two approximations here: Regardless of the distribution of X, the unknown sampling distribution of $Z_{\overline{X}_n}$ approximates the standard normal distribution when $n \to \infty$. For some distributions of X, the approximation is

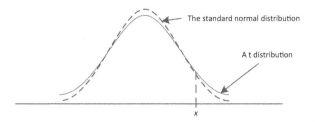

Fig. 13.5 t-distributions are lower at the peak and fatter at the tails than the normal distribution. t_k approximates the normal distribution as $k \to \infty$. For our purposes, the approximation is already close when $k = 100$

already close when $n = 30$. For others, the approximation gets close only for large values of n.

The second approximation is that $T_{\overline{X}_n} \to Z$ as $n \to \infty$. The distribution of $T_{\overline{X}_n}$ is the exact distribution of $Z_{\overline{X}_n}$ when X is normally distributed. For our purposes, the distribution of $T_{\overline{X}_n}$ is very close to the standard normal distribution already when $n = 100$.

If T has a t_k distribution, then by convention, $t_{k,0.025}$ denotes the value of T that cuts off 2.5 % of the area under its distribution at the right tail. $t_{k,0.025}$ has different values for different degrees of freedom k. There are tables and web applications of the t_k distribution for different values of k that allow you to look up $\mathbb{P}(T \geq t)$ for given values of t and k and to look up the value of t for which $\mathbb{P}(T \geq t) = p$, for given values of k and p.[3]

If a sample size is less than 100 and we want to use a t-test, we must make a normality assumption. How do we know whether the distribution of X is normal? The Kolmogorov–Smirnov and Shapiro–Wilk tests test whether a random sample could have been selected from a normal distribution, but these tests do not give certainty. They are hypothesis tests, which you may not want to use after reading the next section.

If the distribution of X is nearly symmetric (has a mean close to the center of the distribution) and has only a single peak, it is customary to use a t-distribution to describe the sampling distribution of $\overline{X}_n$ when $n < 100$.

Still talking about samples less than 100 elements, what if we know that the distribution of X is not nearly symmetric or has more than one peak? Or if we do not know anything about the distribution of X? In these cases, you should use methods that do not make a normality assumption, such as nonparametric or computer-intensive methods. Cohen [13], Wasserman [51], and Wilcox [52] give useful information about these methods. Here we proceed on the sunny day scenario that the distribution of X is normal or the sample size is larger than 100.

13.3 Testing a Statistical Hypothesis

There are three strategies to test statistical hypotheses. In Fisher significance testing, we test a single statistical hypothesis and try to explain the result. In the Neyman–Pearson hypothesis testing, we decide which of two or more hypotheses are to be taken as true in a series of tests, optimizing our error rate. In null hypothesis significance testing (NHST), both strategies are combined, and used to test a null hypothesis of no difference.

13.3.1 Fisher Significance Testing

Statistical significance testing was developed by the statistician Ronald Fisher in the 1920s based on earlier work by Karl Pearson and William Gosset [19, 23, 33]. Statistical significance tests can be done for any statistical hypothesis, including hypotheses about distribution means, correlations, regression coefficients, and other statistical models. The methodology of significance testing is the same for all these statistics, and here we only discuss statistical significance testing for distribution means. Significance testing is very controversial [29, 41], and what follows is what I consider to be a valid version that stands up to the critique. I briefly summarize some main points of criticism at the end of this section.

The goal of significance testing is to see if sample data provide evidence against a statistical hypothesis. Hence, the hypothesis is called the **null hypothesis**, because our aim is to "nullify" it.

p-Values

Suppose we do not know the distribution mean and variance of X and we formulate the statistical hypothesis that

$H_0 : \mu_X = \mu_0$

for some value μ_0. We know from the CLT that the sample means drawn from the X-box can be approximated by a normal distribution. If H_0 is true, then this normal distribution has mean μ_0 as in Fig. 13.6. The approximation for large samples is better than that for small samples.

If we observe sample mean $\overline{x}_n$, then the probability to observe a sample mean at least as large as $\overline{x}_n$ from μ_0 is

$$\mathbb{P}(\overline{X}_n \geq \overline{x}_n).$$

We do not know this probability, as we do not know the real distribution of $\overline{X}_n$. But if we assume that H_0 is true, then according the CLT we can approximate it with

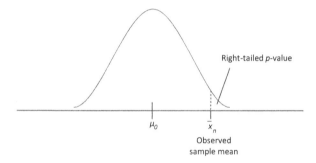

Fig. 13.6 Statistical significance tests using a normal distribution of sample means. The normal curve with mean μ_0 and standard deviation σ_X approximates the random fluctuations that the sample mean would have around the distribution mean μ_0, if H_0 is assumed to be true. The approximation is better for larger samples. If H_0 is true, the right-tailed p-value estimates the probability that $\bar{x}_n$ or a larger value of the sample mean is observed

$$\mathbb{P}_{\mu_0,\sigma_X^2}\left(\overline{X}_n \geq \bar{x}_n\right),$$

where $\mathbb{P}_{\mu_0,\sigma_X^2}$ is the probability computed using a normal distribution with mean μ_0 and variance σ_X^2. The approximation gets better for larger n.

But we do not know σ_X, and so we cannot compute this probability. To get rid of σ_X, we first standardize the variable, still assuming that H_0 is true. The above probability is then equal to

$$\mathbb{P}_{0,1}\left(\frac{\overline{X}_n - \mu_0}{\sigma_X/\sqrt{n}} \geq \frac{\bar{x}_n - \mu_0}{\sigma_X/\sqrt{n}}\right),$$

where $\mathbb{P}_{0,1}$ is the probability computed using the standard normal distribution. Now we can compute the probability, but the event between brackets cannot be detected, because we do not know σ_X.

Next, we transform to the t_{n-1} scale with

$$T_{\overline{X}_n} = \frac{\overline{X}_n - \mu_0}{S_n/\sqrt{n}} \quad \text{and} \quad t_{\bar{x}_n} = \frac{\bar{x}_n - \mu_0}{S_n/\sqrt{n}}.$$

The event $T_{\overline{X}_n} \geq t_{\bar{x}_n}$ can be detected, and if H_0 is true, it approximates the event $\overline{X}_n > \bar{x}_n$ that we are interested in. Moreover, if X is normally distributed, its probability can be computed using the t_{n-1} distribution. And if X is not normally distributed but $n > 100$, its probability can be approximated using the t_{n-1} distribution. Either way, the probability:

$$\mathbb{P}_{t_{n-1}}\left(T_{\overline{X}_n} \geq t_{\bar{x}_n}\right),$$

approximates the probability $\mathbb{P}(\overline{X}_n \geq \overline{x}_n)$ we are interested in, where $\mathbb{P}_{t_{n-1}}$ is computed using the t_{n-1} distribution. It is called the **right-tailed** p**-value** of $\overline{x}_n$ under H_0.

To sum up, if H_0 is true and if X is normally distributed or $n > 100$, the right-tailed p-value approximates the probability that $\mathbb{P}_{\mu_0,\sigma_X^2}(\overline{X}_n \geq \overline{x}_n)$, which approximates $\mathbb{P}(\overline{X}_n \geq \overline{x}_n)$, the probability to observe a sample mean at least as large as $\overline{x}_n$. The approximations get better as n gets larger.

The **left-tailed** p**-value** of $\overline{x}_n$ under H_0 is defined in an analogous manner. The **two-tailed** p**-value** $\mathbb{P}_{t_{n-1}}(|T_{\overline{X}_n}| \geq |t_{\overline{x}_n}|)$ approximates, if H_0 is true, the probability to observe a sample mean at least as far away from μ_0 as $\overline{x}_n$ is. The two-tailed p-value of a statistic is twice the one-tailed p-value. Unless otherwise stated, henceforth p-values are right-tailed p-values.

Statistical Significance

It is customary to call an observed sample mean $\overline{x}_n$ **statistically significant** if its p-value is 5 % or lower. This is a very misleading term, as a single p-value is not significant at all. Rare events do happen. So what?

What would be remarkable is if, on repeated random sampling from the same distribution with a mean of μ_0, all values of $\overline{x}_n$ would have a low p-value. Such a sequence of events would be very rare if $\mu_X = \mu_0$. It would then be reasonable to conclude that $\mu_X \neq \mu_0$.

But Fisher significance testing is usually done without replication. How then can we draw a conclusion from a single occurrence of a sample statistic?

Explaining Low Statistical Significance

In order to draw a conclusion from a single significance test, we have to *explain* it. Explanation is an ampliative inference in which we use our prior knowledge, and knowledge of the research setup, to explain an unusual observation or more precisely an observation that would be unusual if H_0 were true. In the next chapter, we discuss explanations in terms of causes, mechanisms, or reasons. Here, we discuss statistical explanations. A **statistical explanation** accounts for the data by showing how it results from statistical properties of sets of numbers such as mean and variance of the numbers in the set. For example, the statistical explanation of the small variance of the means of large random samples is provided by the CLT. It is not a property of the real world but is a consequence of the fact that we select large sample randomly from the same population.

There are three possible explanations of a low p-value [24, 26]:

- H_0 is false.
- The hypothesis is true, and the observed sample mean is a random fluctuation around the true population mean μ_0.
- The observed sample mean is an outlier.

The first two explanations are statistical, because they explain a p-value in terms of properties of a distribution mean and the standard normal curve. They are mutually exclusive because they say that H_0 is false and true, respectively. The third explanation is not a statistical explanation, because it says that there is a measurement mistake. This explanation says nothing about the truth or falsehood of H_0; it simply says that the measurements cannot be used. We now discuss these three options in more detail.

H_0 Is False

If H_0 is false, then the distribution mean of X is not μ_0. Our statistical explanation of the low p-value is that it is a wrong p-value, because it is computed under a wrong assumption. If the real distribution mean is different, then the real p-value is different too. Note that if H_0 is false, we do not know the real distribution mean, and so we do not know the real p-value of $\overline{X}_n \geq \overline{x}_n$, not even an approximation of it. It might be lower or higher than the p-value that we computed on the assumption that H_0 is true.

H_0 Is True

If H_0 is true, then the distribution mean of X is μ_0, and we computed the true p-value of the event $\overline{X}_n \geq \overline{x}_n$. If this p-value turned out to be low (i.e., statistically significant), then we have made an unusual observation. This is improbable but possible. Our statistical explanation of the low p-value is that the sample mean will fluctuate randomly around μ_0 and that occasionally, we will observe improbable sample means. The best way to test this explanation is to draw another random sample from the same population, in other words to repeat the study.

Outliers

The third option is compatible with both truth and falsehood of H_0, because it says that the measurement is wrong. An **outlier** is a measurement that is a mistake of the researcher, caused, for example, by an incorrect use of a measurement instrument, an incorrect reading, a mistake in a computation, an error in a measurement instrument, etc. [48, pp. 278–280]. If a measurement is treated as an outlier, it is discarded because it injects a foreign element in a mass of measurements. It adds a ticket to the sample that was not in the X-box.

How do we identify outliers? To see this, we have to consider the possible sources of variation in sample means. The statistical explanation for random fluctuations of the observed sample means $\overline{x}_n$ around the distribution mean μ_X is mathematical: The mean of a finite sample will not be exactly equal to the distribution mean. But why do the numbers in the X-box differ in the first place? If they would differ less, then the fluctuations of $\overline{x}_n$ around μ_X would be smaller.

If we are measuring a property X of population elements, then we are faced with the diversity of population elements, which probably all have a different value for X. Our measurement will also be influenced by interactions among the parts of the measurement instruments and by interactions between the instruments and the researcher and the research setup. The world, including our research setup, is full of *ambient correlational noise* by which repeated measurements of the same property differ [37]. The fluctuations of the sample means about the true distribution mean μ_X are created by sampling error and by ambient correlational noise in the real world. This may create unusual observations, such as a sample mean with a probability of less than 5 %.

These unusual observations are *not* outliers. They are normal but rare events. Outliers, by contrast, are mistakes of measurement in which the connection between a measurement and the measured phenomenon has been lost or at least is different from the way all other measurements are connected to phenomena.

Mistakes may produce data that are widely out of range, but not all out-of-range data are necessarily produced by mistakes. Judgment whether something is an outlier is sometimes subjective. There may be clear outliers that could not have possibly be produced by sampling error or ambient noise. But there are sometimes measurements of which it is not clear if they are instances of random fluctuations about μ_X or of measurement mistakes. The advice that the great mathematician Carl Friedrich Gauss gave to the astronomer Heinrich Wilhelm Olbers in 1827 is useful [48, pp. 279–280]:

> In that case one should proceed as one thinks correct, but—and this is a law—one should not conceal anything, so others can make their own calculations.... Cases like these are analogous, it seems to me, to making decisions in everyday life. One has rarely or never mathematical rigor and certainty, and has to be satisfied to act according to one's best judgment.

Choosing an Explanation

So far, we have three possible explanations of a low p-value: H_0 is false, or H_0 is true, but we have observed a rare event, or we made a mistake. How to choose between these explanations? This depends in part on our prior knowledge. If there is almost no reason to believe H_0 in the first place, then in the face of a low p-value it would be rational to conclude tentatively that H_0 is false.

If we had very strong reasons to believe H_0 in the first place, then a low p-value may not put a very big dent into the support for H_0. The conclusion could be that H_0 is true, and we have made a rare observation. If we had a sufficient research budget, we could replicate the research with a fresh randomly drawn sample to see if we again observe an event that would be improbable if H_0 were true. Such a replication with a low p-value would be stronger evidence against H_0. It should prompt us to reconsider the reasons why we believed H_0 in the first place.

The situation may not be so clear-cut as the previous two paragraphs suggest, because H_0 may be supported by a complex argument. We may have hypothesized a distribution mean μ_0 that is produced by the phenomenon of interest plus any systematic deviations introduced by our measurement instruments, research setup, and other relevant factors that we could think of. The computation of μ_0 then has many components, some of which may be well supported and others of which may be very badly supported. Did we really have a random sample? If we used a t-test, is X really normally distributed? If it is nearly normally distributed, how close is it? How do we know? Are the instruments correct? Were they used correctly? Did anything happen during the experiment that could have influenced our results?

What we are really testing in a hypothesis test is a theory of the phenomena and of the research setup. Which part should we give up if we repeatedly find a low p-value? This is abductive reasoning, in which we try to explain the measurements causally, architecturally, or rationally. We return to this in Chap. 14 on abductive inference. Here we look at an example of the Fisher significance testing:

☐ Suppose company WorldCorp considers to take over a software development firm high quality software, HQ for short. As part of the preparations, they investigate the quality of software developed by HQ. In the experience of company HQ, the software they produce usually has a defect density of about 0.75 per function point, but they have never investigated this systematically. Independently from each other, all project managers mention roughly this number, without being able to give hard evidence for it.

   WorldCorp wants to test the null hypothesis that the defect density of software produced by HQ is 0.75 and draws a random sample of 15 software systems developed by HQ. The sample shows an average defect density 0.84 with a sample variance of 0.18. So $\overline{X}_{15} = 0.84$ and $S_{15} = 0.18$. What is the p-value of this observation, given $H_0 : \mu_X = 0.75$?

   If we assume random sampling, then assuming the null hypothesis, the means of large samples drawn from this population are approximately normally distributed around 0.84. We have a small sample, and so we assume that defect density is normally distributed over the population of software developed by HQ. Under this assumption, it is meaningful to compute the t-statistic of the sample under H_0:

$$T_{14} = \frac{\overline{X}_{15} - 0.75}{S_{15}/\sqrt{15}} = 1.94.$$

   Because WorldCorp has no clue about the true average effect density, we must assume that it can be higher or lower than 0.75, and so we will compute a two-tailed p-value. The two-tailed p-value of the sample is 0.07. This is a rare observation, but according to statistical custom it is not rare enough to reject H_0. WorldCorp respects statistical custom and so does not use this result to reject HQ's claim that defect density is 0.75.

☐ However, suppose that the sampling frame consisted of a list of 100 software systems. Now we must apply the correction for small populations. The correction factor is 0.93. This raises the t-statistic to 2.09 and reduces the probability of observing a sample mean this far from 0.75 to 0.06. Very respectful of statistical custom, WorldCorp does not regard this as rare enough to reject H_0.

☐ Suppose now that we know from earlier empirical research across many companies that defect densities cannot be lower than 0.75 per function point. So the true average defect density of software produced by HQ must be 0.75 or higher. So we do a right-tailed t-test. Now the p-value, rounded to two decimal points, is 0.04. According to statistical custom, this observation is rare enough for WorldCorp to be considered evidence against H_0.

HQ now has something to explain. Why is the p-value so low? First, is H_0 false? But then why did all project managers give approximately the same defect density? Did they conspire? Without evidence of a conspiracy, this is hard to accept.

Second, is H_0 true and did we observe a rare event? Possibly. A sample of 15 is small and can show large random fluctuations. And measuring defect density is not very reliable. Where did the data come from? If we had enough time and money, we might repeat the research with a freshly drawn random sample to see if this leads again to a low p-value.

But there is also a third option. Did we make a mistake, and should we put aside the result as an outlier? Is the sample really random? Perhaps there was a systematic bias for more complex and error-prone programs? Again, was there a mistake in measurement? And how is defect density distributed? Can we assume that it is close enough to normally distributed so that we can use the t-test? A minute's thought makes clear that in the population of all programs, defect density is not symmetrically distributed around its mean. Perhaps it is so skewed that using the t-distribution is not justified.

The Significance-Testing Inference Rule

The above inference strategy, based on explaining a low p-value, contrasts with the inference rule given in most applied statistics books:

If the p-value of a test, given H_0, is low, then reject H_0.

I call this the **significance-testing inference rule**. It is combined with the injunction to set the significance level in advance, for example, at 5 %, and to keep it fixed.

However, as eloquently argued by Abelson [1], a low p-value should be the start of a discussion and not the end of it. Fisher himself late in his career made clear that a low p-value should be combined with other knowledge in order to draw conclusions about our null hypothesis [18]. Cox [15] and Birnbaum [8] too emphasized the importance of weighing in prior knowledge following a statistical test of a scientific hypothesis. The significance-testing inference rule should not be applied mechanically.

A possible source of misunderstanding is that the significance-testing inference rule resembles Popper's rule of falsification: If $p \rightarrow q$ and if we observe $\neg q$, then we must conclude that $\neg p$. But there is no valid rule of probabilistic falsification. If H_0 implies that some events are rare, then observing such an event does not falsify H_0 [16]. All events are possible, but some events are less probable than others. As an aside, I should remark that Popper [44] did not intend his rule of falsification to be applied mechanically either.

Another source of misunderstanding is the term "statistical significance," which is by many authors abbreviated to "significance." A statistically significant result can be substantially insignificant, because it can be the result of sampling error and the random correlational noise by which we are surrounded [37]. This critique on the term "statistical significance" is almost as old as the practice of the Fisher significance testing. The first reference I have been able to trace is from 1931 [50], and it has been repeated over and over again [7, 11, 35, 37, 39, 46].

Yet another misunderstanding is the 5% rule. Why is a p-value of 0.04 statistically significant and a value of 0.07 not statistically significant? Whether or not a rare event is important depends on our prior knowledge. In the words of Fisher [19, p. 45],

> ...no scientific worker has a fixed level of significance at which from year to year, and in all circumstances, he rejects hypotheses; he rather gives his mind to each particular case in the light of his evidence and his ideas.

Hacking [26] gives a carefully argued introduction in these issues, and Gigerenzer gives a historical account [22, 24].

13.3.2 Neyman–Pearson Hypothesis Testing

In response to Fisher's significance tests, Neyman and Pearson developed a way to choose between two or more hypotheses [36]. The goal is not to find out which hypothesis is true or is best supported by the evidence and our current knowledge, but to choose a hypothesis that optimizes our error rates when we repeatedly take random samples from the same distribution.

Error Rates

In the simplest decision problem, you have two specific hypotheses:

$$H_0 : \mu_X = \mu_0$$
$$H_1 : \mu_X = \mu_1$$

We must fix a criterion c that distinguishes these two hypothesis according to the decision rule:

If $\overline{X} \le c$, then select H_0; otherwise, select H_1.

See Fig. 13.7, which shows the normal approximations of the distribution of sample means if H_0 is true and if H_1 is true. The figure shows a right-tailed test of H_0 versus a left-tailed test of H_1. The set of values right of c is called the **rejection region** of H_0, and the complement is called the **acceptance region**. (For continuous variables, $\mathbb{P}(\overline{X}_n = c) = 0$ and $\mathbb{P}(\overline{X}_n \le c) = \mathbb{P}(\overline{X}_n < c)$. So it does not matter if we test for $< c$ or $\le c$.)

We do not know whether H_0 or H_1 is true, and so we have two error rates:

- If H_0 is true, rejecting it because $\overline{X}_n > c$ is called a **type I error**. The type I error rate α is defined as $\alpha = \mathbb{P}_{H_0}(\overline{X}_n > c)$. This corresponds to the significance level of significance testing.
- If H_1 is true, rejecting it because $\overline{X}_n \le c$ is called a **type II error**. The type II error rate β is defined as $\beta = \mathbb{P}_{H_1}(\overline{X}_n \le c)$.

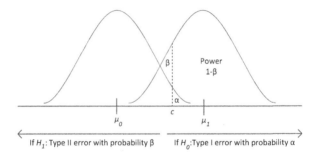

Fig. 13.7 The distributions of sample means if $H_0 : \mu = \mu_0$ is true and if $H_1 : \mu = \mu_1$ is true. If the sample mean $\overline{x} < c$, then H_0 is chosen; otherwise, H_1 is chosen. If H_1 is true, the error rate α is the probability of incorrectly rejecting H_0. If H_1 is true, the error rate β is the probability of incorrectly rejecting H_1

One error rate can be reduced by increasing the other one. Both error rates can be reduced at the same time by increasing the sample size, because this reduces the variance σ^2/n of the distributions in Fig. 13.7. Both error rates will also be smaller if σ is smaller or if the difference $d = \mu_1 - \mu_0$ is larger.

You can avoid making a type I error by always selecting H_0, but then $\beta = 1$: If you always choose H_0, you are sure to make the right choice on the occasions when H_0 is true, and you are sure to make the wrong choice when H_1 is true. Conversely, if you always choose H_1, then $\beta = 0$ but $\alpha = 1$. You could call these extreme decision criteria the criteria of blind belief: no empirical data can influence your decision.

If you let empirical data influence your decision, then you will make errors occasionally, and you have to decide which error levels are acceptable for this decision problem. By convention, H_0 is the hypothesis that you want to make the least errors about. This is called the **null hypothesis** of the decision. H_1 is called the **alternative hypothesis**. Deciding which hypothesis is the null and which is the alternative is a risk assessment that precedes the design of the test.

Following this convention, the **power** of the test is $1 - \beta = \mathbb{P}_{H_1}(\overline{X}_n > c)$. If H_1 is true, this is the probability that we accept H_1. Informally, $1 - \beta$ is the power of the test to discern, in the situations where H_1 is true, that it is true:

☐   Suppose a company produces printer cartridges with a mean life μ of 2,000 p., with a standard deviation of 300 p. in a normal distribution. The product development department has produced a new cartridge that they claim to have a mean life of 2,200 p. This claim is tested on a sample of ten cartridges, with $\alpha = 0.05$, where

$H_0 : \mu = 2{,}000$ versus $H_1 : \mu = 2{,}200.$

What is the decision criterion, and what is the power of this test?

We assume that the distribution of the life of new cartridges has the same variance as the population of old cartridges and that the distribution is normal too. The decision criterion can then be found by assuming that H_0 is true:

$$c = \mu_0 + t_{9,0.05}\frac{\sigma}{\sqrt{n}} = 2000 + 1.83\frac{300}{\sqrt{10}} = 2173.89.$$

If we now assume that H_1 is true, we can compute the error rate β by transforming this to a t value, given H_1, with 9 degrees of freedom:

$$T_9 = \frac{c - \mu_1}{\sigma/\sqrt{n}} = \frac{2173.6 - 2200}{300/\sqrt{10}} = -0.28.$$

The corresponding left-tailed error probability, given H_1, is $\beta = \mathbb{P}(t \leq T_9|H_1) = 0.39$, so the power of the test is $1 - \beta = 0.61$. In the long run, with this kind of test, in 61 % of the times that H_1 is true when the test is done, the test will lead to a correct decision that H_1 is true.

By doubling the sample size, the test becomes more accurate. The number of degrees of freedom becomes 19, and

$$c = \mu_0 + t_{19,0.05}\frac{\sigma}{\sqrt{n}} = 2000 + 1.73\frac{300}{\sqrt{20}} = 2115.98$$

which is closer to μ_0:

$$T_{19} = \frac{c - \mu_1}{\sigma/\sqrt{n}} = \frac{2116.0 - 2200}{300/\sqrt{20}} = -1.25.$$

$\mathbb{P}(t \leq T_{19}|H_1) = 0.11$, so the power increases to 0.89, which means that in the long run, when H_1 is true, the test will show this in 89 % of the times.

A more complex kind of decision problem is the test of a **composite hypothesis** $\mu > \mu_0$ or $\mu < \mu_0$. Consider the one-sided test:

$H_0 : \mu = \mu_0$ versus $H_1 : \mu > \mu_0$.

Now there are infinitely many values of μ that satisfy H_1. Figure 13.8 shows three possible distributions of the sample mean corresponding to three population means greater than c. The criterion c separates the values of $\overline{X}_n$ considered to be statistically the same as μ_0 from those considered to be statistically greater than μ_0. This means that the power of the test is not a probability, but a function,

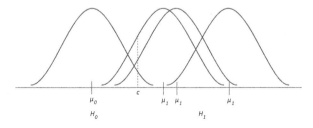

Fig. 13.8 Choosing between a specific hypotheses $H_0 : \mu = \mu_0$ and a composite hypothesis $H_1 : \mu > \mu_0$. Three possible values of μ_1 are shown, with the distributions of their sample means. Distribution means further to the right can be distinguished from μ_0 with greater power

parameterized by μ, that assigns the probability $\mathbb{P}_\mu(\overline{X}_n \in R)$ that a sample mean will be in the rejection region. We do not pursue this further here. Wasserman [51, p. 151] gives mathematical details and an example. Cohen [13, p. 95] gives an algorithm to construct an approximation to the power function by simulation.

Inductive Behavior Versus Inductive Inference

Neyman [42] called the above decision procedure **inductive behavior**. You are repeatedly sampling from the same distribution, and your goal is to optimize error rates in your decisions, regardless of whether or not you believe that the chosen hypothesis is true every time. You know that you will make the wrong decision occasionally, and you have chosen the error rates in such a way that you manage your risks rationally. It is important that you do not change these rates along the way. The error rates are error frequencies in the long run, and to realize these rates in the long run, you should not change the decision criterion in the short run.

This model of decision-making is applicable to signal recognition, quality control, acceptance testing, and other situations where you can repeatedly sample from the same distribution. What is tested in these situations is not a hypothesis but a sample. Does the sample of measurements come from friendly airplane or from an enemy airplane? Is the batch of products above or below a quality norm?

Fisher [18] argued acrimoniously that this model of decision-making does not apply to scientific inference. In scientific research, we often do only one test and combine the results with our other knowledge to draw a conclusion about the null hypothesis. Fisher called this **inductive inference**.

Other authors too have pointed out that statistical testing of a scientific hypothesis can be followed by a revision of our knowledge in the light of the test results [8, 9, 49]. This revision may even include a revision of our conceptual framework, including a redefinition of the chance model of random variables and a reformulation of some of our causal and architectural knowledge. If that happens, we are far removed from the repeated sampling from the same distribution, with fixed error rates and decision criterion, envisioned by Neyman.

The contrast and conflict between the Fisher and Neyman–Pearson theories of statistical testing have been explained with great clarity by Halpin and Stam [28] and by Lenhard [36]. Tukey [49] emphasizes the important difference between acceptance of a conclusion based on evidence, which is what Fisher was after, and deciding to act on the provisional acceptance of a hypothesis, which is what Neyman was after.

Our conclusion is that the Neyman–Pearson hypothesis testing is useful in situations where we repeatedly draw samples from the same distribution, where each time we have to decide mechanically among hypotheses according to a fixed criterion. Scientific hypothesis testing is not such a situation.

13.3.3   Null Hypothesis Significance Testing

In the social sciences, Fisher significance testing came to be merged with Neyman–Pearson hypothesis testing in a procedure called **null hypothesis significance testing** (NHST). Gigerenzer et al. [23–25] give an account of how this happened. Halpin and Stam [28] give a compatible but less polemic account.

NHST combines elements of three strategies: Fisher significance testing, Neyman–Pearson hypothesis testing, and statistical difference-making. To understand statistical difference-making, I give a preview of statistical difference-making experiments, treated more elaborately in Chap. 20.

Statistical Difference-Making Experiments

The goal of a statistical difference-making experiment is to provide evidence that treatments A and B have a different effect, on the average, on some measured variable X:

☐   For example, the goal may be to test which of two effort estimation techniques A and B provides, on the average, more accurate estimations. One way to test this is to select a random sample of program designs, randomly allocate technique A or technique B to each sample element, apply the techniques, and compare the average accuracy of the results once the software has actually been implemented.

The role of statistical inference in this argument is that it must be shown that two sample means are so different, statistically, that it is likely that the populations from which they were selected have different means. In other words, it must be shown that statistically, it is plausible that the mean of the population treated by A differs from the mean of the population treated by B. Let us call this difference between population means δ.

Once it is established with sufficient plausibility that δ is different from 0, the next part of the argument is a causal inference. In causal inference, we try to show that the only possible cause of the difference δ is the difference in treatments A and B. This is part of abductive inference, discussed in the next chapter. From a statistical point of view, causality plays no role, and we are trying to infer something about an unobserved population difference from an observed sample difference.

Before we discuss NHST, one terminological point is in order. The difference δ is usually called the **effect size** of treatment A with respect to treatment B. This already assumes that we know that the difference between A and B will have an effect. Until we know this, it is misleading to use this term. Recall the critique of the terminology of independent and dependent variables when we were discussing research design in Chap. 11 (p. 127).

The NHST Procedure

The NHST procedure tests the null hypothesis of no difference

$H_0 : \delta = 0$

against an alternative that there is a difference. In the simplest case, the alternative is a specific hypothesis

$H_1 : \delta = e$

for some constant e different from 0. We can then proceed as in Neyman–Pearson decision-making and choose a criterion to distinguish 0 from e with the desired error rates α and β. However, we do not talk about accepting H_0 (as is done in Neyman–Pearson decision-making) but about *not rejecting* H_0 (as in Fisher significance testing).

Often, we cannot predict a specific effect size, and so we cannot formulate a specific alternative hypothesis. We may then specify a directional hypothesis such as

$H_1 : \mu_A > \mu_B$

or a bidirectional alternative, such as

$H_1 : \mu_A \neq \mu_B$.

Depending on the alternative hypothesis, we then proceed with a one-tailed or two-tailed significance test in the Fisher style. We compute the p-value of the observed sample difference d under the null hypothesis that $\delta = 0$, using a one-tailed test if H_1 is directional and a two-tailed test if H_1 is bidirectional. If the p-value is below 5 %, we regard H_0 as rejected at the 5 % significance level and accept H_1. Some authors do not report the p-value but only report whether or not a null hypothesis is rejected at the 5 % level or even at the 1 % level if $p < 0.01$.

The NHST procedure has received a lot of criticism, sometimes hilarious, sometimes desperate, but always devastating [11,12,22,25,31,35,39]. Here I discuss three of the many criticisms.

The Null Hypothesis of No Difference Is Always False

It would be a miracle if two sample means were the same. Even if A and B have the same effect on the population, the means of different samples are probably different, because of sampling fluctuation and ambient correlational noise [37,40].

If A and B are different treatments, they are sure to have a different effect. There is bound to be some small difference between the mean of the population treated by A and the population treated by B. And if sample sizes are large enough, we are sure to statistically discern any effect size, no matter how tiny it is, because the sampling variance σ^2/n will be very small. So what we test in NHST is not if two sample means are different—we already know that they are different—but if our samples are big enough to see the difference. This may be statistically highly significant (a very small p-value) but substantially unimportant:

☐ Bakan [2] partitioned a database of 60, 000 subjects into groups according to arbitrary attributes, such as living east of the Mississippi or west of the Mississippi, in Maine versus in the rest of the country, etc. For each of these pairs of samples, he tested arbitrary variables. For each of these variables, the means in the two samples were different with a statistical significance better than 5 %. None of these statistically significant differences had any substantial meaning. They are ambient correlational noise between two variables.

☐ Meehl [38] identifies a casual influence of the religion of the father on a child's ability to name colors that runs through social class, personality trait of father, economic success of father, education level of children in a family, sex differences in color naming, feminine occupations of father, child's general intelligence and father's occupation, general intelligence, and color naming competence. All of these influences are weak, but each of them is known to exist.

☐ The connectedness of the real world is not restricted to the social world. Robins and Wasserman [45, p. 318] report that epidemiologists learn early in their career that in studies with large sample sizes, "one typically observes highly significant statistical associations between variables which are firmly believed, on biological grounds, not to be causally associated."

These examples relate to the point made earlier that a statistical inference rule must never be applied mechanically but must be combined with other knowledge to draw defensible conclusions.

There Are Many Alternatives to a Null Hypothesis

There are infinitely many specific alternative hypotheses that can be compared with the null hypothesis of no difference. Statistical rejection of the null does not imply truth of any particular one of these alternatives. In the Neyman–Pearson-inspired version of NHST, the hypothesis is selected that best explains the observed difference as compared to the other specified hypotheses. In the Fisher-inspired version, whatever the alternative is, it is selected when the observed difference is improbable given H_0. Either way, the conclusion from rejecting the null hypothesis would be different for every different alternative hypothesis. What conclusion is best supported depends on all the other things that we know or believe, and it does not follow mechanically that the best-supported conclusion is the alternative hypothesis that we were testing.

Rejecting a Null Is Not Rejecting a Scientific Hypothesis

Earlier, we saw that Fisher significance testing should not be confused with Popper's rule of falsification, because there is no rule of probabilistic falsification. Here, we see a second difference with Popper's rule of falsification: What we test is the null hypothesis of no difference, rather than a substantial research hypothesis postulating a difference. We are testing something that does not follow from a scientific theory and that we know is false. Popper wants to test scientific theories, but NHST is never a test of a scientific theory.

13.3.4   Conclusions About Hypothesis Testing

Summing up our discussion of statistical hypothesis testing, I conclude that Fisher significance testing can be useful if used properly, combined with prior knowledge, but is sterile when used mechanically.

Neyman–Pearson testing is useful in practical decision-making situations where we can and must make decisions mechanically when sampling repeatedly from the same distribution, such as in signal recognition or quality control. Long-term error probabilities matter here. But scientific inference is not such a situation.

NHST is a procedure in which we test a hypothesis of which we know that it is false and that does not follow from any scientific insight. When the null is rejected, this does not imply anything about the alternative hypothesis. Despite its widespread use, this is not a useful procedure.[4]

Some methodologists argue for Bayesian hypothesis testing, in which probabilities are seen as measures of strength of evidence, as measures of strength of belief, or as measures of your willingness to gamble [26, 27]. This makes sense as an alternative for significance tests, which somehow try to quantify the strength of evidence but, as a frequentist approach, cannot quantify the strength of a statistical hypothesis. For large samples, Bayesian and frequentist inference agree, but Bayesian methods do not give long-run performance guarantees [51, pp. 176 ff]. They must also make additional assumptions that are not required in frequentist inference, such as assumptions about a prior belief distribution or about the size of a quasi-sample that does not exist but must be assumed to characterize prior knowledge [54]. We will not pursue Bayesian inference techniques here.[5] Instead of trying to quantify strength of belief with numbers and then choosing the belief with the highest number, in this book we try to justify beliefs with arguments and then proceed to tentatively adopt the belief with the best arguments.

13.4   Estimating Confidence Intervals

We now turn to the other kind of statistical inference, using sample data to estimate a property of a statistical model of the distribution from which the sample was selected. Some of the pitfalls of hypothesis testing, such as confusion with Popperian falsification of a research hypothesis, disappear, because no hypotheses are tested. Others, such as the danger of mechanical application of a decision rule when this is not appropriate, are still present and must be avoided by intelligent application of confidence interval estimation.

13.4.1 Confidence Intervals

The reasoning for confidence interval estimation is straightforward. We know that

$$\overline{Z}_{\overline{X}_n} = \frac{\overline{X}_n - \mu}{\sigma/\sqrt{n}}$$

approaches a standard normal distribution when $n \to \infty$. Therefore,

$$\mathbb{P}(-z_{0.025} \leq \overline{Z}_{\overline{X}_n} \leq z_{0.025}) \approx 0.95,$$

where the approximation is bad for small n and gets better for larger n. Expanding $\overline{Z}_{\overline{X}_n}$ and rearranging, this implies

$$\mathbb{P}(\overline{X}_n - z_{0.025}\frac{\sigma}{\sqrt{n}} \leq \mu \leq \overline{X}_n + z_{0.025}\frac{\sigma}{\sqrt{n}}) \approx 0.95.$$

In this approximation, μ and σ are unknown distribution parameters, and $\overline{X}_n$ is a known sample statistic. The interval

$$(\overline{X}_n - z_{0.025}\frac{\sigma}{\sqrt{n}}, \overline{X}_n + z_{0.025}\frac{\sigma}{\sqrt{n}})$$

is called a **95 % confidence interval for the population mean.** A confidence interval quantifies the random fluctuation of the sample mean around the population mean. It is customary to write it as an open interval, with round brackets, because the probability that an open interval contains μ is the same as the probability that a closed interval contains μ.

We would like to get rid of σ, which is usually unknown, and estimate it with S_n. We can do this if the sample size is larger than 100 or if X is normally distributed and the sample size is smaller than 100. Switching to the t-distribution with $n - 1$ degrees of freedom, a 95 % confidence interval for the population mean estimated with a t-distribution is

$$(\overline{X}_n - t_{n-1,0.025}\frac{S_n}{\sqrt{n}}, \overline{X}_n + t_{n-1,0.025}\frac{S_n}{\sqrt{n}}).$$

This interval is larger, so less accurate, than a 95 % confidence interval estimated with the standard normal distribution and σ. However, for large samples, the t and z distributions are almost the same.

13.4.2 The Meaning of Confidence Intervals

What does a confidence interval estimation mean? The accepted interpretation is this [4, 26, 51]:

> In all of the 95 % confidence interval estimates that are done in the world, in the long run the real distribution mean will be in this interval in approximately 95 % of the estimates.

The reason is that an infinitely long sequence of decisions to accept or reject hypotheses about parameters μ and σ with a risk of 5 % of being wrong each time has in any finite prefix an error ratio that in the long run converges in probability on 0.05 [3, p. 23]. This follows from the weak LLN.

Of course, no one knows which 5 % of the confidence interval estimations will be out of range. You may have bad luck and score out of range for a while. And if the sequence of confidence interval estimations gets very long, a small percentage out-of-range estimations is a very large absolute number. And how long must we wait until the percentage of out-of-range estimations will get close to 5 %? As Keynes famously said, in the long run, we are all dead. Confidence intervals give us confidence, not certainty.

Acknowledging the fallibility of statistical inference, confidence intervals can give us useful information about population distributions:

☐ We return to the example of WorldCorp who wants to know what the quality of the software developed by takeover candidate HQ is. The project managers of HQ all say that it about 0.75 per function point.

   WorldCorp randomly selects a sample of 15 software systems developed by HQ. The sample shows an average defect density 0.84 with a sample variance of 0.18, so $\overline{X}_{15} = 0.84$ and $S_{15} = 0.18$. What is the estimated 95 % confidence interval for the mean defect density in the population?

   Assuming random sampling and assuming that defect density is normally distributed over the population of software developed by HQ, the $T_{\overline{X}_{15}}$ statistic has a t_{14} distribution, and we can estimate the 95 % confidence interval for the mean defect density as

$$(\overline{X}_{15} - t_{14,0.025}\frac{S_{15}}{\sqrt{15}}, \overline{X}_{15} - t_{14,0.025}\frac{S_{15}}{\sqrt{15}}) = (0.74, 0.94).$$

This just includes the 0.75 given by the project managers, but the confidence interval suggests that the mean may be a bit larger.

   If the sampling frame had 100 elements, the correction factor for sampling without replacement would be about $\sqrt{\frac{100-15}{100-1}} = 0.93$, which makes a negligible difference in the estimation.

☐ Suppose the sample would have consisted of 30 software systems rather than 15 and that $\overline{X}_{30} = 0.84$ and $S_{30} = 0.18$. Still assuming random sampling and normal distribution of defect density, the 95 % confidence interval for the mean defect density now is

$$(\overline{X}_{30} - t_{29,0.025}\frac{S_{30}}{\sqrt{30}}, \overline{X}_{30} - t_{29,0.025}\frac{S_{30}}{\sqrt{30}}) = (0.78, 0.91).$$

The sample contains more information because it has 29 degrees of freedom, and the estimation interval is therefore narrower than the one constructed from $\overline{X}_{15}$. Larger samples give more accurate estimations.

   The new confidence interval does not contain 0.75, suggesting that the project managers are too optimistic, but not by much.

If we assume a sampling frame of 100 software systems, then this sample needs a correction factor of $\sqrt{\frac{100-30}{100-1}} = 0.84$, which gives a slightly smaller confidence interval.

13.4.3   Fisher Significance Tests and Confidence Intervals

There is a systematic relation between confidence interval estimation and statistical significance testing: The 95 % confidence interval around a particular observed sample mean $\overline{x}_n$ is the set of null hypotheses that would not be rejected by $\overline{x}_n$ according to the significance-testing inference rule at the 5 % level. To illustrate this graphically, panel (a) of Fig. 13.9 shows a 95 % confidence around $\overline{x}_n$. Panel (b) shows a distribution mean on the same number line and the acceptance region that cuts off 95 % of the standard normal curve centered on μ_0. The sample mean $\overline{x}_n$ is outside this region and so would be rejected according to the significance-testing inference rule at the 5 % significance level, using $H_0 : \mu_X = \mu_0$ as null hypothesis. The same decision would be made for any distribution mean outside the 95 % confidence interval around $\overline{x}_n$.

In panel (c), the distribution mean μ_0' is inside the confidence interval, and it would not be rejected by the significance-testing inference rule at the 5 % significance level. The same decision would be made about any distribution mean inside the 95 % confidence interval around $\overline{x}_n$.

We can strengthen the analogy between statistical significance tests and confidence intervals by introducing one-sided confidence intervals to correspond to one-sided statistical significance tests, but we will not pursue this further. See, for example, Wonnacott and Wonnacott [54, p. 317].

13.4.4   Methodological Comparison with Hypothesis Testing

Confidence interval estimation gives us a plausible range around $\overline{x}_n$ for the distribution mean. For any distribution mean μ_0 in this range, the probability to

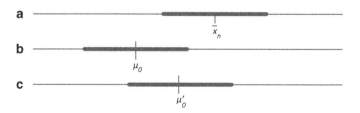

Fig. 13.9 (a) A 95 % confidence interval around the sample mean $\overline{x}_n$. (b) $\overline{x}_n$ is in the 95 % region of μ_0. According to the significance-testing inference rule, $\overline{x}_n$ would not reject $H_0 : \mu = \mu_0$. (c) $\overline{x}_n$ is in the 5 % region of μ_0'. According to the significance-testing inference rule, $\overline{x}_n$ would reject $H_0 : \mu = \mu_0'$

observe a sample mean as far away from μ_0 as $\overline{x}_n$ is more than 5 %, and so according to the significance-testing inference rule, $H_0 : \mu_X = \mu_0$ would not be rejected. The sample mean $\overline{x}_n$ rejects H_0 exactly if μ_0 is outside the confidence interval around $\overline{x}_n$.

Confidence interval estimation gives us more information than significance testing, because it gives us a range of estimations, where the size of the range depends on the sample variance and the desired level of confidence. If the sample size is larger, the estimate is more accurate (the interval is smaller). If the desired confidence is larger, the estimate will be less accurate (the interval will be larger).

Just as there is no other reason than custom to choose 5 % significance in significance testing, there is no reason other than custom to choose 95 % in confidence interval estimation. We may require higher or lower levels of confidence, as the research context requires.

Confidence interval estimation is simple mathematics, but drawing conclusions from it is not mechanical. As we have seen in the example, the position of a hypothetical mean just inside or just outside a confidence interval gives useful information that must be combined with other knowledge to draw conclusions.

13.5   Statistical Conclusion Validity

Statistical conclusion validity is the validity of the statistical inference from sample data to a statistical model [47, p. 512]. Assuming that no mistakes have been made in computations, the validity of this inference depends on the validity of the assumptions made by them. The assumptions of confidence interval estimation are listed in Table 13.5. Note that these assumptions are empirical. A particular population, sample, or variable may violate them [5,6,20]. Other statistical inference techniques make other assumptions that we do not list here. Textbooks on statistical inference always discuss the assumptions made by the different statistical inference techniques.

For statistical difference-making experiments, there are additional important requirements for statistical conclusion validity: The allocation of treatments to sample elements must be random (Table 13.5). Only if allocation is random can we treat the sample treated with A and the sample treated with B as random samples of the population treated with A and the population treated with B, respectively.

There are yet other threats to conclusion validity, which are not really empirical assumptions about the sample of the population or X, but requirements for reporting about research. These are customarily regarded as threats to conclusion validity, and so we list them here (Table 13.5).[6]

Table 13.1 Assumptions of confidence interval estimation

- *Stable distribution.* Does X have a stable distribution, with fixed parameters?
- *Scale.* Does X have an interval or ratio scale?
- *Sampling.* Is sample selection random or does it contain a known or unknown systematic selection mechanism?
- *Sample size.* If the z distribution is used, is the sample sufficiently large for the normal approximation to be used?
- *Normality.* If the t-distribution is used, is the distribution of X normal, or is the sample size larger than 100?

Table 13.2 Assumption of statistical difference-making experiments

---

- *Treatment allocation.* Are the treatments allocated randomly to sample elements?

Table 13.3 Things to avoid when reporting about statistical difference-making experiments

---

- *Effect size.* Seeing a very small difference, but not telling that it is small
- *Fishing.* Seeing no difference most of the time, but not telling this
- *Very high power.* Not telling about a reason why you can see a difference (very large sample size makes very small differences visible)
- *Sample homogeneity.* Not telling about another reason why you can see a difference (groups are selected to be homogeneous, so that any intergroup difference stands out)

If *effect size* is small, this is important information for the reader, and it should be reported. With a large sample, even a small effect size can be statistically significant. But substantial significance depends on the size of the effect.

Another requirement for reporting is that all results are reported. If we *fish* for differences, we will always catch one. Just repeat the experiment until you finally hit a confidence interval that does not contain 0. Or ask your students to do as many experiments as possible and report the ones where the confidence interval for the population difference does not contain 0.

Another way to catch a difference is to increase the sample size. The *power* to discern a difference statistically can be made as high as you wish this way. So if you expect the difference to be small, select a sample so large that the confidence interval around the sample difference still excludes 0.

Another way to find a difference is to make a sample *homogeneous*. If there is little variation within samples, any difference between samples will stand out. This does not imply that there is anything wrong about the statistical inference used. Maybe the population is extremely homogeneous, as it is in some engineering applications. If the population is not homogeneous, random sampling delivers a homogeneous sample only by extreme coincidence, and this should be reported. In the long run, random sampling will not give us homogeneous samples from a heterogeneous population.

13.6 Summary

- Statistical inference is the inference of properties of a statistical model from sample observations.
- Statistical inference is based on the CLT, which says that the means of samples selected randomly from a distribution with mean μ and variance σ^2 are distributed normally around μ with variance σ^2/n.
- In statistical hypothesis testing, we assume one or more hypotheses about a statistical model and then compute the conditional probability of the sample data given these hypotheses:

  - Fisher significance testing tests one hypothesis. This can be useful when the results are combined with prior knowledge.
  - Neyman–Pearson testing tests two or more hypotheses and can be useful in situations of repeated sampling where error rates must be controlled.
  - NHST tests a null hypothesis of no difference against an alternative. This is not useful.

- A 95 % confidence interval for the population mean is an interval that is claimed to enclose the population mean. In the long run, this claim is true in 95 % of the 95 % confidence interval estimations.
- Conclusion validity:

  - Confidence interval estimation makes a number of assumptions about the sample, how it was selected from the population, and about the variable.
  - Estimation of the difference in population means makes the same assumptions. It additionally assumes random allocation.
  - Conclusion validity includes assumptions about proper reporting about statistical inference.

Notes

[1]**Page 143, statistics textbooks** A classic reference on statistical experiments in software engineering is the book by Juristo and Moreno [34], giving all required details about statistical research design and statistical inference. More compact is the book by Wohlin et al. [53]. Cohen [13] gives a comprehensive introduction to statistical inference, including computer-intensive nonparametric methods such as bootstrap methods and randomization tests. It gives examples from artificial intelligence, but all of the techniques are applicable in software engineering and information systems too.

An extremely readable introduction to the statistics of business research is given by Wonnaccott and Wonnaccott [54]. They have a clear explanation of the relation between estimating confidence intervals and testing hypotheses. They also have chapters on Bayesian inference and nonparametric inference, but not on computer-intensive methods. Cooper and Schindler [14] give a textbook introduction to business research methods, giving the full picture of the empirical research cycle, including chapters on hypothesis testing and analysis of variance.

Field [17] is a well-written but very verbose introduction to statistics for psychologists, with many humorous examples. It discusses all of the statistical software package SPSS. There is now also a version of his book using R. The R language and programming environment for statistical computing and graphics are freely available from http://www.r-project.org/.

Freedman [20] is a careful introduction to descriptive statistics, hypothesis testing, and confidence interval estimation for sociologists that is also very verbose but nevertheless never gets boring. His endnotes give a lot of additional useful information for teachers. This is recommended reading, even for the mathematically inclined, because it gives sharp intuitions about what you can do with statistical inference and under which assumptions.

Along the same lines but more wide-ranging and less verbose is the online text published and maintained by Philip Stark, SticiGui (http://www.stat.berkeley.edu/~stark/SticiGui/index.htm). It gives an introduction to probability, hypothesis testing, and confidence interval estimation and adds a lot of practical examples of informal but structured argumentation. It is a joy to read.

If you want to understand the mathematics of statistical inference, Wasserman [51] provides a comprehensive introduction in classical parametric statistics as well as more modern methods such as bootstrapping and causal modeling. My exposition follows Freedman for the intuitions and Wasserman [51] for the mathematics.

[2] **Page 149, simulations of the CLT.** Philip Stark provides many useful simulations in his online statistics textbook at http://www.stat.berkeley.edu/~stark/SticiGui/index.htm.

[3] **Page 151, web applications for t-distributions.** Two useful sites are http://stattrek.com/online-calculator/t-distribution.aspx and http://www.danielsoper.com/statcalc3/default.aspx. You could also use the R environment, mentioned in note 1 above, to compute p-values.

[4] **Page 166, critique of NHST**. The debate about NHST has been raging for a long time in psychology. Some authors have become desperate about the continued use of NHST in some disciplines. Already in 1967, the renowned psychologist Paul Meehl [38, p. 114] called a researcher who produces a string of statistically significant results, very unkindly:

> an eager-beaver researcher, undismayed by logic-of-science considerations and relying blissfully on the 'exactitude' of modern statistical hypothesis-testing .... In terms of his contribution to the enduring body of psychological knowledge, he has done hardly anything. His true position is that of a potent-but-sterile intellectual rake, who leaves in his merry path a long train of ravished maidens but no viable scientific offspring.

This was in 1966. Eleven years later, he was less rude but not less clear [39, p. 817]:

> I suggest to you that Sir Ronald [Fisher] has befuddled us, mesmerized us, and led us down the primrose path. I believe that the almost universal reliance on merely refuting the null hypothesis as the standard method for corroborating substantive theories in the soft areas is a mistake, is basically unsound, poor scientific strategy, and one of the worst things that ever happened in the history of psychology.

In 1982, the outgoing editor of the *Journal of Applied Psychology* [10] tried it with humor:

> Perhaps p-values are like mosquitos. They have an evolutionary niche somewhere and no amount of scratching, swatting, or spraying will dislodge them. Whereas it may be necessary to discount a sampling error explanation for results of a study, investigators must learn to argue for the significance of their results without reference to inferential statistics.

In 1994, the top-ranking applied statistician Cohen [12], of statistical power and Cohen's κ fame, stated that NHST has seriously impeded the advance of psychology as a science and confessed to the temptation to relabel it into *statistical hypothesis inference testing,* which has an easy to remember acronym.

[5] **Page 166, Bayesian statistical hypothesis testing**. Nola and Sankey [43] give a two-chapter introduction, a Bayesian reconstruction of scientific inference. Wonnacott and Wonnacott [54] show how to do Bayesian hypothesis testing and confidence interval estimation. Wasserman [51] explains the difference mathematically and discusses the problem of priors.

Bayesian and frequentist methods answer different questions [51, p. 189]. Bayesian methods can be used to answer the question how to combine numerical quantifications of prior belief, prior strength of evidence, or prior willingness to gamble, with newly obtained data. The real problem here is how to get these quantifications in the first place. Frequentist methods can be used to answer the question how to infer a statistical model of one or more variables that has guaranteed long-run performance. The real problem here is that we do not know how long the run must be before it is stable. We may not live long enough to see this, and the world on which the estimations are based may have changed before it has run long enough for our estimates to be stable.

[6]**Page 170, threats to conclusion validity.** Shadish et al. [47, p. 45] mention three additional threats not listed here. *Unreliability of measures* and *restriction of range* are in this book discussed as part of threats to analogic inference, in particular threats that are posed by measurement design. *Unreliable treatment implementation* is a threat to analogic inference too, this time a threat posed by treatment implementation. These threats are discussed in Chap. 15 on analogic inference.

References

1. R.P. Abelson, A retrospective on the significance test ban of 1999 (If there were no significance tests, they would be invented), in *What If There Were No Significance Tests?*, ed. by L.L. Harlow, S.A. Mulaik, J.H. Steiger (Lawrence Erlbaum, Mahwah, 1997), pp. 117–141
2. D. Bakan, The test of significance in psychological research. Psychol. Bull. **66**(6), 423–437 (1966)
3. J.O. Berger, *Statistical Decision Theory and Bayesian Analysis*, 2nd edn. (Springer, Heidelberg, 1980)
4. J.O. Berger, Could Fisher, Jeffreys and Neyman have agreed on testing? Stat. Sci. **18**, 1–32 (2003)
5. R.A. Berk, Toward a methodology for mere mortals. Sociol. Methodol. **21**, 315–324 (1991)
6. R.A. Berk, D.A. Freedman, Statistical assumptions as empirical commitments, in *Law, Punishment, and Social Control: Essays in Honor of Sheldon Messinger*, 2nd edn., ed. by T.G. Blomberg, S. Cohen (Aldine de Gruyter, Berlin, 2005), pp. 235–254. Reprinted in [21, pp. 23–43]
7. J. Berkson, Tests of significance considered as evidence. Int. J. Epidemiol. **32**, 687–691 (2003). [Originally published in J. Am. Stat. Assoc. **37**, 325–335 (1942)]
8. A. Birnbaum, The Neyman-Pearson theory as decision theory, and as inference theory; with a criticism of the lindley-savage argument for Bayesian theory. Synthese, **36**(1), 19–49 (1977)
9. R.C. Bolles, The difference between statistical hypotheses and scientific hypotheses. Psychol. Rep. **11**, 639–645 (1962)
10. J.P. Campbell, Some remarks from the outgoing editor. J. Appl. Psychol. **67**, 691–700 (1982)
11. R.P. Carver, The case against statistical significance testing. Harv. Education. Rev. **48**(8), 378–399 (1978)
12. J. Cohen, The earth is round ($p < 0.05$). Am. Psychol. **49**(12), 997–1003 (1994)
13. P.R. Cohen, *Empirical Methods for Artificial Intelligence* (Bradford Books, Cambridge, 1995)
14. D.R. Cooper, P.S. Schindler, *Business Research Methods*, 8th edn. (Irwin/McGraw-Hill, Homewood/Singapore, 2003)
15. D.R. Cox, Some problems connected with statistical inference. Ann. Math. Stat. **29**(2), 357–372 (1958)
16. R. Falk, C.W. Greenbaum, Significance tests die hard. The amazing persistence of a probabilistic misconception. Theory Psychol. **5**(1), 75–98 (1995)
17. A. Field, *Discovering Statistics Using SPSS*, 3rd edn. (Sage, Thousand Oaks, 2009)
18. R.A. Fisher, Statistical methods and scientific induction. J. R. Stat. Soc. B **17**, 69–77 (1955)
19. R.A. Fisher, *Statistical Methods and Scientific Inference* (Oliver & Boyd, Edinburgh, 1956)
20. D. Freedman, R. Pisani, R. Purves, *Statistics*, 4th edn. (Norton & Company, New York, 2007)

21. D.A. Freedman, *Statistical Models and Causal Inference: A Dialogue With the Social Sciences*, ed. by D. Collier, J.S. Sekhon, P.B. Stark (Cambridge University Press, Cambridge, 2010)
22. G. Gigerenzer, Mindless statistics. J. Socio Econ. **33**, 587–606 (2004)
23. G. Gigerenzer, D.J. Murray, *Cognition as Intuitive Statistics*. (Lawrence Erlbaum, Mahwah, 1987). Chap. 1, The Inference Revolution
24. G. Gigerenzer, Z. Swijtink, T. Porter, L. Daston, J. Beatty, L. Krüger, *The Empire of Chance: How Probability Changed Science and Everyday Life* (Cambridge University Press, Cambridge, 1989)
25. G. Gigerenzer, S. Krauss, O. Vitouch, The Null ritual: what you always wanted to know about significance testing but were afraid to ask, in *The Sage Handbook of Quantiative Methodology for the Social Sciences*, ed. by D. Kaplan (Sage, Thousand Oaks, 2004.), pp. 391–408
26. I. Hacking, *An Introduction to Probability and Inductive Logic* (Cambridge University Press, Cambridge, 2001)
27. A. Hájek, Interpretations of probability, in *The Stanford Encyclopedia of Philosophy*, Winter 2012 edn., ed. by E.N. Zalta, (2012). http://plato.stanford.edu/cgi-bin/encyclopedia/archinfo.cgi?entry=probability-interpret
28. P.G. Halpin, H.J. Stam, Inductive inference or inductive behavior: Fisher and Neyman-Pearson approaches to statistical testing in psychological research (1940–1960). Am. J. Psychol. **119**(4), 625–653 (2006)
29. L.L. Harlow, S.A. Mulaik, J.H. Steiger (eds). *What If There Were No Significance Tests?* (Lawrence Erlbaum, Mahwah, 1997)
30. C. Hildebrand, G. Häubl, A. Herrmann, J.R. Landwher, When social media can be bad for you: community feedback stifles consumer creativity and reduces satisfaction with self-designed products. Inf. Syst. Res. **24**(1), 14–29 (2013)
31. R. Hubbard, M.J. Bahyarri, Confusion over measures of evidence (p's) versus errors (α's) in classical statistical testing. Am. Statistician **57**(3), 171–182 (2003)
32. T. Huynh, J. Miller, An empirical investigation into open source web applications' implementation vulnerabilities. Empir. Softw. Eng. **15**(5), 556–576 (2010)
33. H.F. Inman, Karl Pearson and R.A. Fisher on statistical tests: a 1935 exchange from Nature. Am. Statistician **48**(1), 2–11 (1994)
34. N. Juristo, A. Moreno, *Basics of Software Engineering Experimentation* (Kluwer, Dordrecht, 2001)
35. C. Lambdin, Significance tests as sorcery: science is empirical—significance tests are not. Theory Psychol. **22**(1), 67–90 (2012)
36. J. Lenhard, Models and statistical inference: the controversy between Fisher and Neyman-Pearson. Br. J. Philos. Sci. **57**, 69–91 (2006)
37. D.T. Lykken, Statistical significance in psychological research. Psychol. Bull. **70**(3), 151–159 (1968)
38. P.E. Meehl, Theory-testing in psychology and physics: a methodological paradox. Philos. Sci. **34**(2), 103–115 (1967)
39. P.E. Meehl, Theoretical risks and tabular asterisks: Sir Karl, Sir Ronald, and the slow progress of soft psychology. J. Consult. Clin. Psychol. **46**, 806–834 (1978)
40. P.E. Meehl, Why summaries of research on psychological theories are often uninterpretable. Psychol. Rep. **66**, 195–244 (1990)
41. D.E. Morrison, R.E. henkel (eds.) *The Significance Test Controversy: A Reader* (Aldline Transaction, Piscataway, 2006)
42. J. Neyman, "inductive behavior" as a basic concept in the philosophy of science. Rev. Int. Stat. Institute. **25**(1/3), 7–22 (1957)
43. R. Nola, H. Sankey, *Theories of Scientific Method* (Acumen, Stocksfield, 2007)
44. K.R. Popper, *The Logic of Scientific Discovery* (Hutchinson, London, 1959)
45. J.M. Robins, L. Wasserman, On the impossibility of inferring causation from association without background knowledge, in *Computation, Causation, and Discovery*. P. Glymour, G. Cooper (eds.) (The MIT Press, Cambridge, 1999), pp. 305–321

46. W.W. Rozeboom, The fallacy of the null-hypothesis significance test. Psychol. Bull. **57**(5), 416–428 (1960)
47. W.R. Shadish, T.D. Cook, D.T. Campbell, *Experimental and Quasi-Experimental Designs for Generalized Causal Inference* (Houghton Mifflin Company, Boston, 2002)
48. Z. Swijtink, The objectification of observation: measurement and statistical methods in the nineteenth century, in *The Probabilistic Revolution. Volume I: Ideas in History.* L. Krüger, L.J. Daston, and M. Heidelberger (eds.) (MIT Press, Cambridge, 1987), pp. 261–285
49. J.W. Tukey, Conclusions vs decisions. Technometrics **2**(4), 423–433 (1960)
50. R.W. Tyler, What is statistical significance? Educ. Res. Bull. **10**(5), 115–118, 142 (1931)
51. L. Wasserman, *All of Statistics. A Concise Course in Statistical Inference* (Springer, Heidelberg, 2004)
52. R.R. Wilcox, *Introduction to Robust Estimation and Hypothesis Testing*, 2nd edn. (Academic Press, Waltham, 2005)
53. C. Wohlin, P. Runeson, M. Höst, M. C. Ohlsson, B. Regnell, A. Weslén, *Experimentation in Software Engineering*, 2nd edn. (Springer, Heidelberg, 2012)
54. T.H. Wonnacott, R.J. Wonnacott, *Introductory Statistics for Business and Economics*, 4th edn. (Wiley, Hoboken, 1990)

Chapter 14
Abductive Inference Design

Abductive inference is inference to the best explanation(s). The traditional definition of abduction is that it traverses deduction in the backward direction: From $p \rightarrow q$ and q, we may tentatively conclude that p. We know that fire implies smoke, we see smoke, and we conclude that there is fire. There is no deductively certain support for this, and there may be other explanations of the occurrence of smoke. Perhaps a Humvee is laying a smoke screen? Douven [5] gives a good introduction into abduction as a form of reasoning, and Schurz [24] provides an interesting overview of historical uses of abduction in science, with examples.

Abduction is used in case-based research and sample-based research to explain case observations and statistical models, respectively. Examples are given in Sect. 14.1. We distinguish three kinds of explanations, namely, causal explanations, architectural explanations, and rational explanations, which are treated in Sects. 14.2, 14.3, and 14.4, respectively. Some phenomena may be explainable in all three ways. Which explanations are relevant for us depends on our research goals.

We do not consider statistical models to be abductive explanations. A statistical model *describes* some property of the distribution of one or more variables over a population but does not explain it causally, architecturally, or rationally. It does explain sample observations statistically, but these explanations are computational. In a very literal sense, statistical explanations of data *account* for the data. For example, the variance of a distribution statistically explains, i.e., accounts for, the variance found in a random sample from the distribution. This explanation is numerical and does not tell us what is the cause, mechanism, or reason for the sample variance.

Just as the other forms of inference that we discuss, abduction may deliver a false conclusion from true premises and is therefore ampliative. We discuss guidelines for validity of abductive inference throughout the chapter and summarize them in Sect. 14.5.

© Springer-Verlag Berlin Heidelberg 2014
R.J. Wieringa, *Design Science Methodology for Information Systems and Software Engineering*, DOI 10.1007/978-3-662-43839-8_14

14.1   Abduction in Case-Based and in Sample-Based Research

Figure 14.1 shows that there are two possible starting points for abduction. In case-based research, we try to find plausible explanations of case observations, and in sample-based research, we try to find plausible explanations of a statistical model, i.e., of a statistical generalization. Here are two examples:

☐   First, an example explanation in case-based research. Sabherwal [23] defined four kinds of coordination mechanisms for global outsourced information systems development projects, namely, coordination by standards, by plans, by formal adjustment, and by informal adjustment. This was his theoretical framework.

   In a series of case studies, he interviewed senior executives at six vendors and at four client organizations about the evolution of these coordination mechanisms during a recent project they were involved in. One observation extracted from these interviews is that at the start from the project, vendors desired greater formalization of coordination mechanisms but clients preferred things to be left flexible. This observation is the result of a descriptive inference from the interview data.

   Next, abductive inference starts. The first explanation offered by Sabherwal for this observation is that vendors sold outsourcing arrangements as "partnerships," causing the clients to think that formal coordination mechanisms are unnecessary [23, p. 179]. A second explanation is that at the start of a development project, during requirements engineering, informal relationships are more important than formalized relationships [23, p. 182]. Sabherwal does not view this as competing with the first explanation but as a second explanation that can be true at the same time as the first and that should be pursued in further research.

☐   As an example of explanation in sample-based research, we return to the study of Hildebrand et al. [9]. In the previous chapter, we saw that the researchers estimated a statistical model of the relation between a change in consumer preferences and the feedback they received (p. 145). This relation was assumed to be linear and can then be represented as a straight line through a point cloud. The researchers estimated the coefficients of the linear equation representing this line by a statistical inference technique, linear regression.

   Next, abductive inference starts. The slope of the line was positive, meaning that consumers' final preference is closer to the feedback that they received than their initial preference. A qualitative explanation given by the theoretical framework of Hildebrand et al. is that people in general tend to seek approval of others. People discount the opinion of distant others but will tend to conform to the opinion of others who are perceived as experts and of those whom they like.

   A second qualitative explanation of the slope of the line is that the subjects of the field study self-selected into the treatment (receiving an advice from someone else) and could have been more susceptible to the influence of others than those who did not self-select themselves into this treatment. Hildebrand et al. think this explanation is implausible [9, p. 27].

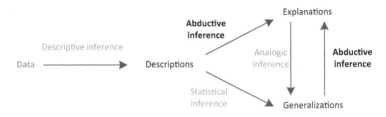

Fig. 14.1   Abductive inference produces explanations of descriptions or of generalizations

Yet other explanations can be given too. Perhaps the subjects shared other characteristics that can explain the observation, such as their age, sex, or education level. More information is needed to assess which of these explanations is most plausible or whether several of them are equally plausible.

In research, there is often an interplay between prediction, description, and explanation. The researcher first *predicts* the outcome of a treatment, using a theoretical framework. Next, the research is done, and results are *described,* possibly statistically. Finally, the results are *explained.* If the outcome happened according to the prediction done in advance, then most likely the theory used for prediction will now be used to give an explanation. But there might be other explanations too, and the researcher should assess them on plausibility and include them in the research report.

14.2   Causal Explanations

Recall from Chap. 9 (Scientific Theories) that a *causal explanation* of a change in a variable Y has the following form:

Y changed because, earlier, a variable X changed in a particular way.

This is a *difference-making* view of causality, in which we explain a change in Y causally by referring to an earlier event that made a difference to Y. We can illustrate this with the two examples given above:

☐ In the example of Sabherwal [23] above, the two explanations are causal. The fact that coordination at the start of an outsourcing project is informal was explained causally by the earlier event that vendors present outsourcing as partnerships. This explanation itself was backed up by reference to agency theory [23, p. 180]. The second explanation was that requirements engineering activities at the start of a project caused many informal exchanges between client and provider [23, p. 182]. Both explanations point at an earlier event which made a difference to the variable *level of formality of coordination*. As it happens, in both explanations, the earlier event made a difference to this variable in the same direction.

☐ In the study by Hildebrand et al. [9], a change in customer preference was explained as the causal effect of feedback received earlier. Receiving feedback made a difference to consumer preference. We have seen that here too there may be additional causal explanations and that here too all point in the same direction.

Causal inference is the reasoning process that produces a causal explanation of observed phenomena. As all forms of abductive inference, it is fallible. The examples illustrate a fundamental problem for causal inference, namely, that difference-making explanations are counterfactual [10]. If we say that an earlier event made a difference to a variable, we are comparing what actually happened with what would have happened if the earlier event had not taken place. For any individual case, this is an unverifiable statement:

☐ If we observe that a particular consumer changes or her preference after receiving feedback, we cannot know what this consumer would have done if he or she had received other feedback or no feedback at all. Perhaps the consumer would have changed his or her preference anyway.

Under some assumptions, we can deal with this problem by comparing the behavior of an object of study at different points in time, and under other assumptions, we can deal with it by comparing the behavior of similar objects of study. Below, these research designs are shown. First, we discuss three reasons for inferring the *absence* of a causal influence between X and Y.

14.2.1   Arguments for the Absence of Causality

To check whether causality can be present, we must check at least three conditions: covariation, temporal precedence, and spatial possibility [16]. If any of these conditions is absent, it is safer to conclude that there is no causality.

Covariation

If differences in X make a difference to Y, then X and Y must covary. So if X and Y do not covary, then differences in X apparently do not make a difference to Y.

☐   If there is no covariation between a consumer preferences and feedback received earlier, we can assume that there is no causal relation between the two.

For causal inference, it is important to deal with four possible explanations of covariation of X and Y:

1. Changes in X cause changes in Y.
2. Changes in Y cause changes in X.
3. A possibly unknown variable U causes changes in both X and Y.
4. Observed covariation is a coincidence.

In complex situations, the first three explanations may all be true:

☐   Feedback from a friend X may influence a consumer's preference, consumer's preferences may influence the feedback that a friend gives, and both can be influenced by advertisements that they both have been exposed to.

Temporal Precedence

Causation cannot work backward in time. This is an easy way to exclude causal influences:

☐   Feedback on a consumer choice can influence later changes in preferences, but not earlier changes. Of course, a consumer can form expectations about likely feedback, and these expectations can influence the consumer's preferences. But then all causal influences still happen from past to future: Past events influence the consumer's expectations, and these expectations may influence the consumer's later preferences.

Spatial Possibility

There is no action at a distance. Gravity and quantum entanglement are spectacular exceptions that confirm the rule. In the physical world, usually, cause and effect must be physically close. In the worlds of people and software, there is a similar principle of action by contact: People and/or software that do not have a channel of communication cannot influence each other. If differences in X make a difference to Y, there must be a chain of action-reaction steps that transfer the influence. If there is no conceivable *mechanism* that leads from a change in X to a change in Y, it is hard to see how differences in X could make a difference to Y:

☐   Feedback received by a consumer may impact the consumer's beliefs and expectations, which may influence the consumer's preferences. Even if we would not know how any of this happens, it is conceivable that some psychological mechanism like this happens. Before doing their experiment, Hildebrand et al. [9] used theories from social psychology to make it plausible that such a causal effect could exist.

14.2.2   Research Designs for Causal Inference

After we established that causal influence is not impossible, we must provide positive evidence for its existence. We can do this in two ways. In **cross-sectional** studies, we take a cross section of the population to show that across cases in otherwise similar circumstances, a change in X leads to a change in Y. In **longitudinal** studies, we take a sequence of snapshots of a case for a while, to show that in otherwise similar circumstances, changes in X are always followed by changes in Y. Combining this with our distinction between case-based and sample-based research, we get the classification of research designs shown in Table 14.2.2. We look at the logic of these designs in the sections to follow.

Most of these designs are experimental, but a few are observational. In all research designs, causal inference is done by assessing the plausibility of causal explanations. We design the research setup in such a way that if we do observe a change in Y, we can list all possible causal explanations of this change. In the

Table 14.1 Research designs to support causal inference. All sample-oriented designs, except the randomized controlled trial, are quasi-experiment designs

	Cross-sectional	**Longitudinal**
Case	• Comparative-cases causal experiment	• Single-case causal experiment
Sample	• Nonequivalent group design	• Interrupted time-series design
	• Regression discontinuity design	
	• Randomized controlled trial	

ideal case, the change in X is the only plausible explanation of the observed change in Y, and all other explanations are implausible. More realistically, more than one explanation will be plausible, but we hope to be able to argue that it is plausible that the change in X too has contributed to the observed change in Y.

Single-Case Causal Experiment

There are two ways to use a single-case experiment, one to support causal inference, discussed here, and one to support architectural inference, discussed later in this chapter. In a **single-case causal experiment,** we assume that the effect is transient and time independent [10]. We expose a single population element to two different values for X in sequence and measure the values of Y each time. The causal inference is like this:

- If the effect of a difference in X is transient,
- and independent of time,
- and all other conditions are held constant,
- a difference in Y measured after X changed, must have been caused by the difference in X.

Transience, time independence, and identity of conditions over time are strong assumptions that must be ascertained by the researcher. And if the population elements are all identical in their response to X—another strong assumption—then we can generalize this conclusion to the population.

In engineering, this kind of single-case causal reasoning occurs quite often, usually combined with architectural reasoning about the components of the object of study, as we will see later. In the social sciences, single-case experiments cannot support causal reasoning because the necessary assumptions are violated when people are involved:

☐ We can test a device or software system by exposing it to different inputs and measuring its outputs. If the effect of a previous input is transient and the effects of input are not influenced by time and we keep all other inputs constant, then this gives an accurate picture of the effect of the input on the output.

☐ Suppose a student maintains programs first using technique A, then using technique B, and then again with A, and we measure maintenance effort to see if the difference in maintenance techniques makes a difference for maintenance effort. Quite likely, after the first maintenance task with A, the student has built up experience in maintenance, which influences the effort of later maintenance tasks. So the effect of doing a maintenance task is not transient. And the effect of using A to do maintenance is not transient either. The second time will be easier.

Depending on the student, the time of day may influence maintenance effort too, which violates the time-independence assumption. And every maintenance task will be performed on a different program, which means that the conditions of maintenance are not identical across the experiments. All of this makes single-case causal inference unreliable if the object of study involves people.

Comparative-Cases Causal Experiment

In a **comparative-cases causal experiment,** we assume that different population elements are identical in their behavior with respect to X and Y. We expose two different elements to two different values of X and measure the values of Y in the two elements. Causal inference from a comparative-cases experiment has the following form:

- If different population elements respond identically to differences in X,
- and two population elements have been exposed to different levels of X,
- and all other conditions are identical for the two elements,
- then a difference in Y in the two population elements must have been caused by the difference in X.

The assumptions of identical response and identical conditions are very strong. If they are true, they allow us to generalize from two population elements to the entire population of identical elements. As above, this can be applied in engineering, but it is very unreliable in social science:

☐ Destructive testing of hardware can be done this way. Different copies of a device are exposed to different levels of X, keeping all other conditions identical across devices, to see at which level the device breaks.

☐ Software that accumulates its earlier stimuli and responses, and therefore never returns to an earlier state, can also be tested this way. Different copies are exposed to different values of X, keeping other conditions identical, to see what the effect of the difference is.

☐ If we include human subjects in the study, then the assumption of identical response across human subjects is very strong. We would need additional knowledge that assures us that people do respond the same to the stimuli applied in the experiment. It is safer to assume that different people respond differently to the same stimuli, although the differences may be small.

Randomized Controlled Trials

If there is variation across population elements in the behavior with respect to X or conditions are hard to keep identical, then comparison of two elements will not give us information about the effect of a difference in X. We then need to switch our reasoning from the case level to the sample level and assume that *on the average* there is a stable response to differences in X in a sample. The price we pay for this move to the sample level is that we establish difference making on the average. It does not tell us for a given population element, whether X makes a difference to Y.

In a **randomized controlled trial** (RCT), causal reasoning is based on random allocation. In the two-sample setup that we discuss in this book, we assume that the treatment variable X has two values, A and B. We select a sample randomly and randomly allocate treatments A and B to the sample elements, so that we have a subsample exposed to A and a subsample exposed to B. The treatments are applied, Y is measured, and we compute the statistic $d_{AB} = \overline{Y}_A - \overline{Y}_B$ and statistically estimate a confidence interval for the population parameter $\delta_{AB} = \mu_A - \mu_B$. If the interval contains 0, we assume that the difference between A and B had no effect on Y. Otherwise, the confidence interval is an estimate of the effect that difference between A and B has on $\overline{Y}$. This is the difference-making experiment sketched earlier when discussing the NHST inference strategy. It is described in full in Chap. 20 on statistical difference-making experiments.

There are different RCT designs, but the above two-sample setup suffices to explain the logic of causal inference in RCTs. The logic of causal inference from an RCT is this [25]:

- If the sample has been selected randomly,
- and treatments A and B have been allocated randomly,
- then a difference between μ_A and μ_B must have been caused by the difference between A and B.

Random sampling and random allocation jointly ensure that we have two randomly selected samples, from two versions of the population, namely, the population treated by A and the population treated by B. This licenses the application of the central-limit theorem in statistical inference from these samples to these populations. Random allocation additionally allows us to conclude, in our causal inference, that the difference between A and B is the only possible stable cause of a difference between μ_A and μ_B. This cause is called stable because in the long run, all other possible causes cancel out:

☐ A new drug is tested by comparing it with another drug (or a placebo) in double-blind randomized controlled experiments. Doctors and patients do not know who receives which treatment, which excludes two possible influences on the outcome. If the researcher is able to randomize all other possible influences on the outcome, then in the long run, these other influences average out, and a difference in average outcomes between treatment and control group that is stable in the long run can only be attributed to the treatment.

☐ Double-blind testing is not possible in software engineering, because it is not possible for a software engineer to be unaware of the technique that he or she is using [14]. Randomization is still a powerful basis for causal inference, but the researcher must allow for some influence on the outcome variable of the fact that subjects knew that they were using a particular technique in an experiment.

Random treatment allocation is a very strong requirement, and in quasi-experimental designs, allocation is not randomized. This means that in statistical inference, the the estimation of the population difference δ_{AB} contains a systematic displacement (bias). To get the true value of δ_{AB}, this displacement has to somehow be estimated. If this is not possible, qualitative reasoning may still be possible:

☐ For example, if we observe a large productivity increase in the experimental group that used a new software engineering technique in a randomized controlled trial, then we may conclude that part of this is due to the new technique and part of it is due to the novelty of the technique, even though we cannot quantify these different contributions.

Quasi-Experimental Designs

In **quasi-experiments,** assignment of a treatment to objects of study is not random. This means that the sample itself is not selected randomly from the population, and/or the treatments are not allocated randomly to elements of the sample.

One kind of quasi-experimental design is the a **nonequivalent group design,** in which the researcher does not do the allocation at all, but nature does. For example, participants may select themselves into one or the other group. The researcher must now measure relevant variables in a pretest and compare outcomes only for subjects that have similar pretest scores:

☐   Janzen and Saiedian [11] describe a number of quasi-experiments in which test-driven development was compared with traditional development. In test-driven development, tests are developed before coding, and in traditional development, tests are developed after coding. The goal was to find any differences in simplicity, cohesion, and coupling of the code developed by these methods.

   The experimental groups included practitioners who volunteered for the experiments and graduate and undergraduate students who participated in a course. Pretests were used to detect any relevant differences between test-first and test-last groups, i.e., differences in variables that could influence the outcomes. Variables tested for were programming experience, age, and acceptance of test-driven development [11, p. 79].

   Any effect of detected differences were blocked out by only comparing test-first and test-last groups with similar pretest scores. Other conditions were held constant. Instruction in the relevant test-first and test-last methods was done as impartially as possible to avoid any influence of teacher preference for one or the other method.

   One outcome was that test-first programmers tended to write smaller and simpler methods and classes. This suggests a causal influence of test-first programming on writing smaller methods and classes. Perhaps the mechanism for this is that programmers who once did test-first programming will always keep attention for the testability of their programs and write simpler programs that are better testable than more complex programs.

In a second kind of quasi-experimental design, the researcher allocates treatments nonrandomly, according to a criterion. This is called a **regression discontinuity design,** because the researcher hopes that at the cutoff point of the criterion, a discontinuity in outcomes will appear. If it appears, the researcher will try to reason that this discontinuity can be attributed to the experimental treatment:

☐   Suppose you want to investigate whether your new experimental programming technique has an effect on programming effort. In your software engineering class, there is a group of highly competent students who finish 1 week ahead of the rest, and you decide to test the technique on them. They do a programming assignment using your technique. Suppose that you have managed to keep all relevant conditions identical to the conditions in the rest of the class: task difficulty, program size, time of day, and teaching method. A plot of programming effort against student competence reveals that higher competence corresponds to lower effort but that for the treatment group there is an additional drop in programming effort that is unlikely to be explainable by the higher competence of these students alone. This is evidence that for these highly competent students, your new technique reduces programming effort compared to the other techniques used in the class.

A third quasi-experimental design is the **interrupted time-series design.** This is a longitudinal design in which objects of study are monitored for a while before and after a treatment is applied, and it is hoped that at the time of the treatment a discontinuity in outcomes will appear that can be attributed to the experimental treatment:

☐   Kitchenham et al. [13] investigated the quality of reports on human-centric software engineering experiments published in the periods 1993–2002 and 2006–2010, to see if the intervening period, 2003–2005, can be viewed as break in a quality trend. Well-known guidelines for software engineering experimentation have been published from 2000 to 2002 [12, 14, 31] and would have had effect from about the year 2006 and later. This is an interrupted time-series design.

> The authors took care to construct a homogeneous sample from the two time periods, avoiding a selection effect as much as possible. Each paper was assigned randomly to three authors, and the three assessments were done according to objective scoring rules, to avoid assignment effects. Interrater agreement was assessed and found to be acceptable. The authors found a steady increase in quality over the two time periods but no clear break in the trend (acceleration or otherwise) in the intervening period.

Shadish et al. [26] give an exhaustive overview of quasi-experimental designs. Cook and Campbell [3] give more information on statistical inference in quasi-experimental designs, as does the more recent treatment by West [30]. Berk [2] provides an insightful methodological analysis of quasi-experimental designs. Treatments of quasi-experimental designs in software engineering are given by Juristo and Moreno [12] and by Wohlin et al. [32].

Whatever the sampling or allocation mechanism, in quasi-experimental designs the researcher must do at least one pretest to measure systematic differences between treatment groups and do at least one posttest to check if these variables have changed and could therefore have influenced the outcome. Causal reasoning now takes the following form:

- If all relevant variables U_i are included in the pretest and posttest measurements,
- and two samples are exposed to A and B, respectively,
- and the difference between the pretest and posttest values of U_i does not provide a full explanation of a measured difference $d_{AB} = \overline{Y}_A - \overline{Y}_B$, then
- the difference between A and B must have caused part of the difference d_{AB}.

There are some very important differences with RCTs. First, there is no requirement of random sampling. This means that if we use statistical inference to infer a statistical model, there is a displacement (bias) with respect to the true statistical model. Second, there is no requirement of random allocation. This too introduces a displacement in any statistical model that we would infer from the samples.

If all relevant variables U_i have the same values in both samples and in pretest and in posttest measurements, they did not change and cannot have had an influence. The causal conclusion is then that

> at the measured levels u_i, the effect of the difference between A and B on the sample is d_{AB}.

Otherwise, if the measured levels of U_i differ across samples or have changed during the experiment, we must assume that they may have had an effect. If we cannot quantify this effect, we can still use qualitative reasoning as illustrated above.

One of the assumptions of causal inference from quasi-experiments is that we have included all relevant variables. But when is a variable "relevant"? For this we need a **theory of the experiment** that includes all factors that may influence A. The discussion of the validity of a causal inference is in fact a discussion of this theory and of the degree of support that this theory gives to a claim that the difference between A and B contributed to the difference in Y:

☐ In the quasi-experiment of Janzen and Saiedian described above, variables measured in pretests were programming experience, age, and acceptance of test-driven development [11, p. 79]. The theory of the experiment is that differences in these variables could influence the simplicity, cohesion, and coupling of the code and that to detect any relevant differences between test-first and test-last groups, the effects of these other variables should be kept constant. The theory also includes the assumption that the effect of the difference between test-first and test-last development is independent of these other variables.

14.2.3 Validity of Causal Explanations

Causal inference is ampliative and has to be supported by arguments that do not provide total certainty. Many of the factors that should be considered when searching for a causal explanation of outcomes are listed in Table 14.2.[1] These factors should be controlled when designing and executing the research, and any factors that could not be controlled should be included in the list of possible causal explanations of the outcome.

An *ambiguous relationship* between X and Y makes it hard to exclude the possibility of a causal relationship between X and Y. Correlation could be nonzero but low, temporal precedence may be ambiguous, and a spatial connection may be present but tenuous.

The *object of study* may experience various mechanisms that may disturb or invalidate causal inference. The checklist in Table 14.2 mentions the following:

- *Unit interaction:* Objects of study may interact during a study.
- *History:* Events in the context of the experiment, unrelated to the treatment, may influence the OoS.
- *Maturation:* Some components of an object of study, e.g., people, can change during the study, for example, by getting older or by getting tired.
- *Dropout* (also called *attrition* or *mortality*): People can drop out of an investigation too early, influencing the sample statistics and their variance.

Table 14.2 Some threats to internal validity of a causal inference

- *Ambiguous relationship:* ambiguous covariation, ambiguous temporal ordering, ambiguous spatial connection?
- *OoS dynamics:* could there be interaction among OoSs? Could there be historical events, maturation, dropout of OoSs?
- *Sampling influence:* could the selection mechanism influence the OoSs? Could there be a regression effect?
- *Treatment control:* what other factors than the treatment could influence the OoSs? The treatment allocation mechanism, the experimental setup, the experimenters and their expectations, the novelty of the treatment, compensation by the researcher, resentment about the allocation?
- *Treatment instrument validity:* do the treatment instruments have the effect on the OoS that you claim they have?
- *Measurement influence:* will measurement influence the OoSs?

Sampling may involve some mechanisms that are relevant for causal inference too. If subjects are selected on a criterion, or if they self-select, there may be systematic differences among groups that will affect outcomes. Even random selection and allocation may influence the subjects of these selection decisions. For example, subjects may feel flattered and work extra hard. This is called a **selection effect.**

Different, but equally relevant, is the so-called **regression effect.** If selected objects score extremely low (or high) on some property before being selected into a sample or into a treatment, then they are likely to perform better (or worse) on the same property during the experiment. This is called regression toward the mean. In the long run, this is a random fluctuation, but in the short run, it might be mistaken for a treatment effect.

Treatment must be *controlled,* which means that the experimenter must control other influences than the treatment. The checklist in Table 14.2 mentions the following:

* *Selection.* Nonrandom selection or allocation introduces systematic bias into a sample or group.
* *Experimental setup.* Subjects may respond to the experimental setup: the location in a special room, lighting, noise, special equipment, etc.
* *Experimenter expectation.* Experimenters may hope for a particular outcome, causing them to behave in a certain way. This may influence the outcome.
* *Novelty.* Subjects who perceive the treatment to be novel may respond to this novelty.
* *Experimenter compensation.* Experimenters who know that a subject is getting a treatment believed not to be effective may compensate for this by providing extra care for these subjects.
* *Subject rivalry or demoralization.* Subjects who know that they have not been selected into a promising treatment may compensate for this by working extra hard. Or they may get demoralized and work less hard.

Shadish et al. [26, p. 73] classify these factors as threats to construct validity. If any of them is present, the researchers are in fact applying another treatment than they think that they are applying.

All of the above threats can be mitigated by keeping both experimenter and subjects unaware of which treatment is being applied. This is not possible in software engineering, where subjects know which technique they are applying. These threats to treatment validity can still be mitigated by repeating the treatment but now with switched allocations, which is called a crossover design. This may create maturation effects in the objects of study, because they may learn something from the first treatment that they can apply in the second. In Chap. 20 on statistical difference-making experiments, we show a design that has dealt with a number of these threats. Any threats that remain after designing the experiment must be blocked out computationally in some way in the statistical and causal inferences.

Returning to Table 14.2, *treatments* need *instruments,* and these need to be validated on their effectiveness. Will instruction sheets or lessons be understood as intended? Are they clear and unambiguous? Will they be used or ignored? If the treatment requires software, would this provide occasion for the students to chat online with other subjects or with their friends?

Measurement is relevant for causal reasoning, because measurement can influence the measured phenomena. If such an influence occurs, it is called a **testing effect.** Measurement instruments like interviews and questionnaires have some influence on subjects, and the relevance of this effect should be assessed in causal inference.

14.3 Architectural Explanations

Recall from Chap. 9 (Scientific Theories) that an *architectural explanation* says that

phenomenon E happened in the object of study because components $C_1, \ldots, C_n$ of the object of study interacted to produce E.

The interactions that produced E are collectively called the **mechanism** that produced E. Mechanisms may be deterministic or nondeterministic, i.e., they can produce their phenomenon always, or according to some possibly unknown probability distribution. Architectural explanation of E is also called **architectural inference.**

To give an architectural explanation of a phenomenon in an object of study, we need to show that the OoS has an architecture with components whose interaction produced the phenomenon. To do this, we need to analyze which interactions are possible given the capabilities/limitations of the components and the architecture of the object of study. This is an analytic activity, as we analyze an architectural structure to understand how global phenomena were produced.

Note also that the capabilities of components are unobservable. We can observe how a component behaves in a particular situation, but we cannot observe its capabilities. In architectural explanation, we often make assumptions about component capabilities that must be verified when we apply the explanation on a particular case:

☐ In the MARP problem [17], a simulation was run of a busy day at Schiphol airport, and delays experienced by aircraft in the simulation were measured. Delays were smaller than on the real airport at a similarly busy day. A *causal explanation* of this is that the aircraft were intelligent agents that could dynamically adapt their taxi route planning to incidents. The delay reduction was caused by the MARP treatment.

But why does the MARP treatment reduce delays? This question became urgent once it became evident that in random route networks, the MARP treatment did not reduce delays at all. Can this be explained? The analysis of the simulations revealed two architectural explanations why MARP reduced delays at airports:

– A small set of starting points and destinations at the edge of the infrastructure produces queues of agents moving in the same direction.
– An even spread of arrival and departure times produces small queues.

These phenomena reduced the number of incidents in which an agent had to wait for a higher-priority agent to enter a resource first and made it possible to respond to incidents that did occur in a way that would not cause delays in other aircraft. Note that these explanations are analytic and qualitative. They follow from a logical analysis of the architecture of a airport-aircraft system, the physical layout of the routes, and the behavior of aircraft, but they cannot explain the exact delay reduction numerically. Note also that in this case, component capabilities are known. The components have been designed by the researcher to have multi-agent route planning capabilities.

☐ A report in a Dutch IT magazine about failures of government IT projects focused on the tendering process [8]. Tendering seems to cause projects to finish over time and over budget.

   To give an architectural explanation of this, we decompose the tendering process into one client (a government organization) who puts out a call for tender and two or more vendors competing in the call. Several mechanisms for failure in this architecture have been identified, including the following two:

   – In an attempt to eliminate risks, government organizations specify requirements in a call for tender in great detail. This makes tendering more expensive than it would otherwise have been. And if requirements are not known in detail in advance of the project, it will cause problems later on, for example, when requirements change.
   – In order to get their project proposal accepted by decision-makers higher up in government, government organizations tend to estimate project cost too low. Suppliers tend to go along with this in order to win the tender: They know they can bill extra time later on. This mechanism is almost guaranteed to lead to time and budget overruns.

   In this example, we assume that all governments have these capabilities and limitations. When we apply this explanation to a particular tendering process, we must verify them. Perhaps we encounter a case where government organizations do not have these limitations.

☐ The study by Sabherwal [23] explained informal coordination at the start of an outsourcing project causally by the fact that vendors present outsourcing as an informal partnering relationship. We can now reframe this explanation architecturally. The architecture of the situation is simple. Its components are vendors and clients, and they interact by marketing, searching, contracting, and outsourcing activities. The causal explanation can be explained architecturally if we assume that vendors want to acquire clients even if these misunderstand the coordination requirements of out-sourcing and if we assume that clients have no experience with outsourcing. This would explain that vendors misrepresent coordination requirements and that clients believe this misrepresentation. This architectural explanation refers to components and their capabilities and limitations. It also makes the scope of the original causal explanation clear, as the causal explanation will not be valid in cases where vendors and clients have other capabilities and limitations.

☐ The causal explanation of the phenomena studied by Hildebrand et al. [9] is that a consumer preference change was caused by feedback. As we have seen earlier, Hildebrand et al. give an explanation of this in terms of the capabilities and limitations of people, e.g., the tendency to conform to the opinion of peers. Prior scientific research makes plausible that most people have this particular capability/limitation.

These examples illustrate that architectural explanations can explain causal relationships and do so analytically in terms of architectural components and their capabilities and in terms of mechanisms by which these components interact to produce the phenomenon of interest.

As an aside, note also that threats to validity of causal explanations (Table 14.2, p. 187) are themselves architectural explanations of possible causal influences.

14.3.1   Research Designs for Architectural Inference

If architectural explanations are analytical, why do we need empirical research? We can give an architectural explanation once we have an architectural model.

The following examples illustrate that we need empirical research to check the assumptions made by an architectural explanation. Some of these assumptions are idealizations about the capabilities of components, and these have to be checked in each case to which the explanation is applied.

In addition, in the case of real-world research, we need to check if the mechanisms postulated by the explanation still occur when other potentially interfering mechanisms are present too. Just as for purely causal explanations a multitude of factors not mentioned in the explanation can drown the causal relationship that we are interested in, for architectural explanations a multitude of mechanisms not mentioned in the explanation can interfere and eventually kill the mechanisms that we are interested in [19]:

☐ In the DOA project, an analysis of the architecture of the context of array antennas allows one to prove that $\phi = 2\pi (d/\lambda)\sin \theta$, where d is the distance between adjacent antennas, λ is the wavelength, θ is the angle of incidence, and ϕ is the phase difference of a wave between two adjacent antennas. The assumptions of this analysis are that waves are plane, i.e., that the wave source is infinitely far away, and that if more than one plane wave arrives at an antenna, these do not interfere. These assumptions are strictly false in the real world, but in the intended application domain (TV reception by cars), they are nearly satisfied. Empirical research is still needed to check whether the formula still holds for antenna's and waves in the real world.

☐ In the MARP project, architectural explanations were developed in two rounds. In the first round, an analytical argument made plausible that multi-agent route planning could reduce delays. This argument was architectural, as it referred to components (agents) and their capabilities (dynamic route planning) and interactions (incidents). In the second round, empirical data from simulations showed that delays sometimes reduced and sometimes increases. A new analytical argument was found that explained this in terms of agent behavior in airports and in random networks.

☐ In the government tendering example, the architecture of tendering processes was known in advance, and empirical research showed that tendering caused projects to be over time and budget. Architectural analysis explained this in terms of capabilities and limitations of government organizations and software vendors. This analysis made assumptions based on the behavior of these actors that were observed in case studies.

The examples illustrate that architectural inference is case based, not sample based. It is about the architecture of population elements, not about the properties of samples of population elements or about the population distribution of a variable.

Table 14.3 shows three case-based research designs that we have briefly discussed in Chaps. 5 and 7 on implementation evaluation and treatment validation. In an *observational case study,* the researcher studies a single case without intervening and explains observations in terms of the case architecture. This can be used in implementation evaluation. In a *single-case mechanism experiment,* the researcher experiments with a single case and explains observed behavior in terms of the case architecture. This can be used to evaluate implementations as well as to validate treatments. In *technical action research,* the researcher uses an artifact to help a client and explains the outcome architecturally in terms of the case. We illustrate these methods in detail in Chaps. 17 to 19. Here, we discuss guidelines for how to infer mechanisms and architectures.

Table 14.3 Three research designs to support architectural inference. The numbers between brackets refer to the chapters where these designs are explained

	Observational	Experimental
Case	• Observational case study (17)	• Single-case experiment (18)
		• Technical action research (19)
Sample	—	—

14.3.2 Inferring Mechanisms in a Known Architecture

When you investigate an artifact in a context, then the architecture of the artifact has been designed, and the architecture of the context is given. What knowledge can we use to infer mechanisms in these architectures and mechanisms in the interaction between these architectures? In our examples, we have seen several kinds of knowledge sources:

☐ *Scientific theory and design knowledge.* In the DOA example, the architectural analysis is done using knowledge from physics, design properties of an antenna, and some mathematical theory.

☐ *Scientific theory.* In the consumer feedback example, there is an architectural analysis too, in terms of social mechanisms of human actors [9]. These mechanisms arise from affective capabilities and limitations of the human actors that are known to exist from social psychology.

☐ *Useful facts and design knowledge.* Architectural analysis in the MARP example was done based on useful facts about airports and design knowledge about the capabilities of actors in an MARP system.

☐ *Primary documents and practical knowledge of subjects.* The mechanisms in the government by studying primary documents in these cases and interviewing subjects.

☐ *Practical knowledge of subjects.* The conceptual models of the ARE project [20] were found by interviewing subjects and reading the professional literature about agile projects.

This is the knowledge context of design science research as listed in Chap. 1 (p. 7), extended with subject knowledge from the context of the artifact itself. In social systems, we often need subject knowledge to infer social mechanisms.

14.3.3 Inferring Architectures

Inferring unknown architectures is more difficult than inferring mechanisms in known architectures. Major breakthroughs in the history of science are often discoveries of previously unknown architectures. For example, astronomers made a major breakthrough when they finally understood the architecture and mechanisms of the solar system [15], and biologists made a major breakthrough when they finally understood the components and mechanisms of fermentation [1]. In the social sciences, discovery of an architecture is often less dramatic. Often, the people participating in a social system are aware of architectural structures of the system. Here are two examples. The first example shows how a social architecture can

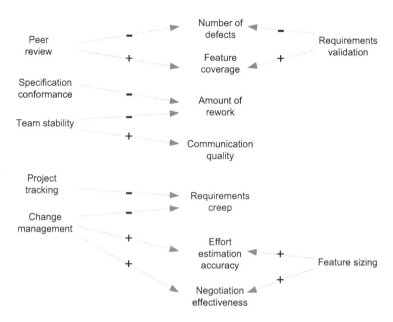

Fig. 14.2 Some perceived influences of requirements engineering improvement, reported in a case study by Damian and Chisan [4]

be uncovered; the second is a spectacular example of discovery of a biological architecture:

☐ Damian and Chisan [4] studied a software development organization in which requirements engineering was introduced. Figure 14.2 shows the results of opinion surveys of developers in the organization about the impact of the introduction of requirements engineering. The nodes in the graph are variables; the arrows are causal influences perceived by stakeholders in the development organization. In other words, the diagram represents the theory that developers in the studied organization have about the effects of the introduction of requirements engineering in their organization. It is a causal theory.

  Figure 14.3 shows the architecture of the organization after requirements engineering practices had been implemented. This diagram is extracted from the descriptions by Damian and Chisan, who in turn acquired the information from primary documents and from interviews with developers:

– Change management is implemented by the change control board. Previously, customers could contact developers directly with requests for new requirements, which is a mechanism that contributes to requirements creep. The change control board prevents this mechanism to occur and so reduces requirements creep, which in turn makes effort estimates more accurate.
– All other root variables in Fig. 14.2 are activities performed by the cross-functional team, which is a team of representatives from design, programming, testing, and product management that meets weekly to discuss requirements, design, tests, and coding. Compared to the period before the introduction of cross-functional teams, this improved effort estimation too, as well as feature coverage, and the quality of communication among developers, and it reduced requirements creep, the amount of rework, and the number of defects.

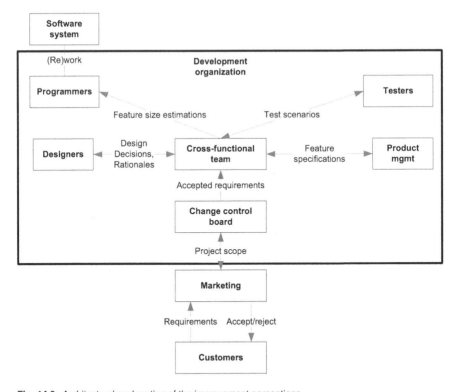

Fig. 14.3 Architectural explanation of the improvement perceptions

The causal model in Fig. 14.2 says which variables are believed by developers to influence which other variables. The architectural model in Fig. 14.3 explains how these perceived influences came about. The variables in the causal model are properties of the components or of interactions between components in the architectural model.

☐ In the mid-nineteenth century, John Snow inferred that cholera was transmitted by invisible agents, now called germs. The then dominant theory was that cholera was transmitted by poisonous particles in the air, the so-called miasma theory. Snow's proposed mechanism of transmission is that small organisms (germs) pass into the alimentary system by means of food or drink and then spread a poison that causes the body to expel water. The organisms pass out of the body with these evacuations, contaminating water supplies, from which it infected new victims. The problem is that all of this assumes invisible components (germs) with unknown capabilities that interacts with the body to produce a disease by a hitherto unknown mechanism. Snow's reasoning is an exemplar of architectural inference, which is why we frame it in Table 14.3.3 [6, 27–29].

14.3.4 Validity of Architectural Explanations

An architectural explanation explains a phenomenon in terms of component inter-actions. There are three ways in which an architectural explanation is fallible: It

Table 14.4 Architectural inference strategies used by Snow to support his theory that cholera is transmitted by germs

- *Multiple case studies:* Snow investigated individual disease cases. However, one case study, e.g., one patient history, is not enough, and he studied many
- *Detailed data collection:* each case is investigated in detail. Snow talked to every surviving patient that he could track and to family and neighbors of patients who had died and collected data about the physical location of water wells, sewers, water inlets of water companies, sewage disposal locations, and the effect of the tides in rivers on sewage floating in the river
- *Selection of positive and negative cases:* Snow investigated a great number of positive cases, i.e., patients who contracted the disease, and negative cases, i.e., cases that could have contracted the disease but did not. The positive cases could all be explained by his hypothetical mechanism, e.g., because they drank from a polluted water supply. The negative cases could be explained by their avoidance of such sources of pollution
- *Analytical reasoning:* Snow's reasoning is analytical: In each individual case, he tried to show that the case phenomena could only be explained by his hypothetical mechanism. His reasoning resembles that of a lawyer trying to prove that an actor is guilty, trying to maintain the highest standards of analytical rigor because the accused was hitherto unknown and is still invisible
- *Alternative explanations:* for each individual case, Snow considered all possible alternative explanations and showed in each case that they cannot explain his observations
- *Reasoning by analogy:* an important source for Snow's germ hypothesis is the analogy and disanalogy of the phenomena of transmission of cholera with the phenomena of transmission of other diseases. Snow takes the most similar phenomena and hypothesizes a similar mechanism compatible with the data
- *Consistency with statistics:* most of Snow's arguments are qualitative, but he does give some simple descriptive statistics to show that the locations of the patients match the location of polluted water supplies. The statistics also show that the mechanism of germ transmission is nondeterministic. Not all who drink from polluted water supply get cholera, and not all of those who get cholera die. Neither Snow nor the rival "miasma" theory offers explanations for this nondeterminism

may contain errors of analysis, the simplifying assumptions of the architecture may be violated in a real-world case, and the real-world case contains additional mechanisms that interfere with our conclusions (Table 14.3.4).

First, mistakes of *analysis*. We may have made mistakes when deriving that an architecture will produce some effect. Mathematical proofs are usually analyzed by mathematicians until they stand beyond unreasonable doubt, but for non-mathematical arguments, reasonable doubt is already quite a stringent standard.

Second, the world is full of *variation*, and architectures are seldom encountered in their pure form. The explanation may assume capabilities that the real-world components may not have, and some components assumed by the explanation may be entirely absent.

Third, every architectural explanation is an *abstraction* because it ignores many components and mechanisms present in the real world but not mentioned in the

Table 14.5 Requirements for the internal validity of an architectural explanation

---

- *Analysis:* the analysis of the architecture may not support its conclusions with mathematical certainty. Are components fully specified? Are interactions fully specified?
- *Variation:* do the real-world case components match the architectural components? Do they have the same capabilities? Are all architectural components present in the real-world case?
- *Abstraction:* does the architectural model used for explanation omit relevant elements of real-world cases? Are the mechanisms in the architectural model interfered with by other mechanisms, absent from the model but present in the real world case?

---

explanation. These may interfere with the components and mechanisms mentioned in the explanation, rendering the explanation false in a real-world case:

- ☐ In the requirements engineering improvement example, the interaction between the cross-functional team and the change control board may not have been analyzed properly, and the conclusion that they prevent requirements creep does not follow literally from the definition of these two teams.
- ☐ Even if there is no mistake of analysis, in a new case with a similar architecture, we may find that the cross-functional team may not have the authority to make decisions as assumed by the architectural model. In this variant of the architecture, not all phenomena that occur may be explainable in the same way as in the previous case.
- ☐ In a new case with a similar architecture, we may find that even though the components have the same capabilities as in the previous case, there are additional mechanisms, not mentioned in the explanations so far, that interfere with the explanatory mechanisms of the previous case. For example, members of a change control board in the new case may have to deal with pressures from the sales department to favor particular customers.

14.4 Rational Explanations

14.4.1 Goals and Reasons

A *rational explanation* explains the behavior of an actor in terms of the goals of the actor. It says that

a phenomenon occurred because the actor wanted to achieve a goal.

This sounds somewhat like the contribution arguments discussed in Chap. 6 (Requirements Specification), but there is an important difference. A contribution argument says that an artifact that satisfies the requirements will contribute to stakeholder goals. This argument is given by the designer and agreed on with the stakeholders. In empirical research, by contrast, the researcher does not have to agree with the goals of the actors, and he or she does not have to believe that the actions performed by the actors contribute to their goals. The researcher just simply explains actions of an actor in terms of the actor's belief that they will contribute to their goals.

Table 14.6   Threats to the internal validity of a rational explanation

---
* *Goals:* The actor may not have the goals that the explanation says it has
* *Motivation:* a goal may not motivate an actor as much as the explanation says it did
---

To do this, the researcher does have to adopt some of the concepts used by the actors that he or she studies. The following example takes an architectural point of view, where the architecture components are social actors with goals:

☐   Myers [18] explains the failure of an information systems implementation project performed for the New Zealand government. Goals of different stakeholders motivated actions that were rational compared to these goals. However, the combined effect of all these locally rational actions led to a very expensive project failure, which became all the more disastrous because it was the goal of one of the stakeholders to make this failure visible to as many members of the general public as possible [18, p. 197].

This illustrates that architectural explanations can be combined with rational explanations. We have already seen an example of this earlier when we discussed the ARE project in Chap. 9 (p. 99).

14.4.2   Validity of Rational Explanations

Table 14.4.2 lists threats to the validity of rational explanations. For example, the explanation may attribute goals to an actor in a case that the actor does not, in fact, have. Or the explanation may suppose that an actor performed an action to achieve a goal while the actor in fact did not have that motivation:

* In the highly politicized situation that Myers [18] investigated, actors may have misrepresented their goals and may have had other motivations than the ones they stated to the researcher.

14.5   Internal Validity

Abductive reasoning is fallible, and the **internal validity** of an explanation is the degree of support for the abductive inference that has led to it.[2] Threats to the validity of causal, architectural, and rational explanations have been listed in Tables 14.2, 14.3.4, and 14.4.2. They are all parts of our checklist.

14.6   Summary

* Abductive inference is searching for the best possible explanation of a case description or statistical model.

- Causal explanations explain a phenomenon by an earlier phenomenon that caused it. Various cross-sectional and longitudinal designs can support such an explanation, among which are the classical randomized controlled trial and quasi-experiments.
- Architectural explanations explain a phenomenon by a mechanism that produced it. The mechanism is an interaction among architectural components. There is a variety of research designs that can provide data to support an architectural explanation.
- Rational explanations explain an actor's actions in terms of reasons for those actions, which are defined in terms of the actor's goals. Rational explanations usually assume a social architecture in which the actor plays a role.

Notes

[1]**Page 187, threats to the validity of causal inference.** This is the list of important threats to internal validity given by Shadish et al. [26, p. 55], minus the threat of instrumentation, plus the threat of unit interaction. Instrumentation has been listed in this book earlier, both as a threat to treatment validity and as a threat to measurement validity. The absence of unit interaction is part of Rubin's [22] **stable unit treatment value assumption** (SUTVA), the other part being the absence of a allocation effect. The absence of selection effects is called **strong ignorability** by Rubin [21].

[2] **Page 197, internal validity.** Shadish et al. define *internal validity* as the validity of inferences about whether the relationship between two variables is causal (p. 508). It is called *internal* to contrast it with validity outside the study setting, which is called external [3, p. 37]. Because we recognize three different kinds of explanations, internal validity in this book includes the validity of causal, architectural, and rational explanations.

References

1. W. Bechtel, R.C. Richardson, *Discovering Complexity: Decomposition and Localization as Strategies in Scientific Research* (MIT Press, Cambridge, 2010). Reissue of the 1993 edition with a new introduction
2. R.A. Berk, Causal inference for sociological data, in *Handbook of Sociology*, ed. by N.J. Smelser (Sage, Thousand Oaks, 1988), pp. 155–172
3. T.D. Cook, D.T. Campbell, *Quasi-Experimentation: Design and Analysis Issues for Field Settings* (Rand-McNally, Skokie, 1979)
4. D. Damian, J. Chisan, An empirical study of the complex relationships between requirements engineering processes and other processes that lead to payoffs in productivity, quality and risk management. IEEE Trans. Softw. Eng. **32**(7), 433–453 (2006)
5. I. Douven, Abduction, in *The Stanford Encyclopedia of Philosophy*, ed. by A.N. Zalta. Spring 2011 Edition (2011)
6. D.A. Freedman, Statistical models and shoe leather. Sociol. Methodol. **21**, 291–313 (1991). Reprinted in [7, p. 45–62]
7. D.A. Freedman, *Statistical Models and Causal Inference: A Dialogue With the Social Sciences*, ed. by D. Collier, J.S. Sekhon, P.B. Stark (Cambridge University Press, Cambridge, 2010)
8. N. Groen, Overheid krijgt geen grip of IT-projecten. Automatiseringsgids, 11th April 2013, pp. 22–23

9. C. Hildebrand, G. Häubl, A. Herrmann, J.R. Landwher, When social media can be bad for you: Community feedback stifles consumer creativity and reduces satisfaction with self-designed products. Inf. Syst. Res. **24**(1), 14–29 (2013)
10. P.W. Holland, Statistics and causal inference. J. Am. Stat. Assoc. **81**(396), 945–960 (1986)
11. D.S. Janzen, H. Saiedian, Does test-driven development really improve software design quality? IEEE Softw. **25**(2), 77–84 (2008)
12. N. Juristo, A. Moreno, *Basics of Software Engineering Experimentation* (Kluwer, Dordrecht, 2001)
13. B. Kitchenham, D.I.K. Sjøberg, R. Dybå, O.P. Brereton, D. Budgen, M. Höst, P. Runeson, Trends in the quality of human-centric software engineering experiments—a quasi-experiment. IEEE Trans. Softw. Eng. **39**(7), 1002–1017 (2013)
14. B.A. Kitchenham, S.L. Pfleeger, D.C. Hoaglin, K.E. Emam, J. Rosenberg, Preliminary guidelines for empirical research in software engineering. IEEE Trans. Softw. Eng. **28**(8), 721–733 (2002)
15. T. Kuhn, *The Structure of Scientific Revolutions*, 2nd enlarged edn. (University of Chicago Press, Chicago, 1970)
16. M. Mooney Marini, B. Singer, Causality in the social sciences. Sociol. Methodol. **18**, 347–409 (1988)
17. A.W. ter Mors, *The World According to MARP*. PhD thesis, Delft University of Technology, March 2010. http://www.st.ewi.tudelft.nl/~adriaan/pubs/terMorsPhDthesis.pdf
18. M.D. Myers, A disaster for everyone to see: An interpretive analysis of a failed IS project. Account. Manag. Inf. Technol. **4**(4), 185–201 (1994)
19. R. Pawson, N. Tilley, *Realistic Evaluation* (Sage, Thousand oaks, 1997)
20. Z. Racheva, M. Daneva, A. Herrmann, A conceptual model of client-driven agile requirements prioritization: Results of a case study, in *IEEE International Symposium on Empirical Software Engineering and Measurement (ESEM)*, ed. by G. Succi, M. Morisio, N. Nagappan, Bolzano. (ACM, New York, 2010), pp. 39:1–39:4
21. D.B. Rubin, Bayesian inference for causal effects: The role of randomization. Ann. Stat. **6**(1), 34–58 (1978)
22. D.B. Rubin, Which ifs have causal answers. J. Am. Stat. Assoc. **81**(396), 961–962 (1986)
23. R. Sabherwal, The evolution of coordination in outsourced software development projects: A comparison of client and vendor perspectives. Inf. Organ. **13**, 153–202 (2003)
24. G. Schurz, Patterns of abduction. Synthese **164**, 201–234 (2008)
25. P. Sedgwick, Random sampling versus random allocation. Br. Med. J. **343**, d7453 (2011). http://dx.doi.org/10.1136/bmj.d7453
26. W.R. Shadish, T.D. Cook, D.T. Campbell, *Experimental and Quasi-Experimental Designs for Generalized Causal Inference* (Houghton Mifflin, Boston, 2002)
27. J. Snow, On the mode of communication of cholera (1849)
28. J. Snow, On the model of propagation of cholera, part 1. Med. Times **24**, 559–562 (29 November 1851)
29. J. Snow, On the model of propagation of cholera, part 2. Med. Times **24**, 610–612 (13 December 1851)
30. S.G. West, J.C. Biesanz, S.C. Pitts, Causal inference and generalization in field settings: Experimental and quasi-experimental designs, in *Handbook of Research Methods in Social and Personality Psychology*, ed. by H.T. Reis, C.M. Judd (Cambridge University Press, Cambridge, 2000), pp. 40–84
31. C. Wohlin, P. Runeson, M. Höst, M. C. Ohlsson, B. Regnell, A. Weslén, *Experimentation in Software Engineering: An Introduction* (Kluwer, Dordrecht, 2002)
32. C. Wohlin, P. Runeson, M. Höst, M. C. Ohlsson, B. Regnell, A. Weslén, *Experimentation in Software Engineering*, 2nd edn. (Springer, Heidelberg, 2012)

Chapter 15
Analogic Inference Design

Analogic inference is generalization by similarity. In our schema of inferences (Fig. 15.1), analogic inference is done after abductive inference. What we generalize about by analogy is not a description of phenomena, nor a statistical model of a population, but an explanation. In Sect. 15.1, we show that it can be used in case-based and in sample-based research. In Sect. 15.2, we contrast feature-based similarity with architectural similarity and show that architectural similarity gives a better basis for generalization than feature-based similarity. Analogic generalization is done by induction over a series of positive and negative cases, called analytical induction (Sect. 15.3). We discuss the validity of analogic generalizations in Sect. 15.4 and generalize the concept of generalization to that of a theory of similitude in Sect. 15.5.

15.1 Analogic Inference in Case-Based and in Sample-Based Research

In case-based research, after explanations for case observations have been found, we assess the generalizability of these explanations by assessing in which architecturally similar cases similar mechanisms could produce similar phenomena. In sample-based research, after explanations for a statistical model have been found, we assess if these models could also be valid for similar populations. Here are two examples, the first case based and the second sample based:

☐ Take again the case study of Sabherwal [14]. We saw that if vendors want to acquire clients even if these misunderstand the coordination requirements of outsourcing, and if clients have no experience with outsourcing there is an architectural mechanism that produces a low level of formalization early in the outsourcing project. We now infer analogically that this mechanism could happen in cases with a similar architecture too. We cannot predict with certainty that this will happen in all similar cases, because the components in these other cases may have other capabilities and limitations, and there may be additional mechanisms, such as legal requirements

© Springer-Verlag Berlin Heidelberg 2014
R.J. Wieringa, *Design Science Methodology for Information Systems and Software Engineering*, DOI 10.1007/978-3-662-43839-8__15

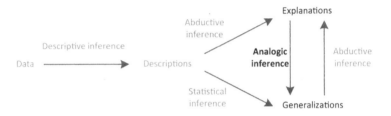

Fig. 15.1 Analogic inference generalizes to similar cases or populations

   on outsourcing, that can interfere the mechanism generalized about. We have to check this on a
   case-by-case basis.

☐ The other example discussed at the start of the previous chapter is the sample-based study
   by Hildebrand et al. [5]. We saw that feedback causes consumers to change their preferences
   in the direction of the feedback, and an architectural explanation of this refers to the social-
   psychological mechanism that people tend to conform to the opinion of peers. This allows the
   analogic generalization that other people in the same situation will behave similarly. Note that
   these explanations and generalizations are sample based. They are about what people do on
   the average. Since they are based on sample averages, the explanation and generalization are
   nondeterministic. Some people behave differently. We have to check this on a case-by-case basis.

These examples illustrate that analogic generalization is qualitative: We indicate
to which other cases, or populations of cases, an explanation can be generalized,
without indicating to how many of them we can generalize. The examples also
illustrate that what we really generalize about is the explanations, more in particular
about the mechanisms that are referred to in our architectural explanations.

   An analogic generalization is always case based and has the following form:

   In cases similar to this, it is plausible that this explanation is true.

This leaves us with the question how to define similarity. We can do this in a
feature-based and an architectural way.

15.2   Architectural Similarity Versus Feature-Based
Similarity

In the above examples, analogic generalization is done by looking at architectural
similarity. If we would restrict ourselves to variables, we would only be looking at
feature-based similarity, such as similarity in size, number, age, volume, speed,
etc. But similarity of features alone is a weak basis for generalization.

☐ Walnuts have a similar appearance to brains, but this does not imply that walnuts are intelligent.
   The magical belief that eating walnuts improves your brain is based on feature similarity, but this
   belief is false.

☐ On rare occasions, feature-based analogies may lead to correct conclusions. For example, in
   1749, Benjamin Franklin saw many shared features between lightning and "electric fluid" in his

laboratory [1, p. 197]: They both gave light, were crooked and swift, made a crackling noise, killed animals, and melted metals. In the laboratory, "electric fluid" was attracted by a metal rod. His conclusion by analogic inference was that lightning would be attracted by a metal rod too. An experiment proved him right.

Both examples contain feature-based analogies, because these analogies are not based on an understanding of mechanisms in the underlying architecture that could justify the analogy. The basis of both arguments is similarity in features, which is also the basis of sympathetic magic and wishful thinking. Very rarely, that kind of reasoning can lead to a correct conclusion, as in the second example. We now know that the composition of lightning and of "electric fluid" in Franklin's laboratory is the same, and it contains a mechanism that produces a similar effect in both cases. Franklin did not know that and coincidentally produced a correct conclusion for reasons not known to him.

We will require that analogic inference be based on **architectural similarity**: Source and target of the generalization must be cases with similar architecture that have components with similar capabilities and limitations so that they will respond to stimuli in a similar way. All examples of architectural explanations given in this book are candidates for analogic generalization:

☐ The DOA example defines an architecture for antenna arrays that the researchers then generalize about.
☐ The MARP example defines an architecture of airport logistics, which is then generalized about.
☐ Damian and Chisan's [3] case study of requirements engineering defines an architecture of development organizations that is generalized about.
☐ The two case studies by Mockus et al. [10], which we will describe below, define an architecture of open source projects generalized about.

Whenever we can give an architectural explanation, we are in a position to generalize to architecturally similar cases. The general form of analogic generalization is now this:

In cases with an architecture like this, it is plausible that this explanation is true.

The explanation itself can still be causal or architectural.

How do we know what the relevant similarity predicate is? For this we need analytical induction.

15.3 Analytical Induction

In **analytical induction**, an explanatory theory is tested by selecting cases with varying architectures, all similar to each other, but different enough to run the risk of not being able to reproduce the phenomenon.[1] Replications as well as falsifications are used to revise the theory so that it can explain all confirmations as well all falsifications. When a case falsifies a theory, the theory can be revised in two ways:

- The conceptual framework of the theory can be changed so that the falsifying case is not in the scope of the theory anymore.
- The generalization of the theory can be changed so that it is valid for all cases in scope so far.

Here are three examples:

☐ A nonstandard example from mathematics may clarify the process of analytical induction. The philosopher and historian of science Imre Lakatos analyzed and rationally reconstructed the history of the proof of Euler's conjecture that for a regular polyhedron, $V - E + F = 2$, where V is the number of vertices, E the number of edges, and F the number of faces [8]. The proof is explained in terms of physical polyhedra made of rubber. Let us view these polyhedra as members of a population of similar physical polyhedra, some made of rubber, others made of wood, etc. Due to architectural similarity, what can be shown to be true of the polyhedra made of rubber, where the conclusion only depends on the architectural properties of the polyhedra, can be generalized to polyhedra made of wood too.

Lakatos' [8, p. 7] initial proof goes as follows. First, the researcher removes one face of a polyhedron. For the remaining form, it remains to be proven that $V - E + F = 1$. The researcher flattens the rest of the rubber polyhedron by stretching it out and then systematically removes parts of it according to a procedure that does not affect the equation $V - E + F = 1$. An analytic argument shows that when the removal procedure ends, i.e., cannot be applied anymore, a triangle is left. For this triangle, $V - E + F = 1$ is true. Reasoning back, for the original polyhedron, $V - E + F = 2$ is true.

To see this as an example of analytical induction, consider the removal procedure as a mechanism, executed by the researcher, that has a predicted effect, namely, preserving the truth value of $V - E + F = 1$.

Lakatos shows that the proof has a history, in which mathematicians found counterexamples to the proof, namely, examples of polyhedra for which the removal mechanism does not produce the desired effect. One such counterexample is a hollow polyhedron, consisting of a large one containing a smaller one. There is a surprising number of counterexamples. Let us view these counterexamples as negative cases: They are examples for which the generalization $V - E + F = 2$ is false.

Each counterexample is dealt with by either *changing the definition of the concept* of a regular polyhedron, so that the counterexample is not element of the population of regular polyhedra anymore, or with *changing the mechanism description*, i.e., the removal procedure, so that the counterexample, and all previously tried cases, behaves properly under the redefined mechanism. This is analytical induction over a series of thought experiments in which imaginary mechanisms are tested in a mathematical structure. In this analytical induction, the generalization itself is saved, but the conceptual framework and mechanism descriptions are changed when negative cases are encountered.

☐ In the MARP example, simulations showed that multi-agent planning causes delay reduction during a busy day on Schiphol airport. By analogy, we infer that it will cause delay reductions on a busy day on any airport. What about a large airport during a strike, so that only three planes land that day? Or a small airport consisting of one runway, receiving 600 airplanes? These extreme cases falsify the claim of delay reduction. We can solve this by restricting our definition of airports to exclude extreme cases like this, e.g., by requiring a minimum number of runways for a given number of arriving airplanes. It is not unreasonable to exclude these extreme cases as not being similar enough to the airports for which these algorithms are intended to be useful. So we save the generalization by changing the definition of "airport."

☐ Mockus et al. [9] analyzed development and maintenance of the Apache and Mozilla open source projects. In the Apache case, they observed that the project has a core of about 10–15 developers who controlled the code base and created approximately 80 % or more of new functionality. This is a descriptive inference.

They explained this architecturally by the following mechanism [9, p. 9]:

- (Apache mechanism): "The core developers must work closely together, each with fairly detailed knowledge of what other core members are doing. Without such knowledge they would frequently make incompatible changes to the code. Since they form essentially a single team, they can be overwhelmed by communication and coordination overhead issues that typically limit the size of effective teams to 10–15 people."

This is an abductive inference.

To check whether we can generalize to architecturally similar projects, they investigated the Mozilla project. This is architecturally similar, yet different from the Apache project. It had a core of 22–36 developers who coordinated their work according to a concretely defined process and used a strict inspection policy and who each had control of a module and created approximately 80 % or more of new functionality. The authors therefore refined their explanation [10, p. 340]:

- (Apache and Mozilla mechanism): Open source developments have a core of developers who control the code base, and will create approximately 80 % or more of the new functionality. If this core group uses only informal ad hoc means of coordinating their work, the group will be no larger than 10–15 people.

Note that this refined explanation addresses both cases. The generalization is saved by reducing its scope.

Confirmation of a generalization in a new case study is gratifying and strengthens the support for the generalization. Falsification is more interesting, because it allows us to sharpen our conceptual framework, redefine a mechanism, or limit the scope of our generalization. Analytical induction proceeds until no negative cases can be found anymore or when the research budget is finished, whichever occurs first.

Analytical induction is used in case-based research, but as we saw above nothing prevents it from being used in sample-based research as well. After generalizing an architectural explanation of a statistical model to architecturally similar populations, we can investigate similar as well as dissimilar populations to check this generalization. If a confirmation is found, this is gratifying, and if a falsification is found, we redefine the concepts or restrict the scope of the analogic generalization. I am not aware of any examples of this in the literature.

15.4   External Validity

External validity is the degree of support for the generalization of a theory beyond the cases or populations on which a theory has been tested.[2] Table 15.1 lists requirements for the external validity of a research design.[3]

To support analogic generalization, the *object of study* must satisfy the population predicate. There will always be some mismatch, and the impact on this on generalizability must be assessed. In addition, the object of study may be an instance of more than one population predicate, and you have to check if your intended

Table 15.1 Requirements for external validity of a research design, repeated from the validity of research design (Chap. 11) and the validity of architectural explanation (Chap. 14)

- *Object of study*

    - *Population predicate*: will the OoS satisfy the population predicate? In which way will it be similar to the population elements? In which way will it be dissimilar?
    - *Ambiguity*: will the OoS satisfy other population predicates too? What could be the target of analogic generalization?

- *Representative sampling*

    - Sample-based research: will the study population, described by the sampling frame, be representative of the theoretical population?
    - Case-based research: in what way will the selected sample of cases be representative of the population?

- *Treatment*

    - *Treatment similarity*: is the specified treatment in the experiment similar to treatments in the population?
    - *Compliance*: is the treatment implemented as specified?
    - *Treatment control*: what other factors than the treatment could influence the OoSs? Could the implemented treatment be interpreted as another treatment?

- *Measurement*

    - *Construct validity*: are the definitions of constructs to be measured valid? Clarity of definitions, unambiguous application, avoidance of mono-operation and mono-method bias?
    - *Measurement instrument validity*: do the measurement instruments measure what you claim that they measure?
    - *Construct levels*: will the measured range of values be representative of the population range of values?

---

generalization would be valid for any of these predicates. Could you be generalizing to other populations too?

Sampling must satisfy some requirements too. In case-based research, to generalize by analogy from the studied cases to the unstudied cases, we must assess how representative the studied cases must be of the unstudied cases in the population. But when is a case representative? Representativeness must be defined in terms of architecture, and part of the goal of case-based research is to find out what architecture is essential for the phenomena being studied. If a case has this architecture, it can be regarded as representative of the population.

In sample-based research, statistical inference and interpretation of the results will take us from the sample to the study population, which is the population described by the sampling frame. Further generalization to the theoretical population will be by analogy. To support that inference, the study population should be representative, in a relevant sense, of the theoretical population.

To generalize about a *treatment*, the specified treatment must be similar to treatments in the target population, and the implemented treatment must be compliant to its specification, i.e., it must be implemented as specified. Third, the control requirements that support abductive reasoning also support generalization by analogy. If any additional influence is present in the experiment, we could interpret the experimental treatment differently from what is intended.

Measurements support analogic reasoning if constructs are operationalized and measured in a valid way. So the requirements of construct validity as described in Chap. 8 should be checked. In addition, instruments should be tested to check that they measure what they should measure. If these requirements are not met, then similarities may crumble away on closer inspection.

Finally, when generalizing the results to a population, we should consider whether the measured data are representative of the data that could be found in the population. If only a small range is measured, this is called **construct level confounding**.

☐   For example, X and Y may have a linear relation when we measure only a small range of values of a variable Y, but in the entire population the relationship may be nonlinear.

☐   If you measure the change in productivity of a new programming method and you test it only on novice programmers, then it is hard to draw conclusions about effects on productivity of expert programmers.

All of these requirements can be satisfied to a degree but not perfectly. Mismatches between the research design and these requirements are threats to the validity of an analogic inference from this research.

15.5   Beyond External Validity: Theories of Similitude

In design science, we often study a validation model of an artifact in context, which consists of a model of an artifact interacting with a model of a context. Here we are not always interested in similarity of the model and its target, and external validity is not exactly what we are after. It is sufficient to be able to learn something about the implemented artifact in a real-world context by studying the behavior of the validation model. This can be done by similarity, but also by difference. Here are four different ways that have been used in design sciences to study the relation between a validation model and its target:

☐   *Mathematical similarity*: In the years 1865–1867, the British engineer William Froude studied the relation between the resistance to surface waves of a scale model of a boat in a water tank and the resistance to surface waves of a real boat in open waters. If the dimensions of the real boat are n times the dimensions of the model, the behavior of the real boat is similar to that of the model if model velocities are multiplied by $\sqrt{n}$ and resistance to surface waves with n^3 [19, pp. 140, 292]. In the ensuing period, the method of dimensional analysis was developed, in which behavior is expressed in formulas with dimensionless terms that are valid for scale models as well as real-world artifacts [16]. Study of the scale model can thus yield information about the target of the model. Dimensionless formulas describe the relevant similarity between scale models and their targets.

☐   *Architectural similarity*: In drug research, animals are used as natural models to study how the human body would respond to a drug. This is done by identifying the biochemical and physiological mechanism triggered by a drug and investigating whether this mechanism also occurs in human beings. For example, Willner [20] reviews a number of physiological mechanisms that are shared between humans and other species. If the effect of a drug is known to be produced by such a shared mechanism, then the response of an animal of that species can be used as a model for the response of humans to that drug. Theories based on the study of animals can thus be *externally valid* with respect to human beings.

☐ *Extreme cases*: Another way to generalize from validation models to real-world targets is to test extreme cases in the laboratory and reason that if something has been shown for an extreme case in some dimension, it will probably also be true for less extreme cases. For example, in the study of Prechelt et al. [11], the effect of a source code commenting technique on maintenance effort was studied in a laboratory experiment. They reasoned that if this positive effect occurs in the relatively small and well-documented programs in the laboratory, the effect may be even more pronounced for larger and ill-documented programs in the real world [11, p. 604]. This is called **exterme-case reasoning**. It generalizes by *dis*similarity.

☐ *Empirical similarity*: Generalizability from a validation model to its real-world target is an empirical problem: If you want to know if generalization G about population A of laboratory models is also valid for population B of real-world targets, you test it on a sample of population B [4]. A number of software engineering researchers have done this to check if results obtained for students are valid for professionals too. Holt et al. [6], Höst et al. [7], Runeson [13], and Svahnberg et al. [17] all gave some task to different groups of students and professionals and measured the outcomes. They found some difference between graduates and professionals but found a larger difference between freshmen and professionals, for example, in the spread of some performance characteristics and difference in the mental models of programs.

All of these approaches require a **theory of similitude** between a validation model and its target. A theory of similitude has the following form:

- If the validation model and its real-world target have similarities S *and differences* D,
- and if the validation model has been observed to have properties P,
- then the target has possibly different properties P', other things being equal.

This generalizes analogic generalization, because the argument can be based on similarities or differences, and the target of generalization may show similar or dissimilar behavior. The theory of similitude should tell us how similar or how different. A theory like this requires empirical support like any other scientific theory. It is itself a generalization and is fallible, as expressed by the "other things being equal" phrase. Each of the above examples yields a theory of similitude.

The mathematical approach illustrated above is very precise about what needs to be similar and what can be different between model and target and can make precise predictions about P'.

Dimensional analysis is restricted to some domains of physical engineering and cannot be used for the virtual and social systems that we work with in software engineering or information systems engineering.

The architectural approach to developing a theory of similitude is common in drug research and aeronautical engineering, as illustrated by examples given by Willner [20] and Vincenti [19]. I am not aware of examples from software engineering and information systems engineering.

The extreme case approach makes a claim about what happens if you move from an extreme to less extreme cases along some dimension. This claim is a theory of similitude too. It needs to be supported by evidence that shows that the expected effect is not interfered with by other mechanisms that may happen in practice.

The empirical approach, finally, builds a statistical, descriptive theory of similitude in the form of a statistical model that relates student performance with the performance of professionals. For example, the papers mentioned in the example above test whether a property observed in students also occurs in professionals.

15.6 Summary

- Analogic inference is generalizing an explanation to cases or populations not yet investigated but that are similar to the ones already investigated.
- Architecture-based analogies give more support to analogic generalizations than feature-based analogies do, so we only consider architectural analogies:

    - The reasoning in architectural analogy is that if the target of the generalization has a similar architecture, then similar mechanisms will produce similar phenomena, other things being equal.

- Analogic generalization gains support by analytical induction, in which the theory is tested on a series of similar and dissimilar cases or populations.
- Generalization from a validation model to a real-world target can be supported by stronger means, namely, by a theory of similitude. This theory can itself gain support from architectural similarity or extreme case reasoning and in a few physical engineering branches by dimensional analysis. Theories of similitude can be tested empirically.

Notes

[1]**Page 203, analytical induction.** Analytical induction was introduced in sociology by the Polish sociologist Znaniecki, who attributes it to Plato and Galileo [22, p. 237]. Yin [21, p. 32] mentions analytical induction in his book on case study methodology but calls it "analytic generalization" and does not really explain it. The best description of analytical induction is given by Robinson [12]. Less well known but very informative too is the review by Tacq [18].

[2]**Page 205, external validity.** Shadish et al. [15, p. 507] define external validity as the validity of, i.e., the degree of support for, claims that a causal relationship holds for variations in research setups, called units, treatments, outcomes and settings (UTOS). The term UTOS was taken from Cronbach [2]. In this book, a research setup consists of an artifact U interacting with a context S, of which the outcomes O are measured, and that possibly receives a treatment T. So our research setup has the UTOS structure. External validity is then the degree of support for the claim that a causal, architectural, or rational explanation is valid for similar research setups.

[3]**Page 205, threats to external validity.** This list does not resemble the standard one from Shadish et al. [15], but it is in fact very similar. Shadish et al. mention the following threats:

- *Variation of causal relationship over units.* An effect found for some population elements may not hold for other population elements:

- Table 15.1 requires the OoS to be similar to the other population elements. So if we are able to explain a causal relationship architecturally and the population elements are architecturally similar, then it is plausible that the effect will occur in other population elements too. Failure to meet these requirements is a threat to external validity.

- *Variation of the causal relationship with variation over treatments*:

  - We require in Table 15.1 that experimental treatments are similar to treatments in the population.

- *Variation of the causal relationship with variations in outcome measures*. For example, a new technique may improve the reliability of a program but may make it slower to execute:

  - This does not correspond to a requirement in Table 15.1. Generalizing from one outcome variable to another outcome variable would be an example of feature-based similarity, which is a weak basis of analogic reasoning that is not supported here.

- *Variation of the causal relationship with settings*:

  - This is part of the requirements in Table 15.1, but indirectly. In our approach, the object of study consists of the artifact *and its context*. So this threat is already captured by our requirements on the object of study.

- *Context-dependent mediation*. In the words of Shadish et al. [15, p. 87], "an explanatory mediator of a causal relationship in one context may not mediate in another context":

  - In the terminology of this book, the mechanism that produced a causal effect in one case may not do so in another. This was mentioned as a threat to internal validity in Chap. 14. There, one threat to the validity of an architectural explanation was that the architecture could be the wrong abstraction of a case, and another threat was that in a real-world case, several mechanisms could interfere to give an unexpected result. These are also threats to external validity. An explanation may succeed in one case and fail in another.

References

1. P. Bartha, *By Parallel Reasoning* (Oxford University Press, Oxford, 2010)
2. L.J. Cronbach, *Designing Evaluations of Educational and Social Programs* (Jossey-Bass, San Francisco, 1982)
3. D. Damian, J. Chisan, An empirical study of the complex relationships between requirements engineering processes and other processes that lead to payoffs in productivity, quality and risk management. IEEE Trans. Softw. Eng. **32**(7), 433–453 (2006)
4. G. Gigerenzer, External validity of laboratory experiments: the frequency-validity relationship. Am. J. Psychol. **97**(2), 185–195 (1984)
5. C. Hildebrand, G. Häubl, A. Herrmann, J.R. Landwher, When social media can be bad for you: community feedback stifles consumer creativity and reduces satisfaction with self-designed products. Inf. Syst. Res. **24**(1), 14–29 (2013)
6. R.W. Holt, D.A. Boehm-Davis, A.C. Shultz, Mental representations of programs for student and professional programmers, in *Empirical Studies of Programmers: Second Workshop*, G.M. Olson, S. Sheppard, E. Soloway (Ablex Publishing, Norwood, 1987), pp. 33–46 http://dl.acm.org/citation.cfm?id=54968.54971
7. M. Höst, B. Regnell, C. Wohlin, Using students as subjects - a comparative study of students and professionals in lead-time impact assessment. Empir. Softw. Eng. **5**(3), 201–214 (2000)
8. I. Lakatos, *Proofs and Refutations*, ed. by J. Worall, E. Zahar (Cambridge University Press, Cambridge, 1976)

9. A. Mockus, R.T. Fielding, J. Herbsleb, A case study of open source software development: the Apache server, in *Proceedings of the 22nd International Conference on Software Engineering (ICSE 2000)* (ACM Press, New York, 2000), pp. 263–272

10. A. Mockus, R.T. Fielding, J.D. Herbsleb, Two case studies of open source software development: Apache and Mozilla. ACM Trans. Softw. Eng. Methodol. **11**(3), 309–346 (2002)

11. L. Prechelt, B. Unger-Lamprecht, M. Philippsen, W.F. Tichy, Two controlled experiments assessing the usefulness of design pattern documentation in program maintenance. IEEE Trans. Softw. Eng. **28**(6), 595–606 (2002)

12. W.S. Robinson, The logical structure of analytic induction. Am. Sociol. Rev. **16**(6), 812–818 (1951)

13. P. Runeson, Using students as experiment subjects–an analysis on graduate and freshmen student data, in *Proceedings of the Seventh International Confonference Empirical Assessment and Evaluation in Software Engineering (EASE '03)*, pp. 95–102 (2003)

14. R. Sabherwal, The evolution of coordination in outsourced software development projects: a comparison of client and vendor perspectives. Inf. Organ. **13**, 153–202 (2003)

15. W.R. Shadish, T.D. Cook, D.T. Campbell, *Experimental and Quasi-Experimental Designs for Generalized Causal Inference* (Houghton Mifflin, Boston, 2002)

16. S. Sterrett, Similarity and dimensional analysis, in *Handbook of the Philosophy of Science, Volume 9: Philosophy of Technology and the Engineering Sciences*, ed. by A. Meijers (Elsevier, Amsterdam, 2009), pp. 799–824

17. M. Svahnberg, A. Aurum, C. Wohlin, Using students as subjects – an empirical evaluation, in *Proceedings of the Second ACM-IEEE International Symposium on Empirical Software Engineering and Measurement (ESEM '08)* (ACM, New York, 2008), pp. 288–290

18. J. Tacq, Znaniecki's analytical induction as a method of sociological research. Pol. Sociol. Rev. **158**(2), 187–208 (2007)

19. W.G. Vincenti, *What Engineers Know and How They Know It. Analytical Studies from Aeronautical History* (Johns Hopkins, Baltimore, 1990)

20. P. Willner, Methods for assessing the validity of animal models of human psychopathology, in *Neuromethods Vol. 18: Animal Models in Psychiatry I*, ed. by A. Boultin, G. Baker, M. Martin-Iverson (The Humana Press, New York, 1991), pp. 1–23

21. R.K. Yin, *Case Study Research: Design and Methods* (Sage, Thousand Oaks, 1984)

22. F. Znaniecki, *The Method of Sociology* (Octagon Books, New York, 1968). First printing 1934

Part V
Some Research Methods

Chapter 16
A Road Map of Research Methods

16.1 The Road Map

The road map of this book was shown in outline in the Preface and is here shown with more detail in Fig. 16.1 (Research Goals and Research Questions). As stated in the Introduction, design science research iterates over solving design problems and answering knowledge questions. Design problems that need novel treatments are dealt with rationally by the design cycle, which has been treated in Part II. Knowledge questions that require empirical research to answer are dealt with rationally by the empirical cycle, which has been treated in Part IV. Design and empirical research both require theoretical knowledge in the form of conceptual frameworks and theoretical generalizations, which enhance our capability to describe, explain, and predict phenomena and to design artifacts that produce these phenomena. Theoretical frameworks have been treated in Part III.

The outcome of the design cycle is a validated artifact design, not an implementation in the intended social context of use. Implementation in the social context of use is transfer of technology to a stakeholder context of which the original designers of the technology are not part. Technology transfer is not part of design science research but may be a sequel to it. Even technical action research (TAR), in which the newly designed artifact is tested by using it to treat real-world problems, is not technology transfer. Technology transfer is adoption of the artifact by stakeholders without involvement of the design science researcher.

The empirical cycle goes beyond research design by executing the design and analyzing the results. The results are then used to answer the knowledge questions that triggered the empirical cycle.

The different tasks in the empirical cycle have been discussed at length in Part IV, and Appendix B summarizes the cycle in the form of a checklist.

© Springer-Verlag Berlin Heidelberg 2014
R.J. Wieringa, *Design Science Methodology for Information Systems and Software Engineering*, DOI 10.1007/978-3-662-43839-8__16

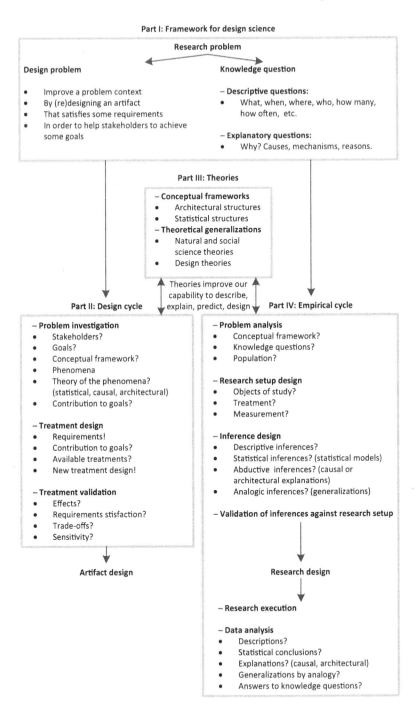

Fig. 16.1 Summary of the design science approach of this book

16.2 Four Empirical Research Methods

In this final part of the book, we show how the checklist can be used to construct four different research methods:

- In *observational case studies*, the researcher studies individual cases to investigate how phenomena in the case are produced by the architecture of the case. The researcher performs no intervention. Observational case studies are done in the field, or at least they are based on information produced in the field. Observational case studies are useful for doing implementation evaluations and problem investigations. They cannot be used to validate new technology because in validation research, by definition, validation models rather than real-world implementations are studied.
- In *single-case mechanism experiments*, the researcher studies individual cases, just as in observational cases studies, to investigate how phenomena in the case are produced by the architecture of the case. But in single-case mechanism experiments, the researcher intervenes, i.e., experiments, with the case. Single-case mechanism experiments are often done in the laboratory, for example, to test an artifact prototype or to simulate real-world phenomena, but they can also be done in the field, for example, to investigate a real-world implementation. Single-case mechanism experiments are useful for validating new technology, for evaluating implementations, and for investigating problems in the field.
- In *TAR*, the researcher experiments with single cases, just as in single-case mechanism experiments. But in contrast to single-case mechanism experiments, this is not only done to answer a knowledge question, but also to help a client. This is useful when validating new technology under real-world conditions. TAR is always done in the field.
- In *statistical difference-making experiments*, the researcher gives two samples of population elements different treatments in order to find out if the difference in treatments causes a difference, on the average, in this population. This can be done in the laboratory or in the field. Statistical difference-making experiments are useful to evaluate implementations in the field, to learn more about problems in the field, and to validate new technology on a large scale in the lab or in the field.

There are additional research methods, not discussed in the chapters that follow. For example, *survey research* is useful for implementation evaluation and problem research but is not discussed here. *Expert opinion* is an effective way to validate new artifact designs at an early stage but is not discussed here. Other important research methods not treated here are *systematic literature surveys* and *meta-analysis*.

The four methods discussed here have many variants too. Observational case studies can be done for cases with a simple or complex nested structure, and it can be done for one or more cases in series. Single-case mechanism experiments can be done with software prototypes, role-play with students, simulations of real-world phenomena, etc. TAR can be done with various levels of involvement of the researcher. Statistical difference-making experiments have many variants, depending on the number of treatments and samples and on the sampling methods. In the chapters to come, we discuss only a few illustrative examples and show how these examples can be reconstructed using the checklist for empirical research. This should provide enough inspiration for you to construct your own research method based on the checklist.

16.3 One Checklist

The checklist is a list of possible choices but does not prescribe how these choices are to be made. The start of the checklist contains questions to position yourself in the goal structure of design science projects that we discussed earlier in Chap. 2. The checklist then goes to ask what the research problem is, how it is to be investigated, how valid this design is for this problem, etc.

To keep in touch with the top-level structure of your research, it is important to ask yourself early on how your research is positioned along the following four dimensions. These dimensions correspond to major choices in the checklist and can be viewed as a high-level version of the checklist. Two of the dimensions are shown in Fig. 16.2:

- **What is studied.** Do you want to study single cases in-depth, or do you want to study statistics of samples? In other words, do you want to know by what mechanisms single phenomena were produced, or do you want to know what the average value of a variable in a sample is, to compare it with other averages? To answer this question, you should be aware of what the population of interest is and what its elements are.

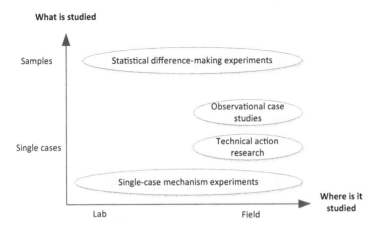

Fig. 16.2 Two dimensions along which to classify research methods

If you are studying a single element at a time, then you are studying single cases. Typically, you want to know how phenomena in the case are produced, and you will generalize by analogy to similar cases, which are the other elements of the population. Case-based research allows you to focus on systematic similarities among population elements. Explanations of phenomena should be architectural. If you are studying sets of elements at a time, then you are studying samples. Typically, you want to know what sample statistics tell you about distribution parameters such as the population average of the variable. Sample-based research allows you to average out nondeterministic differences among population elements. Explanations of phenomena can be causal.

- **Where it is studied**. Whatever you are studying, you may want to study it in the laboratory or in the field. If the phenomenon of interest cannot be produced in the laboratory, you are restricted to do field studies. This is expensive. The population elements that you study may be heterogeneous, and it may be hard to control the factors that influence these elements.

  If the phenomenon of interest can be produced in the laboratory, then you have to specify how to do this and how to control the factors that may influence the objects of study. Laboratory studies can be generalized to other laboratory studies. But if your goal is to learn something about phenomena in the real world, then you also have to think about the (dis)similarity of the laboratory setup with real-world setups.

- **How it is studied**. A third dimension, not shown in Fig. 16.2, is whether or not to intervene in the objects of study. In observational studies, you do not intervene; in experimental studies, you do intervene. Observational case studies, surveys, and focus groups to collect expert opinion are observational studies. Observational studies can support architectural explanations, but to provide support for causal explanations, experimental interventions are needed.

- **Why it is studied**. Your choices made along the above dimensions are motivated by your research goals. Do you want to investigate a real-world problem or evaluate an implementation in the real world? Then you should do field research. Do you want to test a prototype of a newly designed artifact? Then case-based or sample-based experimental research in the lab or field should be done.

Additional considerations in choosing a research design include the available resources and possible risks. Your available resources will constrain what you can do. How much time do you have for the research? What resources would you need for a particular research design, and what is the cost of these resources?

Resources of other stakeholders will play a role too. How much time do they have to wait for your results? How much time would subjects have to participate in the research? Can they afford to spend this time?

Risks must be assessed too. Can stakeholders in the research, such as sponsors or you, afford the risk of failed research? For example, can they, or you, afford to run the risk of doing an experiment that has inconclusive results? And is there a risk of harming people's interests in the research?

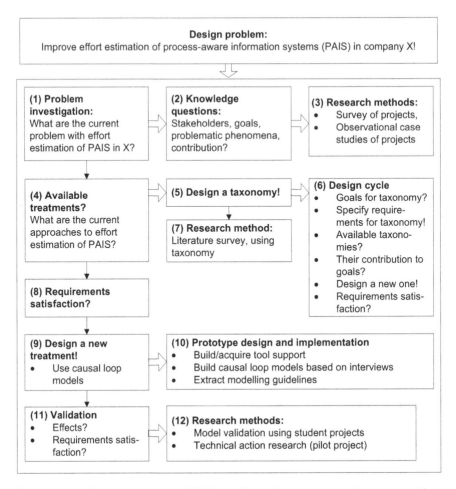

Fig. 16.3 Methodological structure of a PhD thesis. The *hollow arrows* are problem decompositions, the *single arrows* roughly indicate temporal sequence of problem-solving, and the numbers indicate the sequence in which tasks were performed

The following examples illustrate how in different stages of the design cycle different empirical research methods have been selected:

☐ Mutschler's [2] research goal was to improve effort estimation techniques for process-aware information systems (PAIS). A PAIS is a software system that manages and executes operational business processes. Examples are workflow management systems, case management systems, and enterprise information systems. Figure 16.3 shows the structure of the research project. The boxes represent tasks, double arrows indicate task decompositions, and numbers indicate the sequence in which tasks were performed. The boxes at the left-hand side of the figure are connected by single arrows to indicate that they correspond roughly to the tasks in the design cycle and have been executed from top to bottom.

One of the stakeholders was the large multinational manufacturing company who sponsored Mutschler's research. The problem that triggered the research project was that effort estimations for PAIS development projects were often over budget, which means their effort estimations were inaccurate. To investigate this problem, Mutschler performed two observational field studies, namely, a web-based survey among project managers and some observational case studies of individual projects. They were studied in the field, because the relevant phenomena could not be produced in the laboratory. They were studied observationally, because experimental interventions in the projects would probably destroy the relevant phenomena. The web-based survey is sample based and gives an impression of the extent of the problem. The case studies are case based and give information about the possible reasons and mechanisms why effort estimations are inaccurate. Part of the treatment design task is to make a survey of available effort estimation methods, and for this, Mutschler performed a literature survey. There turned out to be several conflicting taxonomies of effort estimation methods, and before conducting the survey, he constructed a taxonomy based on available taxonomies and his own research goals.

The effort estimation technique designed by Mutschler is based on causal loop models that represent various factors that influence project effort. Altogether, Mutschler made about 20 of these models for different stages of a PAIS development project, based on information collected from project managers.

To validate the models, he performed an experiment in the laboratory with students. Different student projects developed two PAIS each, and the causal loop models were validated by using them to predict the effort that student projects would spend to develop these systems and comparing this with the actual effort spent. This validation was done with students to reduce the risk of burdening project managers in the field with a possibly inaccurate effort estimation technique.

The second validation was done by a real-world project, whose project manager used the causal loop models to estimate project effort. This is an example of TAR. After the project was finished, the estimations were compared with actual effort.

☐ Gorschek et al. [1] described a design science research project in which researchers worked with practitioners to identify relevant problems experienced by the practitioners and to select one to solve. Their research process follows the design cycle, followed by the first step of implementation, as shown in Table 16.3. In the following, we use the numbering of steps by Gorschek et al.

(1) Problem investigation was done by observational case studies. One of the problems identified was how to deal with the large volume of requirements, originating from different sources, in market-driven product development, and this problem was selected for treatment.

(2) Selecting a problem for treatment was done jointly with the industrial stakeholders. This is part of research management, and so it is not included in the engineering cycle.

(3) Treatment design consisted of a literature survey of the state of the art of requirements engineering, followed by the specification of a candidate solution.

(4) Validation was done in three iterations. First, the requirements engineering method was used by students in the laboratory. The results motivated an improvement of the method.

(5) Second, software engineers were asked to express their opinion about the method in focus groups. This is not only a validation but also a part of research management to gain support from important stakeholders. To gain further support, the method was also presented to decision-makers, again for validation as well as for gaining support. These expert opinions led to further improvements of the method, in particular by simplifying it to improve its usability in practice.

(6) Management gave the go-ahead for the project, and the third validation task was to use the method in two pilot projects. This is an example of two TAR projects. Lessons learned from these projects was used to further improve and finalize the method.

(7) The final task was to hand over the method to practitioners. This was the start of an implementation process, which is not part of the research project.

Table 16.1 Technology transfer process described by Gorschek et al. [1]

Engineering cycle	Technology transfer model of Gorschek et al. [1]
Problem investigation	1. Identify potential improvement areas based on industry needs
• Observational case study	
	• Observations
	• Process assessment
	2. Formulate research agenda
	• Identify problems to be treated
	• Formulate problem
Treatment design	3. Formulate candidate solution
	• Survey state of the art
	• Formulate candidate solution
Validation	4. Laboratory validation
• Laboratory experiment	• E.g. by laboratory experiment
	5. Static validation
• Expert opinion	• By expert opinion
	6. Dynamic validation
• Technical action research	• By pilot projects
Implementation	7. Release the solution

Both examples illustrate some frequently made choices in design science research. Problem investigation is often done by observational case studies and surveys. Often the problems cannot be reproduced in the laboratory, and so they must be studied in the field. There is usually no need or no possibility to do experiments to understand the problem, and so the problems are investigated using observational field research. Statistical knowledge about the extent of the problem is obtained by doing a survey; architectural knowledge is obtained by doing observational case studies. A literature study helps to collect what is already known about the problem.

Treatment design always involves making a survey of the state of the art, and this is done by a literature study too.

Treatment validation consists usually of an iteration of validation studies, where early on, laboratory research is done to reduce the cost of research and reduce the risk of harming stakeholders with ineffective treatments. As a preparation for field tests, expert opinion is a cheap and effective method. Prior to releasing a treatment design for implementation in the real world, TAR is used to increase confidence in the validity of the treatment. We recognize here the process of scaling up from the lab to the real world, described in Chap. 7 (Treatment Validation).

References

1. T. Gorschek, C. Wohlin, P. Garre, S. Larsson, A model for technology transfer in practice. IEEE Softw. **23**(6), 88–95 (2006)
2. B. Mutschler, Modeling and simulating causal dependencies on process-aware information systems from a cost perspective. Ph.D. thesis, University of Twente, Enschede, January 2008. http://eprints.eemcs.utwente.nl/11864/

Chapter 17
Observational Case Studies

An **observational case study** is a study of a real-world case without performing an intervention. Measurement may influence the measured phenomena, but as in all forms of research, the researcher tries to restrict this to a minimum.

The researcher may study a sample of two or even more cases, but the goal of case study research is not to acquire knowledge about samples, but about individual cases. Generalization from case studies is analytical induction over cases, not statistical inference from samples.

Observational case studies are needed to study phenomena that cannot be produced in the laboratory. Because you do not intervene, observational case studies are a useful research method for implementation evaluation and problem investigation, where you investigate the real world as you find it.

There are several checklists and handbooks for doing case study research in information systems and software engineering research. The checklist of this book includes the others but gives more attention to architectural explanations of case studies and to the possibility of generalization by architectural analogy.[1]

The description of the context, research problem, and design of your case study should be documented in a *case study protocol*. Events during research execution and details of data analysis can be collected later in a separate document, sometimes called a *case study log* or *diary*. The full protocol and diary will be your source for reports in conference and journal papers, and you may consider making them available to other researchers if confidentiality restrictions allow this. The rest of this chapter shows how the checklist of Appendix B is applied to the design and analysis of observational case studies.

© Springer-Verlag Berlin Heidelberg 2014
R.J. Wieringa, *Design Science Methodology for Information Systems and Software Engineering*, DOI 10.1007/978-3-662-43839-8_17

Table 17.1 The checklist for the research context of observational case study research, written from the point of view of the researcher preparing to do the research

1. Knowledge goal(s)

   - What do you want to know? Is this part of an implementation evaluation, a problem investigation, a survey of existing treatments, or a new technology validation?

2. Improvement goal(s)?

   - If there is a higher-level engineering cycle, what is the goal of that cycle?
   - If this is a curiosity-driven project, are there credible application scenarios for the project results?

3. Current knowledge

   - State of the knowledge in published scientific, technical and professional literature?
   - Available expert knowledge?
   - Why is your research needed? Do you want to add anything, e.g. confirm or falsify something?
   - Theoretical framework that you will use?

17.1 Context

Table 17.1 gives the checklist to position your research in context, written from the point of view of the researcher preparing to do the research. An observational case study has a *knowledge goal* and may or may not have an *improvement goal*. If it has an improvement goal, it is part of an implementation evaluation or problem investigation of a higher-level engineering cycle. Otherwise, it is a curiosity-driven study that aims to increase our knowledge about some topic. Finally, the checklist asks about *current knowledge* about this topic.

In a report, you typically provide this information in an introduction that summarizes your research goals and explains why it needs to be done. If there is a lot of related work to discuss, then this could be a separate section, to support your claim that this case study needs to be done.

In the following two examples, I extracted the answers to the checklist questions from two research reports. The example of Warne and Hart [11] is new and the example of Damian and Chisan [1] has been used in Chap. 14 (Abductive Inference Design) to illustrate architectural explanation. Here we analyze these papers in full:

☐ (1) Warne and Hart [11] report on an observational case study of the impact of organizational politics on information system project failure. Their knowledge goal was to contribute to knowledge about the relation between politics and project failure.

   (2) This knowledge may be useful, for example, to assess the possible impact of politics on project failure in future projects. But there was no improvement goal in the sense of a goal to develop

an artifact that would treat this problem. Also, no artifact implementation was being evaluated, so I would classify this study as a curiosity-driven problem investigation.

(3) A brief review of related work reveals that causes of failure are rarely technical and more usually organizational [11, p. 191]. The authors aimed to contribute to the knowledge about the impact of political factors on project success.

☐ (1) Damian and Chisan [1] report on an observational case study of the introduction of requirements engineering in a software development organization. This was an implementation evaluation, in which the artifact consisted of a number of requirements engineering methods and techniques and the context was a software development organization. The knowledge goal was to find out what the effects are of introducing requirements engineering practices in a development organization and to understand why they occur.

(2) There was no stated improvement goal in the sense that a follow-up project was planned to improve requirements engineering practice further, in this company or elsewhere. But the knowledge and understanding acquired in this project were expected to be useful both for practitioners who are interested in improving their requirements engineering practices and for researchers interested in understanding the effects of requirements engineering in practice.

(3) A review of related work reveals that requirements engineering improvement is tightly bound up with other systems engineering processes and that the impacted variables discussed most often in the literature are developer productivity, software quality, and risk mitigation. The review also revealed that there is little knowledge of the benefits of requirements engineering in concrete cases.

17.2 Research Problem

Table 17.2 gives the checklist for the problem statement. In order to specify your knowledge questions and population of interest, you need to define a *conceptual framework*. For case studies, this should define the architectural structures that you are looking for in a case.

Operationalization of constructs may be done at any point before defining the measurement procedures. Whenever it is done, the resulting definitions are part of the conceptual research framework, so the checklist item is listed here. If you define indicators for constructs, then you should check for mono-operation and mono-method bias, at least before you define your measurement procedures.

Knowledge questions help you to prevent drowning in the potentially infinite mass of data that you could collect about a case. The questions can be exploratory or can be focused on testing some hypotheses. Some authors distinguish intermediary kinds of questions, about which you have expectations that are not yet formulated in measurable hypotheses to test. These expectations are expressed as the *propositions*. Just as the knowledge questions themselves, these propositions are intended to focus your attention to relevant case phenomena.

Whether open, closed, or intermediary, case study knowledge questions should not only be descriptive but also explanatory. Case studies are performed in order to gain understanding, not only facts.

Table 17.2 The checklist for the research problem, written from the point of view of the researcher preparing to do the research

4. Conceptual framework

   - Conceptual structures? Architectural structures, statistical structures?
   - Chance models of random variables: Semantics of variables?
   - Validity of the conceptual framework? Clarity of definitions, unambiguous application, avoidance of mono-operation and mono-method bias?

5. Knowledge questions

   - Open (exploratory) or closed (hypothesis-testing) questions?
   - Effect, satisfaction, trade-off or sensitivity questions?
   - Descriptive or explanatory questions?

6. Population

   - Population predicate? What is the architecture of the elements of the population? In which ways are all population elements similar to each other, and dissimilar to other elements?
   - Chance models of random variables: Assumptions about distributions of variables?

A similar remark can be made about generalization from a case study. You select a case study because it is an element of a *population* of interest. A report of facts about a case with no potential for generalization could be relevant as a piece of journalism, but it would not be relevant as research:

☐   For example, you select an information system implementation project because it is, precisely, an information system implementation project. So you are interested in the population of information system implementation projects. If the case would not contain facts relevant for other cases, then there is no reason why another researcher should read your case study report.

As pointed out before, at the start of commencing a series of case studies, the population predicate may not be defined very clearly. This does not mean that there is no target of generalization. It only means that the required similarity across targets of generalization is not so clear yet. Because the similarity predicate and relevant theories may be revised between case studies, it would be misleading to call these case studies *replications* of each other. Rather, the series of case studies is an example of *analytical induction*. It is the purpose of analytical induction over a series of cases to test and improve an architectural theory and get more clarity about the population predicate:

☐   (4) Warne and Hart [11] use the concepts of information system, business-IT alignment, system development project, etc. in the way common to the information systems literature and known to the readers, so they are not defined. *Failure* is defined explicitly, as abandonment of the project. They also define the concept of an *information ward*, as the set of data and processes "owned" by an organizational actor (i.e., a manager), in the perception of that actor. A *political information*

ward is the subset of an information ward that its owner will defend if ownership is threatened.
(6) The population of interest seems to be:

> all large information system development projects for which the major success factors have been satisfied: Alignment with business needs, top management support, user involvement, effective project management, use of a system development methodology.

These conditions have been collected in a literature study [11, p. 193]. The success factors refer to a case architecture that has as components the business, project, top management, users, and project management. The case study report describes some of the interactions between these components in the case.

(5) The authors do not state their knowledge questions explicitly, but the introduction states the top-level knowledge question as "What are the causes for project failure?" That is a question about the case with only local interest. Given the population of interest, a possible corresponding population-level knowledge question is:

– What are the mechanisms that can lead to failure of large information system development projects of which the major conditions of success are satisfied?

This question is about the population, as it should be, not about the case. It has a middle-range scope, as it asks for mechanisms that *can* lead to failure. Also, the requested explanation is now architectural, as I think is appropriate for case studies, rather than causal.

☐ (5) The knowledge question stated by Damian and Chisan [1, p. 435] is:

– How do improvements in requirements engineering processes relate to improvements in productivity, quality, and risk management?

This is a population-level question. There is no explicit mention of causal, architectural, or motivational explanations, but we will see later that both causal and architectural explanations have been found.

(4) The relevant concepts of *developer productivity*, *software quality*, and *risk mitigation* have already been defined by the authors when discussing related work.
(6) The population is not explicitly stated but can be taken to be:

> all software development organizations that introduce requirements engineering processes [1, p. 437].

The case of interest has an architecture consisting of a development organization, users, and a marketing organization. Requirements come from the marketing organization, and help requests come from the users. The case organization actually selected was expanding its capability from CMM level 1 to CMM level 2. Whether or not this expansion of capabilities is essential for the generalizations to be made is not known and must be investigated by additional case studies.

In Chap. 8 (Conceptual Frameworks), we have seen that within a case study you can do a statistical study, for example, by doing a statistical survey of the population of software engineers in a company. In that case, you will need to define a statistical structure too, listing the variables of interest to be studied statistically, and a chance model that defines their meaning, assumptions, measurement procedures, and the sampling procedure. If you are planning to do a statistical study inside a case study, it is best to consider that as a local research project for which you use the checklist afresh. Using the checklist for that local study, you will again define what the research problem of *that* project is, specify a research design, etc.

17.3   Research Design and Validation

In observational case study research, we study cases as we find them in the real world, but the study itself must be designed. This requires decisions about case selection, sampling, and measurement. It also requires alignment of these decisions with the planned inferences from the data. The checklists for inference design are given in Sect. 17.4, but we illustrate their application to research design here.

17.3.1   Case Selection

Table 17.3.1 gives the checklist for selecting a case. Cases are selected, not constructed, and they are selected according to some population predicate that specifies architectural properties of the cases in the population of interest. If we want to give *descriptive statistics* of a case, then we should ensure that the chance model of the variables about which we want to give statistics is defined. The chance model tells us what the meaning of the variables is in terms of case phenomena.

In case study research, the population predicate may not be very clear, and the goal of research may precisely be to gain more clarity about it. This makes it all the more important to think in advance of how you will know that a case that you found has the architecture specified by the population predicate.

We need this because during case selection we should consider how much support a case could give to abductive and analogic inferences. A study of a unique unrepeatable case cannot support *causal inference,* because one case can only show one of the two measurements needed to show a difference. Only if

Table 17.3 The part of the checklist for the acquisition of an object of study that is relevant for case selection, written from the point of view of the researcher preparing to do the research

7.1 Acquisition of Objects of Study (cases)

- How do you know that a selected entity is a case? How do you know it satisfies the population predicate?
- Validity of OoS

  - *Inference support.* Which inferences would be valid with respect to this design? See checklists for validity of descriptive statistics, abductive and analogic inferences.
  - *Repeatability.* Could other researchers use your report to construct or select a similar OoS?
  - *Ethics.* Are people informed that they will be studied, and do they consent to this? Are they free to stop at any time without giving reasons, and do they know this?

different cases would behave identically, or if behavior is time independent, can we do comparative-cases or single-case causal experiments, as described in Chap. 14 (Abductive Inference Design). Real-world observational cases do not satisfy these very strict assumptions. However, case studies can support architectural and rational inferences. For *architectural inference,* the following considerations are relevant (Table 17.4):

- *Analysis.* Can enough information about the case architecture be acquired to be able to analyze relevant case mechanisms? Can information about capabilities and interactions of case components be acquired to be able to explain how the phenomena of interest are produced? Think of information that you can acquire about people, roles, organizational units, projects, systems, etc.
- *Variation.* The world is full of variation, and most real-world cases match the population predicate somewhat but not completely. An architectural component specified in the population predicate may be absent from the case actually acquired. Or it may be present but with somewhat different capabilities from those assumed by the architectural model of the population predicate. You have to assess whether all components and capabilities assumed by the model are essential for the explanations that you can foresee. The ability to do such an assessment depends on your prior knowledge, and if this knowledge is absent, it may be your research goal to find this out in a series of case studies:

  ☐   In a follow-up case study to confirm the findings of Damian and Chisan, we may find that there
      is a team similar to the cross-functional team but that it does not contain a representative from
      product management and does not keep a record of design rationale. Is this essential? Or can
      we still expect similar phenomena produced by similar mechanisms? The best way to find out
      is to do the case study.

- *Abstraction.* The case architecture as specified in the population predicate abstracts away components and mechanisms that may be present in real-world cases. What would happen if the architecture specified in the population predicate does not match the components of the case actually acquired? What is the impact of components present in the case but absent from the architecture specified in the population predicate? It is an important goal of case studies to find out how robust a mechanism is under the impact of other mechanisms with which it may coexist in practice:

  ☐   For example, suppose we are studying coordination in outsourcing projects. Suppose you
      are considering to select a case in which you know that outsourcing is coordinated by an
      independent external consultant. If your population predicate does not specify this additional
      case component, you have to consider whether this case is relevant for your research goal or
      not. If you want to confirm findings from previous case studies, you may not want to select this
      case. But if you want to falsify findings from previous case studies in a process of analytical
      induction, you may on the contrary want to select this case.

To support *rational inference,* the following considerations are relevant already when selecting a case (Table 17.4):

- *Goals.* To which extent you can get information about the true goals of actors in the case?
- *Motivation.* Even if you know what the true goals of the actors are, it may be hard to discover their motivations. Can you get information about the true motivations of actions observed in a case?

To assess support of a case for *analogic inference,* the following questions are relevant (Table 17.4):

- *Population predicate.* Does the case satisfy the population predicate? In which way is it similar to the other cases in the population? In which way is it dissimilar?
- *Ambiguity.* Does the case satisfy other population predicates too? What could be the target of analogic generalization?

The answers to these questions tell us what the potential targets of analogic generalization can be:

☐   Suppose again that you are interested in outsourcing projects. The population predicate then specifies a required case architecture: an outsourcing client interacting with an outsourcing vendor. During acquisition of a case, you may have to ask if a candidate case has the required characteristics to count as an outsourcing case with this architecture. Does a virtual organization of a small client company and an individual programmer count as an outsourcing case? Does the size and location of the participants matter?
All of these aspects of a case have been abstracted away in the population predicate. They are not only important for architectural inference but also for analogic inference. In the end, it will be the architectural explanation of observed phenomena that will determine to which population(s) we can generalize by analogy.

In addition to support for inferences, the two other requirements for validity of case selection are repeatability and ethics. Case selection should be *repeatable* in the sense that other researchers could use the population predicate to select similar cases. If similar case studies done by other researchers confirm your findings, then you can consider those case studies to be *replications.* If they falsify your findings, then it is better to see those studies as a continuation of your *analytical induction* process.

The checklist also tells us that you need to prepare information for the case participants so that they can express *informed consent* and know that they are *free to stop* their participation at any time.

The rationale for case selection and the case architecture must be included in any published report, because they help the reader to understand the explanations that can be given and the generalizations that can be made from the case data. Here is the information that I extracted from the two example case study reports:

☐   (7.1) Warne and Hart [11] do not describe their selection criteria, but their report implies that they were looking for a large failed information system development project that satisfied the major success factors: alignment with business needs, top management support, user involvement, effective project management, and the use of a system development methodology. This is the population predicate that we identified earlier in this chapter (p. 229). They had access to information about the case architecture and the goals and motivations of actors, which allowed them later on to explain phenomena architecturally and indicate a corresponding target of analogic generalization.

☐   (7.1) Damian and Chisan [1] do not describe their selection criteria, but their report implies that they were looking for an organization that introduced an explicit requirements engineering process. This is their population predicate. One of the researchers (Chisan) worked at the organization for a year and had access to sufficient information about the case architecture and goals and motivations of the actors to be able to give architectural explanations of observed phenomena. (The architectural explanations presented in Chap. 14 on abductive inference (p. 193) have been constructed by me based on the published report.) This in turn governs the choice of the target of analogic generalization: organizations with a similar structure.

17.3.2   Sampling

Table 17.3.2 lists the checklist for sampling in case study research. In case study research, cases are sampled in series, where each case is analyzed separately, and a case study may be finished, and the theoretical framework revised, before the next case is started. This is analytical induction.

Scanning the checklist for the validity of abductive inference (Table 17.4), we find the following validity considerations:

- *Sampling influence.* Could the selection mechanism influence the selected cases? Could there be a regression effect?

Being selected for a case study may affect the case organization so that the researcher may observe phenomena that would not occur when the organization would not be studied. And if you study an extreme case, such as a very large project, you must consider in your generalization that most other cases will be less extreme

Table 17.4 The part of the checklist for sampling objects of study in case study research, written from the point of view of the researcher preparing to do the research

7.2 Construction of a sample

- – What is the analytical induction strategy? Confirming cases, disconfirming cases, extreme cases?
- – Validity of sampling procedure

  - - *Inference support.* Which inferences would be valid with respect to this design? See the applicable parts of the checklists for validity of statistical, abductive and analogic inferences.
  - - *Repeatability.* Can the sampling procedure be replicated by other researchers?
  - - *Ethics.* No new issues.

in size. This feature is used in extreme-case reasoning, explained earlier in Chap. 15 (Analogic Inference Design).

In the checklist for the validity of analogic inference (Table 17.4), we find the following question about sampling for analogic inference:

- *Representative sampling,* case-based research. In what way will the selected sample of cases be representative of the population?

Representativeness may be a matter of similarity, but more sophisticated representation relationships can arise if you have a theory of similitude that relates behavior in a model to behavior in the target of a model.

17.3.3   Measurement Design

Table 17.5 lists the decisions you should make when designing your measurements in an observational case study. First, you need a conceptual framework that defines *variables* and their *scales.* You may have already have defined these from the start in the conceptual framework, but often you need to spend additional attention to reach the level of detail needed for doing a case study. In many case study reports, measurement specification is described in a separate section.

Table 17.5 The part of the checklist for measurement that is relevant for case selection, written from the point of view of the researcher preparing to do the research

9. Measurement design

- Variables and constructs to be measured? Scales, chance models.
- Data sources? People (e.g. software engineers, maintainers, users, project managers, politically responsible persons, etc.), primary data (e.g. source code, log files, bug tracking data, version management data, email logs), primary documents (e.g., project reports, meeting minutes, organization charts, mission statements), etc.
- Measurement instruments? Interview protocols, questionnaires, video recorders, sound recorders, clocks, sensors, database queries, log analyzers, etc.
- What is the measurement schedule? Pretests, posttests? Cross-sectional or longitudinal?
- How will measured data be stored and managed? Provenance, availability to other researchers?
- Validity of measurement specification:

  * *Inference support.* Which inferences would be valid with respect to this design? See the applicable parts of the checklists for validity of abductive and analogic inferences.
  * *Repeatability.* Is the measurement specification clear enough so that others could repeat it?
  * *Ethics.* Which company data must be kept confidential? How is privacy of persons respected?

The case architecture defined in the population predicate can now be used to indicate what the *data sources* are, such as:

- People (e.g., software engineers, maintainers, users, project managers, politically responsible persons, etc.)
- Primary data (e.g., source code, log files, bug tracking data, version management data, email logs)
- Primary documents (e.g., project reports, meeting minutes, organization charts, mission statements)

To do measurements, you must acquire or construct *measurement instruments,* such as interview protocols, questionnaires, video recorders, sound recorders, clocks, sensors, database queries, log analyzers, etc. This is an engineering problem in itself, and you may have to test these instruments on real-world phenomena before you use them in a case study.

The *measurement schedule* can only be finalized after you acquire a case, but in order to negotiate with the case organization, you need to make a preliminary plan first. *Data management* includes tools for collecting, storing, and managing data and for maintaining provenance (traceability of data to its sources). You may want to use tools for online surveys, for scanning and processing paper questionnaires, etc. And you may want to use computer-aided qualitative data analysis software or CAQDAS for short.

To assess validity of measurement procedures with respect to abductive inferences from the data, we first need to consult the checklist for *causal inference* (Table 17.4). Observational case studies cannot provide support for causal inferences, but we should still ask what causal influence we may have on the case. We should not end up studying case phenomena caused by ourselves. We should ask the following question about measurement:

- *Measurement influence.* Will measurement influence the case?

Second, to facilitate generalization to other cases by *analogic inference,* the following questions from the checklist of validity of analogic inference are relevant (Table 17.4):

- *Construct validity.* Are the definitions of constructs to be measured valid? Clarity of definitions, unambiguous application, and avoidance of mono-operation and mono-method bias?
- *Measurement instrument validity.* Do the measurement instruments measure what you claim that they measure? Interviewers may be biased, questionnaires may be misleading, queries of databases with primary data may be incorrect, etc. You should validate measurement instruments before you use them.
- *Construct levels.* Will the measured range of values be representative of the population range of values? This is a classical threat to validity in statistical research, but it is relevant for case studies too. For example, collecting data about

only small successful projects in an organization may not give you knowledge that can be generalized to projects of arbitrary size.

In addition to the support for inferences, measurements should be repeatable and ethical. Using your measurement specification, other researchers should be able to *repeat* the same kind of measurements in other organizations. And you will have to establish rules for *confidentiality* of organizational data and for respecting *privacy* of participants. These rules can only be finalized in your negotiations with the case company, but you must prepare a preliminary set of rules first. Maybe your own organization has templates for nondisclosure agreements, as well as a procedure and forms for ethical aspects of research.

The case study protocol will contain all your decisions about measurement. Published reports usually do not report the measurement procedures *as designed* but describe the measurement procedures *as realized*. Here are the measurement procedures reported by our two examples:

☐ (9) Important constructs in the study by Warne and Hart [11, p. 192] were *alignment with business need* and *top management support*. From the report, it appears that these were operationalized by asking case participants about their opinion about the extent to which these phenomena were present. Since one case is studied, it may not be possible to investigate a representative range of levels of these variables. But it is possible to collect data from a wide range of sources in the organization so as to avoid getting a one-sided image of the case organization.

The data sources included all project developers, the managers responsible for the project, and primary documents of the investigated project (e.g., steering committee minutes, project management methodologies). Measurement instruments included interviews and questionnaires. Presumably, these instruments were tested before used, but this is not reported in the paper [11]. The paper also does not report information about the measurement schedule or about data management. Interviews and questionnaires always have some influence on subjects, which needs to be minimized during the case study.

☐ (9) The relevant constructs in the study by Damian and Chisan [1] are *developer productivity*, *product quality*, and *project risk*. The meaning of these concepts in related work is discussed. The authors settle on a number of variables that may impact productivity, quality, and risk, such as *feature sizing*, *change management*, *specification conformance*, etc. These concepts are taken from the literature and are supplemented with measures used in the case organization itself [1, pp. 447–448].

Data were collected in three rounds from several samples of software engineers, team leaders, senior engineers, and managers by means of interviews and questionnaires [1, pp. 438, 440]. The surveys can be considered statistical studies within a case and have their own research design and interpretation. Data from these studies were made available on request to readers of the report.

In addition, primary documents were studied, such as change requests, project development estimation data, and entries in the requirements management tool. Finally, one researcher was on-site for 12 months and could participate in meetings. The variety of sources reduced the threat of construct level confounding and may also have reduced influence on the subjects, as the presence of the researcher was normal. Interviews and questionnaires, though, remain inherently disturbing instruments.

Table 17.6 Checklist for descriptive inference, written from the point of view of the researcher designing a case study

---

10.1 Descriptive inference design

- – How are words and images to be interpreted? (Content analysis, conversation analysis, discourse analysis, analysis software, etc.)
- – What descriptive summaries of data are planned? Illustrative data, graphical summaries, descriptive statistics, etc.
- – Validity of description design

  * *Support for data preparation.*

    - Will the prepared data represent the same phenomena as the unprepared data?
    - If data may be removed, would this be defensible beyond reasonable doubt?
    - Would your scientific opponents produce the same descriptions from the data?

  * *Support for data interpretation.*

    - Will the interpretations that you produce be facts in your conceptual research framework? Would your scientific peers produce the same interpretations?
    - Will the interpretations that you produce be facts in the conceptual framework of the subjects? Would subjects accept them as facts?

  * *Support for descriptive statistics.*

    - Is the chance model of the variables of interest defined in terms of the population elements?

  * *Repeatability:* Will the analysis repeatable by others?
  * *Ethics:* No new issues.

17.4 Inference Design and Validation

Case-based inference consists of three steps, namely, description, architectural explanation, and generalization by analogy. We give the checklists here. Examples of the validity considerations have already been given in the section on research design. Examples of the inferences themselves are given later, in the section on data analysis.

Table 17.4 gives the checklist for descriptive inference design and validity. Descriptive inference from case data may require considerable time and effort, because there is a lot of data to collect and manage, and interpretation may require labor-intensive coding, replicated by more than one coder. You should be sure that you have these resources before you start the case study. The validity requirements of descriptive inference all ask in one way or another whether you will add information to the data that is not warranted by the observed phenomena.

Table 17.7 Checklist for abductive inference design in observational case studies, written from the point of view of the researcher designing a case study

10.3 Abductive inference design

- What possible explanations can you foresee? What data do you need to give those explanations? What theoretical framework?
- Internal validity

  * *Causal inference*

    - *Sampling influence.* Could the selection mechanism influence the selected cases? Could there be a regression effect?
    - *Measurement influence.* Will measurement influence the case?

  * *Architectural inference*

    - *Analysis:* The analysis of the architecture may not support its conclusions with mathematical certainty. Components fully specified? Interactions fully specified?
    - *Variation:* Do the real-world case components match the architectural components? Do they have the same capabilities? Are all architectural components present in the real-world case?
    - *Abstraction:* Does the architectural model used for explanation omit relevant elements of real-world cases? Are the mechanisms in the architectural model interfered with by other mechanisms, absent from the model but present in the real world case?

  * *Rational inference*

    - *Goals.* An actor may not have the goals assumed by an explanation. Can you get information about the true goals of actors?
    - *Motivation.* A goal may not motivate an actor as much as assumed by an explanation. Can you get information about the true motivations of actors?

Table 17.4 gives the checklist for abductive inference. You have to take care that sampling and measurement do not influence case phenomena, as discussed above. Explanations will be architectural and refer to components and mechanisms.

Table 17.4 shows the checklist for analogic inference. To generalize from a case study, you need information about the case architecture and the mechanisms that you have observed operating in a case. As all generalizations, support is not total, there may be exceptions, and the generalization may be refined and revised when more case studies are done. Generalization from a single case is called *analytical generalization,* and generalization from a series of cases is called *analytical induction.*

Table 17.8 Checklist for analogic inference design in observational case studies, written from the point of view of the researcher designing a case study

---

10.4 Analogic inference design

- – What is the intended scope of your generalization?
- – External validity

  * *Object of Study similarity.*

    - *Population predicate.* Does the case satisfy the population predicate? In which way will is it similar to the population elements? In which way will is it dissimilar?
    - *Ambiguity.* Does the case satisfy other population predicates too? What could be the target of analogic generalization?

  * *Representative sampling,* case-based research: In what way will the selected sample of cases be representative of the population?
  * *Treatment.*

    - *Treatment similarity.* Is the specified treatment in the experiment similar to treatments in the population?
    - *Compliance.* Is the treatment implemented as specified?
    - *Treatment control.* What other factors than the treatment could influence the OoS's? Could the implemented treatment be interpreted as another treatment?

  * *Measurement.*

    - *Construct validity.* Are the definitions of constructs to be measured valid? Clarity of definitions, unambiguous application, avoidance of mono-operation and mono-method bias?
    - *Measurement instrument validity.* Do the measurement instruments measure what you claim that they measure?
    - *Construct levels.* Will the measured range of values be representative of the population range of values?

17.5 Research Execution

We now switch perspective from a researcher designing a case study to that of a researcher executing a case study and reporting about it. You have finished writing the case study protocol and have started doing the study. You now start with the case study diary in which you document what happened during execution and what you did during analysis. The case study diary will be your basis for reporting to other researchers. The diary will be much more detailed than an external report.

Table 17.5 lists the checklist for reporting about case study execution. The questions ask about the implementation of the different elements of your research design: the case(s) actually selected, sampling (analytical induction), and measurement. Case acquisition is a lengthy process in which you must build up trust with a case organization. Trust comes by foot but leaves on horseback, and building up trust can

Table 17.9 The part of the checklist for research execution that is relevant for case studies, written from the point of view of the researcher preparing to write a report about the research

---

11. What has happened?

    – What has happened during selection? Did the cases eventually selected have the architecture that was planned during research design? Have there been any unexpected events during the study?

    – What has happened during analytical induction (i.e. sampling)? Could you study the kinds of cases that you originally planned?

    – What has happened during measurements? Data sources actually used, response rates?

---

take months or even years. Beware also that trust comes and goes with people. If your organizational contact leaves his or her job, you may be back at square one.

Related to the difficulty of getting access to a case, you may not be able to get access to a case with exactly the architecture that you hoped for. You cannot always get what you want. In your diary and external case study reports, you should acknowledge mismatches between acquired case architecture and the architecture specified in the population predicate. In your abductive and analogic inferences, you should take this mismatch into account. In a process of analytical induction, case variety may actually strengthen the generalizability of your results.

Measurements too may be subject to the vagaries of the real world. People may cancel interview appointments, and respondents may misunderstand questionnaires or return incomplete answers. Response rates may be low. Data sources promised to be available may turn out to be out of reach. Primary documents may be hard to understand without guidance, and the key stakeholders may be unreachable or have left the organization. Data collected for practical use often has not had the quality needed for scientific research and may have to be cleaned before you can use it.

All of this is important to note in the case diary, and the reader of your research report should be informed of events that may influence the meaning of the data. Here are our two running examples:

☐ (11) Warne and Hart [11] acquired a project in the public sector that failed after nine years. They give a brief overview of organization, of the system developed, of the stakeholders involved, and of important events during these nine years. After describing their measurement procedures, they report on the sample of subjects to whom questionnaires were sent and about the response rates obtained.

☐ (11) Damian and Chisan [1] acquired a medium-sized software development organization (130 employees) responsible for a software product that has been on the market for about 20 years. The organization was located in Australia, is part of a multinational company with customers worldwide, and received its requirements from a marketing department in Canada. They give a description of the software product, the software processes, and the improvement process from CMM level 1 to CMM level 2, during which requirements engineering was introduced. For each of the three sequential case studies performed at this organization, they report on data sources and response rates obtained.

Table 17.10 The part of the checklist for data analysis that is relevant for case studies, written from the point of view of the researcher preparing to write a report about the research

12. Descriptions

- Data preparations applied? Data transformations, missing values, removal of outliers? Data management, data availability.
- Data interpretations? Coding procedures, interpretation methods?
- Descriptive statistics. Demographics? Graphics, tables.
- Validity of the descriptions: See checklist for the validity of descriptive inference.

14. Explanations

- What explanations (causal, architectural, rational) exist for the observations?
- Internal validity: See checklist for the validity of abductive inference.

15. Generalizations

- Would the explanations be valid in similar cases or populations too?
- External validity: See checklist for the validity of analogic inference

16. Answers

- What are the answers to the knowledge questions? Summary of conclusions, support for and limitations of conclusions.

17.6 Data Analysis

In data analysis, you perform the inferences that you planned earlier. During research, unexpected things may have happened, and so you may have to adapt the inference procedures that you designed earlier to changed circumstances, and you have to revisit the validity questions in the light of the data and of the events of research execution.

Table 17.6 shows the checklist for data analysis. The part about statistical inference is absent because from a series of case studies you cannot infer statistical models. Without further discussion, we present the data analysis of our examples.

17.6.1 Descriptions

- ☐ (12) Warne and Hart [11] describe the alignment of the system with the business, the project management, and the system development method used in the case and give descriptive statistics of top management support and user involvement.
- ☐ (12) Damian and Chisan [1] provide descriptions of the requirements engineering practices in their case organization and give some descriptive statistics of the results of the interviews and questionnaires filled in during their third case study.

17.6.2   Explanations

☐   (14) Warne and Hart [11] formulated the theory of information wards before doing their case study. This theory provides a conceptual framework by which an organization is modeled as a collection of stakeholders who own processes and data, called an "information ward," and will defend some of their ward when it is threatened. This is an architectural theory. The organization is modeled as a collection of components (stakeholders, processes, information systems, information wards) with capabilities, and the phenomenon of information system development will trigger a mechanism in stakeholders (defending their ward) that will produce other phenomena (sabotage). The research goal was to explore the effect of organizational conflict on information system development, and prior to doing the case study, they intended to use the theory of information wards as theoretical framework [11, p. 191].

☐   (14) Damian and Chisan [1] did not start with a particular theory about requirements engineering improvement. Their case study was exploratory. They describe a sequence of three case studies done in the same organization, where after each study, new knowledge questions were formulated based on knowledge acquired in the previous study. After the second study, the conceptual framework was expanded to include interactions between requirements engineering and other practices as well as social processes, and the third study produced a theory of requirements engineering process improvement that we have discussed earlier in Chap. 14 (Abductive Inference Design). Damian and Chisan described the theory in causal form, but their paper contains sufficient information to extract an architectural explanation of this causal theory, as we did in Chap. 14.
Damian and Chisan noted other possible explanations of their observations, namely, that new management was responsible for the improvements and that changes in some other working procedures could also have affected the improvements that they observed [1, pp. 447–448].

17.6.3   Analogic Generalizations

☐   (15) Warne and Hart [11] selected a failed project for which the major conditions of success were satisfied. This corresponds to their population predicate and so reveals their intended target of generalization. Their generalization is that the larger the scope of a proposed information system, the more likely it is to intersect with political information wards, which would produce political conflict and sabotage of the development project. After an analysis of the literature on types of organization, they propose to narrow down the population to projects in divisionalized bureaucracies, for which the major conditions of success were satisfied.

☐   (15) Damian and Chisan [1] selected an organization that had introduced requirements engineering, and this seems to be their originally intended scope of generalization. After the case study, this scope had narrowed down to organizations that introduced requirements engineering as part of a move in software engineering maturity from CMM 1 to CMM 2 and that have a similar architecture consisting of a development organization, users who interact with the development organization, and a marketing department who provides requirements [1, p. 448]. The generalization is not claimed to hold for smaller organizations nor for organizations that do not develop software products.

17.6.4   Answers

The answers to the knowledge questions should summarize the conclusions of the data analysis and add nothing new:

☐   The knowledge question of Warne and Hart [11] was:

– What are the mechanisms that can lead to failure of large information system development projects of which the major conditions of success are satisfied?

Their answer is that in divisionalized bureaucracies, the larger the scope of a proposed information system, the more likely it is to intersect with political information wards, which would produce political conflict and sabotage of the development project.
☐   The knowledge question of Damian and Chisan [1] was:

– How do improvements in requirements engineering processes relate to improvements in productivity, quality, and risk management?

The causal part of their answer is a list of factors impacted positively by the introduction of requirements engineering. The architectural part, as constructed in Chap. 14 (Abductive Inference Design), is that the introduction of cross-functional teams and a change control board improves productivity of developers and the quality of the product and reduces project risk.

17.7   Implications for Context

Table 17.7 lists the checklist items about implications for context. Question 1 of the checklist asked for the knowledge goal, and question 2 about any improvement goal. If there is no improvement goal, implications for the improvement goal are interpreted as implications for practice:

☐   (17) Warne and Hart [11] observe that they have contributed to the knowledge about organizational causes of project failures.
(18) Their implication for practice is that not only should developers beware of political problems, but should realize that the scope of the system itself can create these problems.
☐   (17) Damian and Chisan's [1] observe that they have contributed to knowledge about the costs and benefits of requirements engineering in practice. Their conclusion for research is that collaboration between developers is an important subject for further research [1, p. 445].
(18) For practitioners, the case study results describe a number of practices that can increase the benefits of requirements engineering, such as cross-functional teams and change management.

Table 17.11   The checklist for implications of the research results

17. Contribution to knowledge goal(s) Refer back to items 1 and 3.
18. Contribution to improvement goal(s)? Refer back to item 2.

– If there is no improvement goal: is there a potential contribution to practice?

Notes

[1]**Page 225, checklists for observational case study research.** The classic reference for case study methodology is still Yin, in several editions [14, 15]. Denscombe [2] gives a practical introduction to observational case study research in one chapter plus some supporting chapters about measurement methods. Robson [8] gives a more extensive but still very practical introduction. Flyvberg [4] defends case studies as a valid research theory for theory building and generalization.

Kitchenham et al. [7] and Glass [5] give checklists for software engineering method and tool evaluation from the point of view of a company considering the adoption of new technology. From this point of view, case studies are *pilot studies*. In this book, we take the point of view of researchers who want to learn about the experiences of using technology in practice.

Eisenhardt [3] describes an approach to theory building in case study research that emphasizes open questions, multiple case studies, and integrating conflicting results from the literature. Data analysis commences as soon as the first case study is done. She emphasizes the selection of confirmatory cases, which she calls "theoretical sampling."

Verner et al. [10] provide a workflow for doing case studies where the main line of activity is similar to the top-level structure of our checklist, and parallel activities are research management tasks such as data management and relationship building with potential case study sites. Their checklist contains advice on practical matters but is less detailed on inference and validity than the checklist of this book.

Runeson et al. [9] provide checklist for case studies in software engineering research. I have compared this checklist in detail with a precursor of the one used in this book [12, 13]. The checklists are similar, but in the one by Runeson et al. no attention is spent on architectural explanation and analogy. They provide an extensive version of the checklist for researchers and summaries of the checklist for writers and readers of research reports.

Relatively unknown but very useful is a checklist for generalization from case studies given by Kennedy [6] for evaluation researchers.

References

1. D. Damian, J. Chisan, An empirical study of the complex relationships between requirements engineering processes and other processes that lead to payoffs in productivity, quality and risk management. IEEE Trans. Softw. Eng. **32**(7), 433–453 (2006)
2. M. Denscombe, *The Good Research Guide For Small-Scale Social Research Projects*, 4th edn. (Open University Press, Maidenhead, 2010)
3. K.M. Eisenhardt, Building theories from case study research. Acad. Manag. Rev. **14**(4), 532–550 (1989)
4. B. Flyvberg, Five misunderstandings about case-study research. Qual. Inq. **12**(2), 219–245 (2006)
5. R.L. Glass, Pilot studies: What, why, and how. J. Syst. Softw. **36**, 85–97 (1997)
6. M.M. Kennedy, Generalizing from single case studies. Eval. Q. **3**(4), 661–678 (1979)
7. B. Kitchenham, L. Pickard, S.L. Pfleeger, Case studies for method and tool evaluation. IEEE Softw. **12**(4), 52–62 (1995)
8. C. Robson, *Real World Research*, 2nd edn. (Blackwell, Oxford, 2002)
9. P. Runeson, M. Höst, A. Rainer, B. Regnell, *Case Study Research in Software Engineering: Guidelines and Examples* (Wiley, Hoboken, 2012)
10. J.M. Verner, J. Sampson, V. Tosic, N.A.A. Bakar, B.A. Kitchenham,   Guidelines for industrially-based multiple case studies in software engineering, in *Research Challenges in Information Science, 2009. RCIS 2009. Third International Conference on*, 2009, pp. 313–324

11. L. Warne, D. Hart, The impact of organizational politics on information systems project failure-a case study, in *Proceedings of the Twenty-Ninth Hawaii International Conference on System Sciences*, vol. 4, 1996, pp. 191–201

12. R.J. Wieringa, Towards a unified checklist for empirical research in software engineering: first proposal, in *16th International Conference on Evaluation and Assessment in Software Engineering (EASE 2012)*, ed. by T. Baldaresse, M. Genero, E. Mendes, M. Piattini (IET, Ciudad Real, 2012), pp. 161–165

13. R.J. Wieringa, A unified checklist for observational and experimental research in software engineering (version 1). Technical Report TR-CTIT-12-07, Centre for Telematics and Information Technology University of Twente (2012)

14. R.K. Yin, *Case Study research: Design and Methods* (Sage, Thousand Oaks, 1984)

15. R.K. Yin, *Case Study research: Design and Methods*, 3rd edn. (Sage, Thousand Oaks, 2003)

Chapter 18
Single-Case Mechanism Experiments

A **single-case mechanism experiment** is a test of a mechanism in a single object of study with a known architecture. The research goal is to describe and explain cause-effect behavior of the object of study. This can be used in implementation evaluation and problem investigation, where we do real-world research. It can also be used in validation research, where we test validation models. In this chapter we restrict ourselves to validation research, and in the checklist and examples the object of study is a validation model.

Single-case mechanism experiments are at the same time single-case causal experiments (Chap. 14, Abductive Inference Design). They investigate the effect of a difference of an independent variable X (e.g., angle of incidence) on a dependent variable Y (e.g., accuracy). But not all causal experiments are mechanism experiments. In a mechanism experiment, the researcher has access to the architecture of the object of study and explains the behavior of the object of study in terms of this architecture. This is not true of other kinds of causal experiments.

In this chapter, I use the phrase *mechanism experiment* to indicate single-case mechanism experiments. The description of the research context, research problem, and design of a mechanism experiment should be documented in an *experiment protocol*. Events during execution of the experiment and details of data analysis should be documented in a separate report, sometimes called an *experiment log*. In the rest of this chapter, we discuss how the checklist of Appendix B is applied to single-case mechanism experiments used in validation research.

18.1 Context

Table 18.1 gives the checklist for the research context, written from the point of view of the researcher preparing to do the research. Mechanism experiments can be done at any point in the engineering cycle. Researchers may evaluate

© Springer-Verlag Berlin Heidelberg 2014
R.J. Wieringa, *Design Science Methodology for Information Systems and Software Engineering*, DOI 10.1007/978-3-662-43839-8_18

Table 18.1 The checklist for the research context. Initial questions to position your research, written from the point of view of the researcher preparing to do the research

1. Knowledge goal(s)

   – What do you want to know? Is this part of an implementation evaluation, a problem investigation, a survey of existing treatments, or a new technology validation?

2. Improvement goal(s)?

   – If there is a higher-level engineering cycle, what is the goal of that cycle?
   – If this is a curiosity-driven project, are there credible application scenarios for the project results?

3. Current knowledge

   – State of the knowledge in published scientific, technical and professional literature?
   – Available expert knowledge?
   – Why is your research needed? Do you want to add anything, e.g. confirm or falsify something?
   – Theoretical framework that you will use?

---

implementations, investigate problems, and study validation models by single-case mechanism experiments:

☐ In an implementation evaluation, a researcher may test a tool used by a manufacturer in its manufacturing design process, with the goal of analyzing the current architecture of the tool. An example was given in Chap. 5 on implementation evaluation and problem investigation (p. 47).

☐ In a problem investigation, a researcher may be interested in the architecture of a particular social network, and the curiosity-driven research goal may be to find out what groups or social actors are components of this network, what their capabilities are, and how they interact. To learn about a social network, the researcher may send messages to a network or may ask experimental subjects to perform actions in the network. This would be single-case research because it concerns one social network, and it would be mechanism research because the researcher can track and trace mechanisms of interaction in the network.

☐ In validation research, researchers may test algorithms in the laboratory in a simulated context or may do a serious game within an artificial project to investigate the effects of a new way of developing software.

In this chapter, we restrict our attention to mechanism experiments that are used in validation studies, and so in our examples, the *knowledge goal* of the research project is to validate new technology. The *improvement goal* in our examples is to develop some new technology. *Current knowledge* about a new technology may be based on earlier versions of the same technology and on earlier research in the new technology. We will use two examples in this chapter, one of which is our old friend the DOA algorithm:

☐ The direction of arrival estimation algorithm developed in the DOA project [5] was tested with a simulated array antenna and a wave arrival scenario. The first three checklist questions were answered as follows:

  (1) The knowledge goal was treatment validation.
  (2) The higher-level engineering goal was the development of an accurate estimation algorithm. The project was utility driven, with an industrial sponsor.

(3) The knowledge context consisted of a problem theory described in Chap. 5 on implementation evaluation and problem investigation (p. 44) and of design theories described in Chap. 7 on treatment validation (p. 63).

☐   Kumar et al. [1] describe a set of simulations of different organizational coordination mechanisms for scheduling medical tests of patients in a hospital. This is a problem of workflow and information system design, as the mechanisms differ in the order of activities, the allocation of tasks to actors, and the information flow between actors. Each coordination mechanism is an artifact whose properties need to be investigated. Four mechanisms in total were compared. The first three checklist questions were answered as follows:

(1) The knowledge goal was to learn which of these four mechanisms would produce the best combination of patient flow (time taken by the medical tests) and tardiness (time after due date that test result becomes available). This is a validation research goal.
(2) The research was utility driven, with the improvement goal to better utilize hospital resources.
(3) The knowledge context is general scheduling knowledge and domain-specific knowledge about patient scheduling in hospitals.

18.2   Research Problem

Table 18.2 gives the checklist for research problems. Because we restrict ourselves to validation research, the object of study consists of an artifact prototype interacting with a simulation of the context. The *conceptual framework* therefore will include the framework already developed when the artifact was designed. This framework may have to be extended with constructs and indicators needed to measure the performance of the validation model.

In validation research, the *knowledge questions* may be about different aspects of performance of the artifact in context:

• Effect questions: What effects are produced by the interaction between the artifact prototype and the simulated context? Why?
• Requirements satisfaction questions: Do the effects of the simulation satisfy requirements? Why (not)?
• Trade-off questions: What happens if the artifact architecture is changed? Why?
• Sensitivity questions: What happens if the context is changed? Why?

The *population* of validation research is not the set of similar validation models, but it is the set of all real-world instances of artifact × context. The validation model is investigated to learn something about real-world behavior and is not interesting in itself. The trade-off and sensitivity questions help to clarify the population predicate. For which classes of artifacts can we expect similar performance? In which class of contexts?

☐   (4) The conceptual framework of validation research in the DOA project [5] consists of a conceptual framework for signal reception, described earlier in Chap. 5 on implementation evaluation and problem investigation (p. 44), and of the conceptual framework for the DOA estimation algorithm, described earlier in Chap. 7 on treatment validation (p. 63).
(5) There are two groups of knowledge questions:

Table 18.2 The checklist for the research problem, written from the point of view of the researcher preparing to do the research

4. Conceptual framework

    – Conceptual structures? Architectural structures, statistical structures?
    – Chance models of random variables: Semantics of variables?
    – Validity of the conceptual framework? Clarity of definitions, unambiguous application, avoidance of mono-operation and mono-method bias?

5. Knowledge questions

    – Open (exploratory) or closed (hypothesis-testing) questions?
    – Effect, satisfaction, trade-off or sensitivity questions?
    – Descriptive or explanatory questions?

6. Population

    – Population predicate? What is the architecture of the elements of the population? In which ways are all population elements similar to each other, and dissimilar to other elements?
    – Chance models of random variables: Assumptions about distributions of variables?

☐ What is the execution time of one iteration of the DOA algorithms? Is it less or more than 7.7 ms? Why?

☐ What is the accuracy of the DOA estimations? Can they recognize angles of at least $1°$?

(6) The intended population is the set of DOA estimation algorithms running in a satellite TV system in cars.

☐ (4) Kumar et al. [1] use general scheduling concepts taken from the operations research literature, such as *earliest due date, tardiness, slack*, and *patient flow time*. In this particular problem context, *tardiness* is a measure for how late a test is completed after its due date, *slack* is the difference between the due date of a test and the current date, and *patient flow time* is the time between release time of the earliest test of a patient (the earliest date at which the earliest test of the patient can be taken) and completion time of the last test for that patient.

(5) Kumar et al. do not state their knowledge questions, but they investigate tardiness and flow time for different coordination mechanisms. So apparently the knowledge questions are:

– What are the tardiness and flow time of patient test scheduling for each coordination mechanism? Why?

These are effect questions, and trade-offs are analyzed for the compared mechanisms.

(6) The population is not specified explicitly, but from the motivating introduction we can conclude that it is the set of all hospitals, defined by the following architecture: They consist of the so-called medical units providing medical care to patients, such as neurosurgery and cardiology, and of ancillaries such as radiology and the blood laboratory, which perform tests on patients as ordered by the medical units. Units and ancillaries have their own objectives, such as providing comfort to patients and using resources optimally. The compared coordination mechanisms allocate decisions about when to do a test variously to units, ancillaries, or a central coordinator and assume different kinds of information flows between units and ancillaries.

18.3 Research Design and Validation

The design of mechanism experiments requires decisions about the acquisition of validation models, sampling, treatment, and measurement. It also requires alignment of these decisions with the planned inferences from the data. The checklists for inference design are given in Sect. 18.4, and we illustrate their application to research design here.

18.3.1 Constructing the Validation Model

Table 18.3 gives the checklist for the OoS, which in validation research is a validation model, consisting of an artifact prototype and a model of the context. The artifact prototype is constructed by the researcher, and the model of the context may be constructed by the researcher too, or it may be acquired by the researcher in some other way. For example, the artifact prototype may run in a real-world context used as model of other real-world contexts. Before we discuss validity of a validation model, we look at the examples:

☐ (7.1) Two prototypes were made of the estimation algorithms in the DOA project [5], one in Matlab and one programmed in C on an experimental processor. In both cases, the simulated context consisted of sources that transmit waves, a uniform linear antenna array that receives waves, a beamsteering component that calculates time delays across antennas, and a beamforming component that composes the signal to be processed by the rest of the system. Simulations with Matlab were done with 5 wave sources located at angles of $-30°$, $-8°$, $0°$, $3°$, and $60°$ with respect to the vector orthogonal to the antenna array. Between simulations, the number of antennas, the signal-to-noise ratio, and the number of snapshots taken from the antennas was varied.

Table 18.3 The checklist for the object of study, written from the point of view of the researcher preparing to do the research. The OoS is a validation model

7.1 Acquisition of Objects of Study (validation models)

    – How do you construct a validation model? What architecture should it have?
    – Validity of OoS

        - *Inference support.* Which inferences would be valid with respect to this design? See checklists for validity of descriptive statistics, abductive and analogic inferences.
        - *Repeatability.* Could other researchers use your report to construct or select a similar OoS?
        - *Ethics.* Are people informed that they will be studied, and do they consent to this? Are they free to stop at any time without giving reasons, and do they know this?

□   (7.1) The artifacts validated by Kumar et al. [1] were coordination mechanisms between medical
    units and ancillaries to schedule patient tests:

-   In a decentralized mechanism, each ancillary schedules patient tests independently.
-   In a balanced coordination mechanism, the requesting medical unit imposes a patient flow due
    date.
-   In a centralized mechanism, ancillaries additionally coordinate their schedules among each
    other.
-   In a totally centralized mechanism, all coordination is done by a single scheduler [1, pp. 225–
    228].

These four artifacts were tested in a simulation of a hospital with three units, four ancillaries, and
30 patients [1, pp. 225].

To be valid, the validation model must support descriptive, abductive, and analogic inferences. Remember that we are using the term "validation" in two ways. In the engineering cycle, we assess the *validity of a treatment design* with respect to the problem it is designed for, and in the empirical cycle, we assess the *validity of inferences*. Here, we are interested in the second kind of validity. To increase the validity of inferences based on a validation model, the validation model must satisfy some requirements.

For *descriptive inference*, it is important that the chance model for variables is defined (Table 18.7). The meaning of indicators is defined in terms of observable properties of the validation model, i.e., of the artifact prototype and the model of the context. If symbolic data will be produced, then interpretation procedures have to be agreed on too.

Next, consider *abductive inferences* (Table 18.8). Validation models can support causal inference if the conditions for single-case causal experiments or comparative-cases causal experiment, listed in Chap. 14 (Abductive Inference Design), are satisfied. If the validation model contains people and you want to do causal inference, you have to assess possible threats to internal validity related to psychological or social mechanisms of people in the validation model or across validation models:

• *OoS dynamics.* Could there be interaction among validation models? Could there be interaction among people in a validation model? Could there be historical events, maturation, and dropout of people?

Whether or not we can do causal inference, we should also try to explain phenomena architecturally. To assess support *architectural inference,* the following questions are relevant:

• *Analysis.* Is there enough information about the architecture of the artifact and context available to do an interesting analysis later? Is the information exact enough to do a mathematical analysis? You may want to specify software, methods, techniques, etc., formally enough and list exactly the assumptions about entities and events in the context, to be able to do a precise analysis. This will also facilitate explanatory analysis of observed phenomena later on.

- *Variation.* What is the minimal validation model that you can construct to answer your knowledge questions? Can you omit components that have been specified in the population predicate? Can the components in a model that you constructed have restricted capabilities and still provide sufficient information to answer your knowledge questions? Which generalizations will be licensed by the similarity between the validation model and an artifact implemented in the real world? Varying the architecture of the artifact prototype, we actually do a trade-off analysis. Varying the architecture of the context simulation, we do a sensitivity analysis.
- *Abstraction.* The artifact prototype and context simulation will contain components not specified in the artifact design but required to run the simulation. Do these influence the behavior of the validation model? Will there be unwanted influences from parts of the model of the context that cannot be controlled? If we want to study the effect of mechanisms in their pure, undisturbed form, we should eliminate the influence of components and mechanisms not specified in the architecture. On the other hand, if we want to test the robustness of the architectural mechanisms under various disturbing influences, we should keep them.

A validation model may contain human actors, such as students who simulate a real-world software engineering project. In that case, you may want to be able to give *rational explanations* of observed behavior. If you want to do this, you must prepare for it by ensuring that you can get information about goals and motivations of actors in the simulation. The threats to validity of rational explanations are these:

- *Goals.* Actors may not have the goals that the explanation says it has. Can you get accurate information about the true goals of actors?
- *Motivation.* A goal may not motivate an actor as much as the explanation says it did. Can you get information about the motivation of actors in the simulation?

Generalization from a single-case experiment is done by architectural analogy. The following questions are important to assess support for *analogic inference* (Table 18.9):

- *Population predicate.* Will the validation model satisfy the population predicate? In which way will it be similar to implemented artifacts operating in a real-world context? In which way will it be dissimilar?
- *Ambiguity.* What class of implemented artifacts in real-world contexts could the validation model represent? What could be the target of analogic generalization?

In addition to supporting inferences, construction of the OoS must be repeatable and ethical. Other researchers must be able to *repeat* the construction, and if people are participating, the demands of *ethics* require that participants sign an informed consent form and must be informed that they are free to stop at any time:

☐ (7.1 continued) The architecture of the DOA validation model has been specified mathematically, and the expected effects produced by it can be proven mathematically. The model contains all information to provide architectural explanations of phenomena.

But the model abstracts from many components present in the real world. A car moving on a highway will pass many obstacles that may distort the waves, and these influences have been idealized away in the simulation. And the model idealizes away variation that is present in the real world: slightly unequal distances between antennas in an array, waves that are not quite plane, etc. Support for analogic generalization to the real world is not unlimited, and field tests in real-world contexts must be done to find out if these idealizations matter.

☐ (7.1 continued) The hospital architecture assumed by the study of Kumar et al. does not allow mathematical analysis, but it does allow analysis of events generated during a simulation. It contains sufficient information to give architectural explanations of phenomena.

But architectural components and capabilities in the model may have capabilities not present in their real-world counterparts. For example, the model assumes uncertainty about inputs, e.g., about due dates, and they do not claim effectiveness when inputs are uncertain, and it assumes that the hospital departments will not resist change [1, p. 235]. This limits generalizability to real-world hospitals.

In addition, real hospitals may contain components that are abstracted away in the model, such as independent practitioners working on the premises of the hospital and independent labs who do medical tests for the hospital. These additional components of real-world cases may disturb phenomena produced in a simulation.

18.3.2 Sampling

It may come as a surprise, but in single-case mechanism experiments, we sample objects of study too. In validation research, we construct a sample of validation models in sequence. As explained in Chap. 7 (Treatment Validation), this is a process of scaling up from the laboratory to the field, so the sequence of validation models studied starts in the lab and ends in the field. As in all processes of analytical induction, we construct confirming as well as disconfirming cases. Confirming validation models aim to replicate phenomena produced by earlier models; disconfirming models are extreme models used to explore the boundary of the conditions under which the phenomena can and cannot be produced.

The checklist for sampling is given in Table 18.4. The relevant validity consideration is the one for analogic inference:

• *Representative sampling*, case-based research. In what way will the constructed sample of models be representative of the population?

At the start of a process of scaling up to practice, our models are not representative of implemented artifacts in real-world contexts. They are tested under idealized conditions in the laboratory to assess feasibility of a design idea. Later, when we scale up to conditions of practice, the models become more realistic. During the process of scaling up, generalizability to the real world will become increasingly important, possibly supported by a theory of similitude.

Table 18.4 The part of the checklist for sampling objects of study for single-case mechanism experiments, written from the point of view of the researcher preparing to do the research. Objects of study are validation models

---

7.2   Construction of a sample

- What is the analytical induction strategy? Confirming cases, disconfirming cases, extreme cases?
- Validity of sampling procedure

    - *Inference support.* Which inferences would be valid with respect to this design? See the applicable parts of the checklists for validity of statistical, abductive and analogic inferences.
    - *Repeatability.* Can the sampling procedure be replicated by other researchers?
    - *Ethics.* No new issues.

Table 18.5 Checklist for treatment design of a mechanism experiment in a validation study, written from the point of view of the researcher preparing to do the research. The OoS is a validation model. A treatment of a validation model is a scenario in which the context provides stimuli to the artifact

---

8.   Treatment design

- Which treatment(s) will be applied?
- Which treatment instruments will be used? Instruction sheets, videos, lessons, software, computers, actuators, rooms, etc.
- How are treatments allocated to validation models?

    * Are treatments scaled up in successive validation models?

- What is the treatment schedule?
- Validity of treatment design:

    * *Inference support.* Which inferences would be valid with respect to this design? See the applicable parts of the checklists for validity of statistical, abductive and analogic inferences.
    * *Repeatability:* Is the specification of the treatment and the allocation to validation models clear enough so that others could repeat it?
    * *Ethics.* Is no harm done, and is everyone treated fairly? Will they be informed about the treatment before or after the study?

18.3.3   Treatment Design

Table 18.5 gives the checklist for designing treatments of a validation model. A validation model consists of an artifact prototype and a model of the context, and treatments are *scenarios* that the validation model is exposed to. There are some surprising confusions here that I will illustrate using a simple example of drug research. Consider a test of an experimental medicine, in which subjects are instructed to take the medicine according to some medical protocol, e.g., every morning before breakfast for the next 6 weeks. The medicine is the artifact; the

patient and his or her environment are the context. In this situation, there are three
different interpretations of the term "treatment":

- The patient is treated by an experimental medicine. In other words, the context is
  treated by the artifact.
- An experimental medicine is tested by treating it to a realistic context. In other
  words, the artifact is treated by the context.
- The patient is instructed to take an experimental medicine according to a medical
  protocol. In other words, the artifact and context are treated to a scenario.

In validation research, we use the word "treatment" in the third sense. For example,
an experimental software prototype may be treated to an input scenario from a
simulated context, or in a serious game the participants may be treated to a scenario
from a simulated context.

To deliver the treatment scenario, *treatment instruments* may be needed, such
as software to generate scenarios, sensors to collect data from a simulated context,
instruction sheets, videos or lessons for human participants, equipment and rooms
to put them in, etc.

Treatments must be *allocated* to objects of study, which in validation research
means that the researcher must decide which application scenarios to test on which
models. When scaling up from lab to practice, the first models are exposed to toy
scenarios, and the final models are exposed to realistic scenarios.

All of this must be *scheduled*. This is a practical and important matter because
the schedule is limited by research budgets and research project deadlines.

For *causal inference*, the following questions are relevant to assess the degree of
support of a treatment for causal explanations (Table 18.8):

- *Treatment control.* What other factors than the treatment could influence the
  validation models? If a validation model contains people, then possible influences
  are the treatment allocation mechanism, the experimental setup, the experimenters and their expectations, the novelty of the treatment, compensation by
  the researcher, and rivalry or demoralization among subjects. For software or
  hardware in the validation model, we would have to consider virtual or physical
  factors that could influence their behavior.
- *Treatment instrument validity.* If you use instruments to apply the scenario, do
  they have the effect on the validation model that you claim they have?

To conclude something about the target of the validation model, we do *analogic
inference*. To assess support for analogic inference, the following questions are
relevant (Table 18.9):

- *Treatment similarity.* Is the specified treatment scenario in the experiment similar
  to treatments in the population? Or are you doing an extreme case study and
  should it be dissimilar?
- *Compliance.* Is the treatment scenario implemented as specified?
- *Treatment control.* What other factors than the treatment could influence the
  validation models? This is the same question as mentioned above for causal

inference. The relevance for analogic generalization is that if there are factors that we could not control, we should ask if the implemented treatment should be interpreted as another treatment, namely, as the intended treatment plus uncontrolled factors.

Increased control over extraneous factors improves support for causal inference (internal validity) but decreases support for analogic inference to field conditions (external validity) because it makes the simulation less realistic.

In addition to support for inferences, treatment validity includes repeatability and ethics. The experiment protocol must specify the treatment scenarios explicitly, so that other researchers could *repeat* the test using their own validation model. These tests are replications: The results obtained earlier must be reproducible.

If people are involved, *ethical* considerations apply. People must be treated fairly, and no harm must be done. If deception is used, for example, by withholding some information from the subjects, this must not be unfair or harmful either. In a debriefing after the experiment, subjects must be informed of the true research goal, questions, design, and results of the experiment:

☐   (8) In the DOA test, the scenarios are all combinations of values for signal-to-noise ratios, numbers of snapshots, and number of antennas. No treatment instruments were needed other than the Matlab tool. The treatment scenarios were not intended to be fully similar to real-world scenarios, but they were realistic enough to be able to assess which algorithm was most promising in the intended context and could therefore be selected for further investigation. The researcher had full control of all factors that could influence the validation model. This improved support for causal inference but decreased support for analogic inference to real-world conditions.

☐   (8) Kumar et al. [1, p. 225] tested many scenarios in which six parameters were varied: number of tests per patient, test start times, processing time, due dates, load of ancillaries, and patient flow and test tardiness objectives. These are all representative of real-world scenarios. No treatment instruments were needed. The level of control was high, which in this example too improved support for causal inference but decreased support for analogic inference to the real world.

18.3.4   Measurement Design

Table 18.6 gives the checklist for measurement specification. Measurement requires the definition of *measured variables and scales*, and these are usually defined already in the conceptual framework of the research, which for validation research has already been designed as part of artifact design.

The *data sources* are components of the validation model from which you will acquire data, e.g., software or hardware components or people participating in the simulation. *Measurement instruments* include clocks, sensors, probes in software, log analyzers, as well as interviews and questionnaires for people participating in the experiment. There should be an infrastructure for *storing and managing measurement data*. Traceability of data to its source (provenance) and availability of the data to other researchers should be decided on.

Table 18.6 Checklist for measurement design of a mechanism experiment, written from the point of view of the researcher preparing to do the research

---

9. Measurement design

  - Variables and constructs to be measured? Scales, chance models.
  - Data sources? People (e.g. software engineers, maintainers, users, project managers, politically responsible persons, etc.), primary data (e.g. source code, log files, bug tracking data, version management data, email logs), primary documents (e.g. project reports, meeting minutes, organization charts, mission statements), etc.
  - Measurement instruments? Interview protocols, questionnaires, video recorders, sound recorders, clocks, sensors, database queries, log analyzers, etc.
  - What is the measurement schedule? Pretests, posttests? Cross-sectional or longitudinal?
  - How will measured data be stored and managed? Provenance, availability to other researchers?
  - Validity of measurement specification:

    * *Inference support.* Which inferences would be valid with respect to this design? See the applicable parts of the checklists for validity of abductive and analogic inferences.
    * *Repeatability.* Is the measurement specification clear enough so that others could repeat it?
    * *Ethics.* Which company data must be kept confidential? How is privacy of persons respected?

Validation models may support *causal inference* if they are used in single-case and comparative-cases causal experiments. But even if they are not used this way, the validity threats of causal inference are still relevant because you want to avoid disturbance of the validation model. The important question with regard to measurement is then the following (Table 18.8):

- *Measurement influence.* Will measurement influence the validation model?

If it does, then this should be subtracted from the data in order to identify treatment effects.

To assess support for generalization by *analogic inference*, the following questions must be answered (Table 18.9):

- *Construct validity.* Are the definitions of constructs to be measured valid? Clarity of definitions, unambiguous application, avoidance of mono-operation and mono-method bias?
- *Measurement instrument validity.* Do the measurement instruments measure what you claim that they measure?
- *Construct levels.* Will the measured range of values be representative of the population range of values?

Finally, measurements should be *repeatable* by other researchers and should be *ethical* for any human subjects. Confidentiality and privacy should be respected:

☐ The variables measured in the DOA project [5] are *degrees* of incidence and *decibels* of the signal. Their definitions are taken from the literature and need not be included in a research report.

    The artifact prototype itself and the simulation of the context are at once the source of data and the measurement instruments.

    The researcher took care to spread the angles of incidence, signal-to-noise ratios, and numbers of antennas to have a reasonable coverage of the ranges of these values in real-world situations. This reduces the construct level validity threat mentioned above. Practical aspects of research design, such as data storage and management, are not reported.

☐ Kumar et al. [1] measure variables like *patient blocked time*, *test processing time*, and *ancillary blocked time*. These are defined in their conceptual research framework, and the authors provide arguments toward the validity of these variables as indicators of the efficiency of the coordination mechanisms studied.

    The simulation software at once generates the simulations, is the source of data, and is the measurement instrument. Parameters of the simulation are *patient load*, *mean inter-arrival time*, *due date*, etc., and these were set to values for a small hospital [1, p. 225]. This introduces a construct level validity threat. Practical aspects of research design, such as data storage and management, are not reported.

18.4 Inference Design and Validation

Single-case mechanism experiments are case based, and inferences from them are done in three steps: description, architectural explanation, and generalization by analogy. The construction of validation models is done with the goal of supporting these kinds of inference, and validity considerations for them have already been given above. Examples of the inferences themselves are given later, in the section on data analysis. Here we have a brief look at the relevant parts of the checklist.

Table 18.7 gives the checklist for descriptive inference. Descriptive inference in single-case mechanism experiments is often the presentation of data in digestible form such as graphs or tables with aggregate information. As usual, data may be transformed, and symbolic data such as images or text must be interpreted. The validity requirements for descriptive inference all ask in one way or another whether the researcher added information to the data that is not warranted by the observed phenomena or by prior knowledge.

Table 18.8 gives the checklist for abductive inference. If the behavior of the validation model is time independent and if effects are transient, then you can do single-case causal experiments with them. And if they can be replicated, you can do comparative-cases causal experiments with them. Since the architecture of the validation model is known, you should try to explain causal relations established this way architecturally. If the validation model contains people, then you may be able to explain their behavior rationally.

Table 18.9 gives the checklist for analogic inference. Generalization from mechanism experiments is done by architectural analogy: In objects with a similar architecture, similar mechanisms will produce similar phenomena. The purpose of experimenting with validation models is to assess the required similarity between model and target. This goes both ways: How similar must a validation model

Table 18.7 Checklist for descriptive inference, written from the point of view of the researcher preparing to do the research. The OoS is a validation model

---

10.1   Descriptive inference design

- How are words and images to be interpreted? (Content analysis, conversation analysis, discourse analysis, analysis software, etc.)
- What descriptive summaries of data are planned? Illustrative data, graphical summaries, descriptive statistics, etc.
- Validity of description design

    * *Support for data preparation.*

        - Will the prepared data represent the same phenomena as the unprepared data?
        - If data may be removed, would this be defensible beyond reasonable doubt?
        - Would your scientific opponents produce the same descriptions from the data?

    * *Support for data interpretation.*

        - Will the interpretations that you produce be facts in your conceptual research framework? Would your scientific peers produce the same interpretations?
        - Will the interpretations that you produce be facts in the conceptual framework of the subjects? Would subjects accept them as facts?

    * *Support for descriptive statistics.*

        - Is the chance model of the variables of interest defined in terms of the population elements?

    * *Repeatability:* Will the analysis repeatable by others?
    * *Ethics:* No new issues.

---

be to real-world implementations to learn something from the model about those implementations? Conversely, how similar must an implementation be to show behavior similar to the validation model? You test models that represent different artifact versions and with variations of the context. Testing prototypes of different artifacts in the same context is trade-off analysis, and testing different contexts with the same artifact is sensitivity analysis. If the mechanism experiment is part of a process of scaling up from the laboratory to the field, then at every step, the research goal is to acquire sufficient certainty about the repeatability of behavior at the current scale, so as to justify the step to the next level of scaling up.

Table 18.8 Checklist for inference design of a mechanism experiment in validation research, written from the point of view of the researcher preparing to do the research. The OoS is a validation model

---

10.3   Abductive inference design

- What possible explanations can you foresee? What data do you need to give those explanations? What theoretical framework?
- Internal validity

  * *Causal inference*

    - *OoS dynamics.* Could there be interaction among OoS's? Could there be historical events, maturation, and drop-out of OoS's?
    - *Treatment control.* What other factors than the treatment could influence the validation models? The treatment allocation mechanism, the experimental setup, the experimenters and their expectations, the novelty of the treatment, compensation by the researcher, rivalry or demoralization about the allocation?
    - *Treatment instrument validity.* If you use instruments to apply the scenario, do they have the effect on the validation model that you claim they have?
    - *Measurement influence.* Will measurement influence the validation models?

  * *Architectural inference*

    - *Analysis:* The analysis of the architecture may not support its conclusions with mathematical certainty. Components fully specified? Interactions fully specified?
    - *Variation:* Do the real-world case components match the architectural components? Do they have the same capabilities? Are all architectural components present in the real-world case?
    - *Abstraction:* Does the architectural model used for explanation omit relevant elements of real-world cases? Are the mechanisms in the architectural model interfered with by other mechanisms, absent from the model but present in the real world case?

  * *Rational inference*

    - *Goals.* An actor may not have the goals assumed by an explanation. Can you get information about the true goals of actors?
    - *Motivation.* A goal may not motivate an actor as much as assumed by an explanation. Can you get information about the true motivations of actors?

Table 18.9 Checklist for inference design of a mechanism experiment in validation research, written from the point of view of the researcher preparing to do the research. The OoS is a validation model

---

10.4   Analogic inference design

- What is the intended scope of your generalization?
- External validity

  * *Object of Study similarity.*

    - *Population predicate.* Will the validation model satisfy the population predicate? In which way will it be similar to implemented artifacts operating in a real-world context? In which way will it be dissimilar?
    - *Ambiguity.* What class of implemented artifacts in real-world contexts could the validation model represent? What could be the target of analogic generalization?

  * *Representative sampling,* case-based research: In what way will the constructed sample of models be representative of the population?
  * *Treatment.*

    - *Treatment similarity.* Is the specified treatment scenario in the experiment similar to treatments in the population?
    - *Compliance.* Is the treatment scenario implemented as specified?
    - *Treatment control.* What other factors than the treatment could influence the validation models? Could the implemented treatment be interpreted as another treatment?

  * *Measurement.*

    - *Construct validity.* Are the definitions of constructs to be measured valid? Clarity of definitions, unambiguous application, avoidance of mono-operation and mono-method bias?
    - *Measurement instrument validity.* Do the measurement instruments measure what you claim that they measure?
    - *Construct levels.* Will the measured range of values be representative of the population range of values?

Table 18.10 The part of the checklist for research execution relevant for mechanism experiments, written from the point of view of the researcher preparing to write a report about the research

11.   What has happened?
– What has happened when the OoS's were selected or constructed? Did they have the architecture that was planned during research design? Unexpected events for OoS's during the study?
– What has happened during sample construction? Could you build or acquire all objects of study that you planned to study?
– What has happened when the treatment(s) were applied? Mistakes, unexpected events?
– What has happened during measurement? Data sources actually used, response rates?

18.5   Research Execution

We now switch perspective from designing your research to executing it and reporting about it. Collecting a report starts as soon as you start executing the experiment. Table 18.10 lists the checklist items for reporting about research execution. Not everything that happens during execution of a research design needs to be reported. What information about events during research execution did you use to interpret your results? What information would be useful to provide if someone wants to repeat your research? The reader of a report must trust that the writer included all relevant information, so as a writer you will have to be honest:

☐   (11) The report about the DOA project gives no information about the Matlab models. However, it contains detailed information about the construction of the C program that implemented the MUSIC algorithm and the relevant properties of the experimental Montium2 processor on which it was executed [5, Chap. 5].

☐   (11) Kumar et al. [1] give no information about the construction of their simulation or about the events during simulation.

18.6   Data Analysis

We now perform the inferences planned, point no: 13 is missing. Please check and provide the same. for in our research design. Table 18.11 shows the checklist for data analysis. The part about statistical inference is absent because we are studying single cases, e.g., single simulations and single prototypes, and not samples of cases.

In the rest of this section, we give examples without further comments. I should repeat here that written reports may present information differently. For example, validity has been considered during research design and inference design and should

Table 18.11 The part of the checklist for data analysis that is relevant for a mechanism experiment, written from the point of view of the researcher preparing to write a report

---

12. Descriptions

    – Data preparations applied? Data transformations, missing values, removal of outliers? Data management, data availability.
    – Data interpretations? Coding procedures, interpretation methods?
    – Descriptive statistics. Demographics, sample mean and variance? Graphics, tables.
    – Validity of the descriptions: See checklist for the validity of descriptive inference.

14. Explanations

    – What explanations (causal, architectural, rational) exist for the observations?
    – Internal validity: See checklist for the validity of abductive inference.

15. Generalizations

    – Would the explanations be valid in similar cases or populations too?
    – External validity: See checklist for the validity of analogic inference

16. Answers

    – What are the answers to the knowledge questions? Summary of conclusions, support for and limitations of conclusions.

---

be reviewed again during data analysis. A written report may present the result of all validity considerations only once, for example, in a separate section; it may distribute the discussion over the different parts of research design, as we did here; or it may distribute the discussion over the different parts of the data analysis.

18.6.1 Descriptions

☐ (12) Vrielink [5] reports sensitivity of a 16-element antenna in different directions, the spectrum recognized by DOA algorithms in different directions, and DOA estimation errors in different directions. Execution times on the intended Montium processor were estimated, not observed, because the processor was not implemented yet. There are in addition qualitative observations such as that changing the number of antennas does not result in a significant difference in performance between the different estimation algorithms [5, p. 24]. This is a sensitivity property.

☐ (12) Kumar et al. [1] reported the percentage improvement (reduction) in tardiness of the different mechanisms over the base configuration of decentralized ancillaries. All improvement data are given in an appendix, and the paper contains numerous graphs visualizing the improvement trends for different settings of the parameters.

18.6.2   Explanations

☐ (14) The functional correctness of the output of the tested algorithms in the DOA project is explained by the algorithm structure. This is what the algorithms were designed for. The time performance properties are explained by the computational complexity of various steps [5, pp. 20, 55, 58]. He explained measured accuracy of different algorithms in terms of physical properties of the waves [5, p. 23]. These are architectural explanations.

There are also causal explanations. For example, the number of antennas is positively correlated with the spatial resolution of the tested algorithms, and this is interpreted causally: Increasing the number of antenna causes an increase in spatial resolution of the compared algorithms [5, p. 24]. Presumably, this causal explanation in turn can be explained architecturally by the structure of the algorithms and architectural properties of the antenna-wave system.

Other observations remain unexplained, such as that one algorithm performed better than the other in tests where the signal-to-noise ratio was low [5, p. 27].

☐ (14) As explained earlier, Kumar et al. studied four coordination mechanisms, a decentralized, balanced, centralized, and totally centralized one. See the discussion of item (7.1) above. The data showed that the totally centralized solution improved on the centralized ancillary solution, which improved on the balanced solution, which improved on the decentralized ancillary solution. The authors explain this by the fact that each of these mechanisms includes those that follow it in this list. Note that the quantitative amount of the observed improvements cannot be explained, but their ordering can.

18.6.3   Analogic Generalizations

☐ (15) The results of the DOA experiments are generalized to real-world implementations of the algorithms, running in a satellite TV system that is part of a car driving on a road. This generalization is supported by the similarity of algorithms in the laboratory and in the field. The laboratory simulation of the context may be less similar to the real-world context, because in the real world, various conditions of practice may disturb the results obtained in the laboratory simulation. Field tests are needed to give more support to the generalization.

☐ (15) The simulations by Kumar et al. can probably be replicated by other researchers, in which case they are generalizable, by architectural analogy, to other simulations. Generalization to real hospitals is less well supported. The simulation ignores uncertainty about inputs and resistance to change. There are many architectural capabilities, limitations, and mechanisms in a real hospital that may interfere with the simulated coordination mechanisms in a way that makes the results unreproducible in the real world. To learn more about this, real-world case studies should be done. If a hospital decides to implement one of these coordination mechanisms, then we may be able to study the resulting mechanisms in detail in this case. This would be an evaluation study [2].

Some generalizations may not be based on architectural similarity but on feature-based similarity. If we think that an observed phenomenon generalizes to similar cases without understanding the mechanism behind it, then we have postulated an **empirical regularity.** The phenomenon may indeed be regular, so that we can use it as a prediction. But if it remains unexplained, we should treat it as an empirical regularity that may be broken for reasons that we do not understand.

When practitioners use an empirical regularity for which we have no architectural explanation, they can manage the risk that the regularity is violated by moving in small steps. Designs that have been proven to work in practice are used in new situations with only small differences from proven cases. This will make the set of proven cases expand gradually. This is one of the motivations behind evolutionary design [3,4]:

☐ For example, the observation in the DOA project that one algorithm performed better than the other in tests where the signal-to-noise ratio was low [5, p. 27] is unexplained. Suppose that this phenomenon cannot be explained in terms of the different structures of the algorithms. Then we can still treat it as an empirical regularity. There is a slight architectural flavor to this generalization, because the generalization is that in cases with similar architecture, the same phenomenon will occur. But as long as we do not understand how this architecture produces this phenomenon, we should treat it as an empirical regularity. When it is used, it is safe to use it in situations that only differ incrementally from situations where it has shown to be true.

18.6.4 Answers to Knowledge Questions

☐ (16) The DOA project has a number of effect questions:

  – What is the execution time of one iteration of the DOA algorithm? Is it less or more than 7.7 ms? Why?
  – What is the accuracy of the DOA estimations? Can they recognize angles of at least 1°?

The data analysis provides answers to these questions for two algorithms that can be tentatively generalized from the laboratory to the field. One of the algorithms was shown to satisfy the requirements on execution speed and accuracy.

☐ (16) Kumar et al. did not state a knowledge question, but we assumed it to be the following:

  – What are the tardiness and flow time of patient test scheduling for each coordination mechanism? Why?

The data analysis provided support for the generalization that in the absence of disturbing mechanisms and for a simulation of a small hospital, the four coordination mechanisms increasingly reduce tardiness, where total centralization gave the best results. Without further research, this cannot be generalized to real hospitals.

18.7 Implications for Context

Table 18.12 lists the checklist for relating the research results to the knowledge context and improvement context. The knowledge context in validation research is what is known so far about the artifact being validated. The improvement context is the engineering cycle of the artifact:

Table 18.12 The checklist for implications of the research results

17. Contribution to knowledge goal(s) Refer back to items 1 and 3.
18. Contribution to improvement goal(s)? Refer back to item 2.

    – If there is no improvement goal: is there a potential contribution to practice?

☐ (17) The DOA mechanism experiment [5] added knowledge about the performance of the estimation algorithms in the particular context of satellite TV reception.

    (18) The research was sponsored by a hardware manufacturer, who used the results in the design and development of a new satellite TV system for cars.

☐ (17) Kumar et al. [1] were the first to apply their centralized and decentralized coordination mechanisms to patient test scheduling. So this was the first knowledge about these artifacts in this context.

    (18) Their research was motivated by one particular hospital, and each of their mechanisms improved patient test scheduling performance compared to current performance in the hospital. The paper does not report if one of these mechanisms was actually adopted by the hospital.

References

1. A. Kumar, P.S. Ow, M.J. Prietula, Organizational simulation and information systems design: an operational level example. Manag. Sci. **39**(2), 218–240 (1993)
2. R. Pawson, N. Tilley, *Realistic Evaluation* (Sage, Thousand Oaks, 1997)
3. H. Petroski, *To Engineer is Human: The Role of Failure in Successful Design* (Vintage books, New York, 1982)
4. H. Petroski, *The Evolution of Useful Things* (Vintage Books, New York, 1992)
5. J.D. Vrielink, Phased array processing: direction of arrival estimation on reconfigurable hardware. Master's Thesis, Faculty of Electrical Engineering, Mathematics and Computer Science, University of Twente, January 2009. http://essay.utwente.nl/62065/

Chapter 19
Technical Action Research

Technical action research (TAR) is the use of an experimental artifact to help a client and to learn about its effects in practice. The artifact is experimental, which means that it is still under development and has not yet been transferred to the original problem context. A TAR study is a way to validate the artifact in the field. It is the last stage in the process of scaling up from the conditions of the laboratory to the unprotected conditions of practice:

☐ For example, a researcher may have developed a new effort estimation technique and is now ready to test it in the field. She teaches it to project managers, who then use it in their next project. The researcher observes what happens in order to answer knowledge questions about the technique.

    If no project manager wants to use the technique, the researcher may use it him- or herself to do effort estimations in real-world projects. In this case too, the researcher observes what happens in order to answer knowledge questions about the technique.

TAR studies are single-case studies, because each individual use of the artifact is studied as a case. The difference with observational case studies is that the researcher intervenes in the case to see what happens. The difference with single-case mechanism experiments is that the treatment is not merely applied to see what happens but also to help the client. The combination of these two properties is what makes TAR **action research**.[2]

The difference between TAR and other forms of action research is that TAR is artifact driven. All other forms of action research are problem driven, because they work with the client to solve a problem without the goal of testing a particular artifact. In contrast, TAR is part of the validation of an experimental artifact.

In TAR, the researcher is playing three roles (Fig. 19.1):

- As a *technical researcher,* the researcher designs a treatment intended to solve a class of problems. For example, the researcher designs a new effort estimation technique.
- As an *empirical researcher,* the researcher answers some validation knowledge questions about the treatment. For example, the researcher wants to know how accurate the effort estimation technique is.

© Springer-Verlag Berlin Heidelberg 2014
R.J. Wieringa, *Design Science Methodology for Information Systems and Software Engineering*, DOI 10.1007/978-3-662-43839-8_19

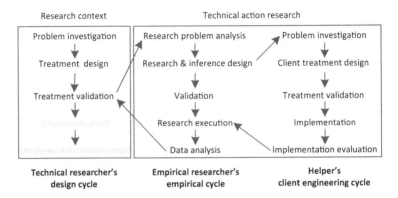

Fig. 19.1 The three-level structure of TAR

- As a *helper,* the researcher applies a client-specific version of the treatment to help a client. For example, the researcher may adapt the effort estimation technique to a client and use it to help the client estimate project effort.

The key to the methodology of TAR is identifying these three roles and keeping them conceptually separate.

Figure 19.1 shows that we start with a design cycle in which we design treatments for a problem. To validate a treatment, we need to answer empirical knowledge questions, and for this we perform an empirical cycle. So far, this is not different from other kinds of validation research. The distinguishing feature of TAR is that we validate a treatment by using it to help a client, in a client's engineering cycle. This requires coordination between the activities done as a researcher and as a helper, which we will discuss later.

After a client cycle is finished, the researcher answers the validation knowledge questions. The answers may provide reasons to improve the artifact in a new iteration through the design cycle, including additional technical action research to validate the improved artifact.

The description of the research context and the research problem, and of the design of the client treatment, should be documented in a *TAR protocol*. This document includes the agreements made with the client about access to the client's organization, treatment, and confidentiality of data. Events during execution of the treatment and details of data analysis should be documented in a separate report that we will call a *TAR log*. In the rest of this chapter, we discuss how the checklist of Appendix B is applied to TAR.

Table 19.1 The checklist for the research context of a TAR project. Initial questions to position your research, written from the point of view of the researcher preparing to do the research

1. Knowledge goal(s)

    – What do you want to know about the treatment?

2. Improvement goal(s)?

    – What is the goal of the treatment?

3. Current knowledge

    – What is currently known about this kind of treatment?
    – Available expert knowledge?
    – Why is your research needed?
    – Theoretical framework that you will use?

19.1 Context

Table 19.1 shows the checklist items for the research context of a TAR project. The *knowledge goal* of a TAR project is to validate a treatment under conditions of practice. The *improvement goal* served by the TAR project is therefore the goal of the treatment to be designed. *Current knowledge* consists of the current version of your design theory of the artifact, plus any prior knowledge about the components that you have used in the design:

☐ Morali and Wieringa [6] designed a method for confidentiality risk assessment when outsourcing data management to a service provider:

   (1) The knowledge goal was to learn whether this method was usable and useful.
   (2) The improvement goal of the method was to allow a company to assess and manage confidentiality risks when data management has been outsourced, so that they can show to their auditors that they are in control of their information assets.
   (3) The method, called CRAC++, had only been used on a toy example, but it was related to methods that computed quantitative risks that had been tested independently. Knowledge about those methods was used to construct CRAC++.

☐ Engelsman and Wieringa [2] describe two TAR studies in the development of a goal-oriented enterprise architecture design method called ARMOR. In between, the method was improved:

   (1) The knowledge goal was to learn whether the method was usable and useful.
   (2) The improvement goal was to achieve better traceability from business goals to enterprise architecture and vice versa.
   (3) Current knowledge about the method was prior knowledge about the enterprise architecture method used (ArchiMate) and about the goal-oriented requirements engineering methods used to define ARMOR.

Table 19.2 The checklist for the research problem of a TAR study, written from the point of view of the researcher preparing to do the research

4. Conceptual framework

  - Conceptual structures? Architectural structures?
  - Validity of the conceptual framework? Clarity of definitions, unambiguous application?

5. Knowledge questions

  - Open (exploratory) or closed (hypothesis-testing) questions?
  - Effect, satisfaction, trade-off or sensitivity questions?
  - Descriptive or explanatory questions?

6. Population

  - Population predicate? What is the architecture of the elements of the population? In which ways are all population elements similar to each other, and dissimilar to other elements?

19.2 Research Problem

Table 19.2 lists the checklist questions for the research problem of TAR, written from the point of view of a researcher preparing for the research. Each treatment has a *conceptual framework* that is developed when the artifact is designed. As we saw in Chaps. 5 (Implementation Evaluation and Problem Investigation) and 7 (Treatment Validation), the conceptual framework of an artifact is used in the design theory of the artifact, and it extends the conceptual framework of the problem.

The *knowledge questions* are validation questions. There are two generic validation knowledge questions:

- What effects are produced by the interaction between artifact and context?
- Do the effects satisfy requirements?

It is convenient for the client to distinguish usability questions from utility questions. *Usability questions* ask whether these effects satisfy usability requirements such as understandability, ease of use, and ease of learning. *Utility questions* take us beyond the requirements to stakeholder goals. Can the users use the artifact to achieve stakeholder goals? The questions can be open or closed and descriptive or explanatory.

The *population* of interest is the set of artifact variants and contexts of use about which you want to generalize. To assess the scope of usability and utility of a method, you need to do a series of TAR projects, and you need to understand by which mechanism effects are produced by the artifact. The generalization that you are after is a claim about which variants of the artifact are effective in which kinds of context, and the justification for such a generalization refers to the mechanisms by which the artifact produces effects in a context:

☐ (4) The CRAC++ method [6] defines a conceptual framework for an outsourcing architecture in which an organization, called the *outsourcing client*, has outsourced data management tasks to an external party, called the *outsourcing provider*. These are problem concepts. The conceptual framework of CRAC++ contains standard risk assessment concepts such as *threat agent*, *asset*, and *vulnerability* and some nonstandard concepts like *ease of access* and *protection level*.

(5) The knowledge questions were:

Q1 Is the method easy to use?
Q2 Does it deliver the same results when used by different persons?
Q3 Does it contribute to the client's understanding of confidentiality risks on an outsourcing relation?

Q3 is relevant because it is the goal of the method to improve understanding of confidentiality risks. Q1 and Q2 are usability questions, and Q3 is a utility question.

(6) The population for which the method is intended is any company that has outsourced some of its data management and is subject to external auditing.

☐ (4) The ARMOR method [2] assumes a problem context in which the concept of an enterprise architecture is defined. The ARMOR method itself extends the conceptual model of the Archi-Mate method with concepts from goal-oriented requirements engineering, such as *stakeholder*, *soft goal* and *hard goal*, and *concern* [3].

(5) The knowledge questions in the first TAR project were about usability:

– What ARMOR constructs are used in practice?
– For which purpose are they used?
– Is this the intended use?

The second TAR project had two questions:

– Are the concepts in the redesigned ARMOR method understandable by architects?
– Does the method help in tracing business goals to enterprise architecture?

This is a usability question and a utility question, respectively.

(6) The intended population consists of all companies with a mature enterprise architecture department who aim to keep their enterprise architecture closely aligned with their business goals.

19.3 Research Design and Validation

The design of TAR studies requires decisions about client selection, sampling, treatment, and measurement. It also requires alignment of these decisions with the planned inferences from the data. The checklists for inference design are given in Sect. 19.4, but we illustrate their application to research design here.

Table 19.3 Checklist for the object of study of TAR, written from the point of view of the researcher preparing to do the research

7.1   Acquisition of Objects of Study (Artifact × Client)

- How do you acquire a client? Which architecture must it have? How do you know it has this architecture?
- How do you customize the artifact to the client?
- Validity of OoS

  - *Inference support.* Which inferences would be valid with respect to this design? See checklists for validity of descriptive statistics, abductive and analogic inferences.
  - *Repeatability.* Could other researchers use your report to construct or select a similar OoS?
  - *Ethics.* Are people informed that they will be studied, and do they consent to this? Are they free to stop at any time without giving reasons, and do they know this?

19.3.1   Client Selection

In TAR, the object of study is a client treated with an experimental artifact. Table 19.3 lists the checklist questions for acquiring a client and customizing the artifact to the client. To acquire an organization where you can apply an experimental artifact, you need to build up mutual trust. Acquiring the trust of a company may require a period of a few months to a few years. The best strategy is therefore to build up a network of possible client companies over a period of years, starting before you are ready to test a method in practice. This also helps you to stay on course with respect to problem relevance [10].

Ways to build up such a network are visits to matchmaking events where researchers and companies meet, visits to practitioners' conferences, membership of professional associations, and asking for referrals to related companies in a snowballing procedure. Student internships are also a good starting point for long-term relationships. You need a match in personality as well as in business goals. Since you need to work with the client company closely, you need a personal relationship with at least a gatekeeper who can provide you access to the relevant parts of the company. The client company will not be primarily interested in your research goal, but they should have a problem to solve for which you can use your method, and they should be convinced that this will help them. For the client company, this is a kind of free consultancy project, but they do take a risk by committing human resources to the TAR project that could have been used for other purposes.

Table 19.7 gives the checklist for *descriptive inference.* You should consider if you can get the data for relevant descriptive statistics and whether chance models for the variables have been defined about which you want to collect statistics.

Causal inferences cannot be supported by a TAR study, because you cannot observe the alternative world in which the treatment was not applied to the client.

To asses support for *architectural inference,* consider the following questions (Table 19.8):

- *Analysis.* Can you collect enough information about the architecture of the client organization to be able to analyze relevant mechanisms? What components of the client organization will interact with the application of the artifact. Will you get access to these components?
- *Variation.* How close must the client organization match the components mentioned in the problem architecture? Must all elements of the problem architecture be present in the client organization? Or do you want to test the robustness of the artifact under variation of real-world contexts?
- *Abstraction.* The problem architecture specified in the conceptual problem framework of the artifact may abstract away potentially relevant structures in a client company. Is this important? Do you want to test the robustness of the artifact against possible influences of components not mentioned in the problem architecture?

To support *rational explanations,* the following considerations are relevant when acquiring a client:

- *Goals.* Can you get information about the true goals of actors?
- *Motivation.* Even if you can get information about goals, would you be able to relate actions to goals? Would actors be open about their motivations?

The checklist for *analogic inference* in TAR studies (Table 19.9) gives us the following:

- *Population predicate.* To which extent do the client organization and the artifact prototype satisfy the population predicate? In which way are the client organization and the customized artifact similar to other organizations and artifact implementations in the population? In which way are they dissimilar?
- *Ambiguity.* Could the client organization and artifact prototype be viewed as instances of other population predicates too? Could you actually be generalizing about the artifact used by the researcher instead of about the artifact? What could be the target of analogic generalization?

Related to the last point, *repeatability* is an issue. You have built up a trust relationship with the client company, and this means that you cannot be simply replaced by any other researcher to do the project. Repeatability is conditional on trust. But we can still ask whether any other researcher with a similar level of trust with a client company from the same population should be able to do a similar TAR project with them.

Finally, *ethics* dictate that the people participating in the TAR project are aware that they participate in a research project and agreed to do so. They should know they are free to stop at any time without giving reasons:

☐ (7.1) The CRAC++ method was applied in a TAR project at a manufacturing company with the required outsourcing architecture [6]. The company was part of the advisory board of the research project in which CRAC++ and other risk assessment methods were developed, so that it had come to know the researchers over a period of time. This allowed us to build up a trust relationship by which we were reasonably aware of the goals and motivations of the important stakeholders in the client organization even before the client cycle started. The company has an unknown number of other processes and components that we assumed would not influence the use of the CRAC++ method.

The CRAC++ method needed a minor adaptation to the client company. CRAC++ requires the helper to estimate frequencies and impact of successful attacks on the outsourcing architecture, and we adapted the scales to the kind of data we could acquire from the client, and we developed a lightweight tool to manage the large amount of data collected.

Generalizability is an issue. Because it was the researcher herself who applied the method, we could not rule out the possibility that we were studying an instance of CRAC++ as used by its developer rather than an instance of CRAC++.

☐ (7.1) The ARMOR research project was performed by a helper who studied for a PhD part-time. The TAR project in which ARMOR was used in a client company, was done with a client that the helper had known for many years. The researcher had access to the relevant components and processes in the client organization and could ascertain that the client organization and the use of ARMOR satisfied the population predicate.

ARMOR was not adapted to the client.

The method was used by others, so there was no threat that we were studying ARMOR as used by its developer. However, because the users know that the method was new, there are still threats to generalizability. We may have been studying ARMOR when it was brand new. We assess the severity of these threats when we discuss generalizations about the treatment.

19.3.2 Sampling

TAR is case-based research, so we have to decide on an analytical induction strategy. However, it is not possible to select disconfirming cases, which is done in analytical induction about observational case studies. It would not be ethical to select a client company in the expectation that the client cycle will result in failure. Failures are a great source of insight in the functioning of artifacts [7], but we cannot intentionally generate failures in TAR studies. Instead of true analytical induction, in TAR we perform improvement cycles. After each client cycle, the artifact may be improved, and each next client is usually selected to show successful use of the updated artifact. Table 19.4 gives the checklist for sampling in TAR.

The checklist for the validity of *abductive inference* (Table 19.8) gives us the following questions:

• *Sampling influence*. Could the selection mechanism influence the client organizations? Could there be a regression effect?

Table 19.4 Checklist for the sampling strategy of TAR, written from the point of view of the researcher preparing to do the research

---

7.2   Construction of a sample of (Artifact × Client) cases

- What is the analytical induction strategy? Confirming cases, extreme cases?
- Validity of sampling procedure

    - *Inference support.* Which inferences would be valid with respect to this design? See the applicable parts of the checklists for validity of statistical, abductive and analogic inferences.
    - *Repeatability.* Can the sampling procedure be replicated by other researchers?
    - *Ethics.* No new issues.

Being selected for a TAR project may affect the client organization so that the researcher may observe phenomena that would not have occurred when the client would not be studied. And if you work an extreme case, such as a very large or very small organization, you must consider in your generalization that most other organizations will be less extreme in size.

For *analogic inference*, the following question is relevant (Table 19.9):

- *Representative sampling*, case-based research. In what way will the selected sample of clients and customized artifacts be representative of the population?

When we search for a client to help with the artifact, this question has a heuristic function because it suggests that we should find a client that will provide us useful information for generalization. After a series of TAR studies, the question can be interpreted empirically: What can we learn from a series of TAR studies about the class of clients where our artifact can be used successfully?

☐ (7.2) In the CRAC++ project, two client cycles were performed with two different client companies. Both projects were successful, but an important shortcomings of the method observed in the first client cycle was the lack of tool support. This was repaired in a quick-and-dirty way by creating some spreadsheet structures. This saved the researcher some time in the second client cycle, but it did not change the effects of using the method to help a client.

   The clients were large manufacturing companies that have outsourced the management of some of their ERP systems. The organizations were too large to be influenced in any way by being selected as a client for our TAR project. This is tentatively the population of clients for which the CRAC++ method would be useful.

☐ (7.2) The ARMOR method too was tested in two client cycles. The first cycle revealed which parts of ARMOR were hard to use. This leads to an update of ARMOR, which was then used in the second cycle.

   The clients were semigovernment organizations with a mature enterprise architecture, so this is tentatively the class of clients to which we can generalize our findings. One organization was large (handling all welfare payments in the Netherlands) and the other relatively small (handling the administration of water supply bills in one province). This suggests that we can generalize independently of the size of the organization.

19.3.3   Treatment Design

In TAR, there are three treatments, corresponding to the roles that the researcher plays. As we move from one role to another, there is a reversal of what is treated by what:

- In the client cycle, the client is treated with an experimental artifact.
- In the empirical research cycle, an experimental artifact is tested by treating it with a real-world context.
- The researcher and client agree on a treatment plan in which, from one point of view, the client is treated by the artifact and, from another point of view, the artifact is treated to the client context.

We have observed this ambiguity earlier when we discussed treatments in single-case mechanism experiments (p. 256).

Figure 19.2 shows in detail how the empirical cycle and the client cycle interact. Before acquiring a client, you determine your conceptual framework, formulate the knowledge questions, and state what the population of interest is. Next, you acquire a client organization and do a client cycle as follows:

- When acquiring a client organization, you will discuss with potential clients what problem they want to solve and which business goals they want to achieve. This is the problem investigation task in the client cycle. In the empirical research cycle, it is part of research design, and it includes customizing the artifact to the client.
- Once you have acquired a client, you will agree a treatment plan with them. You will specify requirements on the treatment, show that this would contribute to their goals, and agree on a plan. In the empirical cycle, this is still part of research design.
- The client treatment must be validated with the client in order to achieve a mutual agreement that this is what you will do to help them achieve their goals. At the same time, in the empirical cycle, you validate that this research design will help *you* to answer your knowledge questions.
- Next, you execute the client treatment. This is part of research execution in the empirical cycle.
- Finally, you evaluate the outcome with the client. This is the last task in the client cycle, and it is still part of research execution in the empirical cycle.

After the client cycle is finished, you analyze the data as part of the empirical cycle.

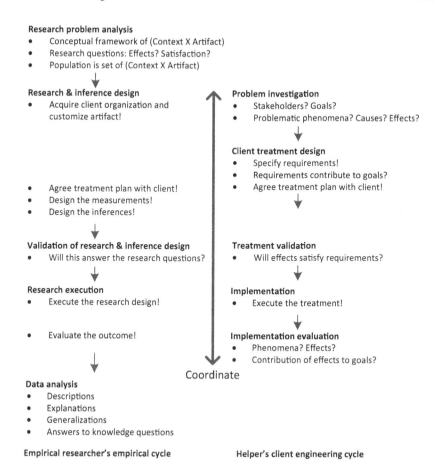

Fig. 19.2 Detailed list of tasks in TAR. Exclamation marks indicate things to do, question marks indicate questions to answer. Coordination with activities in the client cycle starts as soon as a client is acquired and the artifact customized and finishes when the client cycle is evaluated

Switching back to the empirical research cycle, we are currently concerned with the design and validation of the treatment to be applied to the client. Table 19.5 lists the checklist questions for the treatment design and validation in the empirical cycle. Treatment design in TAR is customizing the still-experimental treatment to the client, and this is the first question of this part of the checklist. You may have to make decisions about treatment instruments and treatment schedule, which you need to agree with the client.

To assess support for abductive inference, the checklist for *causal inference* is relevant, not because we want to show the presence of causality, but because we want to assess which causal influences can be assumed to be absent. The relevant questions ask you to check whether or not some capabilities and mechanisms that could influence the results were absent:

Table 19.5 Checklist for treatment design in TAR, written from the point of view of the researcher preparing to do the research

8. Treatment design
– How will the treatment be customized to the client?
– Which treatment instruments will be used? Instruction sheets, videos, lessons, software, computers, actuators, rooms, etc.
– How are treatments allocated to OoS's?
*   Are treatments scaled up in successive cases?
– What is the treatment schedule?
– Validity of treatment design:
*   *Inference support.* Which inferences would be valid with respect to this design? See the applicable parts of the checklists for validity of statistical, abductive and analogic inferences.
*   *Repeatability.* Is the specification of the treatment and the allocation to OoS's clear enough so that others could repeat it?
*   *Ethics.* Is no harm done, and is everyone treated fairly? Will they be informed about the treatment before or after the study?

- *Treatment control.* What other factors than the treatment could influence the outcome of the client cycle? You intervene as a helper in an organization. Possible influences on the outcome are the treatment allocation mechanism, the client-consulting setup, your expectations and expectations of organizational actors, the novelty of the client treatment, compensation by the helper for the willingness of actors to work with you, and rivalry or demoralization among organizational actors.
- *Treatment instrument validity.* Will the treatment instruments have the effect on the client organization that you claim they have? Will they understand your instructions, will they use tools properly?

Since you act as a helper for a client, your control of treatment conditions is probably low, which implies that architectural explanations of outcomes have many threats to their internal validity. On the other hand, this increases support for the external validity of *analogic inference* to field conditions. For this, the following questions are relevant (Table 19.9):

- *Treatment similarity.* Is the customized treatment plan similar to other treatments in the real-world population? Different clients may require different customizations.
- *Compliance.* Will the customized treatment plan that you agreed on be implemented as specified?

- *Treatment control.* What other factors than the treatment could influence the client? This is the same question as mentioned above, and the question is relevant here because you have to be aware what you can actually generalize about, the treatment or the treatment plus other factors.

In addition to support for inferences, treatment validity includes repeatability and ethics. The TAR protocol must specify the client treatment explicitly, so that other researchers with the same level of trust could *repeat* the process with similar clients.

Since people are involved, *ethical* considerations apply. People must be treated fairly, and no harm must be done. If deception is used, for example, by withholding some information from the subjects, this must not be unfair or harmful either. In a debriefing after the project, for example, as part of the client evaluation, the subjects must be informed of any deception that took place:

☐   (8) In the CRAC++ projects, the client problem was this: These companies had to show to external auditors that they were in control of the information assets [6]. However, some of the data was managed by an outsourcing provider, so some employees in the outsourcing provider had permission to access confidential data of the client company. In addition, some of the confidential data of the client company was actually stored on servers located in the premises of the outsourcing provider. Some of these servers were owned by the client company; others were owned by the outsourcing provider. The outsourcing provider would not allow the client's auditors to audit the provider's IT architecture, because this would violate the provider's confidentiality requirements.

The researcher agreed with the client company to do a risk assessment in two calendar weeks, using documents about the architecture of the systems managed by the outsourcing provider. She acquired permission to interview an enterprise architect once to ask clarifications about these documents and agreed on a limited number of appointments with the chief security officer to clarify points regarding sensitivity of data and risk of data loss.

The researcher had no control over conditions in the company during the assessment. She applied the same risk assessment twice in different clients, which increases support for external validity.

A debriefing was planned with the chief security officer in which the results would be reported and the advice to the company would be explained. This debriefing would be part of the client evaluation.

☐   (8) In the ARMOR projects, the client companies had the problem that their budgets were shrinking. Their goal was to get better control of IT expenses by improving the alignment of their enterprise architecture with business objectives. Both clients were (semi)government organizations.

The first client was a government organization who wanted to redesign their enterprise architecture due to changes in the law. These changes had been translated into changed business goals of the client. The researcher taught the ARMOR method to enterprise architects of the client company, who then used it to redesign their enterprise architecture in agreement with the changed business goals. The researcher had no control over what happened when the architects used ARMOR. This made this application realistic.

In the second project, the researcher used an updated version of ARMOR, called Light ARMOR, to model the existing enterprise architecture of the client and then verified this architecture on understandability and utility with the client.

19.3.4   Measurement Design

Table 19.6 lists the checklist questions for measurement design. As usual, you need a conceptual framework that defines *variables* and their *scales*. This may already have been defined in the technical researcher's design cycle, when the artifact was designed. Restricting yourself to a limited set of measured variables is important, because there is an infinite number of aspects that you could measure in a TAR study, and you should restrict yourself to those aspects that are relevant for your design theory of the artifact.

Since the researcher plays an active role in the TAR study, it is important to record any treatment decisions that you make as well as decisions about how to interpret and respond to events. Would an impartial observer who does not know you make the same observations? What would a journalist who follows you write?

Table 19.6 Checklist for measurement in TAR, written from the point of view of the researcher preparing to do the research

9. Measurement design

- Variables and constructs to be measured? Scales, chance models.
- Data sources? People (e.g. software engineers, maintainers, users, project managers, politically responsible persons, etc.), primary data (e.g. source code, log files, bug tracking data, version management data, email logs), primary documents (e.g. project reports, meeting minutes, organization charts, mission statements), etc.
- Measurement instruments? Interview protocols, questionnaires, video recorders, sound recorders, clocks, sensors, database queries, log analyzers, etc.
- What is the measurement schedule? Pretests, posttests? Cross-sectional or longitudinal?
- How will measured data be stored and managed? Provenance, availability to other researchers?
- Validity of measurement specification:

    * *Inference support.* Which inferences would be valid with respect to this design? See the applicable parts of the checklists for validity of abductive and analogic inferences.
    * *Repeatability.* Is the measurement specification clear enough so that others could repeat it?
    * *Ethics.* Which company data must be kept confidential? How is privacy of persons respected?

The client architecture can be used to indicate what the *data sources* are: people, primary documents, and primary data. One of the people who provides data is you. You should note in your diary any event that influences the measured variables and that may influence the outcome of the project. Try to find data that conflicts with your claim, before other people present you with such data. Is the beneficial effect of your consulting perhaps due to your own competence or to the competence of the people you work with? Is the client's problem solved despite your effort rather than thanks to your effort? Do they have the problem that you thought they have, or is the real problem different?

You must also acquire or construct *measurement instruments*, such as interview protocols, questionnaires, video recorders, sound recorders, clocks, sensors, database queries, log analyzers, etc. These may have to be validated before use.

You need to agree on a *measurement schedule* and set up a *data management* discipline so you can maintain traceability (provenance) of data.

To assess validity of measurement procedures, the checklists for the validity of *causal inference* ask this (Table 19.8):

- *Measurement influence.* Will measurement influence the client?

As a helper, you are far from invisible. You are intervening in the client organization. As a researcher, you are also taking measurements; it may be hard for stakeholders to distinguish measurement taking from intervening. This may or may not influence the accuracy of the measurements. Stakeholders interested in a positive outcome of the consulting may find it important to give you accurate information about the state of the consulting process.

To facilitate generalization to similar cases by *analogic inference*, the following questions are relevant (Table 19.9):

- *Construct validity.* Are the definitions of constructs to be measured valid? Clarity of definitions, unambiguous application, and avoidance of mono-operation and mono-method bias?
- *Measurement instrument validity.* Do the measurement instruments measure what you claim that they measure? If you maintain a diary, are you impartial in recording the events of the day? Do you have the energy, at the end of each day, to keep a diary?
- *Construct levels.* Will the measured range of values be representative of the population range of values? Your client organization may be an extremely difficult or an extremely easy one to help.

A further validity requirement is that using your measurement specification, other researchers should be able to *repeat* the same kind of measurements in similar organizations.

Finally, you will have to establish rules for *confidentiality* of client data and for respecting *privacy* of actors:

☐   In the CRAC++ projects, primary documents were consulted, and an enterprise architect inter-viewed, to collect data about the outsourcing architecture. The researcher kept a diary too [6]. For one of the projects, all of this data could be published after anonymization. Data from the other project had to remain confidential.

    Objectivity of the risk assessment (asked about in knowledge question Q2) was operationalized by counting the number of concepts in CRAC++ that needed subjective interpretation to be applied and comparing this with a similar count in alternative methods.

    The evaluation task of the client cycle was done by interviewing the chief security officer. The interview was not only by about how (dis)satisfied the CSO was but also how they used the results. This reduced the threat of socially desirable answers.

☐   In the first ARMOR project, the researcher visited the client company every 2 weeks to observe how ARMOR was used, give feedback on the work products, and answer any questions. The reliability of the evaluation of the client cycle was increased because the enterprise architect was relatively high because the client was paying for this consultancy, which presumably reduces the chance of socially desirable answers.

    In the second project, data about the current enterprise architecture was collected, and an enterprise architect was interviewed twice, once before the project and once after the conclusion of the project. In both projects, the enterprise architectures were confidential.

19.4   Inference Design and Validation

Inferences from TAR studies must be planned as carefully as inferences in other studies and must match your research design. Inference from TAR studies is case based and consists of description, explanation, and analogic generalization. Examples of validity concerns during research design have been given above. Examples of the inferences themselves are given later, in the section on data analysis. Here we briefly review the relevant parts of the checklist.

The checklist for descriptive inference is shown in Table 19.7. Descriptive inference in TAR studies is summarizing the large amount of data that you collected from primary data and primary documents, including all work products produced when applying the experimental artifact. Your diary too will contain a wealth of information about events that needs to be summarized. To avoid adding information in your descriptions that is not contained in the data, you may want to ask other researchers to summarize and code the data. You may also want to ask other researchers to check your interpretations in a privately organized blind peer review process.

Table 19.7 Checklist for descriptive inference design, written from the point of view of the researcher preparing to do the research

---

10.1 Descriptive inference design

- How are words and images to be interpreted? (Content analysis, conversation analysis, discourse analysis, analysis software, etc.)
- What descriptive summaries of data are planned? Illustrative data, graphical summaries, descriptive statistics, etc.
- Validity of description design

  * *Support for data preparation.*

    - Will the prepared data represent the same phenomena as the unprepared data?
    - If data may be removed, would this be defensible beyond reasonable doubt?
    - Would your scientific opponents produce the same descriptions from the data?

  * *Support for data interpretation.*

    - Will the interpretations that you produce be facts in your conceptual research framework? Would your scientific peers produce the same interpretations?
    - Will the interpretations that you produce be facts in the conceptual framework of the subjects? Would subjects accept them as facts?

  * *Support for descriptive statistics.*

    - Is the chance model of the variables of interest defined in terms of the population elements?

  * *Repeatability:* Will the analysis repeatable by others?
  * *Ethics:* No new issues.

Table 19.8 gives the checklist for abductive inference. Explanations of outcomes in a TAR study should be architectural. Your expectation is that the artifact is the mechanism by which the helper will produce a desired effect in the client context. The goal of the study is to find out if this really happens under uncontrolled and possibly disturbing conditions of practice.

Table 19.9 gives the checklist for analogic inference design. Other potential client organizations should have a similar architecture, in other words similar components with similar capabilities and interactions, as the study client organizations. And other customizations of the treatment, of other clients, should still be similar enough to act as target of generalization by analogy. Our generalization will be stronger if it is based on a series of TAR studies with different clients (analytical induction without disconfirming cases) than if it is based on a single TAR study (analytical generalization).

Table 19.8 Checklist for abductive inference design in TAR, written from the point of view of the researcher preparing to do the research

10.3 Abductive inference design

- What possible explanations can you foresee? What data do you need to give those explanations? What theoretical framework?
- Internal validity

  * *Causal inference*

    - *Sampling influence.* Could the selection mechanism influence the client organizations? Could there be a regression effect?
    - *Treatment control.* What other factors than the treatment could influence the outcome of the client cycle? The treatment allocation mechanism, the experimental setup, the experimenters and their expectations, the novelty of the treatment, compensation by the researcher, rivalry or demoralization about the allocation?
    - *Treatment instrument validity.* Will the treatment instruments have the effect on the client that you claim they have?
    - *Measurement influence.* Will measurement influence the client?

  * *Architectural inference*

    - *Analysis:* The analysis of the architecture may not support its conclusions with mathematical certainty. Components fully specified? Interactions fully specified?
    - *Variation:* Do the real-world case components match the architectural components? Do they have the same capabilities? Are all architectural components present in the real-world case?
    - *Abstraction:* Does the architectural model used for explanation omit relevant elements of real-world cases? Are the mechanisms in the architectural model interfered with by other mechanisms, absent from the model but present in the real world case?

  * *Rational inference*

    - *Goals.* An actor may not have the goals assumed by an explanation. Can you get information about the true goals of actors?
    - *Motivation.* A goal may not motivate an actor as much as assumed by an explanation. Can you get information about the true motivations of actors?

Table 19.9 Checklist for analogic inference design in TAR, written from the point of view of the researcher preparing to do the research

---

10.4   Analogic inference design

- What is the intended scope of your generalization?
- External validity

  * *Object of Study similarity.*

    - *Population predicate.* To which extent does the client organization and artifact prototype satisfy the population predicate? In which way are they similar to the population elements? In which way are they dissimilar?
    - *Ambiguity.* Could the client organization and artifact prototype be viewed as instances of other population predicates too? What could be the target of analogic generalization?

  * *Representative sampling,* case-based research: In what way will the selected sample of clients and customized artifacts be representative of the population?

  * *Treatment.*

    - *Treatment similarity.* Is the customized treatment plan similar to other treatments in the real-world population?
    - *Compliance.* Will the customized treatment plan that you agreed on be implemented as specified?
    - *Treatment control.* What other factors than the treatment could influence the client? Could the implemented treatment be interpreted as another treatment?

  * *Measurement.*

    - *Construct validity.* Are the definitions of constructs to be measured valid? Clarity of definitions, unambiguous application, avoidance of mono-operation and mono-method bias?
    - *Measurement instrument validity.* Do the measurement instruments measure what you claim that they measure?
    - *Construct levels.* Will the measured range of values be representative of the population range of values?

Table 19.10 Checklist for execution of the client treatment in TAR, written from the point of view of the researcher preparing to write a report

11. What happened?

    – What has happened when the client was selected? Does the client have the architecture that was planned during research design? Did any unexpected events happen in the client during the study? Personnel changes, organizational changes, etc.
    – What has happened during sampling? Did you do more than one TAR project? In what sequence did you do the client cycles? Was the treatment changed between cycles?
    – What has happened when the client treatment was applied? Mistakes, unexpected events?
    – What has happened during measurement? Data sources actually used, response rates?

19.5   Research Execution

We now switch perspective from designing a TAR project to executing it and reporting about it. Table 19.10 lists the checklist questions for executing the client cycle. This cycle is usually confidential as it is usually a consultancy project. You can probably not report about it, but it is important to keep a record in the project log, which you can use in data analysis. Typical elements of the TAR log are the intermediary work produces of using the artifact, interview records, and your diary containing notes about expected and unexpected events and about decisions that you made about treatment and interpretation.

19.6   Data Analysis

We now apply the inferences designed earlier. Table 19.11 lists the checklist questions for data analysis. There is no part about statistical inference over a sample of TAR case properties, because we are studying single cases, not sample properties. Events during the client cycle, and data actually collected, should be analyzed with the validity questions in mind. The entire validity discussion could be collected in a separate section of a report.

19.6.1   Descriptions

☐ (12) The CRAC++ report [6] contains the key work products of one of the client cases. Since these are work products, they have been verified with the client stakeholders. The major observation is that according to the chief security officers of the clients, the CRAC++ assessment produced more insight into the confidentiality risk position and trade-offs than their current, checklist-based

Table 19.11 Checklist for data analysis in TAR, written from the point of view of the researcher preparing to write a report

12. Descriptions

  – Data preparations applied? Data transformations, missing values, removal of outliers? Data management, data availability.
  – Data interpretations? Coding procedures, interpretation methods?
  – Descriptive statistics. Demographics, sample mean and variance? Graphics, tables.
  – Validity of the descriptions: See checklist for the validity of descriptive inference.

14. Explanations

  – What explanations (causal, architectural, rational) exist for the observations?
  – Internal validity: See checklist for the validity of abductive inference.

15. Generalizations

  – Would the explanations be valid in similar cases or populations too?
  – External validity: See checklist for the validity of analogic inference

16. Answers

  – What are the answers to the knowledge questions? Summary of conclusions, support for and limitations of conclusions.

method. We judged this not to be socially desirable statement, as the clients actually did use the CRAC++ risk assessment to renegotiate their service level agreements with their outsourcing provider. So we accept it as a fact.

☐ (12) The ARMOR report only contains the observations about how ARMOR constructs were used [2]. The observations were about nonuse and even misuse of some constructs in the ARMOR language. This could have been caused by our treatment, e.g., by a confusing instruction of the enterprise architects who used the language. But the nonuse and misuse were consistent across architects and across the two client cycles that we performed. So we accept this as a fact.

19.6.2   *Explanations*

☐ (14) The major observation in the CRAC++ project was that the CRAC++ assessment gave the chief security officers more insight into the confidentiality risk position than their current, checklist-based method. Our earlier discussion of the validity of our research design, together with the events recorded in the researcher's diary, provides support for the belief that the effects were produced by CRAC++ and not by something else. We concluded from this that the CRAC++ method "worked" in the two client cycles that we performed. In the two client cycles, the CRAC++ method was a mechanism for increasing insight in confidentiality risks.

☐ (14) In the ARMOR project, the nonuse and misuse of important language constructs were explained by redundancies in their definitions, so that some concepts were perceived as superfluous and other concepts were confused, and by incompatibility with the way of working of the enterprise architects, so that some definitions were not understood, creating even more confusion.

19.6.3 Analogic Generalizations

☐ (15) The two client organizations where CRAC++ was applied are manufacturing organizations, which are very cost aware, have outsourced data management, and yet must comply with auditing standards. The tentative generalization is therefore that similar effects will be obtained by CRAC++ in similar organizations.

☐ (15) The two clients where ARMOR was applied were a provincial government organization and a semigovernment organization. The pressure for accountability is high in both organizations, and so they are interested in maintaining alignment between business objectives and enterprise architecture, which is what ARMOR supplies. Both organizations were also under pressure of shrinking budgets. In both organizations, the enterprise architects that used ARMOR and that we asked to read ARMOR models has at least 5 years of experience. The tentative generalization is that in similar organizations, the use of ARMOR will produce similar effects.

19.6.4 Answers to Knowledge Questions

☐ (16) The first knowledge question in the CRAC++ project is:

Q1   Is the method was easy to use?

The researcher found the method not so easy to use without a more sophisticated tool, because the method requires a lot of data to be maintained, structured, (re)organized, and graphically presented. This gives a negative answer to Q1. The next question is:

Q2   Does it deliver the same results when used by different persons?

The measurements should provide less room for subjective estimates in CRAC++ than in the current methods, suggesting a positive answer to Q2 about repeatability of the results. The third question is:

Q3   Does it contribute to the client's understanding of confidentiality risks on an outsourcing relation?

As indicated earlier, the response of the clients also suggests a positive answer to Q3 about contribution to understanding.

☐ (16) The knowledge questions in the first ARMOR project were about usability:

–   What ARMOR constructs are used in practice?
–   For which purpose are they used?
–   Is this the intended use?

The observations about nonuse and misuse provided the answers to these three questions. This caused the researcher to simplify ARMOR and test this simplified version in the second client project, which provided occasion to improve the method by simplifying it. This project had two questions:

- Are the concepts in the redesigned ARMOR method understandable by architects?
- Does the method help tracing business goals to enterprise architecture?

The second TAR project provided a preliminary positive answer to the question whether Light ARMOR would be useful to maintain traceability between business objectives and enterprise architecture. The answer has weak support, because it was based on the opinion of one enterprise architect.

19.7 Implications for Context

Table 19.12 lists the checklist questions to feed back your results into the research context. The TAR project will have added to the *knowledge* about the method, and this should be related to items 1 and 3, the knowledge goal and state of knowledge when you started the project.

Relevance to the improvement goal is twofold: The TAR project may have suggested improvement needs for the method, which relates back to item 2. In addition, there may be lessons learned for other companies that may want to use the method. This would be a possible contribution to practice:

☐ (17) The CRAC++ projects contributed to the goal of learning about the usability and utility of CRAC++.

 (18) The major improvement need found was that tool support would be required to make the method usable. On the other hand, the client companies found the method useful but not to the extent that they would invest in a tool to use this method on a regular basis.

☐ (17) The ARMOR projects added knowledge about usability of the method.

 (18) This in turn suggested improvements to the method. However, these could only partially be implemented because by the time the first project was finished, the method was standardized and the standard would not be changed. However, training material was still under development, and this has been adapted based on the results of this TAR project.

Table 19.12 Checklist for implications of TAR, written from the point of view of the researcher preparing to write a report

17. Contribution to knowledge goal(s) Refer back to items 1 and 3.
18. Contribution to improvement goal(s)? Refer back to item 2.
– If there is no improvement goal: is there a potential contribution to practice?

Notes

²**Page 269, action research.** Action research was initiated by Lewin in the 1940s as a method to apply the results of social research to practice and learn from it [4, 5]. A very influential paper by Susman and Evered [9] defined action research as the following cycle:

- Diagnosis
- Action planning
- Action taking
- Evaluating
- Specifying learning

This is roughly our client cycle followed by what we called data analysis.

Davison et al. [1] integrate different approaches to action research into what they call *canonical action research* (CAR). They formulate five principles of CAR:

- There should be a client-researcher agreement.
- The process should be cyclical.
- Theory should be applied.
- The action of the researcher should change the client.
- The researcher learns through reflection.

TAR satisfies these principles too.

Sein et al. [8] define *action design research*, which, like other CAR methods, is problem driven. It starts with a joint problem analysis with the client, performs a search for solutions, implements and evaluates them, and then specifies lessons learned. TAR is described, motivated, and compared with these other approaches in more detail elsewhere [11].

References

1. R.M. Davison, M.G. Martinsons, N. Kock, Principles of canonical action research. Inf. Syst. J. **14**(1), 65–86 (2004)
2. W. Engelsman, R.J. Wieringa, Goal-oriented requirements engineering and enterprise architecture: two case studies and some lessons learned, in *Requirements Engineering: Foundation for Software Quality (REFSQ 2012), Essen, Germany*. Lecture notes in computer science, vol. 7195 (Springer, 2012), pp. 306–320.
3. W. Engelsman, D.A.C. Quartel, H. Jonkers, M.J. van Sinderen, Extending enterprise architecture modelling with business goals and requirements. Enterp. Inf. Syst. **5**(1), 9–36 (2011)
4. K. Lewin, The research center for group dynamics at Massachusetts Institute of Technology. Sociometry **8**(2), 126–136 (1945)
5. K. Lewin, Action research and minority problems. J. Soc. Issues **2**, 34–46 (1946)
6. A. Morali, R.J. Wieringa, Risk-based confidentiality requirements specification for outsourced it systems, in *Proceedings of the 18th IEEE International Requirements Engineering Conference (RE 2010), Sydney, Australia* (IEEE Computer Society, Los Alamitos, California, 2010), pp. 199–208
7. H. Petroski, *The Evolution of Useful Things* (Vintage Books, New York, 1992)
8. M.K. Sein, O. Henfridsson, S. Purao, M. Rossi, R. Lindgren, Action design research. MIS Q. **35**(2), 37–56 (2011)
9. G.I. Susman, R. Evered, An assessment of the scientific merits of action research. Admin. Sci. Q. **23**(4), 582–603 (1978)

10. R.J. Wieringa, Relevance and problem choice in design science, in *Global Perspectives on Design Science Research (DESRIST), 5th International Conference, St. Gallen*. Lecture Notes in Computer Science, vol. 6105 (Springer, Heidelberg, 2010), pp. 61–76
11. R.J. Wieringa, A. Morali, Technical action research as a validation method in information systems design science, in K. Peffers, M. Rothenberger, B. Kuechler (eds), *Seventh International Conference on Design Science Research in Information Systems and Technology (DESRIST)*. Lecture Notes in Computer Science, vol. 7286 (Springer, Heidelberg, 2012), pp. 220–238

Chapter 20
Statistical Difference-Making Experiments

In a **statistical difference-making experiment**, two or more experimental treatments are compared on samples of population elements to see if they make a difference, on the average, for a measured variable. More than two treatments may be compared, and more than one outcome measure may be used. Different treatments may be applied to different objects of study in parallel or to the same object of study in sequence.

The logic of statistical inference in all these designs is the same. If two treatments A and B are compared, the sample treated by A is viewed as a random sample from the population treated by A, and the sample treated by B is viewed as a random sample from the population treated by B. The question to be answered is whether there is a difference between the average of a measured variable Y in the population treated by A and the population treated by B.

There is a different kind of design, in which we do not ask whether a difference between treatments has an effect on a measured variable, but whether a difference in objects of study has an effect on a measured variable. The question to be answered is whether there is a difference between the average of a measured variable in population P treated by A and population Q treated by A. Such a difference could exist if the elements of P and Q have different capabilities and limitations with respect to the treatment:

☐ Several studies have investigated the effect on personality on pair programming [2, 11]. Programmers are coupled in pairs depending on their personality structure, and two groups of pairs are formed, where, for example, pairs in one group have one member who is emotionally unstable and the pairs in the other group do not have a member that is emotionally unstable. Measured variables are duration of the programming task and correctness of the program. The knowledge question is whether the averages of these variables in the two groups are different.

The role of statistical inference in all of these research designs is to establish if there is a statistically discernable difference between the average of a measured variable

© Springer-Verlag Berlin Heidelberg 2014
R.J. Wieringa, *Design Science Methodology for Information Systems and Software Engineering*, DOI 10.1007/978-3-662-43839-8_20

in different populations. The designs differ in the way the populations are defined and the samples are constructed. As explained in Chap. 13, there are two classes of statistical inference: We can test a hypothesis about the difference in Y, or we can estimate a confidence interval for the difference. If a statistically discernable difference exists, we use abductive reasoning to explain this difference causally in terms of the way the groups were constructed. For example, we can explain it causally in terms of a difference in treatments or architecturally in terms of a difference in capabilities of population elements.[1]

There are several checklists for the statistical difference-making experiments. The checklist in this book includes the other ones but spends more attention on architectural explanation and on generalization by analogy.[2] Statistical difference-making experiments require careful preparation. The *experiment protocol* contains your description of the context, the statement of the research problem, and the specification and validation of the research design. The *experiment log* contains a documentation of events during the execution of the research and details of the data analysis. In the rest of this chapter, we discuss how the checklist of Appendix B is applied to statistical difference-making experiments.

20.1   Context

Table 20.1 shows the checklist for the research context. The *knowledge goal* may be to evaluate existing treatments or to validate new, experimental treatments. This may be curiosity driven, or there may be an *improvement goal* of a higher-level engineering cycle. In any case, you have to summarize *current knowledge* to explain and motivate the knowledge goal.

When you decided to do an empirical study, you probably already knew the answers to these questions. But readers of your research report do not know the answers, and so they must be provided with the answers at the beginning of the report:

☐   Briand et al. [1] investigated the effect of using system sequence diagrams (SSDs) and system operation contracts (SOCs) in the quality of unified modeling language (UML) domain models. These two artifacts are recommended by Larman [7] in his textbook on UML and patterns:

  (1) Their *knowledge goal* was to find out whether these artifacts improved modeling.
  (2) There was no *improvement goal*, because this was not part of a higher-level engineering cycle. The study can be classified as an evaluation. It investigates a current practice in teaching UML, namely, using SSDs when producing domain models and extending the domain models with SOCs. Results of this evaluation could be useful for software engineering education and possibly for software engineering practice too.
  (3) Not much was known about this particular question. There was no theory and at the time of writing there was no body of empirical knowledge about the effect of using these techniques.

Table 20.1 Checklist for the research context, written from the point of view of the researcher preparing to do the research

Research context

1. Knowledge goal(s)

   - What do you want to know? Is this part of an implementation evaluation, a problem investigation, a survey of existing treatments, or a new technology validation?

2. Improvement goal(s)

   - If there is a higher-level engineering cycle, what is the goal of that cycle?
   - If this is a curiosity-driven project, are there credible application scenarios for the project results?

3. Current knowledge

   - State of the knowledge in published scientific, technical, and professional literature?
   - Available expert knowledge?
   - Why is your research needed? Do you want to add anything, e.g., confirm or falsify something?
   - Theoretical framework that you will use?

20.2 Research Problem

Table 20.2 lists the checklist questions for stating the research problem. The *conceptual framework* of a statistical difference-making experiment must define a statistical structure. It should define a chance model for random variables that defines the meaning of each variable in the population and lists assumptions about their distribution. The two other elements of chance models, measurement procedures and sampling procedures, are defined later on. Chance models are needed for the validity of descriptive and statistical inference.

Knowledge questions must be stated in terms of the conceptual framework. The first formulation of the questions may not use fully operationalized constructs, but before conducting the experiment, all constructs must be operationalized in measurable indicators. This is subject to the requirements of construct validity.

Questions may be open or closed. In statistical difference-making experiments, they are about a statistical model, such as a hypothesis about a population mean, population variance, or some other property of the population distributions of random variables. To answer an open question, you may want to estimate some parameter of the distribution. A closed question has one or more **statistical hypotheses** as possible answers, and the question is answered by testing these hypotheses.

The conceptual framework must define the constructs to define a *population*. Without a clear population concept, a sampling procedure cannot be defined, and then no inference from the sample to a population is possible. As explained

Table 20.2 Checklist for the research problem, written from the point of view of the researcher preparing to do the research

Research problem

4. Conceptual framework

   - Conceptual structures? Architectural structures, statistical structures?
   - Chance models of random variables: semantics of variables?
   - Validity of the conceptual framework? Clarity of definitions, unambiguous application, avoidance of mono-operation and mono-method bias?

5. Knowledge questions

   - Open (exploratory) or closed (hypothesis-testing) questions?
   - Effect, satisfaction, trade-off, or sensitivity questions?
   - Descriptive or explanatory questions?

6. Population

   - Population predicate? What is the architecture of the elements of the population? In which ways are all population elements similar to each other and dissimilar to other elements?
   - Chance models of random variables: assumptions about distributions of variables?

---

in Chap. 11, sampling requires a sampling frame, which is a list of population elements that can be selected for a sample. The population described by the frame is the study population. If a further inference to the theoretical population is aimed for, then this inference is analogic, and the study population must be representative of the theoretical population:

☐ (4) The conceptual framework of the study by Briand et al. [1] was that of the UML, supplemented by the SSD and SOC concepts as defined by Larman. They compared two methods: In the Unified Process (UP), domain models are designed from use case scenarios. In the extension to the UP defined by Larman, which we will refer to as UP+, SSDs are defined for the most complex use case scenarios, the domain model is designed after SSDs have been designed, and the domain model is extended with SOCs that specify how the domain model changes when an event arrives that is defined in the SSDs.

The objects of study were students who perform system modeling tasks using one of these methods. The researchers measured the quality of the model and the effort of modeling for each student and then average this per sample. The quality of a model was operationalized by indicators such as *number of missing classes, number of useless classes, number of missing relationships*, etc. The effort of modeling was operationalized by the indicator *time to complete domain model*.

For the quality indicators, there is a mono-method construct validity threat because all indicators were measured by grading the model. A different concept of model quality would arise if it would be related somehow to properties of the system built from the model. For effort there is a mono-operation bias: time is only one indicator of effort. Some students will be faster than others anyway, whereas in the same period of time, two students could spend different amounts of cognitive effort to solve a problem. We will see in measurement design that in addition to measuring time, the researchers also asked the students for their *perception* of effort, thus reducing mono-operation bias.

(5) There were two knowledge questions. Since this is sample-based research, the questions were asked about population averages, and we make this explicit here:

RQ1   Does the use of SSDs and SOCs improve the quality of the domain model, on the average?

*   The researchers formulated as null hypotheses for the quality and effort indicators that the *number of missing classes* is the same for both methods, and they formulated directional alternatives such that the *number of missing classes* is better for UP+ than for UP.

RQ2   Does the use of SSDs and SOCs reduce the effort to design the domain model, on the average?

*   Here the null hypothesis was that the *time to complete the domain model* is the same for both methods, and the alternative was that it is better for UP+ than for UP.

(6) The theoretical populations were the set of all student projects using UP and the set of all student projects using UP+.

20.3   Research Design and Validation

The design of statistical difference-making experiments requires decisions about the acquisition of objects of study, sampling, treatment, and measurement. It also requires alignment of these decisions with the planned inferences from the data. The checklists for inference design are given in Sect. 20.4, but we illustrate their application to research design here.

20.3.1   Object of Study

Table 20.3 shows the checklist for the object of study. The object of study in design science is an artifact in context. In validation studies, the artifact is an experimental prototype, and the context can be an artificial one in the laboratory or a natural one in the field. In evaluation studies, both the artifact and its context exist in the field. Fully randomized statistical difference-making field experiments in information systems and software engineering are very expensive and hence very rare.

To support *descriptive inference*, the chance models of variables about which we collect data must be defined (Table 20.7). The meaning of the variables in terms of properties of the population elements should be defined, and assumptions about their distribution over the population should be listed. Sampling and measurement procedures will be defined later in research design.

Table 20.3 Checklist for acquiring objects of study in statistical difference-making experiments, written from the point of view of the researcher preparing to do the research

Object(s) of study

   7.1 Acquisition of objects of study

        – If OoSs are selected, how do you know that a selected entity is a population
           element?
        – If OoSs are constructed, how do you construct a population element?
        – Validity of OoS

               – *Inference support*. Which inferences would be valid with respect to this
                   design? See checklists for validity of descriptive statistics and abductive
                   and analogic inferences
               – *Repeatability*. Could other researchers use your report to construct or
                   select a similar OoS?
               – *Ethics*. Are people informed that they will be studied, and do they consent
                   to this? Are they free to stop at any time without giving reasons, and do
                   they know this?

To support validity of *causal inference* from the experimental data, the following checklist question is relevant (Table 20.9):

- *OoS dynamics*. Could there be interaction among OoSs? Could there be historical events, maturation, and dropout of OoSs?

Interaction, historical events, and maturation of objects of study may influence the outcome of the experiment, which should then be added to any effects of the treatment. Dropouts reduce the sample size, which affects the statistics and their variance.

In addition to causal inference you may want to do *architectural inference* to explain observed phenomena. This would be the case if you want to explain a causal influence, or if you want to compare capabilities of different populations. The following considerations are relevant for architectural inference:

- *Analysis*: Is the architecture of the objects of study specified in the population predicate? What are the components of an object of study, and how do the components interact? What are their capabilities? Do you know enough of the architecture and capabilities of the objects of study to give an analytic explanation afterward?
- *Variation*: How close should the objects of study match the population predicate? Should all architectural components be present in an object of study? What is the variation in capabilities?
- *Abstraction*: The objects of study that you actually acquire have many more components than what is specified in the population predicate, and they may have other capabilities in addition to the ones you are studying. Is this relevant for architectural explanation?

Variations of these consideration are also relevant for supporting *analogic inference* (Table 20.10):

- *Population predicate*. Do all objects of study satisfy the population predicate? In which way are they similar to other population elements? In which way are they dissimilar? What populations can be the target of analogic generalization?
- *Ambiguity*. Will the OoS satisfy other population predicates too? If all objects of study in a sample have multiple classifications, then it can be ambiguous which population is the intended target of analogic generalization.

For the validity of an OoS, it is also necessary that acquiring them be *repeatable* by other researchers. The specification of the way you acquire objects of study should be sufficient for other researchers to replicate your research. Finally, *ethical* constraints must be respected. For example, human subjects must only participate after informed consent, and they should know that they are free to stop any time without giving reasons:

☐ (7.1) The objects of study in the study by Briand et al. [1] are fourth-year students performing a system modeling task. They have received programming courses earlier and will perform the experiment as part of a full-term course on UML-based software modeling.
    Depending on the research setup, students may or may not interact during the experiment. There may also be historical events outside the control of the experimenter that influence the experiment, such as a soccer game or late night party the previous night that left some subjects sleepless and may cause other subjects to drop out of the experiment. This is not reported by the authors, so we assume it did not happen.
    There is no model of cognitive mechanisms that will be used in the experiment, and no architectural inference will be done. The authors do assume that fourth-year bachelor computer science students all over the world are similar in their responses to the experimental manipulations.

20.3.2   Sampling

In the ideal statistical difference-making experiment, sampling is random, so that all extraneous variables are randomized. This gives an unbiased estimate of population parameters. If full randomization is not possible, then extraneous variables that could influence the measured variables must be blocked physically in the experiment or blocked computationally in the statistical analysis.

Table 20.4 gives the checklist for sample design. You need to define a sampling frame and decide on a selection strategy. In a simple random sampling strategy, we randomly select elements from the sampling frame without replacement.

To assess support of the sampling procedure for *statistical inference*, you should check the assumptions of the statistical inference procedures that you plan to use. At least, sample size should be sufficient to discern the expected differences between experimental groups. If sampling is done without replacement and the population is small with respect to the sample, a correction factor should be applied to

Table 20.4 Checklist for sampling in statistical difference-making experiments, written from the point of view of the researcher preparing to do the research

7.2 Construction of a sample

       – Sample-based research: What is the sampling frame and probability sampling strategy? Random with or without replacement, stratified, cluster? What should the size of the sample be?

       – Validity of sampling procedure

           - *Inference support.* Which inferences would be valid with respect to this design? See the applicable parts of the checklists for validity of statistical, abductive, and analogic inferences

           - *Repeatability.* Can the sampling procedure be replicated by other researchers?

           - *Ethics.* No new issues

---

statistical estimations. In Chap. 13, we listed the assumptions of confidence interval estimation, but other procedures may have other assumptions. Some inference procedures have a graceful degradation if some assumptions are violated a bit but give meaningless results if other assumptions are violated. To assess the robustness of the statistical inference procedure that you use, you should consult the literature [14, 18] or, better still, a statistician.

To assess support for *causal inference*, the following question is relevant (Table 20.9):

• *Sampling influence.* Could the selection mechanism influence the OoSs? Could there be a regression effect?

Even in random sampling, being selected for an experimental treatment can change the responses of the objects of study, which could be mistaken for a treatment effect. And being selected nonrandomly surely biases the average of the outcome variables. Also, if objects of study have been selected on an extremely good or bad score on a pretest, it is likely that they will score less extreme on the next test. This is called a regression effect, and it could be mistaken for a treatment effect.

Statistical inference reasons from a sample to the study population. To generalize to the theoretical population by *analogic inference*, the following question is relevant (Table 20.10):

• *Representative sampling.* Will the study population, described by the sampling frame, be representative of the theoretical population?

Support for analogic generalization to the theoretical population increases when population elements have a similar architecture and if this architecture explains the property of the study population that we want to generalize:

☐ (7.2) In the study by Briand et al. [1], the experiment was done four times, and each time the sampling frame was the list of computer science students enrolled in a fourth-year UML course at Carleton University, Canada, doing domain modeling tasks in UP and in UP+. We can conservatively take the theoretical population to be the set of all last year computer science bachelor students at Carleton University in any calendar year, doing domain modeling tasks. The study population is probably representative of this theoretical population. There is less certainty about representativeness of the study population for larger populations, such as the set of all fourth-year computer science students worldwide doing domain modeling tasks, or for the different population of professional software engineers doing domain modeling tasks.

There is no information how the subjects were selected from the sampling frame. If this is not by (simple) random selection, then there might be some unknown systematic displacement (bias) of population estimates.

20.3.3 Treatment Design

Table 20.5 gives the checklist for treatment design. Treatments always require instruments, such as instruction sheets, lessons, help desks, background material, etc. They must be specified before applied, and in statistical experiments they must be allocated to sample elements. There is a large variation of allocation strategies, classified as independent group design, dependent group design, and mixed designs. The example illustrates one of the many possible allocation strategies. More information can be found in the literature [5, 10, 13, 19].

To support inferences, the treatment should satisfy a number of requirements. The core requirement for supporting *statistical inference* is this (Table 20.8):

- *Treatment allocation.* Are the treatments allocated randomly to sample elements?

If we select a sample randomly and allocate treatments A and B randomly to sample elements, we end up with treatment groups A and B that can be viewed as random samples selected from the population treated with A and the population treated with B. The estimation of the difference between the population means will then be without bias (systematic displacement).

Random allocation greatly simplifies *causal inference*. If treatments are allocated randomly, the only remaining systematic difference between treatment groups is the difference in treatments. If on the other hand allocation is not random, then there is a systematic difference between the samples that would lead to a false estimate of the difference between population means. This could be falsely interpreted as a treatment effect. The literature on experiment designs provides guidelines on how to reason about these nonrandom differences, and the example illustrates some of this.

The checklist for causal inference design gives us two other questions about treatments (Table 20.9):

- *Treatment control.* What other factors than the treatment could influence the OoSs? The treatment allocation mechanism, the experimental setup, the experimenters and their expectations, the novelty of the treatment, compensation by the researcher, and rivalry or demoralization about the allocation?
- *Treatment instrument validity.* Do the treatment instruments have the effect on the OoS that you claim they have?

Table 20.5 Checklist for treatment design in statistical difference-making experiments, written from the point of view of the researcher preparing to do the research

---

8. Treatment design

- Which treatment(s) will be applied?
- Which treatment instruments will be used? Instruction sheets, videos, lessons, software, computers, actuators, rooms, etc.
- How are treatments allocated to OoSs?

    * Blocking, factorial designs, crossover designs? Between-subjects or within-subject designs?

- What is the treatment schedule?
- Validity of treatment design

    * *Inference support.* Which inferences would be valid with respect to this design? See the applicable parts of the checklists for validity of statistical, abductive, and analogic inferences
    * *Repeatability.* Is the specification of the treatment and the allocation to OoSs clear enough so that others could repeat it?
    * *Ethics.* Is no harm done, and is everyone treated fairly? Will they be informed about the treatment before or after the study?

To assess support for *analogic inference* from a study population to some other population, three questions about treatments are relevant (Table 20.10):

- *Treatment similarity.* Is the specified treatment in the experiment similar to treatments in the population? For example, if you want to generalize to the real world, is the specified treatment realistic?
- *Compliance.* Is the treatment implemented as specified?
- *Treatment control.* Should the factors that we could not control be viewed as parts of the treatment that is being generalized about? Could the implemented treatment be interpreted as another treatment?

Treatment application must be *repeatable* by other researchers. Finally, if the objects of study contain people, *ethics* dictates that they must not be harmed by the experiment. In the interest of the experiment, the experimenter may hide the research goal or some other aspects of the experiment from experimental subjects. In that case, the subjects must be informed after the experiment has finished:

☐ (8) In the study by Briand et al. [1], the treatments were the assignments to use the two methods UP and UP+. Normal instructional material was used, but students in the fourth experiment received more training in the UP+ constructs SSD and SOC than students in the previous three experiments. Results from the fourth experiment are therefore not fully comparable with those of the first three.

Each experiment except the second consisted of four laboratory sessions of 3 h each, 1 week apart. The second experiment had too many participants to be taught in one lab session, and students were partitioned into two groups that were taught the same material but in two lab sessions 1 week apart. The second experiment therefore lasted 8 weeks, while the other three lasted 4 weeks. This increased interaction possibilities among the students between lab hours in the second experiment. This was a potential influence on the experimental outcome in the second experiment. Other potential influences were history, maturation, and dropout.

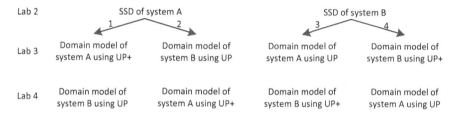

Fig. 20.1   A crossover design for comparing the UP and UP+ methods. Each lab is 3-h practicum in which students must make system models. Lab 1 was spent on learning the relevant techniques. To cancel out order effects, each system is modeled two times in lab 3, with the UP and UP+ methods, and two times in lab 4, with the UP and UP+ methods, in all possible sequences. This defined four experimental groups in total per experiment, identified by the labels of the arrows in the diagram

The measured variables are the six indicators for quality of domain model and the indicator for effort, *time to produce the model.*

The simplest design to test if the difference between UP and UP+ causes a difference in these measured variables is to randomly allocate the treatments to experimental subjects and then compare the average value of the measured variables in the UP group and UP+ group. This mixes the effect of student's software engineering ability with possible effects of the method.

A better design is to have each student use both methods in sequence and measure the measured variables each time, in a *repeated measures design.* This removes variance from the measurement that is due to student variability but introduces the possibility that the second modeling effort will deliver a better quality model anyway, because the system has been modeled already. This is called a *learning effect.* At the same time, students could become tired or bored, producing a worse model, which is called a *fatigue effect.*

To avoid this, the student sample was partitioned into two groups that applied the two methods in opposite order. This would make order effects in the use of methods visible and allows the researchers to average them out in each treatment sample.

To avoid the situation that students would model the same system twice, which would introduce a learning effect again, two systems of comparable complexity were used. As a result, in each lab the students can be given one out of two methods to use and one out of two systems to work on, giving a total of four possible sequences in a *crossover design,* as shown in Fig. 20.1.

Treatment control was thus as high as one could get it in the classroom. One of the treatment instruments as instruction in the SSDs and SOCs is used in UP+, and in the fourth experiment, more time was spent on teaching these techniques than in the first three experiments, to be sure that the students understood and could use these techniques.

Due to the limitations of classroom experimentation, similarity between the experimental treatment and treatments applied in the real world is relatively low, as also acknowledged by the authors.

20.3.4   Measurement Design

Table 20.6 lists the checklist for measurement design. By the time measurements are designed, the researcher should finalize the operationalization of *variables,* including the definition of scales and chance models. The objects of study are the *data sources.* But the objects of study may have a complex architecture, and

Table 20.6 Checklist for measurement design in statistical difference-making experiments, written from the point of view of the researcher preparing to do the research

---

9. Measurement design

  – Variables and constructs to be measured? Scales, chance models
  – Data sources? People (e.g., software engineers, maintainers, users, project managers, politically responsible persons, etc.), primary data (e.g., source code, log files, bug tracking data, version management data, email logs), primary documents (e.g., project reports, meeting minutes, organization charts, mission statements), etc.
  – Measurement instruments? Interview protocols, questionnaires, video recorders, sound recorders, clocks, sensors, database queries, log analyzers, etc.
  – What is the measurement schedule? Pretests, posttests? Cross-sectional or longitudinal?
  – How will measured data be stored and managed? Provenance, availability to other researchers?
  – Validity of measurement specification

  * *Inference support.* Which inferences would be valid with respect to this design? See the applicable parts of the checklists for validity of abductive and analogic inferences
  * *Repeatability.* Is the measurement specification clear enough so that others could repeat it?
  * *Ethics.* Which company data must be kept confidential? How is privacy of persons respected?

---

the researcher has to figure out where exactly the data is generated and which *instruments* are needed to collect the data. In addition, measurements must be *scheduled*, and the data must be stored, transformed, manipulated, and made available, which requires setup of a *data management system*.

Statistical difference-making experiments are used to support *causal inference*, and to assess validity of these inferences, the following question is relevant (Table 20.9):

• *Measurement influence.* Will measurement influence the OoSs?

To find out if a treatment makes a difference to a measured variable, any influence of the measurement procedure itself should be avoided or else subtracted from the data.

To facilitate generalization from the study population by *analogic inference*, three questions about measurement are relevant (Table 20.10):

• *Construct validity.* Are the definitions of constructs to be measured valid? Clarity of definitions, unambiguous application, and avoidance of mono-operation and mono-method bias?
• *Measurement instrument validity.* Do the measurement instruments measure what you claim that they measure?
• *Construct levels.* Will the measured range of values be representative of the population range of values?

Other researchers may want to repeat this kind of research, so measurement procedures must be specified in a *repeatable* way. And some agreements about *ethical* use of data must be made, in particular about confidentiality of company data and privacy of personal data:

☐ In the study by Briand et al. [1], the software engineering *ability* of students was tested at the start of the experiment. This was used in the analysis to check if ability made a difference to the measured variables in the sample.

    Model *complexity* may also make a difference to outcomes, and so an effort was done to keep the two models that the students worked on of similar complexity. Model complexity was measured by counting the number of actors, use cases, classes, associations, and attributes in the system models. This may not fully operationalize the concept of model complexity, as we will see when we discuss the measurements later.

    The *quality* of domain models was measured according to six indicators, as described earlier. These are measured in percentages relative to the correct domain model. The arithmetic average of the six indicator scores is the *overall correctness* of the model.

    The *time* to make the domain model was the time in minutes from entering the lab to the moment of handing in the domain model. Students could spend additional time in the lab because they also has to make SOCs.

    Finally, on exit from a lab, students had to fill in questionnaires about their *perception* of the task performed in that lab. This could be used to supplement measurements of model quality and effort with perceptions of task difficulty.

20.4 Inference Design and Validation

Inference from statistical difference-making experiments is sample based and contains a statistical inference step. Suppose that the experimental treatments A and B are modeled as values of a treatment variable X and that the measured variable is Y. We select a sample of population elements. Treatments A and B are allocated to elements of the sample, giving two *treatment groups*. Then the following inferences are attempted, in the following order:

- Statistical inference: Assuming random sampling and allocation of treatments, a difference in the average value of Y between the treatment groups is used to infer a difference in the mean of the study population treated by A and the mean of the study population treated by B. This step is often done using NHST, but confidence interval estimation is a better alternative, as explained in Chap. 13.
- Causal inference: Suppose that all possible causes of this difference, other than the treatment, have been randomized away or are implausible for other reasons. There is still a small chance that the difference is coincidental, but assuming it is not, then the only plausible cause of the difference in outcomes is inferred to be the difference in treatments.
- Architectural inference: Assuming relevant theories, the mechanism(s) by which the difference between A and B caused a difference in Y is hypothesized. This mechanism will consist of interactions among components of population elements.

Table 20.7 Checklist for descriptive inference design in statistical difference-making experiments, written from the point of view of the researcher preparing to do the research

---

10.1 Descriptive inference design

- How are words and images to be interpreted? (Content analysis, conversation analysis, discourse analysis, analysis software, etc.)
- What descriptive summaries of data are planned? Illustrative data, graphical summaries, descriptive statistics, etc.
- Validity of description design

  * *Support for data preparation.*

    - Will the prepared data represent the same phenomena as the unprepared data?
    - If data may be removed, would this be defensible beyond reasonable doubt?
    - Would your scientific opponents produce the same descriptions from the data?

  * *Support for data interpretation.*

    - Will the interpretations that you produce be facts in your conceptual research framework? Would your scientific peers produce the same interpretations?
    - Will the interpretations that you produce be facts in the conceptual framework of the subjects? Would subjects accept them as facts?

  * *Support for descriptive statistics.*

    - Is the chance model of the variables of interest defined in terms of the population elements?

  * *Repeatability*: Will the analysis repeatable by others?
  * *Ethics*: No new issues.

- **Rational inference:** If the objects of study contain people, rational explanations for their behavior may be sought as well. The causal, architectural, and rational explanations could all be true and mutually supporting each other.
- **Analogic inference:** Assuming that the study population is representative of the theoretical population, the difference and its explanations are generalized to the theoretical population. Further generalization to other, similar populations may be attempted too.

Which of these inferences actually lead to defensible conclusions, and whether their conclusions are mutually inconsistent, consistent, or even mutually supporting depends on the design of the experiment, the acquired data, and the available prior theories. Randomized controlled trials can support this kind of reasoning, but quasi-experiments can too, although one has to be very cautious with causal inference in quasi-experiments [13]. Here we briefly discuss the checklists of all these inferences and their validity requirements.

Table 20.7 gives the checklist for descriptive inference design. Descriptive inference in statistical difference-making experiments starts with data preparation,

Table 20.8 Checklist for statistical inference design in statistical difference-making experiments, written from the point of view of the researcher preparing to do the research

---

10.2 Statistical inference design

- What statistical inferences are you planning to do? What data do they need? What assumptions do they make?
- Statistical conclusion validity

  * Assumptions of confidence interval estimation

  - *Stable distribution.* Does X has a stable distribution, with fixed parameters?
  - *Scale.* Does X have an interval or ratio scale?
  - *Sampling.* Is sample selection random or does it contain a known or unknown systematic selection mechanism?
  - *Sample size.* If the z distribution is used: Is the sample sufficiently large for the normal approximation to be used?
  - *Normality.* If the t distribution is used: Is the distribution of X normal, or is the sample size larger than 100?

  * *Treatment allocation.* Are the treatments allocated randomly to sample elements?

  * Avoid the following omissions in a report about difference-making experiments:

  - *Effect size.* Seeing a very small difference, but not telling that it is small.
  - *Fishing.* Seeing no difference most of the time, but not telling this.
  - *Very high power.* Not telling about a reason why you can see a difference (very large sample size makes very small differences visible).
  - *Sample homogeneity.* Not telling about another reason why you can see a difference (groups are selected to be homogeneous, so that any inter-group difference stands out).

---

which involves deciding what to do with missing data and with extreme data that may be outliers, testing normality and transforming to another scale, etc. Second, qualitative data may have to be interpreted and coded. Finally, descriptive statistics may be given, for example, of the demography of subjects and of important statistics such as sample mean, variance, and correlation between variables. The validity considerations all say in one way or another that no information should be added in data preparation and that any step that could add information should be reported.

The checklist for statistical inference design is listed in Table 20.8. All statistical inference techniques make assumptions, and these should be checked in the data. The only statistical inference techniques discussed in this book are confidence interval estimation and hypothesis testing, and Table 20.8 only lists the assumptions of confidence interval estimation.

Statistical conclusion validity is the degree to which statistical conclusions are supported by the data. This requires not only that the assumptions of the statistical

Table 20.9 Checklist for abductive inference design in statistical difference-making experiments, written from the point of view of the researcher preparing to do the research

---

10.3 Abductive inference design

- What possible explanations can you foresee? What data do you need to give those explanations? What theoretical framework?
- Internal validity

   * *Causal inference*

      - *Ambiguous relationship.* Ambiguous covariation, ambiguous temporal ordering, ambiguous spatial connection?
      - *OoS dynamics.* Could there be interaction among OoS's? Could there be historical events, maturation, drop-out of OoS's?
      - *Sampling influence.* Could the selection mechanism influence the OoS's? Could there be a regression effect?
      - *Treatment control.* What other factors than the treatment could influence the OoS's? The treatment allocation mechanism, the experimental setup, the experimenters and their expectations, the novelty of the treatment, compensation by the researcher, rivalry or demoralization about the allocation?
      - *Treatment instrument validity.* Do the treatment instruments have the effect on the OoS that you claim they have?
      - *Measurement influence.* Will measurement influence the OoS's?

   * *Architectural inference*

      - *Analysis*: The analysis of the architecture may not support its conclusions with mathematical certainty. Components fully specified? Interactions fully specified?
      - *Variation*: Do the real-world case components match the architectural components? Do they have the same capabilities? Are all architectural components present in the real-world case?
      - *Abstraction*: Does the architectural model used for explanation omit relevant elements of real-world cases? Are the mechanisms in the architectural model interfered with by other mechanisms, absent from the model but present in the realworld case?

   * *Rational inference*

      - *Goals.* An actor may not have the goals assumed by an explanation. Can you get information about the true goals of actors?
      - *Motivation.* A goal may not motivate an actor as much as assumed by an explanation. Can you get information about the true motivations of actors?

---

inference techniques be satisfied but also that all data must be reported, so that statistical conclusions can be interpreted in terms of the data.

Table 20.9 lists the checklist for abductive inference. In the ideal case, only one causal explanation is possible, and of this causality only one architectural explanation is possible. In the real world of experimentation, there may be more than one causal explanation, and likewise there may be more than one architectural and

Table 20.10 Checklist for analogic inference design in statistical difference-making experiments, written from the point of view of the researcher preparing to do the research

---

10.4 Analogic inference design

- What is the intended scope of your generalization?
- External validity

  * *Object of Study similarity.*

    - *Population predicate.* Will the OoS satisfy the population predicate? In which way will it be similar to the population elements? In which way will it be dissimilar?
    - *Ambiguity.* Will the OoS satisfy other population predicates too? What could be the target of analogic generalization?

  * *Representative sampling.*

    - Sample-based research: will the study population, described by the sampling frame, be representative of the theoretical population?
    - Case-based research: In what way will the selected/constructed sample of cases be representative of the population?

  * *Treatment.*

    - *Treatment similarity.* Is the specified treatment in the experiment similar to treatments in the population?
    - *Compliance.* Is the treatment implemented as specified?
    - *Treatment control.* What other factors than the treatment could influence the OoS's? Could the implemented treatment be interpreted as another treatment?

  * *Measurement.*

    - *Construct validity.* Are the definitions of constructs to be measured valid? Clarity of definitions, unambiguous application, avoidance of mono-operation and mono-method bias?
    - *Measurement instrument validity.* Do the measurement instruments measure what you claim that they measure?
    - *Construct levels.* Will the measured range of values be representative of the population range of values?

---

more than one rational explanation. This gives us a list of alternative explanations of the outcome, many of which could be true at the same time. Together they constitute one or even more than one theory of the experiment. The assessment of the plausibility of the explanations offered by this theory includes the assessment of the internal validity of your preferred explanation.

Statistical inference takes you from sample statistics to a statistical model of the study population. Abductive inference may add a causal and architectural explanation of this model. Analogic inference can then take you further to the theoretical population and beyond. Table 20.10 gives the checklist for designing analogic inference from the study population.

Table 20.11 Checklist for reporting about research execution

Research execution
11. What has happened?
– What has happened when the OoSs were selected or constructed? Did they have the architecture that was planned during research design? Unexpected events for OoSs during the study?
– What has happened during sampling? Did the sample have the size you planned? Participant flow, dropouts?
– What happened when the treatment(s) were applied? Mistakes, unexpected events?
– What has happened during measurement? Data sources actually used, response rates?

20.5   Research Execution

The real world is very diverse, even in the laboratory. No two objects of study are identical, and artificial objects of study may not be constructed exactly as you planned to. Relevant events during the execution of the research design must be recorded and reported. Events are relevant if they can influence the interpretation of the outcomes. This includes events during acquisition of the objects of study, sampling, treatment, and measurement. A very informative record used in medical research [8, 12] is the participant flow diagram, which shows the events starting from setting up a sampling frame until the last follow-up measurement of the study. The diagram shows sample sizes at each stage and states the reasons of dropout.

Table 20.11 gives the checklist for reporting about execution of a study:

- In the study by Briand et al. [1], four experiments were done with group sizes ranging from 9 to 26. Two systems of comparable complexity were selected, a Car Part Dealer (CPD) system and a Video Store (VS) system. System complexity was measured as specified in measurement design earlier.

  After the first experiment, the indicator for effort *time in the lab* was replaced by the one mentioned earlier, *time to produce the model*. This is a more accurate measure for the effort of domain modeling. Also, the questionnaire filled in by students at the end of each lab was extended with some questions about time. Finally, for experiment 4, the training in the SSD and SOC techniques was improved.

20.6   Data Analysis

In data analysis, the researcher applies the inferences planned earlier. The data actually collected may suggest other inferences to be performed too. All of this must be assessed on validity again, and the resulting validity assessment must be

Table 20.12 Checklist for reporting about data analysis in statistical difference-making experiments

12. Descriptions

- Data preparations applied? Data transformations, missing values, removal of outliers? Data management, data availability
- Data interpretations? Coding procedures, interpretation methods?
- Descriptive statistics. Demographics, sample mean, and variance? Graphics, tables
- Validity of the descriptions. See checklist for the validity of descriptive inference

13. Statistical conclusions

- Statistical inferences from the observations. Confidence interval estimations, hypothesis tests
- Statistical conclusion validity. See checklist for the validity of statistical inference

14. Explanations

- What explanations (causal, architectural, rational) exist for the observations?
- Internal validity. See checklist for the validity of abductive inference

15. Generalizations

- Would the explanations be valid in similar cases or populations too?
- External validity. See checklist for the validity of analogic inference

16. Answers

- What are the answers to the knowledge questions? Summary of conclusions and support for and limitations of conclusions

reported. Table 20.12 gives the checklists, and the following sections discuss the example.

20.6.1 Descriptions

☐ Briand et al. [1] give descriptive statistics of the participants' level of understanding of the two systems, of mean overall correctness in labs 3 and 4, and of the mean time to obtain a domain model in labs 3 and 4. The descriptive statistics show that on the average, the participants' understanding of the CPD system is slightly better than that of the VS system. At the same time, the CPD system is more complex according to the indicators defined earlier. It has almost twice the number of classes and more attributes and associations. However, the difference in complexity is still small, because both models are small. Still, these data do suggest that complexity may not be an objective property of a system but of a system-as-perceived. This is relevant for the construct validity of the complexity indicators.

The descriptive statistics do not show a remarkable difference in average overall correctness or in modeling time between the groups who used UP and the groups who used UP+.

Lab exit questionnaires showed that students felt time pressured.

20.6.2 *Statistical Conclusions*

☐ Briand et al. [1] did an independent sample t-test of the null hypothesis that there is no difference between the UP and UP+ groups. This did not produce statistically significant p-values except in experiment 4. This may have been the result of a smaller variance created by the additional training given to the participants in experiment 4. Or it may have been a coincidence. Further replication of experiment 4 should make this clear.

Briand et al. used analysis of variance (ANOVA) to compare the performance of the four groups identified in Table 20.1 in lab 3 and lab 4. ANOVA tests whether group means are different by comparing within-group variance to between-group variance. If between-group variance is much greater than averaged within-group variance, where the average is weighted by group size, then the groups are considered to have statistically different means. In repeated measures ANOVA, the average difference between the performance of group members at two points in time is compared.

Using these methods, Briand et al. found an improvement in overall correctness for subjects in experiment 4 when UP+ was used. They report a small effect size of a few percent difference in correctness.

Briand et al. also found a reduction in domain modeling time when UP+ was used, in all experiments. In addition, students generally performed faster in the second modeling exercise, regardless the method. Modeling time reduced by roughly half an hour, from about 2 h to about 90 min.

No differences were found between the two systems or for different levels of student ability [1, p. 165].

20.6.3 *Explanations*

☐ The statistical model inferred by Briand et al. [1] says that in the study population (from which the sample was selected), there is no statistically discernable difference in quality between models produced by UP and UP+, except when extra training is given in the techniques of UP+, namely, SSDs and SOCs. A *computational explanation* of this, mentioned above, is that due to additional training, variance among the students was smaller. A *causal explanation* is that the difference observed in experiment 4 is caused by the difference between UP and UP+, assuming that the subjects are well trained in the additional techniques. The *architectural explanation* is that reading SSDs of a system, as required by UP+ but not by UP, improves the student's understanding of the system, which improves his or her ability to create a correct domain model.

Checking the threats to validity of abductive inference, we find at least one more explanation, which is that the students in experiment 4 responded to the extra attention given by the experimenter to SSDs and SOCs, to experimenter expectation, or to the novelty of the method [1, p. 166].

All of these explanations can be true at the same time. It seems plausible that at least the improvement of understanding created by SSDs contributes to the improvement of domain model quality.

Once the subjects had processed the SSDs, they produced the domain model faster than those who had to work directly from use case models. The *causal explanation* of this is that UP+ reduces domain modeling time compared to UP. An *architectural explanation* of this is that a number of decisions that must be made when building a domain model had already been made for the students in the SSDs that they were given.

Faster production of a model the second time, regardless the method, could be the effect of learning or of fatigue: Perhaps they better knew how to make a model, or perhaps they were tired and wanted to finish quickly. This agrees with the finding that students felt time pressured [1, p.

164]. Another possibility is that it is ceiling effect: The deadline was approaching, so the measured time was smaller anyway [1, p. 165].

Note that the explanations of the findings are causal as well as architectural. Attributing an improvement in model quality to the difference between UP and UP+ is a causal explanation. Explaining a reduction in modeling time by learning, fatigue, or deadline pressure is an architectural explanation, as it explains how a phenomenon is produced by capabilities and limitations of components of the object of study, i.e., by capabilities and limitations of students.

20.6.4   Analogic Generalizations

☐ Briand et al. [1, p. 159] indicate that their experimental subjects had a strong background in object-oriented software development and UML-based design. They consider their sample representative of entry-level professional software engineers with significant familiarity with UML-based development.

On the other hand, the tasks were performed on systems that were relatively easy to understand, unlike the systems of high complexity found in industry [1, p. 166]. Considering the threats to external validity, the object of study (a programmer using a method to perform a task on a system) does not satisfy the population predicate of real-world objects in this respect. Related to this, the levels of the construct system *complexity* do not span the full range that they can have in practice. The authors speculate that even if the use of SSDs and SPCs makes little difference in the classroom, they could make a larger difference if they were used for complex systems.

Note that Briand et al. performed a three-step generalization, which can be spelled out as follows:

– The sample was selected from a sampling frame (a list of students that describes the study population). Statistical inference generalized from the sample to the study population.
– By architectural similarity, this is generalized further to the theoretical population to students with a similar level of software engineering knowledge and experience.
– By further architectural similarity, this is generalized to the similar population of entry-level professional software engineers.

20.6.5   Answers

Data analysis has produced, or perhaps failed to produce, answers to the knowledge questions. You do the reader of a report a great favor if you briefly summarize the answers explicitly. This also helps you as a researcher to keep track of the bottom line of the mass of research results:

☐ RQ1   Does the use of SSDs and SOCs improve the quality of the domain model?

* In the study population, provided that additional training in SSDs and SOCs was given, UP+ improves the quality of domain models somewhat. This could be caused by a variety of factors, including small variance, experimenter attention, and the use of SSDs. It seems plausible that at least the use of SSDs contributes to a small improvement of model quality.

RQ2   Does the use of SSDs and SOCs reduce the effort to design the domain model?

Table 20.13 Checklist for reporting implications for context

Research context
17. Contribution to knowledge goal(s), refer back to items 1 and 3
18. Contribution to improvement goal(s), refer back to item 2
– If there is no improvement goal, is there a potential contribution to practice?

> * Time for domain modeling reduces if SSDs are used. This is probably due to improved understanding crated by SSDs. Some of the decisions that must be made in domain modeling have already been made when building SSDs.

20.7 Implications for Context

To close the circle, a research report should return to the motivation for the research. What do we know now that we did not know before? What further studies are needed? What can we do now that we could not do before? What needs to be done before this could be applied in practice? This relates the research results to the prior knowledge context and to possible practical applications. Table 20.13 gives the checklist:

☐ (17) This study provides the first evidence about the effect of using SSDs on domain modeling. To increase the generalizability of the results, the authors call for replication in the field.
(18) The results do not indicate possible usefulness of SDDs for domain modeling in general. To find out if SSDs add benefit for complex systems or for complex use cases, more study is needed [1, p. 166].

Notes

[1]**Page 296, causes and capabilities.** Holland [3, p. 946] emphasizes that in order to speak of causes, all population elements must be potentially exposable to any of the treatments that we are comparing. So a difference in teaching methods can be a cause of differences in learning, but a difference in gender cannot be a cause of differences in learning. If population elements are not potentially exposable to different treatments, we can still do correlational studies but not causal studies. My view is that in a sense all statistical inference is correlational. Causal and architectural reasoning is part of abductive inference, not of statistical inference. If we observe a statistically discernable difference among groups of OoSs that all received the same treatment, then it is reasonable to try to explain this difference by differences in the capabilities of the OoSs.

[2]**Page 296, checklists for difference-making experiments.** Pfleeger [9] and Kitchenham et al. [6] have given guidelines for statistical difference-making experiments in software engineering. Jedlitschka and Pfahl [4] integrated some of the existing checklists in 2005. There is also an important checklist for randomized controlled trials in medical research [8, 12]. I compared all of these checklists and then defined a unification [16, 17]. Empirical evaluation of the result led to a drastic simplification [15]. The checklist in this book is an expansion of the simplified one with more detailed items for inference and validity.

References

1. L. Briand, Y. Labiche, R. Madrazo-Rivera, An experimental evaluation of the impact of system sequence diagrams and system operation contracts on the quality of the domain model, in *International Symposium on Empirical Software Engineering and Measurement* (IEEE Computer Society, Los Alamitos, 2011), pp. 157–166
2. J.E. Hannay, A. Arisholm, H. Engvik, D.I.K. Sjøberg, Effects of personality on pair programming. IEEE Trans. Softw. Eng. **36**(1) (2010)
3. P.W. Holland, Statistics and causal inference. J. Am. Stat. Assoc. **81**(396), 945–960 (1986)
4. A. Jedlitschka, D. Pfahl, Reporting guidelines for controlled experiments in software engineering, in *Proceedings of the 4th International Symposium on Empirical Software Engineering (ISESE 2005)* (IEEE Computer Society, Los Alamitos, 2005), pp. 94–104
5. N. Juristo, A. Moreno, *Basics of Software Engineering Experimentation* (Kluwer, Dordrecht, 2001)
6. B.A. Kitchenham, S.L. Pfleeger, D.C. Hoaglin, K.E. Emam, J. Rosenberg, Preliminary guidelines for empirical research in software engineering. IEEE Trans. Softw. Eng. **28**(8), 721–733 (2002)
7. C. Larman, *Applying UML and Patterns* (Prentice-Hall, Upper Saddle River, 1998)
8. D. Moher, S. Hopewell, K. Schulz, V. Montori, P.C. Gøtzsche, P.J. Devereaux, D. Elbourne, M. Egger, D.G. Altman, for the CONSORT Group, CONSORT 2010 explanation and elaboration: updated guidelines for reporting parallel group randomised trials. Br. Med. J. 340:c869 (2010). http://www.bmj.com/content/340/bmj.c869
9. S.L. Pfleeger, Experimental design and analysis in software engineering. Ann. Softw. Eng. **1**(1), 219–253 (1995)
10. C. Robson, *Real World Research*, 2nd edn. (Blackwell, Oxford, 2002)
11. N. Salleh, E. Mendes, J. Grundy, G.St.J. Burch, The effects of neuroticism on pair programming: an empirical study in the higher education context, in *Proceedings of the 2010 ACM-IEEE International Symposium on Empirical Software Engineering and Measurement (ESEM '10)* (ACM, New York, 2010), pp. 22:1–22:10. http://dl.acm.org/citation.cfm?id=1852816&dl=ACM&coll=DL&CFID=541946863&CFTOKEN=30791837
12. K.F. Schulz, D.G. Altman, D. Moher, CONSORT 2010 statement: updated guidelines for reporting parallel group randomised trials. Ann. Intern. Med. **152**(11), 1–7 (2010)
13. W.R. Shadish, T.D. Cook, D.T. Campbell, *Experimental and Quasi-Experimental Designs for Generalized Causal Inference* (Houghton Mifflin, Boston, 2002)
14. L. Wasserman, *All of Statistics. A Concise Course in Statistical Inference* (Springer, Heidelberg, 2004)
15. R. Wieringa, N. Condori-Fernandez, M. Daneva, B. Mutschler, O. Pastor, Lessons learned from evaluating a checklist for reporting experimental and observational research, in *International Symposium on Empirical Software Engineering and Measurement (ESEM)* (IEEE Computer Society, Los Alamitos, September 2012), pp. 157–160
16. R.J. Wieringa, Towards a unified checklist for empirical research in software engineering: first proposal, in *16th International Conference on Evaluation and Assessment in Software Engineering (EASE 2012)*, T. Baldaresse, M. Genero, E. Mendes, M. Piattini (IET, 2012), pp. 161–165
17. R.J. Wieringa, A unified checklist for observational and experimental research in software engineering (version 1). Technical Report TR-CTIT-12-07, Centre for Telematics and Information Technology University of Twente, 2012
18. R.R. Wilcox, *Introduction to Robust Estimation and Hypothesis Testing*, 2nd edn. (Academic Press, Waltham, 2005)
19. C. Wohlin, P. Runeson, M. Höst, M.C. Ohlsson, B. Regnell, A. Weslén, *Experimentation in Software Engineering*, 2nd edn. (Springer, Heidelberg, 2012)

Appendix A
Checklist for the Design Cycle

This checklist can be used to decide what to include in a technical research report (internal report, published paper, or thesis), as well as to read a research report written by others. In artifact-oriented research, treatment design and validation will receive more attention. In evaluation- and problem-oriented research, the questions under implementation evaluation and problem investigation will receive more attention. Exclamation marks indicate things to do.

Implementation Evaluation/Problem investigation

- Who are the stakeholders?
- How (in)different is this project to them? Why? (Reasons)
- What are the stakeholder goals? Why? (Reasons)
- What conceptual problem frameworks are in use? (Concepts, variables, components, architectures)
- What conceptual problem framework will I use?
- If an implementation is evaluated, what is the artifact and what is its context?
- What are the phenomena? Why do they happen? (Causes, mechanisms, reasons)
- What are their effects if nothing would be done about them? Do they contribute or detract from goals?

Treatment Design

- Specify requirements and context assumptions!
- (Requirements × context assumptions) contribute to stakeholder goal?
- Available treatments?
- Design new ones!

Treatment Validation

- (Artifact × context) produce effects? Why? (Mechanisms)
- Effects satisfy requirements?
- (Alternative artifact × context) produce effects? Why? (Mechanisms)
- (Artifact × alternative context) produce effects? Why? (Mechanisms)

© Springer-Verlag Berlin Heidelberg 2014
R.J. Wieringa, *Design Science Methodology for Information Systems and Software Engineering*, DOI 10.1007/978-3-662-43839-8

Appendix B
Checklist for the Empirical Cycle

This checklist can be used to design your research, write a report about it (internal report, published paper, or thesis), and read a research report written by others. The questions are precisely that: questions. They are not instructions to do something. It is up to you to decide how to design and execute your research, how to write a report, and how to read one. Related to this, the checklist is not a table of contents for a report. But you can use it to get inspiration for a report.

The first ten items can be used to design your research and is also useful when considering what to include in a report. They are stated from a design point of view, in the future tense. The remaining part of the list can be used for reporting and not for designing. The items are written in the past tense.

Research Context

1. Knowledge goal(s)

   - What do you want to know? Is this part of an implementation evaluation, a problem investigation, a survey of existing treatments, or a new technology validation?

2. Improvement goal(s)?

   - If there is a higher-level engineering cycle, what is the goal of that cycle?
   - If this is a curiosity-driven project, are there credible application scenarios for the project results?

3. Current knowledge

   - State of the knowledge in published scientific, technical, and professional literature?
   - Available expert knowledge?
   - Why is your research needed? Do you want to add anything, e.g., confirm or falsify something?
   - Theoretical framework that you will use?

Research Problem

4. Conceptual framework

   - Conceptual structures? Architectural structures, statistical structures?
   - Chance models of random variables: Semantics of variables?

© Springer-Verlag Berlin Heidelberg 2014
R.J. Wieringa, *Design Science Methodology for Information Systems and Software Engineering*, DOI 10.1007/978-3-662-43839-8

- Validity of the conceptual framework? Clarity of definitions, unambiguous application, avoidance of mono-operation and mono-method bias?

5. Knowledge questions

- Open (exploratory) or closed (hypothesis-testing) questions?
- Effect, satisfaction, trade-off, or sensitivity questions?
- Descriptive or explanatory questions?

6. Population

- Population predicate? What is the architecture of the elements of the population? In which ways are all population elements similar to each other and dissimilar to other elements?
- Chance models of random variables: Assumptions about distributions of variables?

Research Design and Validation

7. Object(s) of study

   7.1 Acquisition of objects of study

   * If OoSs are selected, how do you know that a selected entity is a population element?
   * If OoSs are constructed, how do you construct a population element?
   * Validity of OoS

      - *Inference support*. Which inferences would be valid with respect to this design? See checklists for validity of descriptive statistics and abductive and analogic inferences.
      - *Repeatability*. Could other researchers use your report to construct or select a similar OoS?
      - *Ethics*. Are people informed that they will be studied, and do they consent to this? Are they free to stop at any time without giving reasons, and do they know this?

   7.2 Construction of a sample

   * Case-based research: What is the analytical induction strategy? Confirming cases, disconfirming cases, extreme cases?
   * Sample-based research: What is the sampling frame and probability sampling strategy? Random with or without replacement, stratified, cluster? What should the size of the sample be?
   * Validity of sampling procedure

      - *Inference support*. Which inferences would be valid with respect to this design? See the applicable parts of the checklists for validity of statistical, abductive, and analogic inferences.
      - *Repeatability*. Can the sampling procedure be replicated by other researchers?
      - *Ethics*. No new issues.

8. Treatment design

- Which treatment(s) will be applied?
- Which treatment instruments will be used? Instruction sheets, videos, lessons, software, computers, actuators, rooms, etc.
- How are treatments allocated to OoSs?

   * In sample-based research: Blocking, factorial designs, crossover designs? Between-subjects or within-subject designs?
   * In case-based research: Are treatments scaled up in successive cases?

- What is the treatment schedule?
- Validity of treatment design:

      * *Inference support.* Which inferences would be valid with respect to this design? See the applicable parts of the checklists for validity of statistical, abductive, and analogic inferences.
      * *Repeatability.* Is the specification of the treatment and the allocation to OoSs clear enough so that others could repeat it?
      * *Ethics.* Is no harm done, and is everyone treated fairly? Will they be informed about the treatment before or after the study?

9. Measurement design

    – Variables and constructs to be measured? Scales, chance models.
    – Data sources? People (e.g., software engineers, maintainers, users, project managers, politically responsible persons, etc.), primary data (e.g., source code, log files, bug tracking data, version management data, email logs), primary documents (e.g., project reports, meeting minutes, organization charts, mission statements), etc.
    – Measurement instruments? Interview protocols, questionnaires, video recorders, sound recorders, clocks, sensors, database queries, log analyzers, etc.
    – What is the measurement schedule? Pretests? Posttests? Cross-sectional or longitudinal?
    – How will measured data be stored and managed? Provenance, availability to other researchers?
    – Validity of measurement specification:

      * *Inference support.* Which inferences would be valid with respect to this design? See the applicable parts of the checklists for validity of abductive and analogic inferences.
      * *Repeatability.* Is the measurement specification clear enough so that others could repeat it?
      * *Ethics.* Which company data must be kept confidential? How is privacy of persons respected?

Inference Design and Validation

10. Inference design

  10.1 Descriptive inference design

      * How are words and images to be interpreted? (Content analysis, conversation analysis, discourse analysis, analysis software, etc.)
      * What descriptive summaries of data are planned? Illustrative data, graphical summaries, descriptive statistics, etc.
      * Validity of description design

        · *Support for data preparation*

          - Will the prepared data represent the same phenomena as the unprepared data?
          - If data may be removed, would this be defensible beyond reasonable doubt?
          - Would your scientific opponents produce the same descriptions from the data?

        · *Support for data interpretation*

          - Will the interpretations that you produce be facts in your conceptual research framework? Would your scientific peers produce the same interpretations?
          - Will the interpretations that you produce be facts in the conceptual framework of the subjects? Would subjects accept them as facts?

        · *Support for descriptive statistics*

          - Is the chance model of the variables of interest defined in terms of the population elements?

        · *Repeatability*: Will the analysis repeatable by others?
        · *Ethics*: No new issues.

10.2 Statistical inference design

* What statistical inferences are you planning to do? What data do they need? What assumptions do they make?
* Statistical conclusion validity

  · Assumptions of confidence interval estimation

    - *Stable distribution.* Does X have a stable distribution, with fixed parameters?
    - *Scale.* Does X have an interval or ratio scale?
    - *Sampling.* Is sample selection random or does it contain a known or unknown systematic selection mechanism?
    - *Sample size.* If the z distribution is used, is the sample sufficiently large for the normal approximation to be used?
    - *Normality.* If the t-distribution is used, is the distribution of X normal, or is the sample size larger than 100?

  · *Treatment allocation.* Are the treatments allocated randomly to sample elements?
  · Avoid the following omissions in a report about difference-making experiments:

    - *Effect size.* Seeing a very small difference, but not telling that it is small
    - *Fishing.* Seeing no difference most of the time, but not telling this
    - *Very high power.* Not telling about a reason why you can see a difference (very large sample size makes very small differences visible)
    - *Sample homogeneity.* Not telling about another reason why you can see a difference (groups are selected to be homogeneous, so that any intergroup difference stands out)

10.3 Abductive inference design

* What possible explanations can you foresee? What data do you need to give those explanations? What theoretical framework?
* Internal validity

  · *Causal inference*

    - *Ambiguous relationship.* Ambiguous covariation, ambiguous temporal ordering, ambiguous spatial connection?
    - *OoS dynamics.* Could there be interaction among OoSs? Could there be historical events, maturation, and dropout of OoSs?
    - *Sampling influence.* Could the selection mechanism influence the OoSs? Could there be a regression effect?
    - *Treatment control.* What other factors than the treatment could influence the OoSs? The treatment allocation mechanism, the experimental setup, the experimenters and their expectations, the novelty of the treatment, compensation by the researcher, and rivalry or demoralization about the allocation?
    - *Treatment instrument validity.* Do the treatment instruments have the effect on the OoS that you claim they have?
    - *Measurement influence.* Will measurement influence the OoSs?

  · *Architectural inference*

    - *Analysis.* The analysis of the architecture may not support its conclusions with mathematical certainty. Components fully specified? Interactions fully specified?
    - *Variation.* Do the real-world case components match the architectural components? Do they have the same capabilities? Are all architectural components present in the real-world case?

     - *Abstraction.* Does the architectural model used for explanation omit relevant elements of real-world cases? Are the mechanisms in the architectural model interfered with by other mechanisms, absent from the model but present in the real-world case?

    ·   *Rational inference:*

     - *Goals.* An actor may not have the goals assumed by an explanation. Can you get information about the true goals of actors?
     - *Motivation.* A goal may not motivate an actor as much as assumed by an explanation. Can you get information about the true motivations of actors?

10.4 Analogic inference design

  * What is the intended scope of your generalization?
  * External validity

    ·   *Object of study similarity*

     - *Population predicate.* Will the OoS satisfy the population predicate? In which way will it be similar to the population elements? In which way will it be dissimilar?
     - *Ambiguity.* Will the OoS satisfy other population predicates too? What could be the target of analogic generalization?

    ·   *Representative sampling*

     - Sample-based research. Will the study population, described by the sampling frame, be representative of the theoretical population?
     - Case-based research. In what way will the selected/constructed sample of cases be representative of the population?

    ·   *Treatment*

     - *Treatment similarity.* Is the specified treatment in the experiment similar to treatments in the population?
     - *Compliance.* Is the treatment implemented as specified?
     - *Treatment control.* What other factors than the treatment could influence the OoSs? Could the implemented treatment be interpreted as another treatment?

    ·   *Measurement*

     - *Construct validity.* Are the definitions of constructs to be measured valid? Clarity of definitions, unambiguous application, and avoidance of mono-operation and mono-method bias?
     - *Measurement instrument validity.* Do the measurement instruments measure what you claim that they measure?
     - *Construct levels.* Will the measured range of values be representative of the population range of values?

At this point, the checklist for research design ends. From this point on, the checklist describes research execution and analysis. We switch from the future tense to the past tense because this part of the checklists asks questions about what has happened, not about what you plan to do.

Research Execution

11. What has happened?

    - What has happened when the OoSs were selected or constructed? Did they have the architecture that was planned during research design? Unexpected events for OoSs during the study?
    - What has happened during sampling? Did the sample have the size you planned? Participant flow, dropouts?
    - What has happened when the treatment(s) were applied? Mistakes, unexpected events?
    - What has happened during measurement? Data sources actually used, response rates?

Data Analysis

12. Descriptions

    - Data preparations applied? Data transformations, missing values, removal of outliers? Data management, data availability.
    - Data interpretations? Coding procedures, interpretation methods?
    - Descriptive statistics. Demographics, sample mean and variance? Graphics, tables.
    - Validity of the descriptions: See checklist for the validity of descriptive inference.

13. Statistical conclusions

    - Statistical inferences from the observations. Confidence interval estimations, hypothesis tests.
    - Statistical conclusion validity: See checklist for the validity of statistical inference.

14. Explanations

    - What explanations (causal, architectural, rational) exist for the observations?
    - Internal validity: See checklist for the validity of abductive inference.

15. Generalizations

    - Would the explanations be valid in similar cases or populations too?
    - External validity: See checklist for the validity of analogic inference

16. Answers

    - What are the answers to the research questions? Summary of conclusions, support for, and limitations of conclusions.

Research Context

17. Contribution to knowledge goal(s). Refer back to items 1 and 3.
18. Contribution to improvement goal(s)? Refer back to item 2.

    - If there is no improvement goal, is there a potential contribution to practice?

Index

© Springer-Verlag Berlin Heidelberg 2014
R.J. Wieringa, *Design Science Methodology for Information Systems
and Software Engineering*, DOI 10.1007/978-3-662-43839-8

Printed in the United States
By Bookmasters